Emotion AND THE Arts

Emotion AND THE Arts

Edited by

METTE HJORT

& SUE LAVER

New York   Oxford • Oxford University Press   1997

Oxford University Press

Oxford   New York

Athens   Auckland   Bangkok   Bogota   Bombay   Buenos Aires
Calcutta   Cape Town   Dar es Salaam   Dehli   Florence   Hong Kong
Istanbul   Karachi   Kuala Lumpur   Madras   Madrid   Melbourne
Mexico City   Nairobi   Paris   Singapore   Taipei   Tokyo   Toronto   Warsaw

and associated companies in
Berlin   Ibadan

Library of Congress Cataloging-in-Publication Data
Emotion and the arts / edited by Mette Hjort, Sue Laver.
p.   cm.
Includes bibliographical references.
ISBN 0-19-511104-4; ISBN 0-19-511105-2 (pbk)
1. Emotions in art.   2. Arts—Psychological aspects.   I. Hjort,
Mette.   II. Laver, Sue, 1961–
NX165.E45   1997
700'.1'9—dc20   96-9892

1   3   5   7   9   8   6   4   2

Printed in the United States of America
on acid-free paper

Emotion AND THE Arts

Acknowledgments

The contributors' judicious advice and gracious attention to detail greatly facilitated the completion of this intensely collaborative project. Susan Feagin's "Imagining Emotions and Appreciating Fiction" (chapter 3) first appeared in the *Canadian Journal of Philosophy* (vol. 18, no. 3, pp. 485–500) and is published here courtesy of the University of Calgary Press. Robert Solomon's "In Defense of Sentimentality" (chapter 14) first appeared in *Philosophy and Literature* (vol. 14, pp. 304–23) and is published here, in revised form, courtesy of the Johns Hopkins University Press. The section on kitsch in chapter 14 also appeared, in a different form, in the *Journal of Aesthetics and Art Criticism* (vol. 49, pp. 1–14) and is used here courtesy of the editors of the journal. Mette Hjort wishes to acknowledge the generous support of the Social Sciences and Humanities Research Council of Canada. She is also indebted to colleagues at the Institute for Research in the Humanities, Kyoto University, for their hospitality.

Contents

Introduction

METTE HJORT & SUE LAVER

It is generally assumed that art and emotion are inextricably linked, as is shown by even the most cursory account of the history of critical thinking about music, painting, literature, or theatre.

Consider, for example, a few salient moments in the history of the theory and practice of the dramatic arts. Whereas Plato's indictment of poets construes theatre as a source of undesirable and even dangerous emotions, Aristotle's defense of the art hinges on its putative capacity to purge spectators of these very emotions. Plato's conception of theatre and emotion as inextricably intertwined provides support for the antitheatricalist viewpoints espoused by the early Church Fathers, just as it informs the condemnations of theatre articulated in sixteenth-century England and seventeenth-century France.[1] Thus, for example, William Prynne's strikingly vitriolic *Histriomastix* makes theatre a veritable machine of pandemonium fueled by mimetically inspired social emotions.[2] Pierre Nicole, the Jansenist, also charges theatre with undermining social order, but focuses his critique on actors' and playwrights' strategic and selective representation of the emotions, thereby taking issue with the links presented in plays between emotion and action.[3]

Emotion, we have suggested, figures centrally in influential attempts to chart the reception of plays. Yet, if dramatic theorists are to be believed, this phenomenon should occupy a privileged site not only within reception studies, but within studies of performance as well. For example, Denis Diderot argued

3

persuasively that performers should be internally distanced from the characters they play and from the emotional states that these characters experience in the dramatic fiction.[4] This view of inner distance was later forcefully challenged by the method actor's insistence on the need for an empathetic simulation of the fictional character's emotional states.[5]

In the course of the twentieth century, attempts to politicize the theatre through a particular style of acting hinge on the question of emotion. Bertolt Brecht's rejection of what he rather misleadingly refers to as "Aristotelian theatre" in favor of an epic theatre inspired by the principles of Erwin Piscator is designed to promote theatre's revolutionary potential. To assume that the goal of theatre is to enable actors and spectators somehow to simulate the fictional characters' emotional states is, claims Brecht, to endorse the ideologically suspect legacy of an Aristotelian tradition bent only on producing "hypnotic" effects and "culinary" pleasures.[6] What he proposes instead is a properly political theatrical practice based on notions of alienation, a phenomenon allegedly capable of enhancing the role of reason and distance within both the actor's and the spectator's psychic arrangements.

To those moderns steeped in the traditions of Enlightenment thinking, this emphasis on reason may seem wholly salutary. Not surprisingly, however, this same preference for reason over emotion appears in a rather different, and far less appealing, light when viewed from Counter-Enlightenment perspectives. Thus, for example, Antonin Artaud's influential *Theater and Its Double* is at once an indictment of rationalist and representationalist forms of theatrical practice and a passionate attempt to make theatre a liberating site of wholeness. The actor, suggests Artaud, should reach the spectator in much the same way that the snake charmer charms a snake: through the body and its many sensations.[7] A certain nostalgia for aspects of premodern culture, which is so characteristic of Counter-Enlightenment thought, motivates Artaud's conception of the body as a means of contacting some of the deeper and repressed dimensions of human existence.[8] Although the term "body," as used by Artaud and his many followers, is at times tantalizingly ambiguous, there can be little doubt that it valorizes one side of the reason/emotion divide.

Our brief remarks about theatre and emotion are admittedly inconclusive, for the precise nature of the existing or desirable links between these two phenomena, let alone between emotion and the arts more generally, remains quite obscure, as does the nature of emotion itself. What does seem clear, however, is that our thinking about various art forms will be impoverished and even wrongheaded if we fail to take seriously questions having to do with the emotions of those who inhabit and engage with the many worlds of art.

One could argue that emotion has already found its due in contemporary theorizing about art. Is it not the case, after all, that recent studies of the paintings of Gustave Courbet, the films of Alfred Hitchcock, and the writings of Isak Dinesen, for example, find a starting point in concepts derived from Freud? And although Freud, given his clear commitment to science, can hardly be characterized as a Counter-Enlightenment thinker, the centrality in contemporary discourses of castration complexes, anxiety, narcissism, scopophilia, and of the body clearly derives from Freud's influence and is part of a widespread rejection of idealist and rationalist conceptions of agency. Should these discourses not be seen, then, as clearing a space for a properly critical awareness of emotion and its many complexities? The answer to this question, we believe, is both yes and no. Emotion, it seems, should indeed be of genuine interest to critics and theorists who espouse Counter-Enlightenment views. Yet, at the same time, it is important to note that our chances of grasping the complexities of emotion are slim if we remain committed to models derived only from psychoanalysis. This point is made cogently by two of the contributors to *Emotion and the Arts*. In an important study, entitled *Emotion*, William Lyons argues persuasively that "Freud had no single or systematic account of emotion . . . , but tended to restrict himself to giving accounts of the workings of particular emotions, particularly anxiety."[9] In chapter 12 of this volume, Noël Carroll argues that psychoanalytic, humanistic research all but ignores the "garden-variety emotions" that "keep audiences engaged with artworks." Instead, psychoanalytic critics focus exclusively on anxiety or on "ill-defined forces like desire and pleasure." Given that an adequate account of emotion cannot be said to be part of the Freudian legacy, any suggestion that we can grasp the place of emotion within the arts from a purely, or even largely, psychoanalytic perspective seems misguided at best.

There are other reasons why theorists committed to understanding emotion should look beyond the frameworks provided by psychoanalysis. The psychoanalytic emphasis on the body and on desire is part of a wholesale rejection of idealist conceptions of rationality and agency, and of explanatory models centered on the beliefs, intentions, and attitudes of individual agents. Yet, as certain critics of postmodernism and poststructuralism have argued recently, it is wrong to assume that a rejection of Descartes's *cogito* or of Kant's unity of apperception necessarily entails an affirmation of polymorphous perversity. Nor is it clear that holistic models of explanation, in which a notion of desire mediated through language is given absolute priority, can do justice to all aspects of human behavior. What we are witnessing in the work of these critics, then, is an attempt to articulate some modest conceptions of agency that start from the assumption that agents are embodied beings inserted within social and cultural life worlds. *Emotion and the Arts* is designed to take seriously, and to contribute to, this renewed interest in agency. The chapters jointly shed light on some of the ways in which an agent's beliefs, intentions, desires, and attitudes are constitutive of his or her emotional engagements with art. At the same time, the volume is meant to support and further develop some of the intuitions that initially motivated the influential postmodernist turn to the body and related phenomena.

The claim that the link between emotion and art is worthy of intense scrutiny will seem banal to some scholars. *Emotion and the Arts* does not contest the value of works exploring this link in a detailed, historical manner, but it does reflect the contributors' shared assumption that such accounts cannot in themselves exhaust the topic. If thinking about emotion and art is to be more than a form of what Paisley Livingston has called "megaphone criticism"[10] —

an elaborate but uncritical restating of beliefs held by earlier thinkers—it must also attempt to determine the extent to which those thinkers' arguments are valid or true. It follows that thinking about emotion and art also should be a matter of considering carefully, and in an analytic mode, certain recurrent issues or problems. What is more, theorizing about emotion and the arts ideally should be informed by the best available findings of other relevant disciplines, such as psychology and cognitive science.[11]

The contributions to *Emotion and the Arts* display these problem-oriented and interdisciplinary tendencies. Although the chapters deal with arts as diverse as film, painting, music, dance, literature, and theatre, the aim here is not to provide a comprehensive picture of any particular art and its relation to emotion, nor is the goal to do justice to any given historical period's conception of the issues. The volume brings together a number of analytically minded philosophers, psychologists, and literary theorists, all of whom are interested in providing fine-grained accounts of particular problems having to do with emotion and art.

AT THIS POINT, it would be well to say a few words about current conceptions of emotion and the place of our contributors on the conceptual landscape in question. Many contemporary theorists of emotion are aligned with either a cognitive or a social constructivist approach. Although these two approaches are often regarded as rivals, the differences between them are not as extreme as is sometimes suggested. For example, cognitivists and social constructivists both reject the historically important idea that emotion is reducible to a wholly natural and purely subjective registering of some physiological perturbation. This reductive approach is targeted by Rom Harré's contribution, which critiques a "biological" point of view from the "discursive" perspective favored by social constructivists. In the work of a cognitivist, such as William Lyons, this same biological point of view is identified with a "feeling" theory influenced decisively by Descartes, Hume, and William James, and with a "behaviorist" theory shaped by J. B. Watson and B. F. Skinner. Together, these theories provide a foil for William Lyons's own cognitive account, which he refers to as a "causal-evaluative theory of emotions."[12]

Contemporary cognitive theorists of emotion take their lead from Aristotle's incisive discussion, in the *Rhetoric*, of the ways in which emotion, if properly manipulated, can serve the interests of politicians and orators. As Lyons points out, "Aristotle's account is a cognitive account, not because he believed emotions affected our judgment, but because he also believed that judgments or cognitions were central to emotion."[13] According to cognitivists, attitudes generate emotions and may even provide the basis for differentiating one emotion from another. In most cognitive accounts of emotion, a crucial causal role is attributed to agents' *evaluations* of relevant states of affairs. For example, a mother who learns that her child's teacher intends to break her contract in the middle of the school year can be expected to experience certain negative emotions if she believes that the sudden change will be harmful to her child. The fact that beliefs, judgments, or evaluations are now widely held to be constitutive of emotion is due in part to the influential work of many of the contributors to *Emotion and the Arts*, including Ronald de Sousa, William Lyons, and Robert Solomon.[14]

Social constructivists typically accept cognitivists' emphasis on the intentional dimensions of emotion. That is, they agree with the cognitivists that emotions exhibit a certain "aboutness" that involves an agent's attitudes being directed, in the form of beliefs and judgments, toward real or imagined states of affairs. Although social constructivists believe the cognitive approach to emotion presents a definite advance over behaviorism and Cartesianism, they nonetheless consider it impoverished or, as Rom Harré puts it in his introduction to an influential anthology, "anorexic."[15] What makes the cognitive approach overly thin is its alleged failure to do justice to the constitutive role that culture plays in human emotion. According to social constructivists, emotion is a phenomenon that finds its condition of possibility in local languages and moral orders.[16] On this account, the task of the theorist of emotion is not to provide a general analysis of distinct emotions, such as fear, love, or hate, and of the beliefs, judgments, or evaluations that are their defining features. Instead, the theorist should adopt the stance associated with a certain school of anthropology, one that urges "thick descriptions" and eschews theoretical generalizations or abstractions. The focus, claims Harré, should be on "angry people, upsetting scenes, sentimental episodes, grieving families and funerals, [and] anxious parents pacing at midnight."[17] Social constructivists favor the kind of insight yielded by particularist descriptions of the connections between certain contexts and activities, on the one hand, and the use of emotion terms, on the other.

By emphasizing the need for thick descriptions, social constructivists take issue with the idea that the phenomenon of emotion can be properly understood through an analysis of *occurrent* emotional states. Such states, claim the social constructivists, are made possible by a complex set of conditions, which are not only psychological, but also sociocultural and political. Whereas cognitivists tend to focus on the proximal, psychological causes of emotions, social constructivists give priority to the distal, sociopolitical causes of such phenomena. Some social constructivists believe that analyses dedicated to the proximal causes of emotions can provide only an inaccurate and distorted picture of emotion. Others contend that the absence of political awareness in such accounts reflects a form of ideological collusion.

The social constructivist tendency to prefer thick descriptions to theoretical generalizations is motivated, at least in part, by a belief in one of two claims. The first claim is that emotions are culturally diverse in the sense that an emotion found in one culture may be entirely absent from some or all other cultures. The second claim, which, as Robert Solomon has suggested, is much more difficult to prove, is that there are no universal emotions at all.[18] A weaker variant of this claim concedes that there may be some universal emotions, but insists that they are the exception rather than the rule. The premise of widespread and even radical diversity motivates social constructivists to view general and purely conceptual accounts of emotion as expressions of power wielded by dominant groups. Such accounts, it is held, merely attribute a dubious universality to emotions associated with dominant groups supported by certain ethnic categories or by pervasive sexist ideologies. Social constructivists believe that their proposed approach to the study of emotion provides a much-needed means of circumventing the ethnocentric and phallocentric excesses that mark the history of thinking about emotion.

Although there is disagreement among theorists of emotion about what exactly emotions are and about how best to describe them, there is at least some agreement about the centrality of key problems or issues. One such problem is that of determining how emotions should be differentiated from one another. Indeed, all theories of emotion—biological, psychoanalytic, behaviorist, cognitivist, or social constructivist—betray a commitment to providing a solution to this question. Thus, for example, a cognitivist, such as William Lyons, argues that emotions cannot be adequately differentiated in terms of the behavior or physiological changes to which they give rise. Nor, claims Lyons, can emotions be distinguished by means of reference to the contexts in which they occur. According to Lyons, the key to the conundrum of differentiation lies in the beliefs and evaluations that are constitutive of emotion.[19] On this view, the emotion felt by a young child may legitimately be described as anger and not fear if it is generated by a belief that the situation she faces is unfair rather than dangerous.

The social constructivist solution to the problem of differentiation contrasts sharply with the cognitivist solution, for it gives priority, not to the contents of an agent's beliefs or evaluations, but to a set of irreducibly social phenomena, such as the "rights, duties, and obligations" of agents as these are understood within a *particular* culture.[20] To understand fully the difference between certain emotions, claims the social constructivist, it is necessary to enter into a set of language games and into a whole way of life, the constitutive rules of which cannot be adequately conveyed through theoretical formulations or descriptions. So, whereas the cognitivist believes that emotions can be understood only by paying careful attention to the beliefs and attitudes of individual agents (among other things), the social constructivist considers irreducibly social categories and entities to be the essential factor.

In some instances, social constructivism is a matter of urging a hermeneutic stance designed to ensure that theoretical discussions reflect the self-understandings of the agents whose emotions are under scrutiny. The claim that it is important to understand the ways in which agents shape and give meaning to their lives is in no way at odds with the realist goal of accurately grasping and describing certain emotional phenomena. This particular interpretation of the social constructivist project needs to be distinguished, then, from the radically historicist and antirealist versions of social constructivism. In these latter types of accounts, emotions are held to defy explanation for a number of different reasons. For example, the conditions of an emotion's emergence may be considered too complex to render explicit. An additional problem is the alleged absence of a neutral language in which to describe the emotion in question. Given such premises, descriptions or analyses of particular emotions become mere impositions of cultural concepts and frameworks.

Having focused on some of the salient differences between cognitivist and social constructivist approaches, we would like now to suggest that work in these two traditions need not be mutually exclusive and may, in fact, in many cases be mutually supportive. It is worth noting that this idea of complementarity is implicitly inscribed within the conception of social constructivism as somehow adding to, rather than entirely redoing, the picture of emotion that cognitivists provide. Moreover, although debates between cognitivists and social constructivists frequently involve a hyperbolic, separatist rhetoric, it is difficult at times to find any real warrant for the alleged divide. Thus, for example, it is hard to see how many of the influential cognitive theorists of emotion can legitimately be charged with engaging in a project of phallocentric or ethnocentric universalization. Although cognitivists do not typically adopt the anthropological stance associated with thick descriptions and idiographic accounts of particular cultures, they do, at a theoretical level, tend to acknowledge the significance of cultural and social phenomena. In many instances, then, their theories may well be capable of exhibiting the desired sensitivity to cultural variation.

Although work in a social constructivist vein tends to be rich and suggestive, it frequently begs at least as many questions as it answers. For example, Catherine Lutz's extremely influential and in many ways admirable piece entitled "Need, Nurturance, and the Emotions on a Pacific Atoll" (1995) leaves unanswered the question of exactly *how* we are to understand the claim that emotions are constructed in much the same way as the language of ethnicity, ritual, and land tenure. It is hard to see how a full, detailed development of such claims could avoid drawing on the kinds of fine-grained conceptual analyses favored by the analytically minded cognitivists. If social constructivist accounts are to be persuasive, they must demonstrate an ability successfully to mediate between individual and social levels of descriptions. At this stage in our collective thinking about emotion, it seems clear that if we wish to do justice to the psychological as well as social dimensions of emotion, we cannot afford to set aside the cognitive account. For it is this account that provides the most detailed analysis, among many other things, of the different kinds of beliefs that are constitutive of emotion, and of the types of objects that figure centrally in occurrent emotional states.

Although most readers will be inclined to see the contributions to *Emotion and the Arts* as so many exemplifications of the cognitive approach, it is important to note that some of the contributions reveal a social constructivist bent, while others clearly support the idea that constructivist and cognitivist insights can be mutually supportive. Rom Harré's "Emotion in Music" (chapter 7) is clearly of social constructivist inspiration, reflecting his earlier work on the emotions. Thus, he argues that "the emotional aspects of music, as it is performed, be it in the head or in the concert hall," can be understood only if we pay careful attention to the way in which "those involved in an emotional episode" are positioned "in the local moral order, the taken-for-granted structure of rights, obligations, and duties that obtain in some corner of the social world." In "Emotion and Emotions in Theatre Dance" (chapter 8), Francis Sparshott exhibits a deep awareness of the social and cultural dimensions of emotion and dance. Sparshott's decision to develop his views on emotion and dance through a detailed, comparative analysis of classical Indian and Western traditions of expressive movement reflects at least some of the social constructivist premises.

A compelling example of how the two approaches can complement each other is provided by David Novitz's "The Anaesthetics of Emotion" (chapter 15). In his essay, Novitz identifies a critical paradox, which he describes as follows:

> The problem for art criticism is clear. On the one hand, an appropriate response to fictional literature (and, as we shall see, to other art forms as well) requires us to ignore the challenges that these works present to our core beliefs and values. On the other, it is simply irresponsible to overlook the effects that certain works can have on our attitudes and beliefs, and accordingly, on the fabric of our society. It is thus entirely appropriate to respond angrily to some works of art and to do so on account of the threat that they pose to our systems of beliefs and value. From which it follows that it is critically appropriate to respond inappropriately to specific works. This I call the critical paradox.

Novitz's proposed solution to the "critical paradox" that is seemingly generated by emotional responses to art hinges on a distinction between messages that may be discovered "in" a work of art and messages that are somehow conveyed "through" a work of art. Messages in a work of art, claims Novitz, "are derived by responding to a work in terms of the conventions that govern the medium." Messages through art, on the other hand, appear only when agents suspend these very conventions and focus on the ways in which certain favored values and beliefs are affected by a given work. Such messages, says Novitz, have "everything to do with the social location of works of art but have nothing directly to do with what we regard as the content of these works." Novitz argues that the critical paradox dissolves once we realize that it is simply false to assume that "an appropriate response to fiction *as fiction* excludes all other responses to the fiction." Novitz's defense of the legitimacy of emotional responses generated by messages through art relies crucially on the categories of intentional psychology, while simultaneously foregrounding the importance of the specific social contexts in which agents and works are embedded. As Novitz points out, his approach helps to clarify some of the claims about art advanced by feminists and other theorists concerned primarily with ideology, gender, and power.

Emotion and the Arts is designed to reflect the central place that emotion currently occupies in aesthetics and in the work of philosophically minded literary theorists and cognitive psychologists. The importance of emotion is clearly recognized in articles and monographs that contribute to ongoing debates, yet there is no single volume that adequately explores the state of those debates. *Emotion and the Arts* is our attempt to fill this lacuna. Although many other scholars could have been included in a multivolume project, we feel that *Emotion and the Arts* begins to respond, however modestly, to the described need. We hope that Jerrold Levinson's masterful "Emotion in Response to Art: A Survey of the Terrain" (chapter 1) will serve to expand the scope of the volume by identifying other important researchers and topics. The rest of the contributions have been grouped beneath four rubrics, each of which points to a cluster of issues considered crucial to an understanding of emotion and its relation to art. These rubrics are "The Paradox of Fiction," "Emotion and Its Expression through Art," "The Rationality of Emotional Responses to Art," and "The Value of Emotion." We shall now briefly discuss each in turn.

According to Gregory Currie, three plausible but mutually contradictory propositions constitute the paradox of fiction:

1. We have emotions concerning the situations of fictional characters.
2. To have an emotion concerning someone's situation we must believe the propositions that describe that situation.
3. We do not believe the propositions that describe the situations of fictional characters.[21]

Three ways of trying to solve this paradox, each targeting one of its propositions, dominate the literature. *Pretense* theorists deny (1) and replace it with an alternate account of our emotional or "quasi-emotional" response to fiction. *Thought* theorists deny (2) and advance different views of the cognitive constraints on the generation of emotion. *Illusion* theorists deny (3) and defend a stronger thesis concerning the reader's or viewer's cognitive states.

In Part I of this volume, the contributions by Kendall Walton, Susan Feagin, Gregory Currie, and Derek Matravers respond to and build on earlier discussions of the paradox of fiction. In "Spelunking, Simulation, and Slime: On Being Moved by Fiction (chapter 2)," Kendall Walton responds to objections to the pretense solution associated with his influential "Fearing Fictions" and *Mimesis as Make-Believe*. Walton argues that critics have misinterpreted his views on agents' emotional responses to fiction, for his intention was not to deny that the emotions in question are *real*. What is more, his critics are said to have paid undue attention to his "negative claim," in *Mimesis as Make-Believe*, that Charles does not really fear the Slime he sees on the screen. Walton argues that current discussions of mental simulation allow him to respond to the relevant misconceptions and to bring into proper focus important, though often neglected, "positive aspects" of his theory of make-believe.

Susan Feagin's explorations of emotional responses to fictions are oriented by her assumption that the complexity of such responses makes it necessary to resist the temptation to provide simple analyses or explanations, especially in the absence of a systematic and testable theory of emotions. She distinguishes between several different kinds of art-emotions, focusing in particular on sympathetic, empathetic, and meta-level responses, contending that different psychological mechanisms are relevant to each kind.[22] In her essay in this volume, "Imagining Emotions and Appreciating Fiction," Feagin discusses key differences between empathizing with real persons and empathizing with fictional characters. She argues that whereas real-life empathy often depends on our beliefs about the beliefs of the person with whom we empathize, the situation is quite different in the case of art-empathy, which usually does not rely on such second-order beliefs. Feagin claims that art-empathy is best thought of as a kind of imagined emotion, and, much like Walton, she suggests that the imagining in question is a matter of simulating the patterns of thinking underwriting real emotions. She insists that the relevant thoughts may be generated as a result of many different factors, including formal features of the work. Indeed, she argues that these formal features may be more important than any beliefs we may have about what real persons might think or feel in situations similar to those of our fictional characters. Feagin concludes her essay by considering the implications of this line of reasoning for how we think about art's contribution to knowledge. She contends that the important contribution made by art is not a matter of knowledge by acquaintance or propositional knowledge, but of the cultivation of mental complexity through a "restructuration of experience".

In "The Paradox of Caring: Fiction and the Philosophy of Mind" (chapter 4), Gregory Currie draws significantly on his earlier analysis of the paradox of fiction in *The Nature of Fiction*, where he proposed a solution favoring a version of the pretense theory. However, whereas Currie's earlier work on the paradox focused on the logical problems involved, "The Paradox of Caring" foregrounds some key psychological issues. Indeed, Currie's stated aim is to show that his solution to the paradox "is not merely logically satisfactory but psychologically plausible as well." To this end, Currie identifies two psychological problems, both having to do with the way in which agents come to care for fictional characters. The problem of belief, says Currie, arises because agents frequently appear to care for people who they don't believe exist. The problem of personality, on the other hand, is caused by the nature of the caring in question. More specifically, agents frequently seem to care in ways that are at odds with the kinds of persons they are. In an effort to shed light on these two puzzles, Currie turns to cognitive psychology and simulation theory. He argues that readers of fiction "simulate, empathize with, or take on the role of" a hypothetical "reader of fact" who is learning about and empathizing with a fictional character. To become absorbed in a fictional narrative is to simulate this hypothetical reader's imagined states of belief and desire. According to Currie, the real reader's resulting "I-states" resemble real beliefs and desires in terms of their content, but not in terms of their external causal role. That is, these states are "off-line" and do not give rise to the kind of behavior one associates with the relevant beliefs and desires. Currie's approach to the problems of belief and personality thus involves emphasizing a form of imaginative role playing that allows us to avoid attributing a series of false beliefs to readers of fiction.

In "The Paradox of Fiction: The Report versus the Perceptual Model" (chapter 5), Derek Matravers attempts to clarify the particular nature of the game of make-believe that is played by agents when they consume fiction. His central claim is that when reading a novel, agents make believe that they are being given a report of actual events. Matravers begins by describing this "report model" in detail and he then goes on to defend it against objections based on the idea that in certain fictions, such as plays, it is difficult, if not impossible, to identify a narrating character who might legitimately be seen as reporting on events and situations. Matravers's defense of the model hinges on key features of the make-believe itself:

> [T]he situation we are in when reading a novel is sufficiently similar to the situation we are in when reading a report of actual events (made by someone or other) that it is entirely natural for us to imagine that the novel is just that, a report of actual events (made by someone or other).

The report model, claims Matravers, has been accepted by Walton and others as applying to literary works but not visual representations, such as plays or films, which are held instead to require a "perceptual model." Matravers's intention is to show that the report model in fact can deal adequately with visual representations and has clear advantages over the perceptual model. According to Matravers, one such advantage is that the "report model describes exactly the limits of the make-believe we play with visual fiction." Thus, the report model helps explain why there can be psychological interaction, but no physical interaction, between viewers and fictional characters.

Matravers rejects the idea, attributed to Walton, that readers and viewers do not feel real emotions, but only quasi-emotions, for fictional characters. As is well known, Walton's position is based on an alleged absence, in responses to fiction, of a connection between emotion and action. Matravers's contention is that the report model allows us to see that there is no reason to expect quasi-emotions to have a connection to action. After all, the viewer of a documentary or of the evening news does not typically act on the strong emotions he or she may feel. Much like Currie, Matravers's discussion shields consumers of fiction from false beliefs. In addition, his defense of the report model explains why consumers of fiction are right when they claim to experience real emotions in response to films or novels.

It is worth noting in passing that although the contributions just discussed are the only ones to deal single-mindedly with the paradox of fiction, many other pieces include brief discussions of some its aspects. We are thinking in particular of the contributions by Noël Carroll, Robert Solomon, Willie van Peer, and Paisley Livingston and Alfred Mele.

In Part II, the focus shifts to a number of questions having to do with the expression of emotion through art. For example, if art really does express emotion, then *whose* emotion does it express? How, exactly, are the relevant emotions communicated to viewers, listeners, or readers? By what mechanism do these agents identify the particular emotions in question? Is the process of identification subject to constraints or is it a matter largely of idiosyncratic projection? And why would a perceived or imagined expression of emotion generate emotion in viewers, readers, or listeners?

As Jerrold Levinson remarks in "Emotion in Response to Art," abstract or nonrepresentational art presents a particular problem for our understanding of the expression and experience of emotion. The absence in such works of a recognizable world inhabited by characters driven by particular interests and concerns makes it difficult to understand why such works move us. This is so, for example, in the case of pure music, the topic of Stephen Davies's contribution entitled "Contra the Hypothetical Persona in Music" (chapter 6). In this chapter, Davies contrasts two rival approaches, "appearance emotionalism" and "hypothetical emotionalism." The former, he claims, is a view committed to the idea that "musical materials can be literally expressive as a result of presenting to audition sounds with emotion-characteristics." A strong version of hypothetical emotionalism maintains instead that "to understand and appreciate some musical works fully, the listener *must* hypothesize a persona and hear the unfolding of the formal and expressive elements of the music as actions and feelings of, or events affecting, that persona." Davies rejects hypothetical emotionalism on a number of grounds. Most important, he claims that attributions of higher emotions to a hypothetical persona are subjective and idiosyncratic, because they cannot be properly anchored in objective features of the work. What is more, says Davies, hypothetical emotionalism presupposes a level of "imaginative input" that is much higher than that required in order to follow music with understanding. A further problem faced by proponents of hypothetical emotionalism is that it is difficult, if not impossible, to determine just how many personae should be hypothesized in response to a given work.

In "Emotion in Music" (chapter 7), Rom Harré aims to show that a social constructivist conception of "public emotion displays as complexes of judgments and social acts" has "application to music." What is needed, according to Harré, is a set of criteria and a system of categories that would allow us both to recognize and to classify the emotions expressed in music. Having discussed briefly the problem of determining whose emotions are expressed in music, Harré goes on to present the results of what he calls the "Georgetown Experiments." The purpose of these experiments, claims Harré, was to determine "how reliable various musical performances were as instruments of mood (emotion) induction." What these experiments allegedly demonstrate is that musical expression is largely a matter of convention. More specifically, they point to the existence of a "Western tradition of expressive devices through which music manifests judgments." The importance of convention, culture, and social context is further underscored by the fact that participants in the experiments proved unable to identify the emotions expressed in music originating in a culture significantly removed from their own. Harré goes on to examine the relation between the emotional qualities of music and the emotions experienced by listeners. He rejects the "sympathetic account" which sees our emotional responses as simply mirroring the perceived emotional tenor of the music. He concludes by emphasizing the need for a nuanced account of the place of emotion in music and its reception. Whereas formalists are reproved for entirely overlooking the ways in which music expresses and gives rise to emotion, philistines are charged with the reduction" of music to emotion pure and simple.

In "Emotion and Emotions in Theatre Dance" (chapter 8), Francis Sparshott begins by pinpointing the shortcomings of influential views of emotion. He then goes on to suggest that thinking about emotion and dance needs to acknowledge the widely overlooked fact that dance can express and generate emotion because the "transaction between" artists and spectators "inescapably involves their common humanity as well as their performance and appreciation, respectively, of the work that is being performed." While Sparshott's intention clearly is to grasp the significance of the dancer's presence in a dance performance, he does point out that it is the emotions to which the artist gives formal expression, rather than the emotions actually felt by the dancer, that are relevant to a spectator's proper response to art. Sparshott further develops his views on dance and the expression of emotion through a comparative analysis of the *rasa* theory of classical Indian dance drama, and the views and practices of modern, contemporary, and postmodern practitioners of dance in the West. This comparison sheds light on the ways in which radically different cultural self-understandings influence not only dance, but also the emotions that dance can be seen as expressing. *Rasa* theory and its nine basic emotions are specific to a cultural community committed to "the notion of a classical art, deliberately confined to exploiting the possibilities of a culture accepted as definitive." Modern, contemporary, and postmodern dance, on the other hand, find a basis in cultural communities that see themselves as "inherently subject to variation and change."

Part III brings together four chapters that, in one way or another, deal with the rationality of agents' emotional responses to works of art. More specifically, the authors consider whether such emotional responses are subject to certain evaluative criteria, and if so, what these criteria are.

The starting point for William Lyons's discussion of emotion and painting ("On Looking into Titian's *Assumption*," chapter 9) is William James's contention that all acceptable responses to art are either romantic or classic and that all other responses are unacceptably intellectual or philistine. James attributes a philistine response to an English couple whom he saw observing Titian's *Assumption*. Lyons considers James's characterization of the couple's response to be erroneous. His aim in this chapter is thus twofold: "to sketch a different, richer view of the interplay between emotions and paintings" and to put "forward a more liberal and less censorious account of what" should be allowed to count "as a legitimate emotional response to a painting." Lyons's analysis of the complex relations between emotion and painting relies on seven categories that fall under the following three metagroupings: "the painter's own emotion in relation to what he (or she) is painting"; "emotion as depicted in the painting"; and "the viewer's emotion in relation to the painting." Lyons contends that James wrongly rejects as spurious, sentimental, coarse, and philistine all responses belonging to the third of these metagroupings. Lyons insists that James's conception of emotional responses to painting involves a conflation of a "knowing-naive" spectrum and an "acceptable-unacceptable" spectrum. Lyons defends the "rather laissez-faire view" that emotional responses may be perfectly acceptable, even if they reveal a lack of knowledge or understanding on the part of the viewer.

In "Evaluating Emotional Responses to Fiction" (chapter 10), Paisley Livingston and Alfred Mele begin by noting that discussions of the paradox of fiction tend to focus only on the way in which agents are believed to respond to fiction. As a result, claim Livingston and Mele, the question of how agents *ought* to respond to fiction remains largely unexplored. Livingston and Mele seek to identify the conditions under which emotional responses to fiction are rational and aesthetically or artistically appropriate. Having first discussed what makes emotional responses to actual situations rational, Livingston and Mele go on to contend that an analysis of the appropriateness of responses to fiction requires an account of truth in fiction, and they present an intentionalist version of such an account. Livingston and Mele take issue with Gregory Currie's analysis of sophisticated responses to fiction, focusing on the "autonomy of fictional events thesis" on which it depends. They argue that in many cases, agents' responses to fictional truths should be essentially the same as those that would be appropriate to analogous, nonfictional truths.

In "Fetishism and Objectivity in Aesthetic Emotion" (chapter 11), Ronald de Sousa asks three questions:

1. Should our attitude to art be essentially different from our attitude to people?
2. What is the role of the particular in aesthetic experience? . . .
3. Can we isolate components of our experience, in such a way as to separate the aesthetic element from other interests?

In an attempt to respond to these questions, de Sousa develops an account of what he calls "aesthetic akrasia," a typical example of which is fetishism. Drawing in part on anthropological and psychoanalytic concepts, de Sousa defines fetishism as "the valuing of a *particular* object for the sake of its causal link to some other particular, which is held to be of intrinsic (or at least prior) value." An agent's response to a work of art is fetishistic if, for example, it is based to some important extent on the work's monetary value or on its connection with particular persons. Whereas fetishistic responses to people are rational, de Sousa claims, fetishistic responses to art are not obviously so. Yet, says de Sousa, there can "be no systematic basis for making a difference between those of our emotions that are targeted to people and those that are targeted to art." De Sousa argues that although "the objects of aesthetic experience are . . . essentially general," our responses to works of art are often influenced by "the identity of the particular target that gives rise to them." He further contends that "there is not and cannot be any independent criterion for the identity of two experiences," which, in his mind, means that it is impossible to distinguish rigorously between the aesthetic and other dimensions of our emotional responses to art. De Sousa's argument casts a strongly skeptical light on projects dedicated to determining the rationality of emotional responses to art.

In "Art, Narrative, and Emotion" (chapter 12), Noël Carroll draws on a broadly cognitive theory of emotion to argue that our emotional responses to fictional narratives can be assessed in terms of norms that are reflected in the very structure of the narratives themselves. Texts, as he puts it, are "criterially prefocused," thereby encouraging, though not necessarily guaranteeing, a certain kind of response. Horror, for example, combines fear and disgust. Whereas the criterion of fear is the harmful, the criterion of disgust is the impure. Horror narratives thus typically involve descriptions of beings that are both harmful and impure, as well as accounts of characters' horrified responses to the monsters in question. The appropriate emotional response to a narrative that is criterially prefocused in this way is horror. In Carroll's view, eliciting the appropriate emotional response is anything but a trivial matter. On the contrary, this kind of response is the very "condition of our comprehending and following the work." Emotions, then, are not the maladaptive phenomena that Plato and others have taken them to be. Indeed, according to Carroll, emotions, including those elicited by art, possess a certain rationality.

Part IV, entitled "The Value of Emotion," includes contributions dealing with three related topics: the cognitive and broadly ethical value of emotional responses to art; the ethical value of some *specific* emotions traditionally associated with women's writing and with certain forms of low art; and the emotional responses generated by works of art that somehow challenge our most fundamental values.

In "Toward a Poetics of Emotion" (chapter 13), Willie van Peer proposes an account of the value of literature and of the emotions it elicits. He situates his discussion in the context of rival views of art and emotion associated with Plato and Aristotle.

Van Peer contends that the issues raised by these figures are now better understood as a result of empirical, literary, and social-scientific research on emotion. Van Peer's goal is to resolve the conflict between Platonic and Aristotelian conceptions, and to this end he endorses Herbert Simon's contention that the emotions involve "hot cognition." Emotions are held to direct our attention to crucial concerns and to help sustain an unusually intense level of psychological involvement with those concerns. Yet, if "emotions powerfully focus our psychic energies on a particularly pressing problem," they do not identify "some kind of solution to that problem." This inability of the emotions to deal fully with the very concerns they create or foreground may, following van Peer, be described as the "paradox of emotion." Although this paradox seems to support a negative view of emotion as a mere obstacle to effective action, van Peer insists that it in fact helps to identify the unique value of emotions elicited by literature. At times, he says, it is essential to refrain from means-end deliberations and to surrender instead to a contemplative process focused on fundamental concerns. Literature is valuable, then, precisely because it deals with and elicits emotions that enrich our sensibilities and promote a deeper understanding of the things that really matter to us.

In chapter 14 entitled "In Defense of Sentimentality," Robert Solomon examines some of the charges that have been leveled against sentimentality, where the latter is understood as involving an "appeal to tender feelings." Solomon claims that sentimentality came to be seen in a negative light around the same time that moral sentiment theory lost ground to a Kantian conception of ethics. Solomon suggests that Kant's hostility toward the tender emotions was engendered in part by the sentimental writings of European and North American women, in which "virtue and goodness" were equated with "gushing sentiment." Solomon's account of changing attitudes toward sentimentality provides the historical backdrop for his analysis of sweet kitsch, which he takes to be a prime manifestation of sentimentality in art. Solomon admits that there may be ample grounds for dismissing sweet kitsch as bad art, but he takes issue with the widespread assumption that the sentimentality of kitsch should be condemned on ethical grounds. The tender emotions, such as "pity, sympathy, fondness, adoration, [and] compassion," are neither ethically undesirable nor irrelevant, because they provide the basis for a properly human response to ethical issues. The sentimentality of certain kinds of art is of ethical value precisely because it cultivates our moral faculties, stimulating and exercising "our sympathies without straining or exhausting them."

In "The Anaesthetics of Emotion" (chapter 15), David Novitz begins by noting that we tend to respond with strong emotions to challenges to our most deeply held convictions. What is curious and requires explanation, claims Novitz, is the fact that art frequently induces us to abandon our favored values and beliefs *without* giving rise to such emotions. It is this ability of art to block such responses that constitutes what Novitz calls the "anaesthetics of emotion." In the first part of his contribution, Novitz provides a detailed explanation of this phenomenon. He then goes on to deal with the "critical paradox" discussed above, which involves responses other than those dictated by the conventions of art.

Chapter 16, written by Keith Oatley and Mitra Gholamain and entitled "Emotions and Identification: Connections Between Readers and Fiction," exemplifies an influential cognitive approach to reading and emotion. Oatley and Gholamain argue that fiction is best understood as a kind of simulation, not imitation, of life. Much like Currie and Walton, Oatley and Gholamain believe that simulation theory provides a key to understanding the place of emotion in art.

The authors of "Emotions and Identification" aim to clarify the processes involved in reading fiction and to identify related connections between texts and readers. In the course of their discussion, Oatley and Gholamain suggest ways of understanding the value of these connections. The emotions represented in, and provoked by, fiction are crucial in this regard. The authors draw on the cognitive theory of emotion proposed in Oatley's *Best Laid Schemes: The Psychology of Emotions*,[23] where emotions are described as enabling agents to manage actions and goals. Much like van Peer, who relies on this same work, Oatley and Gholamain contend that the value of emotional responses to art lies in their being severed from immediate action. Arts such as literature, theatre, and film allow us to focus intensely on certain emotions, thereby affording us a better understanding of the relation between our emotions, beliefs, desires, and actions.

NOTES

1. For an excellent account of the history of antitheatrical thinking, see Barish 1981.

2. See Prynne [1633] 1972.

3. See Nicole [1667] 1971. The *Traité* was first published in 1667 as part of *Les Imaginaires ou lettres sur l'hérésie*. See also the discussion of Prynne and Nicole in "The Theater of Emotions" in Hjort's *The Strategy of Letters* (1993).

4. See Diderot [1906] 1958.

5. See Stanislavski 1936.

6. See Brecht 1957, 87–90. For an illuminating discussion of Brechtian views of emotion, see Murray Smith 1996.

7. *The Theater and Its Double* (1958).

8. See his reference to the recto and verso of existence in *The Theater and Its Double* (1958).

9. *Emotion* (1980), 25.

10. See his *Literary Knowledge: Humanistic Inquiry and the Philosophy of Science* (1988), 233–34, 238–42.

11. This point is made clearly by Gregory Currie, who characterizes his use of simulation theory as an attempt "to break out of the philosopher's ghetto within which the aesthetician so often finds herself imprisoned."

12. See Lyons's *Emotion* (1980), chap. 1 ("Three classical theories of emotion: the feeling, behaviourist and psychoanalytic theories").

13. Lyons, *Emotion* (1980), 33.

14. See de Sousa's *The Rationality of Emotion* (1987), Solomon's *The Passions* (1976), and Lyons's *Emotion* (1980).

15. "An Outline of the Social Constructionist Viewpoint," in *The Social Construction of Emotions* (1986), edited by Rom Harré, 2–14, 9.

16. See Catherine Lutz's much cited "Need, Nurturance, and the Emotions on a Pacific Atoll" (1995).

17. Harré 1986, 4.

18. See Solomon's "The Cross-Cultural Comparison of Emotion" (1995), 263.

19. See Lyons's critique of the "three classical theories of emotion" and his account of the "causal-evaluative theory" in *Emotion* (1980).

20. Harré 1986, 6.

21. *The Nature of Fiction* (1990), 187. For other discussions of the paradox of fiction, see Charlton 1984; Walton 1978; Dammann 1992; Lamarque 1981; Yanal 1994; and Novitz 1980.

22. See *Reading with Feeling: The Aesthetics of Appreciation* (1996), esp. 140–42.

23. New York: Cambridge University Press, 1992.

I

Emotion in Response to Art

A Survey of the Terrain

JERROLD LEVINSON

Responding emotionally to artworks is a familiar enough occurrence, and hardly seems puzzling, recalled at that level of generality. Why should not works of art, in company with people, animals, natural objects, and political events, produce emotions in us? Philosophers have, however, raised questions about emotional responses to art in particular contexts or when viewed from certain angles. These questions suggest that there is indeed something puzzling about such emotions.

One such context is that of fiction, whether literary, dramatic, or cinematic: emotions appear to be had not only for the work itself, but for the fictional characters or situations represented therein, even though these are understood not to exist. A second such context is that of abstract or nonrepresentational art, with music the preeminent example, where it is unclear both what could elicit such a response and what its object could be. A third context is that in which artworks expressive of negative emotion—for example, tragedies, requiems, and tales of horror—engender parallel responses in perceivers without evoking avoidance or disapproval. And a fourth context in which emotional response to art has struck philosophers as problematic is where the proper appreciation of art is at issue. Is such appreciation compatible with experiencing the familiar emotions that art seems capable of raising in us?

We might formulate the main philosophical questions concerning emotion in response to art as follows: (1) What kind or type of emotions are had in response to works of art? (2) How can we intelligibly have emotions for fictional persons or situations, given that we do not believe in their existence? (This query relates to what is known as "the paradox of fiction.") (3) How and why do abstract works of art, especially musical ones, generate emotions in audiences, and toward what do audiences then have these emotions? (4) How can we make sense of the interest appreciators have in empathetically experiencing art that expresses negative emotions? (A particular form of this query is "the paradox of tragedy.") (5) Is there a tension or conflict between responding emotionally to art and what aesthetic appreciation of art demands?

Answers to these questions depend, to some extent, on the conception of emotion adopted. I begin this essay by sketching a conception of the emotions that mediates between the sensationalist model of early twentieth-century psychology and the cognitivist model generally favored in current philosophy.[1] With that as background, various responses to the above questions will be critically reviewed.

I. The Nature of Emotions

In order fruitfully to assess the varieties of emotional response to art, it is obviously of use to have some account of what exactly emotions (in the occurrent, as opposed to dispositional, sense) are. Philosophical debate on the nature of emotions, informed to greater or lesser degree by available work in psychology, has in the past thirty years or so revolved around an opposition between feeling- (or sensation) based and thought- (or cognition) based approaches. The former holds that at the core of an emotion is an internal feeling or set of sensations, while the latter holds that at the core of an emotion is a particular kind of thought, judgment, or evaluation. While the feeling approach has trouble accommodating the intentionality (or object-directedness) and amenability to reason of many emotions, the thought approach has trouble with the experiential aspect of emotions (that is, with what it is to feel emotions as opposed to merely having beliefs or entertaining thoughts); with the evident inertia and passivity of many emotional conditions; as well as with states of desire, whose connection with many emotions seems more than contingent. Still, while the feeling approach can be faulted for presenting too "mindless" a picture of emotions, it is right to insist on bodily response and inner affect of some sort as a sine qua non of emotion. Similarly, while the thought approach can be faulted for too "mindful" a picture of emotions, it is right to emphasize that many emotions include essentially cognitive elements, that is, thoughts with specific contents, which contents are in many cases socially shaped.

At present there appears to be some consensus that in perhaps the majority of cases an emotion is best thought of as a bodily response with a distinctive physiological, phenomenological, and expressive profile, one that serves to focus attention in a given direction, and that involves cognition to varying degrees and at various levels. The level of cognitive involvement runs from mere registering of presence, to ways of seeing or regarding that which is registered, to propositional conceptions of the object responded to, to articulate beliefs about or attitudes toward the object of response. Alternatively put, an experienced emotion has as its core a bodily reaction—comprising physiological sensations, feelings of comfort and discomfort, and orientings of attention—which is often caused or modified by, and is sometimes necessarily bound up with, cognitions of various sorts and strengths, depending on the type of emotion involved. Such a view of emotion, which sees cognitive representations on the order of beliefs or desires as characteristic of, but not essential to, experienced emotion, preserves the intentionality or directedness of emotions (as opposed to moods) by accepting that a root feature of emotion is the orientation of attention to or focusing of concern on that which the subject registers as significant.[2]

On the other hand, there is also a growing acknowledgment that the pretheoretically recognized emotions constitute an irreducibly heterogeneous class, that is, that they do not form a "natural kind."[3] It seems reasonable to recognize a spectrum of emotional states experienced by humans, from the startle reaction, involving minimal cognition, at one end; to pride, envy, shame, jealousy, grief, remorse, embarrassment and the like, involving complex and often morally conditioned cognitions, at the other end; with hunger, surprise, lust, fear, anger, joy, sorrow, and so on filling in the vast middleground. The emotional responses typical of engagement with art, though, tend to be of the moderately, or highly, cognitively involved sort. This fact is relevant to some recent attempts to dissolve too quickly the paradox of fiction by appeal to what need not be true of all cases of emotion.

Although it is convenient to speak of emotions having elements or components of various sorts, such as thoughts, sensations, desires, feelings, pleasures, pains, or shifts of attention, these should not be thought of as simply bundled together, and the emotion as a mere conglomeration. The truth is, rather, that an emotion is an *ordered* complex or structure of the elements it is taken to comprehend, with *causal* relations prominent among those in which this order consists. For example, my anger at my wife for having carelessly misplaced my keys is a bodily response, rooted in physiology and reflected in countenance, involving a focusing of attention on her and feelings of agitation and displeasure. These feelings result jointly from my thought of her action and my desire that she not have so acted, while fueling, perhaps, my desire that she in some way pay for having so acted.

II. Emotional Response to Representational Art:
The Paradox of Fiction

The much-discussed paradox of fiction can be formulated as a set of three propositions, to each of which we seem to have strong allegiance, but which are jointly inconsistent and thus impossible to maintain as a coherent set. Solutions to the paradox typically take the form of rejecting one or more of the propositions, with a reasoned justification for doing so. The propositions are these: (a) We often have emotions for fictional characters and situations known to be purely fictional; (b) Emotions for objects logically presuppose beliefs in the existence and features of those objects; (c) We do not harbor beliefs in the existence and features of objects known to be fictional. In the extensive discussion of this conundrum in the literature, almost every possible solution to it has been essayed. The following comprise most of the solutions that have found adherents.

1. *The non-intentionalist solution.* Emotional responses to fictions are not, despite appearances, instances of emotions as such, but rather of less complex states, such as moods (e.g., cheerfulness) or reflex reactions (e.g., shock), which lack the full intentionality and cognitivity of emotions per se. This solution involves the denial of (a), but the diagnosis it offers seems to apply comfortably to only a small portion of the full range of developed responses to fictions.

2. *The suspension-of-disbelief solution.* While caught up in fictions, consumers thereof temporarily allow themselves to believe in the nonexistent characters and situations of the fiction, and thus to have bona fide emotions for them, reverting to standing beliefs in the nonexistence of such characters or situations once the fiction no longer actively engages them. Such a solution turns on a denial of (c); though popular in the nineteenth century, it unacceptably depicts consumers of fiction as having both a rather tenuous grip on reality and an amazing ability to manipulate their beliefs at will.[4]

3. *The surrogate-object solution.* Emotional responses to fictions take as their real objects not known-to-be-nonexistent persons and events in fictions, but other objects, both existent and believed to be existent. This solution, in one way or another, thus calls (a) into question.

In one version of this solution, the object of response is simply the fictional work or artistic representation itself, or parts thereof. In another version, the objects of response are rather the descriptions, images, propositions, or thought contents afforded by the fiction or representation.[5] And in a third version, different enough from the preceding two to deserve a separate label—the *shadow-object proposal*—the objects of response are real individuals or phenomena from the subject's life experience, ones resembling the persons or events of the fiction, and of which the fiction puts the subject covertly or indirectly in mind.[6]

The surrogate-object solution in its first two guises distorts the logic and phenomenology of emotional response to fictions. Whatever the nature or status of our response to fictional characters or situations, it is an emotional response to *them*, not to something else. Our responses, however ultimately analyzed, have those characters and situations as their evident objects, and not the vehicles that bring them to us or the thoughts through which they are delineated. Much the same complaint can be brought against the shadow-object proposal, though here it is clear that the sort of response to which the proposal draws attention does indeed often accompany and underlie the emotional response to fictional matters per se. Still, despising a fictional character, for instance, is not simply reducible to despising people of that sort generally, or to despising some actual similar individual of one's acquaintance.

4. *The antijudgmentalist solution.* Emotional responses to objects do not logically require beliefs concerning the existence or features of such objects, but only weaker sorts of cognitions, such as seeing a certain way, or conceiving in a certain manner, or regarding as if such and such. Thus, there is no good reason to categorize the emotional responses had toward fictions as anything other than standard, since they satisfy the demands of a more relaxed cognitivism about emotions. This approach to the paradox, which directly challenges (b), has a growing number of proponents, and merits extended discussion.[7]

The instances of emotional response that challenge judgmentalism—the view that the cognitive element involved in all emotions is a judgment or belief—are mostly of two types. The first type is where there is insufficient time for cognition as such, so that no real representation of the object responded to is formed, there being only a virtually instantaneous reaction, instinctive or reflexive in nature, unmediated by conscious thought (examples: apprehension at a suddenly looming shape, disgust at an accidentally felt slug). A second type is where, though cognition is involved in generating the response, the representation thus formed is either not propositional in nature, or else does not have the status of a judgment, or both (examples: phobic fear of garter snakes, unfounded resentment of female superiors).

As noted earlier, the emotions involved in responding to fictions, ones such as pity, sorrow, love, admiration, anger, hate, and hope, lie in the main in the middle and upper ranges of cognitive complexity for emotions. It thus seems undeniable that, whether or not they involve beliefs, such emotions are centrally mediated by representations of various sorts, such as views, conceptions, or evaluations, that serve to characterize the object of response.

But even if emotions at this cognitive level do not necessarily involve beliefs of a *characterizing* sort about their objects, it seems that such emotions must still involve *existential* beliefs in regard to those objects, or something very close to that—that is, attitudes or stances on the order of *taking to exist* or *regarding as existent.* Otherwise, the state attributed becomes unintelligible, whether as an emotion or anything else. How can one be said to pity, fear, admire, or hate something that one does not, concurrently with one's emotion, at least *take* or *regard* as existing, now or at some other time? If indeed that cannot be said, then the problem resurfaces, despite what is right in the critique of judgmentalism: since sane consumers of fiction do *not* take, regard, or view fictional characters as existing, even when fully engaged with them appreciatively, they cannot really be in the full-fledged emotional states they are casually said to inhabit. The paradox of fiction is proof against antijudgmentalist dissolution, even if we grant that emotions can occur without characterizing beliefs.[8]

The sticking point of the paradox of fiction is the dimension of existence and nonexistence, as this connects to the cognitive characterization that emotions of the sort in question minimally require. When we *view* or *conceive* an object as having such and such properties, whether or not we strictly *believe* that it does, we must, on pain of incoherence, be *taking* said object to exist or be *regarding* it as existent. For nothing can coherently be viewed or conceived as having properties without at the same time being treated as existent. A case of genuine emotion of a cognitively mediated sort, unlike a corresponding emotional response to a fictional character, involves at least viewing or conceiving an object as having such and such features, which thus in turn presupposes regarding it as existent or taking it to exist.

But I do not, when reading Dostoyevsky's *The Brothers Karamazov*, take Smerdyakov to exist, and so cannot strictly be viewing or conceiving him as having properties, such as being base or being a murderer. My evaluative Smerdyakov-thoughts, generated as I read, may largely be what causes my hateful response, directed ostensibly at him, but for that response strictly to have *him* as its object, and so count clearly as an instance of hatred *of* Smerdyakov, requires that I take him to exist—which, once more, I clearly do not.

However, it may be the case that I *imagine* or *make-believe* that someone to that effect exists, and that as a result I imaginarily, or make-believedly, experience toward him an emotion of hate. Elaborating, my response to Dostoyevsky's character can be interpreted, not as truly one of hatred for Smerdyakov, but as various sensations, feelings, and focusings of attention caused in me by my Smerdyakov-thoughts in the course of making believe that he and his world exist, which may as a result amount to my make-believedly, or imaginarily, hating Smerdyakov. (For more on this, see item 7.)

5. *The surrogate-belief solution.* Certain emotional responses to fictions, such as pity, require belief only that, *in the fiction*, the character exists and is or does such and such, and *that* belief is indeed widely held by rational consumers of fiction. This solution thus rejects (c), though not in the manner of suspension-of-disbelief theorists.[9]

However, the beliefs this proposed solution highlights, ones about what is fictionally the case, can only ground the truth of one's *fictionally*, or imaginarily, pitying a character, not of one's *literally* doing so. Furthermore, that such beliefs play a role in generating emotional responses to fictions does not touch the heart of the paradox, which is that intelligible emotions for objects of the sort typical of engagement with fiction conceptually require beliefs in the existence of such objects, or at a minimum, existential stances toward them. Beliefs about how things are fictionally can cause emotional reactions of some sort, but they cannot logically ground intelligible emotions for entities whose existence is denied. They are the wrong sort of beliefs even partly to constitute the sort of emotions that constitutively require beliefs. For example, the beliefs I have in connection with Anna Karenina cannot coherently make her the proper object of any pitiful reaction I might have. Pity involves concern for the welfare of and distress at the suffering of some creature. If one doesn't believe such welfare or suffering is actual, what can one be concerned *for* or distressed *about*? Pity may likewise involve wishes or desires with respect to the thing pitied, but absent a belief in the thing, or more loosely, an existential stance toward it, there cannot coherently be any such wishes or desires.

6. *The irrationalist solution.* While caught up in fictions, consumers of fiction become irrational, responding emotionally to objects that they know do not exist and thus do not have the features they are represented as having.

Irrationalists implicitly deny (c), proposing that we in some manner do endorse the existence of fictional characters and events, while apparently at the same time disavowing them, which qualifies as irrational, in the sense of inconsistent. Alternatively, they implicitly deny (b), holding that we can have emotions for phenomena such as fictional characters and events, toward which we lack the usual beliefs, but qualifying such emotions consequently as irrational, in the sense of unwarranted.[10]

In the first construal, the irrationalist solution approaches closely that of suspension of disbelief, with the difference, perhaps, that no attempt is made to mitigate the clash of existential stances involved by suggesting that they are not simultaneously in full force. In the second construal, the irrationalist solution holds appreciators of fiction at fault, not for believing what they already believe the negation of—that fictional characters and events exist—but for emotionally responding to such characters and events in ways contraindicated by their beliefs.

It might seem that the irrationalist solution, in this second construal, is saved from being a nonstarter by the rejection of judgmentalism, since otherwise it could be held to be simply impossible, rather than just possibly irrational, to experience full-fledged emotions in the absence of certain beliefs. But as suggested earlier, if the critique of judgmentalism, applied to emotions of the sort that fiction typically elicits, shows only that characterizing beliefs, as opposed to existential ones, may be absent in such cases, the logical space this construal hopes to occupy may not be available.

In any event, in the judgment of most commentators, portraying the normal consumer of fiction as fundamentally enmeshed in irrationality, however this be understood, is too high a price to pay for this to be an acceptable solution to the paradox.[11]

7. *The make-believe, or imaginary, solution.* Emotional responses to fictions cannot strictly be instances of the ordinary emotions with whose names we tend to label them, but are instead instances of imaginary, or make-believe, emotions.[12] First, the standard emotions of life arguably have belief or belief-like presuppositions, notably existential ones, that are not fulfilled in normal engagement with fictions; second, such emotions have motivational or behavioral consequences that are not in evidence in the course of such engagement.

The proposal is that in our interactions with works of fiction we experience make-believe emotions, or make-believedly we experience emotions, for fictional characters and situations. Thus, this solution rejects (a). Make-believedly experiencing fear, say, is enough like really experiencing fear, especially internally, that it is easily confused with it, and yet make-believedly experiencing fear can be reconciled, while really experiencing fear cannot, with the absence of existential endorsement and motivational upshot vis-à-vis the fictions that are feared. In this way the paradox is finally resolved.

In considering this solution, it is important to distinguish the claim that what we feel for fictional characters is *some* kind of emotion, or constitutes emotional response in the broad sense, from the claim, here disputed, that what we feel for fictional characters and name as some ordinary emotion is *literally* an example of such emotion. We are indeed moved, this solution affirms, but not strictly to the standard emotions whose names come to our lips. The issue is not whether making-believe can cause various emotional reactions, but whether those reactions, given that certain cognitive conditions are not satisfied, qualify as full-fledged emotions of the ordinary sort. Note also that to classify our emotions for fictions as imaginary is to say that they are ones we *imagine* ourselves to be having, on the basis of experiences, contributory to emotion, that we are *actually* having, but it is not to imply that such emotions are illusory or unreal.

What makes some philosophers reluctant to accept that our emotional relations to fictional objects might be of a different stripe from our emotional relations to objects we take as existent (as the make-believe theory insists) is the sense that, to the person experiencing them, they seem very much the same—they *feel* the same, we might say. But as has been observed, there is more to emotional conditions than feelings. Cognitive and conative commitments play a role in the identity of many, though not all, emotions; thus, if those commitments vary, so may the emotion that is present.[13]

Though the make-believe proposal thus probably provides the best resolution to the paradox of fiction, a full account of our emotional responses when engaged with fictions—as opposed to our emotions for fictional characters per se—will want to acknowledge what is called to our attention by the nonintentionalist and surrogate-object proposals as well.[14] And even the irrationalist proposal, on the first construal, may contain a grain of truth, for perhaps we are, at least at moments of maximum involvement, in the incoherent states of mind it postulates as ours throughout.

III. Emotional Response to Abstract Art:
Music and Feeling

Emotional response to abstract art is puzzling, principally, because the strategies that provide obvious explanations of both *why* we respond emotionally, and *what* we are responding to, in the case of representational art, here seem not to be available. A novel, film, Impressionist landscape, or Greek vase gives me the image of a human world, elements of which I can empathize or identify with, react to sympathetically or antipathetically, or even mirror unthinkingly, by a sort of natural contagion. But with a symphony, sonata, Minimalist sculpture, or Abstract Expressionist painting, such explanations appear to have no purchase. Human beings and their predicaments are notably absent, at least as far as representation is concerned. So why, or how, does perception of such artworks raise emotion, and toward what is such emotion directed?[15] Concentrating for brevity's sake on the art of music, rough answers to these questions follow.

Insofar as music is capable of eliciting emotions in listeners, it appears to work through two different routes or mechanisms, typically operating in tandem. The first we may label the sensory, or cognitively unmediated, route, and the second the perceptual-imaginative, or cognitively mediated, route. It seems undeniable that music has a certain power to induce sensations, feelings, and even moods by virtue of its basic musical properties, virtually without any interpretation or construal on the listener's part. Particular timbres, rhythms, intervals, dynamics, and tempi exemplify this power most clearly. Such properties need only be registered to have their effect, at least for an auditor acclimatized to a given musical culture. The rise in heartbeat caused by rapid tempo, the discomfort occasioned by dissonant intervals, the kinetic impulses induced by dancing rhythms, the excitement produced by quick alternations of soft and loud, or the relaxation engendered by a certain tone color or manner of articulation are all familiar phenomena.

But if the capacity of music to elicit emotion were exhausted by the direct effects of sensing basic musical features, it would be a poor thing, falling far short of the evocation of emotions proper, or even the semblance of such. The gap is filled by the second, or cognitively mediated, route to such evocation.

In addition to presenting an array of sonic features, simultaneously and successively, much music offers the appearance of human emotion, or of persons outwardly manifesting emotional states; arguably, that is what the expressiveness of music largely consists in. In other words, music is often heard as, heard as if, or just imagined to be, the expression of emotion by an unspecified individual, whom we may call the music's "persona." The degree of resemblance between the shape of the music and the behaviors through which emotions are commonly expressed in life will have something, though not everything, to do with our being disposed to hear music in such ways. In any event, once this occurs, the mechanisms mentioned above and familiar from appreciation of representational art—mirroring, identification, empathy, sympathy, antipathy—can come into play, resulting in the arousal in the auditor of those same emotions, or the feelings characteristic of them, or those emotions on an imaginary plane. The sensory aspect of music alone indeed seems capable of inducing in us at least a number of simple states of arousal typically identified as constituent elements of one or another emotion. But it is the perceptual-imaginative aspect, manifested in our disposition to hear emotion or emotional expression in music, that is surely primarily responsible for the complex, more robustly emotional responses to music, whether mirroring or reactive, that so many listeners report.

These mechanisms do not operate in total isolation from each other. The emotion I perceive in a passage of music may soften or accentuate the particular psychological effect some basic musical feature produces on me, while the effect induced in me, largely unthinkingly, by some basic musical feature may influence and constrain the emotion I am disposed to hear an image of in the music.

But if emotions are often produced in listeners by virtue of auditing emotionally expressive music, toward what are such emotions directed? Music neither supplies any objects, nor appears itself to be an appropriate object, for the vast majority of emotions that are putatively aroused. In addition, music does not seem to provide anything that would justify the beliefs or attitudes toward objects that many emotions can be held to require. Among the ways of responding to this difficulty are the following.

It can be held that music produces in listeners only moods, such as anxiety or elation, which intrinsically lack intentionality, or else "objectless" emotions, ones that characteristically take objects but somehow lack them when aroused by music, such as sadness or joy directed toward nothing, or nothing in particular.

Alternatively, it can be held that music produces in listeners just the feeling component of an emotion, together with the sense of focus or directedness inherent in the bodily response at the emotion's core, but not the cognitions that characteristically accompany or even partly constitute the emotion.

Finally, it could be maintained that what music occasions in many listeners are states of imaginary emotion. That is, listeners may readily erect, upon a basis of feelings produced in them by music whose expressiveness they empathetically grasp, imagined emotions of a corresponding sort, and they may do this through imagining, usually tacitly, objects and thoughts suitable to the emotions in question. The object of musical emotion, then, is not missing, but merely indefinitely posited in imagination, or perhaps logically appropriated from the emotion imaginarily ascribed to the music's persona.

IV. Emotional Response to Negatively Emotional Art:
The Paradox of Tragedy

The paradox of negative emotion in art, of which the paradox of tragedy is a classical illustration, is this. Art that is negatively emotional—that is, art that represents, expresses, or otherwise deals with emotions such as shame, grief, horror, sorrow, anger, remorse, and despair, seems to have a propensity to elicit parallel responses in appreciators. But if that is so, one would expect appreciators to avoid, or at any rate, regard as inferior, art of this nature. Yet not only do they not do so, but often they hold such art in the highest esteem, considering it perhaps to be the most rewarding art of all.

A number of possible explanations have been given for why people rationally desire or value the empathic experience of negatively emotional art, given the ostensibly negative character of that experience. Following is a general categorization of such explanations:

- Compensatory explanations: negative emotion aroused by negatively emotional art is, as such, unpleasant, but undergoing it offers other rewards that compensate for this.
- Conversionary explanations: negative emotion, which is initially or ordinarily a disagreeable response, is transformed in the context of artistic appreciation into something that is in fact agreeable, or at any rate, capable of being enjoyed.
- Organicist explanations: negative emotion aroused by negatively emotional art is an essential element in a total experience, an organic whole, that is desired or valued.

- Revisionary explanations: neither negative emotions, nor the feelings they include, are intrinsically unpleasant or undesirable, and thus there is nothing odd about appreciating art that induces such emotions or feelings.
- Deflationary explanations: despite appearances, neither negative emotions, nor the feelings they include, are really aroused in us by negatively emotional art.

Compensatory explanations include Aristotle's doctrine of catharsis, understood as a purging or purification of excess or unruly emotions of pity and fear through engagement with tragic drama, which justifies the raising of such emotions in the course of that engagement. Another such explanation holds that engagement with "tragic" art affords valuable knowledge of important truths of human existence.[16] A third explanation endorses such engagement, not for the knowledge of life it may afford, but rather for the knowledge of the artwork it facilitates, emotional engagement with a work being seen as a necessary cost, in many cases, of fully understanding it.[17] A fourth such explanation invokes the moral exercise that is provided, or the moral deepening that results, as a benefit of engagement with negatively emotional art. And a fifth explanation appeals to purely aesthetic pleasures in the beauty, lifelikeness, virtuosity, or cognitive interest of the representation or expression itself, positing these as enough to outweigh whatever negative emotion is undergone in their appreciation.[18]

Conversionary explanations include Hume's explanation of the appreciation of tragedy; like that just noted, Hume's explanation highlights the pleasure in artistic representation and expression as such, but premises that this pleasure, being greater than the pain of the negative emotions concomitantly raised, does not simply offset that pain, but rather overwhelms and absorbs it, leaving an experience of uniformly positive character. A rather different conversionary explanation proposes that since the negative emotions raised by a work of art have no life implications for spectators, calling for no actions and betokening no real harms, such emotions must evidently be so altered by the artistic conditions under which they issue that, though still recognizable as this or that negative emotion and disagreeable affects intact, they are yet capable of being relished or enjoyed for experience's sake.[19]

An example of an organicist explanation would be one invoking a satisfaction in some negative emotion having been raised in one by a work of art, perhaps because the emotion strikes one as appropriately raised in such circumstances, and oneself as admirably human for being thus susceptible. Such a satisfaction would obviously be inseparable from the negative emotion raised, in the fact of which satisfaction is taken.[20] Another such explanation would appeal to the value of working through negative emotions in connection with a work of art, via immersion in its formal, narrative, or dramatic structure, the emotions raised thus being an essential element in the experience valued as a whole.[21]

Revisionary explanations propose that the experience of negative emotions is not intrinsically unpleasant; the affects—that is, the sensations and feelings—involved are not in themselves disagreeable, and can be unproblematically savored as such, in appropriate contexts. What is negative about negative emotions is only the *evaluation* of their objects that is central to such emotions. Thus, there is no special difficulty about people seeking these emotions from art.[22]

Deflationary explanations come in at least three varieties. One hypothesizes artistic *analogues* of the life emotions, distinct from them in hedonic tone, conative connectedness, and behavioral implication, and proposes that only these are raised in us by engagement with emotional art, and not the life emotions themselves. Another deflationary explanation simply denies that anything like the garden-variety emotions are evoked in subjects in the course of engaging with emotional art, and suggests that the subject's response, insofar as it is emotional, is exhausted by properly *appreciative* reactions, such as being moved by a work's beauty of expression.[23] A third deflationary explanation maintains that spectators are always only make-believedly in states of negative emotion by virtue of engaging with a work of art, and that on the assumption that make-believe emotions of the negative sort are *not* inherently displeasing, there is no special problem about people tolerating, or even actively pursuing, such experiences.[24]

Detailed assessment of these proposals awaits another occasion, but in my view there is more merit in compensatory and organicist explanations, and in the second of the conversionary explanations sketched above, than in revisionary or deflationary ones.

V. Emotion and the Appreciation of Art

Are there emotions unique to the appreciation of art, or aesthetic emotions per se, had when and only when a work is apprehended aesthetically? Past theorists, notably Clive Bell, have posited something of this sort, but such a posit has not lately found favor, nor does it appear to respond to any pressing theoretical problem about art.[25] There may, on the other hand, be an interesting category of positive emotions that, if not had uniquely for art, are both distinctive of the appreciation of art and not of the sort that typically figure in the content of art. Candidates for membership in this category would include admiration for a work's skill, fascination with a work's form, delight in a work's beauty, or awe at a work's depth of insight or expression. What might also figure here are experiences, remarked by many, of momentary will-lessness or self-transcendence occasioned by intense absorption in a work of art.

The question may also be raised as to the appropriateness of emotional responses to art of the ordinary sort. One form of this question concerns an apparent tension between the familiar picture of an emotion as a disturbing derangement of the psyche and the image of aesthetic appreciation as a state of calm and unclouded attention to a work of art.

The traditional notion of the aesthetic attitude, rooted in Kant, Schopenhauer, and the eighteenth-century theorists of taste, depicts a frame of mind characterized by disinterestedness, detachment, and disengagement from the practical. Charitably construed, such a notion demands only that what primarily drives or directs one's response to a work not be one's personal situation or condition, but instead, the humanly significant material that the work presents. In other words, such a notion need not call for suppression of emotional receptivity generally. So long as one's emotional response is a way of connecting to a work, of tracing its expressive contours or grasping its dramatic import, rather than a distraction from it or a springboard to wallowing in one's private concerns, then there is no conflict between responding to a work with a range of ordinary emotions on the basis of one's life experience and individual sensibility, and appreciating a work in an aesthetically appropriate manner, as the specific embodiment of human content that it is. By contrast, disinterestedness or detachment understood not as a principle for maintaining focus on a work rather than one's own circumstances, but as a desired end-state of impassivity or imperturbability, is nothing an account of artistic appreciation need embrace.[26]

Finally, accounts of the value of emotional response to art can be divided roughly into those that exploit the value of emotional experience generally, for example, in contributing to a full life, and those that seek instead to identify a particular value of emotional experience in the context of art and its appreciation, for example, as a mode of understanding a work more fully or a means of reaping more efficiently the benefits a work has to offer.[27]

NOTES

1. See, for example, among recent major studies, Solomon 1976; Lyons 1980; Gordon 1987; de Sousa 1987; and Greenspan 1988. A useful review of this literature, to which I am indebted, is John Deigh 1994.

2. See, most relevantly, Jenefer Robinson 1995b.

3. See on this, in addition to Robinson 1995b, Griffiths 1997.

4. For discussion, see Schaper 1978 and Carroll 1990.

5. See, for example, Lamarque 1981 and Carroll 1990, chap. 2.

6. See, for example, Charlton 1984.

7. See, for example, Morreall 1993. For a response, see Neill 1995.

8. It is a mistake, in particular, to try to assimilate cases of fictional fear to cases of phobic fear, even apart from their evident divergence in behavioral consequences. With phobic fear we can say that although the subject doesn't believe the animal in question is dangerous, the subject at least conceives or views the animal as dangerous, all the while clearly believing that the animal exists, that there is something to be so conceived or viewed. With fictional fear, however, it is not open to us to say that the subject even conceives or views some fictional individual as dangerous or threatening, since the subject does not, if in his right mind, believe that such an individual exists; he does not believe there is any such thing to be so viewed or conceived. Full-blown fear of X has an irreducible cognitive component, one part of which is a viewing or perceiving X as dangerous or threatening, but another part of which is a taking or regarding X to exist, amounting in most, if not all, cases to a belief in X's existence.

9. See, for example, Neill 1993 and Yanal 1994.

10. See Radford and Weston 1975 and Slater 1993.

11. Having now largely completed our survey of responses to the paradox of fiction, it is worth revisiting briefly an issue we may have too quickly settled in setting up the terms of the problem. The issue is this: Is the principle that underlies the paradoxicality of emotional responses to fiction that of the *conceptual impossibility* (or logical impossibility) of a response being an emotion if it does not include, or is not premised on, certain beliefs (as embodied in (b) above in our formulation of the paradox)? Or is it, rather, that of the *irrationality* (or incoherence) of responding with emotion to things believed not to exist or not to be as they are described? We are now in a position to see that this may depend, to some extent, on whether one focuses on existence-beliefs or feature-beliefs regarding creatures of fiction. If the former (e.g., that Anna Karenina exists or existed), the issue is perhaps best understood as one of rationality: it is simply irrational to have an emotional response to something whose existence you don't credit in any measure. If the latter (e.g., that Anna Karenina suffers or suffered), again the issue might be construed as one of rationality—since pitying someone you don't believe suffers or has suffered seems to qualify as irrational—but it is perhaps better understood as concerned with the logical boundaries of the concept in question. So, for example, the logical boundaries of the emotion *pity for x* can reasonably be held logically to presuppose the belief that *x suffers* or *has suffered*, so that whatever one feels for an entity, it can't be pity unless one believes it to be a logically fit object for pity.

12. See Walton 1990 and Currie 1990.

13. But suppose it is replied that consumers of fiction *do* take or regard the characters encountered in fictions as existing, precisely insofar as they *imagine* them to exist as they engage with them. Well and good: this can mean only that, *imaginarily*, they take them to exist, or that *in the fiction*, they take them to exist—not that they take them to exist, *period*.

A dilemma presents itself, in short, for those who resist the make-believe solution to the paradox of fiction. Either such taking-to-exist of their objects as these emotions must be understood to involve amounts to *belief*, in which case the subject, who denies that fictional entities exist, is mired in inconsistency; or else such taking-to-exist amounts to *making-believe*-to-exist, in which case any emotion both based on that stance and directed to its object will be make-believe emotion, of the appropriate sort.

14. For some discussion in this vein, see Levinson 1996a.

15. See, on these matters, Scruton 1983; Budd 1985 and 1995; Kivy 1989 and 1990a; Radford 1989; Levinson 1990b, 1990a, and 1996a; Stephen Davies 1994; Robinson 1994; Sparshott 1994; Alan Goldman 1995; and Ridley 1995.

16. See, for instance, Packer 1989.

17. See, notably, Goodman 1968, 1976, chap. 6.

18. Noël Carroll's resolution of the paradox of horror—a first cousin of the paradox of tragedy—is largely of this sort (see Carroll 1990).

19. See, perhaps, Eaton 1982, and, in a musical context, Levinson 1990c.

20. See, in this vein, Feagin 1983.

21. See, perhaps, Morreall 1985; Robinson 1995a; and again, in a musical context, Levinson, "Music and Negative Emotion" (1990c).

22. A suggestion of this sort can be found in Walton 1990, chap. 7, and also in Gaut 1993.

23. A suggestion of this sort, applied to music, can be found in Kivy 1990a, chap. 8.

24. Suggestions of this sort are also to be found in Walton 1990.

25. But see the debates on this, pro and con, in Beardsley 1982 and Dickie 1974.

26. For further discussion, see Levinson 1996d.

27. See, for example, the discussion, as applied to music, in Stephen Davies 1994, chap. 6.

PART I

THE
PARADOX
OF FICTION

2

Spelunking, Simulation, and Slime

On Being Moved by Fiction

KENDALL WALTON

Works of fiction induce in appreciators thoughts about people, situations and events; let's say that they induce appreciators to *imagine* them. The imagined people, situations, and events are frequently ones that do not really exist or occur, but we can (as we do) speak of them as constituting a "fictional world," the world of the novel or story or film.

This much is not controversial. But it is important to realize how little it comes to, how much remains to be explained. Why should we be interested in these nonexistents? Why should we bother thinking about or imagining them? We haven't yet distinguished novels and other fictions from a mere list of sentences—sentences used in a grammar lesson, for instance. When we read and understand these sentences, they induce us to entertain the thoughts that they express. But that is all. Fictional worlds seem so far to be worlds apart, worlds having nothing to do with us, ones that we merely peer into from afar. As I put it in *Mimesis as Make-Believe:*

> If to read a novel or contemplate a painting were merely to stand outside a fictional world pressing one's nose against the glass and peer in, . . . our interest in novels and paintings would indeed be mysterious. We might expect to have a certain clinical curiosity about fictional worlds viewed from afar, but it is hard to see how that could account for the significance of representations, their capacity to be deeply moving, sometimes even to change our lives." [1]

Consider children's games of make-believe. Children do not peer into worlds apart, nor do they merely engage in a clinical intellectual exercise, entertaining thoughts about cops and robbers, or whatever. The children are in the thick of things; they *participate* in the worlds of their games. We appreciators also participate in games of make-believe, using works as props. Participation involves imagining about ourselves as well as about the characters and situations of the fiction—but not just imagining *that* such and such is true of ourselves. We imagine *doing* things, *experiencing* things, *feeling* in certain ways. We bring much of our actual selves, our real-life beliefs and attitudes and personalities, to our imaginative experiences, and we stand to learn about ourselves in the process.[2]

There have been lively discussions recently, in philosophy of mind and cognitive science, about what is called "mental simulation." Fiction and the representational arts are rarely mentioned in them, but the notion of mental simulation dovetails almost uncannily with my make-believe theory. Insights concerning simulation reinforce and augment my theory of fiction. Indeed, the participation in make-believe that I described is itself a form of mental simulation.[3]

Many discussions of *Mimesis as Make-Believe* have concentrated on my negative claim that it is not literally true, in ordinary circumstances, that appreciators fear, fear for, pity, grieve for, or admire purely fictitious characters. Charles, who fidgets and tenses and screams as he watches a horror movie, does not, I argue, really fear the Slime portrayed on the screen. The reasons that have been advanced against this claim are, in my opinion, very weak. Of even more concern, however, is the undue emphasis that commentators have put on this issue, at the expense of the positive aspects of my make-believe theory. This presents me with the ticklish job of defending the negative claim while directing attention to other more important matters. Simulation theory will be helpful in both parts of this task. In particular, it will help to counter a surprisingly prevalent assumption that imagining (and make-believe, which I understand in terms of imagining), or the kind of imagining central to my theory, can be only a clinical, antiseptic, intellectual exercise, and so cannot have a central role in explaining the genuinely emotional responses to fiction that appreciators (often) experience.

It goes without saying that we *are* genuinely moved by novels and films and plays, that we respond to works of fiction with real emotion. Some have misconstrued my make-believe theory as denying this. "[T]he key objection to Walton's theory," says Noël Carroll, "is that it relegates our emotional responses to fiction to the realm of make-believe."[4] That would indeed be a mistake. In fact, our responses to works of fiction are, not uncommonly, more highly charged emotionally than our reactions to actual situations and people of the kinds the work portrays. My make-believe theory was designed to help explain our emotional responses to fiction, not to call their very existence into question. My negative claim is *only* that our genuine emotional responses to works of fiction do not involve, literally, fearing, grieving for, admiring fictional characters.

LET'S BEGIN WITH an experiment. Imagine going on a spelunking expedition. You lower yourself into a hole in the ground and enter a dank, winding passageway. After a couple of bends there is absolute pitch darkness. You light the carbide lamp on your helmet and continue. The passage narrows. You squeeze between the walls. After a while you have to stoop, and then crawl on your hands and knees. On and on, for hours, twisting and turning and descending. Your companion, following behind you, began the trip with enthusiasm and confidence; in fact she talked you into it. But you notice an increasingly nervous edge in her voice. Eventually, the ceiling gets too low even for crawling; you wriggle on your belly. Even so, there isn't room for the pack on your back. You slip it off, reach back, and tie it to your foot; then continue, dragging the pack behind you. The passage bends sharply to the left, as it descends further. You contort your body, adjusting the angles of your shoulders and pelvis, and squeeze around and down. Now your companion is really panicked. Your lamp flickers a few times, then goes out. Absolute pitch darkness. You fumble with the mechanism . . .

This experiment demonstrates the power of the imagination—the power on me of my imagination, anyway. I did not for a moment, while I was composing the preceding paragraph or reading it over, think I actually was wriggling on my belly in a cave, or really see the dank walls of the passageway close in on me in the flickering light of a carbide lamp. I imagined all of this, *merely* imagined it. Yet my imaginative experience was genuinely distressing, upsetting—loaded with "affect," as psychologists say. Even rereading the paragraph for the umpteenth time gives me the shivers.

The results of the experiment may not be the same for everyone. You may not find it distressing to imagine crawling in a cave—maybe you aren't claustrophobic. In that case, a different experiment would probably demonstrate to you the power of the imagination. Try imagining climbing a nearly vertical rock face, looking down on a valley several thousand feet below, as the wind screams around you. Or imagine being in an automobile accident, or discovering an intruder in your home.

My imagining of the spelunking expedition taps into my actual personality and character. This, I am sure, is why it affects me as it does. It is because of my (dispositional) claustrophobia that I find it distressing to imagine slithering on my belly through the cramped passages of the cave. The slithering is only imagined, but imagining it activates psychological mechanisms I really possess, and brings on genuine distress. What I called the power of the imagination is really the power of dynamic forces of one's actual personality released by the imagination.

To release them is to reveal them. Elevators and small rooms have never bothered me much, even when I experienced them in real life. But imaginative experiments like the one I described make me realize how susceptible to claustrophobia I am. My actual distress exposes psychological mechanisms that would no doubt come into play should I actually embark on a spelunking expedition. As a matter of fact, now that I have experienced imaginary spelunking, I am aware that I am sometimes uncomfortable in elevators and small rooms.

In performing experiments like this one, people are likely to find themselves imagining more than what they are specifically asked to. When, in response to instructions, I imagine having to squeeze through a long, narrow passageway, it will probably occur to me, in my imagination, that the passageway is too small to allow me to pass my companion should I want to retrace my steps. I might then imagine undertaking one or another course of action: pausing to collect my wits, or rushing ahead hoping to find a wider place quickly before I completely lose my nerve, or suggesting to my friend that we try slithering backward, or simply gritting my teeth and going on. I may find myself, in my imagination, reassuring my panicked companion that things will be all right while fearing that they won't be, pretending to a confidence that I don't have. I may imagine cursing her for talking me into going on the trip, or berating myself for not resisting—or for not trying out the adventure in an armchair first. I might find myself, in my imagination, feeling strangely confident of my ability to cope, or being resigned to my fate, or hoping to hear the voice of a rescuer, or hoping not to, wanting to rely on my own resources.

What I go on to imagine beyond what is called for, like the distress that accompanies my imaginings, depends heavily on my character and personality—on how much self-confidence I have, on my propensities to blame myself rather than others, or vice versa, on whether I am fundamentally of an optimistic or a pessimistic disposition. The additional imaginings reveal features of my personality, just as the affect produced by the initial imaginings do. It is I, after all, the real I, who is doing the imagining. And I may be proud or ashamed of what is revealed. I may be proud to find myself imagining acting with cool resolve and unselfish concern for my friend. If I should catch myself abandoning my terrified companion, in my fantasy, searching for a way out of the cave that bypasses her, this may be cause for serious concern about my moral character. I can be wrong about what character traits my imaginings reflect, of course, just as I can misinterpret my real actions and feelings. There is danger of self-deception and other errors in all of these cases. Nevertheless, one needn't be much of a Freudian to accept that when I imagine certain things in response to instructions, what else I then find myself imagining, as well as the kinds of affect I experience, reflect aspects of my real character and personality. (The spontaneity of the additional imaginings may make self-deception less likely, as it sometimes does in the case of dreams and daydreams.)

None of this is news. But it needs to be emphasized to counter the peculiar tendency, in some discussions of fiction and the imagination, to think of imagining as a sterile intellectual exercise.

MY IMAGINING EXPERIMENT is an instance of mental simulation. In imagining as I did, I simulated an experience of a caving expedition. Mental simulation has most often been invoked, in the recent literature, to explain or help explain how we acquire knowledge of the mental lives of other people. The intuitive idea is that we put ourselves imaginatively in the other person's shoes—in the shoes of a real-life spelunker, for instance—and judge, on the basis of our own imaginative experience, what she is thinking and feeling, or what she decides to do. Simulation can also serve to predict what one's own experience would be like should one really go spelunking in the future, for instance.[5] I am interested now mainly in simulation itself, apart from its use in ascertaining or predicting the actual experiences of another person or oneself.

In a study often discussed by simulation theorists, subjects were asked to suppose that a Mr. Crane and a Mr. Tees are scheduled to take different flights, departing at the same time from the same airport. Their limousine is caught in traffic on the way to the airport, and arrives 30 minutes after the departure time. Mr. Crane is told that his flight left on time. Mr. Tees is told that his was delayed and just left five minutes ago. The subjects were then asked which of the two is more upset? Most said that Mr. Tees is.[6] How did they arrive at this conclusion? According to Alvin Goldman, they simulated the experiences of Tees and Crane:

> The initial step, of course, is to imagine being "in the shoes" of the agent, e.g., in the situation of Tees or Crane. This means pretending to have the same initial desires, beliefs, or other mental states that the attributor's background information suggests the agent has. The next step is to feed these pretend states into some inferential mechanism, or other cognitive mechanism, and allow that mechanism to generate further mental states as outputs by its normal operating procedure. For example, the initial states might be fed into the practical reasoning mechanism which generates as output a choice or decision. In the case of simulating Tees and Crane, the states are fed into a mechanism that generates an affective state, a state of annoyance or "upsetness." More precisely, the output state should be viewed as a pretend or surrogate state, since presumably a simulator doesn't feel the *very same* affect or emotion as a real agent would. Finally, upon noting this output, one ascribes to the agent an occurrence of this output state. Predictions of behavior would proceed similarly. In trying to anticipate your chess opponent's next move, you pretend you are on his side of the board with his strategy preferences. You then feed these beliefs, goals, and preferences into your practical reasoning mechanism and allow it to select a move. Finally, you predict that *he* will make this move. In short, you let your own psychological mechanism serve as a "model" of his.[7]

What exactly are the outputs of mental simulations? The inputs are imagined or pretend circumstances and states. Simulation theorists commonly characterize the outputs, the results of the operation of one's psychological mechanisms on this input, as imagined or pretend states also. Goldman, as we saw, prefers to say that what is experienced by the simulator of Mr. Crane and Mr. Tees is a "pretend or surrogate state" of annoyance or upsetness. Others describe outputs as pretended or feigned or imagined or "as if" emotions and other mental states, or speak of the simulator as "continuing the make-believe."[8] Outputs usually include more than imaginings, however. I have already said that when I imagine the spelunking expedition, I experience intense "affect," as well as being induced to engage in further imaginings. My shuddering, my clammy palms, my cold sweat, and the sensations that accompany them, are not merely imagined.

There can be no doubt that among the outputs of simulations are imagined psychological states which the simulator is not actually experiencing. It is only in my imagination that I have beliefs about the topography of the cave—knowing as I do that there is no cave for my beliefs to be about. Only in my imagination does it occur to me that the (nonexistent) passageway in which I find myself when my (nonexistent) companion panics is too narrow for me to pass her. It is not literally the case that I intend to turn around at the next wide spot I come to, or that I decide not to, any more than it is literally true that I continue crawling further, or that I stop. Nor do I actually consider whether to try slithering backwards. What I do in my armchair is imagine forming certain beliefs and intentions concerning my situation in the cave, imagine making certain decisions and performing certain actions.

This is not to deny that the simulation may result in my forming actual beliefs and intentions. It might occur to me that if there is a passage in a real cave configured like the one I am imagining, it would be too narrow to turn around in. I might decide to turn back as soon as possible should I find myself in a pickle like the one I am imagining. I might swear never to go spelunking in real life.[9] But if I am simulating, I will first form beliefs and intentions in imagination, concerning the particular cave I am imagining.[10] I might mutter to myself, "We had better turn around next chance we get" (not "In a real cave like this, it would be best to turn back"), or "Gosh, she is blocking my way out of the cave, so I can't go for help." It is (partly) because of what I find myself imagining believing and intending that I form general or conditional beliefs and intentions (if I do). This is because what I find myself imagining helps me to clarify my interests and desires.

What about feelings and emotions? A person simulating Mr. Tees may really be distressed or upset (in one sense of these terms, anyway). I do not think it is true, literally, that the simulator is *annoyed at having missed her flight*. She *didn't* miss a flight, and she knows it. Imagine being passed over in favor of your best friend for a coveted position. Let's suppose that you conclude from your imaginative experience that, were your friend to be offered the job in real life, you would feel jealous. I do not think it is literally the case that you *are* jealous of him for receiving the offer, when you only imagine that he did.

Looking ahead to the case of Charles and the Slime, we can ask whether, when I negotiate the twists and turns of the cavern in my imagination, I am literally *afraid*. I am claustrophobic, and claustrophobia is a kind of fear. But this claustrophobia is a standing (or dispositional) condition which I had all along and which is merely activated and revealed by my imaginative experience. It is not part of the output of the simulation; it doesn't result from my imagining myself crawling around in the cave. Do I, as I imagine coming to a particularly tight bend in the cave, fear that I won't be able to squeeze through (or worse, that if I do I won't be able to squeeze back when I return)? Do I fear that my (utterly fictitious) carbide lamp will malfunction, or that my (equally fictitious) companion will become hysterical? I think not—although I may experience these specific object-directed fears in imagination, and my genuine (standing) claustrophobia has a lot to do with the imaginings.

These are not pressing questions, from the simulation theorist's perspective. The simulation works in any case. What simulation requires is that the input and the output states be analogous to inputs and outputs of the experience being simulated, and that there be reason to presume a similarity in the processing whereby the inputs produce the outputs. Many of the inputs of the simulation are pretend or imagined versions of the corresponding simulated ones, and the same can be true of the outputs — it obviously *is* true of some of them. You may simulate an experience of being jealous of your friend, whether your condition, when you imagine, qualifies as one of actually being jealous of him or only imagining this. In either case you may predict that you would really be jealous should your friend actually be offered the job you want.

In simulating, one's psychological mechanisms are being run "off line." This means at least that they are disconnected from some of their usual behavioral manifestations. Sitting in my armchair, I do not carry out the decisions I imagine making, nor do I behave, in other ways, as I would if I were actually in a cave. What blocks the behavior is my clear awareness that I am sitting in an armchair and not actually exploring a cave. Whether one's fear or jealousy or annoyance are actual or merely imagined, when one engages in simulation, depends on whether fear or jealousy or annoyance of the relevant kinds require either the usual links to behavior (actual behavior, or the potential for producing it, or an awareness of this potential), or the belief that the situation is actual. Again, the simulation theorist needn't decide.[11]

BACK TO EMOTIONAL responses to works of fiction. The movie induces Charles to simulate an experience of being attacked by a Slime. It induces him to imagine a Slime, and to imagine its going after him. As a result, he enjoys — or undergoes — a complex combination of experiences, including both affective responses (what in *Mimesis* I called quasi-fear sensations) and additional imaginings, beginning with imagining himself to be in grave danger. His initial imaginings engage certain of his psychological mechanisms, and the results reflect aspects of his actual personality and character (perhaps a standing propensity to be repelled by things that are amorphous, shapeless, or slimy, not to mention concern for his own well-being).[12] Different people react differently to horror movies; the differences in reaction reflect differences in their personalities and character. Charles imagines fearing the Slime. This is one of the further imaginings that result from the ones initially induced by the movie.

I stand by my contention that it is *only* in imagination that Charles fears the Slime, and that appreciators do not literally pity Willy Loman, grieve for Anna Karenina, and admire Superman — notwithstanding the consternation these opinions have caused among commentators. Indeed, I believe that these negative claims depart little from common sense, and should not seem either very surprising or very momentous. We are now in a position to dispatch some of the main objections that have been leveled against them.

Concerning Amos Barton, a character in George Eliot's *Scenes of Clerical Life*, Noël Carroll remarks that "given the intensity of our feelings" it "seems counterintuitive" to "give up the idea that we are saddened by the plight of Barton."[13] This does not seem counterintuitive to me at all. Would a similar but less intense reaction not qualify as feeling sad (mildly sad) for Barton? If I have a mild reaction when I put myself in Mr. Crane's shoes, and a stronger one when I imagine being in Mr. Tees's situation, is it plausible to say that I am, literally, more annoyed at missing a flight, when I simulate Tees than when I simulate Crane? The intensity of one's feelings is no reason to insist that the correct description of one's experience has to be that of (literally) being saddened by Amos Barton, or fearing the Slime, or grieving for Anna Karenina. A car on a hoist simulating being driven at breakneck speed up a winding mountain road can spin its wheels like crazy, the engine might over-heat or even blow up, without making it at all counterintuitive to deny that it is actually travelling on a mountain road.

Richard Moran faults my make-believe theory for suggesting a lack of "real-world accountability" in our responses to fiction.[14] He observes that "responses of laughter, lust, indignation, relief, delight in retribution, etc. are normally treated as expressions of genuine attitudes that we actually have, and are es-teemed or repudiated accordingly," as when one chortles at a racist joke. He evidently thinks that responses consisting in imaginative experiences of the kinds I attribute to appreciators—to the spectator of a movie, for instance— would be "as remote from [the appreciator's] real temperament as the events on the screen are remote from his real beliefs about the world." It is obvious from our discussion of simulation how far off the mark this objection is. There simply can be no doubt that imaginings often reflect actual attitudes, desires, values, prejudices, and so forth, and are thus subject to esteem and repudia-tion. Fantasizing about torturing kittens may, depending on the circumstances, indicate a cruel nature as surely as actually doing so would. In order to clarify my interests and desires, it may help to imagine being faced with a choice between accepting a job as an accountant and touring with a rodeo. If I find myself, in imagination, choosing the former alternative, this may teach me something about myself. Will Moran insist that I must have literally decided to accept the (nonexistent) accounting job, that if I merely imagine intending to report to work at the accounting firm, my experience won't have revealed anything about my actual desires?[15]

Moran emphasizes the manner in which one imagines, including imagin-ing with this or that feeling, as opposed to what one imagines. Feelings actually experienced, as we noted in the spelunking case, are part of the output of simulations and are revealing of character. They are also, on my account, an important component of appreciators' imaginative responses to fiction. Noth-ing follows about whether an imaginer is best understood as actually, that is, literally, experiencing a given intentional psychological state or merely experi-encing it in imagination. If I read a story about kittens being tortured, the mere fact that I imagine this probably does not, in this case, reflect badly on my moral character. If I should find myself imagining it with a sense of glee, however, I may have reason to worry. The glee is real. But my experience certainly does not have to be described as actually taking pleasure in the suffering of kittens, in order to signal a cruel streak in my character.

It is the manner in which I imagine that is significant, in this case. But in other cases what I imagine, even apart from any particular accompanying feelings, may reflect on my character. Suppose, for instance, that I find myself imagining kittens being tortured, on seeing the word "kitten" on a spelling test, or simply out of the blue. Our real selves make themselves felt in what we imagine, as well as in what we feel and the manner in which we imagine what we do.

Some objectors seem to think that it is just intuitively obvious that Charles fears the Slime, that readers feel sorry for Anna Karenina, and so forth.[16] This is by no means intuitively obvious to everyone; the simulation theorists I mentioned express contrary intuitions about similar cases. It is true that we—all of us—readily describe appreciators as fearing, feeling sorry for, and admiring characters in fiction, even falling in love with them. Is there a presumption that what is commonly and naturally said, in ordinary circumstances, is true? At most there is a presumption that in thus speaking, people *express something true*. Our question is whether what is said, taken literally, is true. Saying that Charles is afraid of the Slime is a way of expressing the truth that it is fictional ("true" in the world of make-believe) that he fears the Slime. We also express truths about what is fictional when we say, "There is a horrible green slime on the loose," or "Anna threw herself under the wheels of a train." Whether any of these sentences is true when taken literally is another matter; clearly the latter two are not. Is there some presumption that what is commonly and ordinarily said should be taken literally, rather than in some special way? Not in this context, which already involves so much make-believe. If there is a presumption at all about how statements like "Charles fears the Slime" and "John grieves for Anna" are to be taken, it is that they, like "There is a slime on the loose" and "Anna threw herself under the wheels of a train," express what is fictional, what is imagined to be the case.

Moran points out that many common everyday emotional experiences concern "what is known to be in some sense nonactual," or things which are not "in the actual here and now"—that our responses to fiction are not special in this regard. There are feelings directed at modal facts, at "things that might have happened to us but didn't"; there are "spontaneous empathetic reactions such as wincing and jerking your hand back when someone else nearby slices into his hand"; there is "the person who says that it still makes her shudder just to think about her driving accident, or her first date"; and there are backward-looking responses such as relief, regret, remorse, nostalgia.[17] Moran thinks these are all "paradigms" or "central instances" of emotional experience. His idea seems to be that responses to fiction of the kinds under discussion are not essentially different from them, and hence have to be regarded as themselves instances, maybe paradigms, of emotional response. There is certainly no quarrel so far. The word "paradigm" carries unfortunate baggage from the crude "paradigm case arguments" of the 1950s and 1960s, but all of the examples mentioned, including the reactions to fiction, are indeed clear and obvious instances of emotional response. Are they clear instances of emotions whose objects are things not present? Regret, remorse, and nostalgia are, but these are plainly irrelevant to the issue at hand. The fact that regret and nostalgia are feelings about events long past has no tendency to suggest that appreciators literally pity or admire people they know do not exist and never did, or fear things that they are utterly certain pose no present danger.

Some of Moran's other examples are more interesting, and more like the fiction cases, although it is mysterious how they are supposed to contribute to his argument. Is the person who shudders on recalling her automobile accident terrified of the truck that she remembers careening into her car years previously? Moran thinks that, as a "paradigm," this example is not or should not be regarded as "paradoxical." Whatever he means by this, it certainly does not follow that she is, literally, afraid of the truck when she recalls the accident. (Does a person's wincing in empathy with a friend who cuts his finger, indicate that she actually feels pain herself?)

Moran admits that we might find these cases puzzling. But if we do, he says, we "would thereby lose what was supposed to be distinctive about the *fictional* case." [18] That fiction must be understood to be distinctive is a requirement of Moran's own manufacture. To reiterate a prominent theme of *Mimesis*, make-believe and imagining are pervasive in human experience, by no means confined to our interactions with works of fiction. [19] This theme is reinforced by our discussion of mental simulation, as it occurs in everyday life as well as in our experiences of fiction—and by Moran's own examples. A significant advantage of the make-believe theory is that it allows us to see fiction as continuous with the rest of life.

Vivid memories like the ones Moran discusses involve imagining; one *relives* the remembered experience. The shudders result from vividly imagining the truck careening into one's car, despite being fully aware that that is not now happening. One is terrified of the truck in imagination; there is no need to insist that one is (also) actually terrified of it. This is another instance of mental simulation; one simulates one's own past experience. To empathize with another's pain may also be to imagine being cut and feeling pain oneself; one may (automatically, without reflection) imagine oneself in the other's situation.

AFTER ALL THE INK that has been splattered on the question of whether appreciators' experiences include emotions of various kinds vis-à-vis fictional characters and situations, it may be disappointing to learn that it doesn't much matter. It doesn't; not for our purposes. The positive side of my account of appreciators' responses to fiction—their imaginative participation in games of make-believe—is much more important.

This imaginative participation, we now see, consists (in part) in mental simulation. Appreciators simulate experiences of being attacked by monsters, of observing characters in danger and fearing for them, of learning about and grieving for good people who come to tragic ends, of marvelling at and admiring the exploits of heroes. We simulate these experiences, including the fear and grief and admiration, whether these emotions are construed in such a way that appreciators, literally, experience them, or in such a way that they merely imagine doing so. In either case, appreciators bring much of themselves to the make-believe; their actual psychological makeup, attitudes, interests, values, prejudices, hangups, and so forth, come powerfully into play. And this sometimes makes their experience of the fiction a deeply moving one. The connection with simulation is especially helpful in cashing out the suggestion which I reiterated throughout *Mimesis* (and which many others have made as well) that appreciating works of fiction and engaging in other make-believe activities are important in helping us to understand ourselves. So far we have no reason to suppose that Charles literally fears the Slime, or that any of us, in normal circumstances, fears for or grieves for or admires purely fictional characters. There is no reason to cook up a theory specially designed to make it come out true that we do experience these emotions.

Even if we were to hold that appreciators do, literally, experience them, we would need to recognize that they experience them in imagination as well. If an old shed counts as a stagecoach in a game of make-believe, a child sitting on the edge of its roof might imagine sitting on a stagecoach and driving the horses. Suppose that, in place of the shed, the child uses an actual abandoned stagecoach for her game, and imagines driving horses as they pull the coach from one town to another. In this case also she is sitting on a stagecoach, in her imagination, even though she really is doing so as well. Charles imagines a Slime oozing toward him, and, in his imagination, it threatens him. It would be strange to deny that he fears it in his imagination also, even were we to decide that his experience counts as one of actually fearing it.[20] In that case his actual fear would be incorporated in his make-believe in the way that the real stagecoach is incorporated in the child's game. Surely spectators of *Romeo and Juliet* not only realize, in imagination, the tragedy that befalls the young lovers, but also grieve for them in imagination—whether or not we suppose that their experiences amount to grieving for them in reality.

Some who insist that appreciators experience fear or pity or grief toward fictional characters and situations admit that the emotions they experience are of a different kind from the fear or pity or grief that one feels toward real people and situations. We might think of *fear-of-fictions*, for instance, as a variety of fear different from *fear-of-perceived-dangers*. Some hold that the intentional object of fear or pity (what "the Slime" in "Charles fears the Slime" refers to) is something of an entirely different kind in the fiction cases: a Fregean sense, a collection of properties (Carroll), or a "kind of imagining" (Lamarque). Some say appreciators of fiction are frightened by thought contents (Lamarque), or that their pity involves beliefs and desires about what is fictional rather than what is actual (Neill).[21]

The stated rationale for describing appreciators as experiencing fear, pity, and so forth, of different kinds, rather than as imagining fearing and pitying, is to underscore the similarity to the real-life cases. But in one way this exaggerates the differences. Appreciators imagine having pity or fear of ordinary, every-day kinds, with ordinary kinds of objects. I imagine pitying a person who really suffers a tragedy, or admiring someone who actually performs heroic deeds, or fearing a monster that really poses a threat—not thought contents or Fregean senses or collections of properties. The words that may come to me as I imagine are not, "Oh, that poor thought content!," or "Yikes! A horrible fictitious slime," or "What a dangerous collection of properties," but simply, "Oh, that poor waif!," "Yikes, a horrible slime!," or "What a dangerous situation." The view that we really do fear, pity, and admire fictitious entities, but with fear, pity, or admiration of a special kind, fails to account for the phenomenology of our experiences, in particular for the close analogies they manifestly bear to possible "real-life" experiences. To account for this, we need to recognize that we imagine feeling fear, pity, and admiration—fear, pity, and admiration of the kinds we might actually feel in "real life." Once we recognize this, there is little reason to insist that we also, really, fear, pity, and admire fictional characters.

NOTES

1. Cambridge, Mass.: Harvard University Press, 1990, 273.

2. The preceding points are explained much more fully in *Mimesis as Make-Believe* (1990).

3. For discussions of mental simulation, see Gordon 1987, chap. 7, and the essays collected in Martin Davies and Tony Stone 1995a and 1995b.

Mental simulation is related to older notions of empathy, which have figured prominently in the discussions of the arts, but it is their more recent incarnation in the form of mental simulation that exhibits special affinity to my make-believe theory. Gregory Currie links fiction to simulation theory in "Imagination and Simulation: Aesthetics Meets Cognitive Science," in Davies and Stone 1995b. See also Feagin 1996.

4. *The Philosophy of Horror* (1990), 73–74. Carroll may no longer endorse this objection.

5. Simulation theory is controversial in various respects. I simply record my conviction that it is on the right track. Many of the points of controversy are not relevant here anyway, for instance, disputes about whether simulation theory is really distinct from its main rival, the theory theory; worries about the validity of extrapolations from one's simulated experience to an actual experience of another person; and questions about how much of our knowledge of other people is based on simulation. There are different variants of simulation theory as well, which we need not decide among.

6. From an experiment by Daniel Kahneman and Amos Tversky, "The Simulation Heuristic" (1982).

7. Alvin Goldman 1995, 189. Gordon describes the process of simulation rather differently. See his 1995 piece.

8. See Gordon 1987, and the essays by Gary Fuller, Jane Heal, Adam M. Leslie and Tim P. German, Gregory Currie, and Derek Bolton, in Davies and Stone 1995b.

9. William Charlton (1984) holds that to feel for a fictitious person is simply to experience a hypothetical feeling concerning real people.

10. Since I do not recognize purely imaginary entities, this characterization of my imaginative experience is misleading. See *Mimesis as Make-Believe*, part IV.

11. A number of commentators take me to hold that fear requires the belief that one is in danger. I explicitly refrain from endorsing this principle in *Mimesis as Make-Believe*.

12. Cf. Jerrold Levinson 1990d.

13. Noël Carroll, "Critical Study: Kendall L. Walton, *Mimesis as Make-Believe*" (1995), 95. Carroll switches between speaking of being "saddened by (the plight of) Barton" and "feeling sad for Barton." I take him to be treating these as equivalent.

14. "The Expression of Feeling in Imagination" (1994), 93.

15. Confusion is evident in Moran's observation that "although a person typically won't find it a disturbing discovery about himself that he is capable of imagining this or that fictional truth, he might well be disturbed by what he finds himself *feeling* at the movies" (93). What betrays one's character is not what one *can* imagine — one can imagine just about anything, as Moran points out — but what one *does* imagine, especially what one *finds* oneself imagining in given circumstances: what one imagines as a result of mental simulations induced by works of fiction, for instance.

16. This seems the only way to understand Berys Gaut's unexplained declaration that my theory fails to "respect the phenomenology of our responses to art: we sometimes are genuinely afraid of fictional monsters" (1992, 298).

17. "The Expression of Feeling in Imagination" (1994), 78.

18. Moran 1994, 78. See also 80.

19. See, for instance, *Mimesis*, 7. For other applications of notions of pretense or make-believe, see Herbert H. Clark 1996, Herbert H. Clark and Richard J. Gerrig 1990, Mark Crimmins 1995, Thomas G. Pavel 1986, and Gideon Rosen 1994.

20. Those who hold, on ordinary language grounds, that only what is not true or not believed to be true can be imagined, misunderstand ordinary language. To say that a person imagines such and such, sometimes carries a conversational implication that it is not true or not believed. But it is obvious that much of the content of our dreams and daydreams and games of make-believe is known by us to be true. Ordinary language should not be decisive in constructing a theory, in any case. (Cf. *Mimesis*, 13.)

21. Carroll 1990, 84–86; Lamarque 1991, 164; and Neil 1993.

3

Imagining Emotions and Appreciating Fiction

SUSAN L. FEAGIN

The capacity of a work of fictional literature to elicit (some) emotional responses is part of what is valuable about it, and having (relevant) emotional responses is part of appreciating it. These claims are not very controversial; perhaps they are even common sense. But philosophy rushes in where common sense fears to tread, raising questions and looking for explanations.

Are the emotions we have in appreciating fictional works of art, what I call art emotions, of the same sort as those which occur in "real life"? Which emotions are appropriate to the work, and why: what justifies having one emotion rather that another? And why should we think emotionally responding to fiction is desirable, something that should be respected and encouraged, rather than looked at as a little weird or a waste of time?

These questions are given more urgency by the currently well-entrenched view that emotions involve beliefs. For example, fear involves the belief that what one is afraid of is dangerous, pride requires the belief that what one is proud of reflects well on oneself, and anger entails that one believes that there has been an injustice.[1] There will also be beliefs about what makes the situation dangerous, what qualities reflect well on oneself, and what makes something an injustice. These beliefs identify the object of the emotion and help explain why the emotion is a fitting one.

But when reading fiction, precisely because we know it is fiction and we are appreciating it as such, we do not have the relevant beliefs. When reading

Middlemarch, I am afraid that Casaubon will make unreasonable demands of Dorothea, and that she will make promises she will later regret. When reading *The Grapes of Wrath*, I am angry that the growers and their foremen treat migrant workers so callously. The beliefs implicated by each of these emotions are identified by the embedded sentence within the "that"-clause of each statement: "Casaubon will make unreasonable demands of Dorothea," and "growers and their foremen treat migrant workers callously." But Dorothea does not exist, and no life is going to be ruined if the novel were to proceed with her making promises and having deep regrets. Why is it, then, that I am afraid that Casaubon will make unreasonable demands of her? *The Grapes of Wrath* is not a news account but a fictionalized story, and it would be unreasonable of me to base any beliefs about injustices that occurred during the Depression on the basis of reading the novel. So why am I angry that the foremen mistreat the migrant workers?

In this paper I will attempt to analyze one type of emotional response to fiction, emotions that are "empathetic" or in some sense "shared" with a fictional character. The fear I feel empathetically with Dorothea, and the anger I feel empathetically with the migrant workers, both described above, are examples of such emotions. I will begin with a short discussion of the rationale for belief/desire accounts of emotion, and then explore how this applies to empathetic emotions. In the following section I explain why it is misguided to expect that our understanding of empathetic *art* emotions can be increased by trying to figure out whether they are the same as real-life emotions, despite the large amount of attention given to this issue in the literature.[2] Instead, I analyze what it is to empathize with the emotions of a fictional character in terms of the variety of mental acts that constitute *imagining* having an emotion, for example, imagining being afraid, angry, or remorseful. The final section outlines how art emotions may give knowledge, in spite of the fact that they consist largely of imagination and are a response to fiction, with some brief words on the values of literature.

I. Belief/Desire Accounts of Emotion

Something like desires (which vary in strength) or wants (which vary in magnitude) are needed in an analysis of emotion in order to account for its variable intensity. Moreover, conflicts of desire, their resistance to change even when irrational, and the impossibility of "summing up" divergent and conflicting wants or desires by treating them as a single desire all explain parallel features of the "logic" of emotions.[3]

Desires are also the most convenient way of accounting for physiological aspects of emotions. Emotions are typically accompanied by arousal of the autonomic nervous system (ANS)—heart muscles; smooth muscles of the intestines, blood vessels, stomach, and genito-urinary tract; and various glands activated by the nervous system. Moreover, desires establish a link between emotions, motivations for acting, and actions themselves.[4] Physiological arousal and actions performed may be connected: the sympathetic division of the ANS is generally concerned with bodily mobilization and expenditure of energy (whereas the parasympathetic division is concerned with the conservation of bodily energy and resources, and may be implicated in such emotional phenomena as contentment).[5] Subjects who have been "sympathectomized," so that they show no autonomic arousal, engage in "emotion behavior" only which had been learned long before, and avoidance learning is retarded.[6]

Physiological changes produced by stimulation of the ANS during fear, for example, are connected with fight-flight responses, which, in their more primitive forms, do not appear to require cognitive mediation in order to eventuate in behavior. However, the range of actions motivated by, for example, fear, has the potential for being much broader than the range produced by a cognitively unmediated fight-flight response. There is thus some reason to distinguish between fear or other emotions that are manifested by cognitively unmediated responses, and the fears or other emotions that figure in one's reasons for action.[7] What actions are motivated by an emotion in fact depends both on one's wishes or desires and on one's beliefs about the nature of the situation giving rise to the emotion.

Two types of views about how beliefs are involved in emotions should be distinguished. One type of view introduces beliefs as *individuating devices* for different emotions.[8] ANS and central nervous system (CNS) arousals can at best be used as a measure of emotional intensity, and not as a means for differentiating emotions from each other, since there are few receptors for ANS activity and there are virtually no emotion-specific ANS or CNS arousals.[9] Moreover, there are fears, such as my being afraid that it will rain on the picnic, that are relatively unarousing.[10] Thus, it is urged, we identify which emotion one has by whether one has a belief that is definatory of that emotion (and which, depending on one's view, either causes or is "internally related" to the arousal): a belief that the situation is dangerous marks the emotion as fear, a belief that one has been wronged marks it as anger, and so on.

The other group of theories about emotions takes beliefs to be necessary for emotion, but does not take any particular belief(s) to be definatory of an emotion.[11] Belief here serves to identify the *object* of emotion, what the emotion is *about*, rather than to distinguish which emotion it is. I will call these *object-directed* beliefs. Beliefs are responsible for the intentionality, or object-directedness, of emotions, and one can have different emotions about the same (intentional) object. Objects of emotions, what one is afraid *of* (proud of, angry about, etc.), have been identified propositionally, or simply as an object or event. If I am afraid that it will rain (because I believe that if it rains it will ruin the picnic), the object of my emotion is either the rain itself, or the fact that it will rain. If, on the other hand, I (maliciously) want the picnic to be ruined, having the same belief (that if it rains it will ruin the picnic) and the same object of the emotion (the rain or that it will rain), I will nevertheless have a different emotion, say, hope, rather than fear. I could also be angry that it will rain (say, if it seems to me that it always rains on my picnics), again having the same beliefs and the same object of the emotion. In these theories, *desires* can serve as individuating devices for different emotions, rather than beliefs.

II. Empathetic Emotions

Empathy occurs when we in some sense "share" an emotion with someone: we have the emotion we do because the other person has it. "Empathy" does seem to be a "success term": my emotion is not an empathetic emotion unless it *is* what the other person feels, and unless I have it for the right reasons. I may think I am empathizing with someone when I am not: I may have it all wrong. I may also, on the other hand, have the some emotion someone else does, but for reasons that do not include any understanding of why he or she feels that way.

Empathy requires "identifying with" someone, which requires being able to feel as they would feel, because they would feel that way, under those circumstances: I identify with my nephew, because a belief that something may happen to *him* affects me emotionally as if I were him. (Be careful not to read this as saying I respond as I would if I believed that this might happen to me: I may not believe myself to have the vulnerabilities I believe he has, and hence I would *not* be afraid for myself with respect to the things that make me afraid for him.) The beliefs involved in empathetic emotions will thus be slightly different from the beliefs involved in the emotions with which I empathize: if I am empathetically afraid for (and with) my nephew that he will flunk out of school, it is because I believe that *he* believes that he is in danger (identificatory belief), or because I believe that *he* believes that if he doesn't pass the test he will flunk out (object-directed belief) and I believe that he desires not to flunk out (identificatory desire).

My nephew may even have beliefs (and desires) on which his fear depends that I, even though I empathize with his fear, do not share. My nephew's emotions depend on (among other things) how he understands the situation; my empathetic emotions depend on how well I understand my nephew. Empathetic emotions, then, always involve higher order beliefs than those involved in the emotion with which one empathizes: beliefs about someone else's beliefs. Thus, my empathy may be "justified" or reasonable when the person's emotion with which I empathize is not, simply because I understand how he views the situation a lot better than he understands the situation itself.

Empathy seems to be quite different from sympathy in these respects, though I do not wish to place much weight on how the two words are defined. Whereas empathy requires responding as if I were someone else who has certain sorts of beliefs, sympathy does not necessarily require this. My emotion may be sympathetic if I believe that if my nephew fails the exam he will flunk out, even though my nephew is unaware of the danger. My sympathetic responses are dependent upon my beliefs about how he would (if he were being reasonable) respond if he had the beliefs (or knowledge) that I have. The basis for my sympathetic response is not so much how the other person responds and why he or she responds that way, but rather my judgment about how the situation is or would be likely to affect him or her. "Sympathy" at least admits of this broader basis for response than empathy, even though in ordinary language there is no clear distinction between the two.[12]

It may appear as though the differences in beliefs required for empathetic emotions and the emotions with which one empathizes might dissolve the problems raised by emotional responses to fiction, since it is no longer to be expected that one will have the same beliefs as the individual (say a fictional character) with whom one empathizes. But it should not appear so for long. For not only do the "individuals" with whom I identify not exist, but none of their sorrows or joys do either. (Even if one holds a view that such beings exist in possible worlds, it is also true that *everything* possible, good and bad, exists in some possible world, so it seems odd to get worked up over some possibilities and not others.) Furthermore, "real-life" empathy, like other emotions, has the role of motivating action, or at least deliberation about appropriate actions. My beliefs (about the other person's beliefs) in conjunction with my desires are relevant to my decisions about whether to intervene. But my beliefs about fictional characters play no role in motivating intervention or deliberation about intervention on my part. The very idea is absurd. This is in part because of the absurdity of intervening in a fictional story, and in part because the pleasures and pains of fictional characters (*and* those the reader has as part of appreciating the work when empathizing with those characters) have no moral implications, and should not be considered in any "hedonic calculus" (as if Shakespeare were a bad person because he wrote so many tragedies where characters suffer, and because we suffer empathetically when reading about them). If they did have moral implications, I don't think the idea of at least deliberating about how to intervene would be such an absurdity.

III. Real-Life Emotions

Empathetic emotions involve different beliefs from the emotions empathized with, but there is still the urge to say it is the *same* emotion which is "shared" by the two people. There is likewise a strong inclination to use ordinary emotion terms, such as "fear," "anger," or "relief" to describe our emotional responses to art. The temptation, then, is to ask whether art emotions, and empathetic emotions in general, are emotions of the same type and in the same sense as real-life emotions.

Nevertheless, there are two reasons why I think this is an unpromising approach. First, names of particular emotions refer to psychological states or processes whose underlying nature will be elucidated by a theory. That is, the defining features of emotions will be revealed by whatever psychological theory has the greatest explanatory, and where appropriate, predictive value. In point of fact, we don't have anything even close to an understanding of emotions, that is, a systematic, testable theory of emotions, so it is premature to ask if art emotions, and empathetic emotions, meet the definition.[13]

It is even possible that the concept of emotion, and/or concepts of particular emotions, will not even occur within the theoretical vocabulary of such a theory. The most promising analysis of (at least some) emotions, as compounds of beliefs and desires, though reasonably adequate as a conceptual analysis, would be more satisfying as psychological theory if we understood what beliefs and desires were.[14] Whether art emotions, real-life emotions, and empathetic emotions can each be analyzed by concepts showing sufficient integrity to play a systematic role in a science of human behavior, and whether any would be analyzed by the same concepts playing the same roles as any other, is something on which it would, at this point, be foolhardy to pronounce.

A second difficulty in asking whether art emotions and empathetic emotions are the same as real-life emotions is not due to the poverty of current psychological theory but rather to the vagaries of common sense in identifying emotions. If you took a psychological run through what could pass for an ordinary life, you would rarely find emotions and feelings tidily individuated and separated from each other and their surrounding mental environments. They grow out of, feed on, reflect, and are absorbed and compromised by myriad aspects of mental life. If I may borrow an example from literature, George Bernard Shaw, at one point in his play "Widower's House," gives the following stage direction to a character with the wonderful name of "Lickcheese": "Surprised into contemptuous amusement in the midst of his anxiety." How many emotions would a real person have who was surprised into contemptuous amusement in the midst of his anxiety? How many emotions would we have if we were to empathize with Lickcheese (though with a name like that it may be hard to do—which is no doubt significant). There are four words that have emotional connotations. But is contemptuous amusement one emotion or two? If it's only one, is it amusement colored by contempt, or contempt colored by amusement? How would one ever know, and what difference does it make? Is being surprised into contemptuous amusement a single emotion, but different from just being contemptuously amused, or is it the addition of a new emotion to one (or two) that one already has?

I think most people would find these questions a little silly, and it goes to show that identifying and individuating emotions according to "common-sense psychology" is a messy business. And not much is to be gained in the understanding of art emotions by introducing spurious standards of rigor. More progress will be made in understanding art emotions, and ultimately other moods and feeling-responses we have as part of our appreciation of works of fiction, by looking at the multivalent cases such as the above, rather than at emotional capsules such as fear and pity, which crop up in aesthetic discussions with depressing regularity. Though emotional states such as fear may be easier objects for *psychological* analysis, they are not the best models for understanding emotions insofar as they constitute part of our appreciation of fictional literature.

IV. Imagining Having Emotions

So far I have discussed real-life emotions and what it is to empathize with someone's emotions in real life. I have also explained why empathizing with a fictional character's emotions cannot be analyzed like empathizing with real-life emotions: neither the individuals with whom one empathizes nor their emotions exist, and one's empathy plays no role in deliberations about whether to do something about the situation. In addition, art emotions typically do not have rigorously identifiable boundaries, unlike at least some real-life emotions.

In this section I will develop the outlines of an account of what it is to have *art* emotions that consist in empathizing with a fictional character's emotions. I will explicate what it is to empathize with a fictional character's emotions in terms of what it is to *imagine* having emotions. My emphasis will be on what activities one performs in doing the imagining, and on what explains and describes what one is doing *in* doing this imagining. The final section of the paper deals with whether imagining emotions (in response to fiction) can give knowledge of what human experience is like.

As I suggested above, whether we are empathizing with the emotions of a real person depends on what our second-order beliefs are. But whether we are empathizing with a fictional character does *not* depend on what our second-order beliefs are. This is because there aren't any *first*-order beliefs (or desires, or other psychological states) for them to be about, since neither fictional characters, nor their psychological states, exist. The existence of the empathy therefore does *not* depend on whether we "feel" the way the other person feels, and for the right reasons (see section III).

When beliefs are alleged to be individuating devices for different types of emotions, the specifications of what beliefs are involved for different emotions will be indeterminate. Actual instances of emotions involve more determinate beliefs and desires: so-and-so did me an injustice, and the injustice has such-and-such characteristics, and here's why I didn't deserve it, and it's especially noxious coming from him since he's such a hypocrite and gets more than he deserves anyway . . . and so on. On the model where object-directed beliefs are necessary conditions for emotions, these more determinate beliefs will serve to pinpoint the object of the emotion rather than to identify which emotion it is. *Empathizing* with a real-life emotion, on either model, requires understanding its conceptual constituents and background, that is, having second-order beliefs about the determinate beliefs, desires, and so on, involved in the emotion.

When empathizing with the emotions of a fictional character, on the other hand, we don't form second-order beliefs about an individual's first-order beliefs, but rather *imagine* what these beliefs, desires, and so on, might be. I am not suggesting that one imagines *that* if a person (or most people) were in the same situation as this character then he or she would believe this or that. And I am certainly not suggesting that one *believes* this. Nor am I suggesting that one imagines (or believes) *that* if such a person as this character really existed then he or she would believe this or that. What I am saying is that one actually has a number of ideas, such as ideas of actions and inhibitions, impulses and paralyses, facial expressions and gestures, perceptions, thoughts, and judgments, about what one should refrain from doing.[15] I engage in a *pattern* of thinking, or imagining, that simulates or mimics the pattern of thinking one might have when one has, and by virtue of one's having,[16] a given emotion. These imaginings are an example of the kind of thing that goes on when one does imagine having an emotion.

The beliefs and desires (and whatever else is) involved in the emotion must jointly *describe* the set of imaginings one engages in for one to be imagining having the emotion.[17] When we reflect on what we imagine, we may recognize a pattern or "rule" to the imaginings which "unifies" or "describes" the pattern or whole set of them, even though it was not (necessarily) the reason why or the rule by which they were produced. Robert Schwartz has made an analogous point about linguistic competence: even if there are rules that describe the regularities of a speaker's unlimited linguistic competence, performances of that competence are not necessarily generated by the application of those rules.[18] We can discover or find ourselves de facto tracing a mental pattern even when the defining features of that pattern were not the rules or principles that were responsible for it, and hence are not the explanation *why* we thought that whole set of things. Once we notice what we have, perhaps unwittingly, done, or what the individual things we have done add up to, we may subsequently employ that "rule" or description and thereby produce other thoughts or imaginings by employing it. (Sophistication in general comes with recognizing the huge numbers of things one is at any given time in fact doing, and of course, with the attendant ability to control more of what one does with less effort than it takes others to recognize it.)

There may be a lot more thinking or imagining going on when one imagines having an emotion than one is ordinarily aware of. We engage in the formation of lots of ideas which are quickly forgotten as we get to the point. Independent empirical support for this comes, for example, from D. N. Perkins, of Harvard's "Project Zero," who has used contemporaneous and retrospective reporting techniques to show how problem-solving that seems to be an inexplicable, creative "leap" is actually a more extended process of fairly ordinary reasoning, the individual steps of which are in general obscured from our introspective view.[19]

Empathy felt with fictional characters, as an art emotion, does not require making *judgments* about what a possible or actual person believes (desires, etc.), or about what people like that character would feel given those beliefs (desires, etc.), or about how people in general would feel or what they would believe or desire. In one of the now-classic theories of empathy, Vernon Lee proposed that empathy was the process of transferring properties of one's activity to an object.[20] The German word for empathy, *Einfühlung*, translates literally as "feeling oneself into something." Such an account contrasts strikingly with the account of empathy with real-life emotions that I gave above, which does not involve a projection of my activity onto another person or object, but rather involves the formation of second-order beliefs about that person's beliefs, which are either the individuating devices for, or objects of, his or her emotions.

To be having an empathetic art emotion, like real-life empathy, there has to be a temptation to describe one's experience as the same emotion with which one empathizes. But, unlike real-life empathy, the art emotion of empathy is not dependent on (or explained by) our beliefs about what is involved in the beliefs (desires, etc.) of the person with whom we empathize. Reading literature requires a different sort of perceptual attentiveness from "reading" people. Our thoughts occur as a result of many different factors, including the length of sentences, vocabulary and diction, shifts in voice, recurrence of images, allusions, and juxtaposition of episodes. These features of the literary work prompt our emotional responses to it, just as much as, or more than, and even instead of, our beliefs about what anyone would believe, desire, think of, or feel in real life.

Imagining emotions, then, consists of patterns of thinking that can be described or "unified," but not necessarily explained, by the relevant beliefs (desires, etc.). We impose those descriptions as organizational principles on our mental activity in an attempt to understand or make sense of what we are doing. We see them as simulations of a process one might go through if one *did* have the emotion, in *virtue* of one's having the emotion. Recognizing the *pattern* is a matter of identifying at least one thing we are doing, that is, imagining having the emotion. This recognition may involve construction, an imposition of a pattern on what could also be seen as random activity or as having a different pattern. (See n. 24.)

In concentrating on the role of thought patterns, the foregoing overemphasizes the cognitive aspect of emotions at the expense of the "arousal" side, what one might call the "emotionality" of the response. What seems missing is something like "feeling" the emotion. But I am reluctant to use the "phenomenology" of an experience as a defining feature of it, something which would raise philosophical problems inherent in appeals to qualia. All I want to add to the analysis of imagining having an emotion at this point is that the imaginings be produced, and the patterns be recognized, relatively spontaneously. This probably doesn't seem like much, but it does more work than one might initially suspect.

Just as the illusion of motion is created only when frames of a film are projected rapidly enough, something like the "feelings" associated with emotional states emerge only when the imaginings are produced relatively spontaneously.[21] The spontaneity is clearly a matter of degree, as is the amount of imagining, the relative amount of irrelevant imagining, and the facility with which the recognition of the pattern of imagining takes place.

The degree to which I am inclined to say one does *not* actually empathize with a fictional character, that is, imagine having his or her emotion, is the degree to which the thoughts of actions, gestures, and other thoughts have to be dredged up and worked through. (If the character is bored by laborious thinking, one spontaneously imagines the relevant constituents of being bored by laborious thinking. One of the tricks of the playwright is to get you to empathize with a character's boredom without boring you.) It also depends on the number of competing thoughts, and on how many *other* mental acts you have to perform in order to generate the pattern of thoughts described by the relevant beliefs (desires, etc.). The clarity of one's feeling is measured by the degree to which one doesn't *have* to backtrack, reexamine, stop and figure out, or urge oneself on to do the relevant thinking. This point is familiar from Gilbert Ryle. A person who is highly motivated does not have to keep telling herself, "now I am going to get down to work," but she gets down to work without having to tell herself that.[22] Comparably, having an empathetic art emotion requires that one spontaneously produce and recognize the relevant imaginings. If *too* much mental prodding is necessary, then you can't even imagine the emotion: it all gets lost, as it were, in irrelevant thoughts. For those who do not do the requisite imagining spontaneously, reading is a chore, and the labored activity ensures that the experience of reading will not include the art emotions one should have in order to appreciate the work.

V. Knowledge

Very often fictional literature is touted as giving us knowledge of something or other: what it is *like* to be in a certain kind of situation, or to be a certain kind of person, or, relevant to our purposes, what it is like to have a particular kind of experience or emotion. One thing seems fairly clear about whatever the knowledge is that we have of what it is like to have emotions. It can be more or less extensive, accurate, subtle, and thorough: it admits of degrees. Knowing something well or less well *can* be accommodated on propositional accounts of knowledge when it is a matter of knowing more or fewer *facts* about something. But the types of imaginings engaged in when imagining emotions hardly seem to be giving us knowledge of a variety of facts about an emotion. What they do is give us some *specifics* about it: imaginings get down to cases, down to particulars, down to the concrete. Knowing what an emotion is is *not* to know what it is like. The latter requires more determinate and elaborate (and spontaneous) imaginings of injustices, their sources, circumstances, and effects.[23] Imagining an emotion is not a matter of having a mental representation of some fact about the world, in this case, a fact about a type of human psychological state. It is instead a matter of simulating by the pattern of concrete imaginings what we identify as being in that state.

Knowing what an emotion is like requires not merely simulating it, but also identifying it. Identifying it depends on extracting the relevant features of the pattern out of the myriad thoughts and imaginings that occur to you. But the determinate contents of the imaginings that constitute the art emotion affect what constitute relevant similarities and contrasts to the pattern, that is, what one identifies as other versions of the same emotion and other emotions. There's potentially a lot of knowing to be done here, with virtually infinite permutations. Such knowledge admits of degrees in that the potential for making finer and finer discriminations and for seeing more extensive and varied relations between experiences increases with every permutation of thought.

There is, however, something misleading in calling this knowledge. To know what emotions are *like* is not to learn something we should expect to show up in a psychological theory, and hence art emotions cannot give us knowledge of any truths about human psychology.[24] And this is because patterns of imagination, and what constitute relevant similarities to and differences from their structures and particulars, are as much a product of construction as of discovery. They are "conceptual artifacts," not natural kinds. The patterns of imagination we identify may map onto the familiar conceptual terrain of something like fear, involving, perhaps among other things, a belief in the presence of danger and desire to avoid pain or death. But the aesthetically more interesting cases occur when art emotions involve a restructuring of experience, which we can try to capture by sorting out, for example, enmeshed patterns of overlapping emotions (such as "surprised into contemptuous amusement in the midst of anxiety"), or by trying to identify a pattern for which we hitherto had no name. Art educates the emotions not by giving us knowledge by acquaintance of what they are *really* like, but by expanding our knowledge of the myriad ways affective states can be identified and distinguished from one other.

One thing which, you may have noticed, has been absent in this discussion is any attempt to explain emotional responses to fiction in terms of how one would respond to similar situations in real life. Explanations of art emotions in terms of beliefs, desires, or even ideas that a reader already has is a formula for philistinism. Having imaginal and emotional experiences is part of appreciating an artwork, and an important part of what we appreciate about art in general is that it breaks us out of ordinary patterns of thought and feeling. Fiction trades on what we already know and how we can usually be expected to respond, but it shouldn't do *only* that. Art can expand experience by leading us to engage in imaginings whose overall patterns are identified after the fact, but not where beliefs and desires can be appealed to in order to explain *why* we engaged in the particular (set of) imaginings we did. It is unnecessary to suppose that these patterns of thought would have occurred in real life in order to explain them as appropriate responses to art. In fact, I think such a view is not only unnecessary, but also empirically implausible, and simply wrong-headed. Rather than reflect our ordinary responses to real life, art should be a guard against intellectual and emotional myopia—not that it exhibits special insights or hidden truths, but that it keeps us mentally flexible. Each artwork, ideally, should contribute something to our affective and cognitive repertoire.

NOTES

I am grateful to Béla Szabados, Dolores Miller, and Dabney Townsend and an anonymous referee of the *Canadian Journal of Philosophy* for comments on earlier drafts of this paper, one of which was read at the Pacific Division meetings of the American Society for Aesthetics, Asilomar, California, in April 1986.

1. There are debates about what beliefs are required for which emotions. I am citing these just as plausible examples. Nothing in this paper depends on the analysis one gives of the beliefs or desires involved in any *particular* emotion.

2. Works addressing this issue include Radford and Weston 1975, Walton 1978, Novitz 1980, Lamarque 1981, Charlton 1984, Mannison 1985, Best 1985, and Allen 1986.

3. That the "logic" of emotion derives from the "logic" of the underlying desires has been persuasively argued by Jenefer Robinson 1983.

4. Andrew Woodfield's analysis of desire eschews this role for desire, claiming, like Robinson, that it alters the way one thinks about things (the kind of planning or deliberation engaged in), and only via this cognitive activity alters one's actions or behavior. See "Desire, Intentional Content and Teleological Explanation" (1982) 79. A view at the other extreme is exemplified by R. W. Leeper, who takes emotions to act essentially as motives, pervading and organizing behavior. Magda Arnold's "appraisal" view also emphasizes the effects of emotion on behavior. See the discussions in chapters 2 and 4 of K. T. Strongman 1973.

5. See George Mandler 1975, 113–14.

6. See Strongman 1973, 71.

7. Robert M. Gordon 1980 argues persuasively for this distinction, 565–66. See also Roger Scruton 1971, 37.

8. See Gabriele Taylor 1985, 1; William Lyons 1980, 56–67; and O. H. Green 1972, 24.

9. See, e.g., Mandler 1975, 66. However, see also recent work which has attempted to identify emotion-specific ANS activity, e.g., Paul Ekman, Robert W. Levenson, and Wallace V. Friesen 1983, 1208–10.

10. See Robert M. Gordon 1980, 566.

11. See Gordon 1974, 27; and Scruton 1971, 32.

12. I no longer hold that these higher order beliefs are necessary for empathy. Rather, I believe empathy with actual people can be explained along the lines of the model developed for empathizing with fictional characters in section IV. For a fuller account of my revised view of empathy and sympathy, see *Reading with Feeling: The Aesthetics of Appreciation* (1996), chaps. 4 and 5.

13. For an idea of how diverse psychological theories of emotion are, see Robert Plutchik and Henry Kellerman 1980. Also useful is Strongman, which contains descriptions of twenty theories of emotion and related research. For more philosophically oriented surveys see Lyons 1980, and Robert Solomon and Cheshire Calhoun 1984.

14. See, for example, Stephen Stich's by now well-known arguments against any unrelativized correct criterion for ascribing belief, and that belief ascriptions instead take the form of similarity judgments. My conclusions about imagining emotions and having art emotions are very similar to these conclusions of Stich's about belief. See *From Folk Psychology to Cognitive Science: The Case Against Belief* (1983).

15. An analysis of imagination similar to this one is developed by Adam Morton 1980, chap. 3: "Imagination," esp. 65–71.

16. This phrase is meant to be indefinite as to whether the emotion causes, consists in, involves, or is caused by this pattern of thought. Just as we need not, for the purposes of this paper, decide whether beliefs are individuating devices or object-directed, we also need not decide among these or other alternatives.

The point here is that imagining *having* an emotion is different from merely imagining *that* someone or other has the emotion. The former, and not the latter, requires that one's own psychological state(s) mimic or simulate being in a state(s) that counts as having that emotion. The former is *not* a propositional attitude, though propositional attitudes may be components of it.

17. For an explanation of how a desire might describe or explain a pattern of thought, see Woodfield 1982.

18. See Robert Schwartz 1978, 189–90. P. N. Johnson-Laird has advanced a theory about the actual psychological processes involved in problem-solving that do not involve applying inference schemata (such as modus ponens), even though one ends up with the same conclusions that applying inference schemata would produce. See *Men-

tal Models: Towards a Cognitive Science of Language, Inference, and Consciousness (1983), chap. 2. Ultimately, what is at issue here is whether the mind works by applying, say, a propositional calculus (or some other logical apparatus). Whatever turns out to be the truth on this issue, it will have far-reaching implications for aesthetics. The only point being made here, however, is that even if the results of one's mental performance can be *modeled* in a given way, that doesn't mean the mind operates by applying the principles employed in the model.

19. D. N. Perkins 1981, 48–9.

20. Vernon Lee 1970, 757–61.

21. Johnson-Laird has made a point somewhat similar to this in explaining one reason why the infamous "Chinese Room" example fails as a counter-example to functionalism as an adequate theory of mind: the individuals constituting the Chinese room "might not interact quickly enough to maintain its real-time properties," and would thus rapidly lose contact with reality (1983, 475). Likewise, we might say a faltering, overactive, or misdirected imagination leads us to lose contact with the book.

22. Gilbert Ryle 1949, 133.

23. Mandler uses an information-processing account of psychological processes to develop, not really a theory of emotion, but rather a description of how some psychological variables affect certain human actions, experiences, and autonomic activity (1975, vii–ix). His discussions of emotional involvement and aesthetic emotions emphasize the importance of concreteness to emotionality. See especially 236–38.

24. See Michael Tye 1986, 1–17, who argues that knowledge of a particular experience does not constitute knowledge of any new facts. Paul Churchland has given a similar argument against qualia in 1985, and very briefly in 1984, 33–34. A much more general but related point is made by Philip Johnson-Laird in *Mental Models* (1983) about consciousness in general. After pointing out that there are certain algorithms that can be executed only by a parallel processor (455), and arguing that consciousness is a serial process (468), he summarizes, "Consciousness is a property of a particular class of algorithms, not of the functions that they compute: it's not what you do; it's the way you do it" (475).

All these writers emphasize that experiences or qualia are a *way* of knowing, not an *object* of knowledge (not a new fact to be known). I expand on this below by suggesting that our attempts to identify this way of knowing as some fact to be known are therefore "constructions," themselves involving imagination rather than discoveries.

4

The Paradox of Caring

Fiction and the Philosophy of Mind

GREGORY CURRIE

> The sentiments of others can never affect us, but by becoming, in some measure, our own.
>
> —David Hume

Our responses to fictions, their events, and their characters, can seem deeply problematic. A typical statement of the problem raises the question: how is it even logically possible to respond to fictions in the way we seem to? How, more specifically, is it possible to care about people we don't believe in? But to be given an answer to this problem—to be told the conditions that make it possible to do something—is not yet to be told how we actually do it, for actuality is a much narrower condition than possibility. Indeed, mere assurance of possibility can itself be no solution to a problem about what we humans, with our contingent mental makeup, do or don't do; many things that are logically possible cannot be done *by us*. So if our concern is how *we* respond to fiction as we appear to do, we had better be given a plausible story about the mental mechanisms involved.

In earlier work on what I am here calling "the paradox of caring" I had much to say on the logical issues, and relatively little on the psychological detail necessary to fill out the solution I proposed.[1] I think that solution was basically right, and that might be excuse enough for going back to it. But I don't want merely to repeat myself. I shall say something about why the solution I offer is not merely logically satisfactory but psychologically plausible as well.

So one constraint that an acceptable solution to the paradox of caring should satisfy is *coherence*: the solution should cohere with the best psychologi-

63

cal theorizing, and should not postulate any mechanisms or causal pathways not sanctioned by that theorizing. There is another constraint I shall seek to satisfy; I shall call it *Moran's constraint* after the person who, so far as I know, invented it: Richard Moran. Moran's constraint says that a solution to the paradox, while it should deal adequately with cases that arise with respect to fiction, should also deal with the large number of cases of what is essentially the same phenomenon that arises in other areas. For there is, as Moran points out, a class of cases where we respond with emotional feeling to situations that are not our own, current situation, such as when I recall an embarrassing moment or think about the merely possible mishaps that confront my child (1994). If our reactions to fictions are puzzling, these other reactions ought to seem puzzling for the same sorts of reasons. More on this later.

One other preliminary remark. In focusing on caring, I am concentrating on cases of emotional and evaluating responses to fiction that center on the fate of the fictional characters and events themselves. There are other kinds of cases, as when someone says he is afraid of Dracula or some other creature of fiction. I shall not have anything to say about these other cases here. But caring in my sense covers negative as well as positive cases: it covers wanting things to turn out badly for the character as well as wanting them to turn out well.

I. Two Problems about Fiction

In *The Masters*, one of a series of novels by C. P. Snow about intellectual and political life in the middle of this century, an election to the Mastership of a Cambridge College takes place. The present Master is terminally ill, so there is time for candidates to declare themselves, and for alliances to form and shift. Paul Jago is the choice of a peculiar union of leftwingers and academic conservatives. Intellectually mediocre and with few other evident qualifications for the job, he desperately wants the Mastership. But the alliance falls apart and Crawford, an aloof, self-confident, and distinguished scientist is elected. Crawford, though not especially likable, seems eminently the better candidate, and the loyalty of the narrator, Lewis Elliott, to the sometimes pathetic Jago is hard to understand. Nonetheless, I wanted Jago to win, and it was with growing dismay that I watched the decline of his fortunes.

The Masters is competent work, but hardly great literature. Whatever its merits, they are not those of a deeply emotional work. Indeed, the novel's rhetoric seems deliberately understated: cool, analytical, and distant. Yet there I was, hoping that Jago would get the job and generally caring about how things would turn out.

As a piece of reader-response criticism this is dull stuff. But as philosophers well know, it brings us to a difficult problem. In fact I shall argue that there are two problems, one less often remarked on than the other. The first, better known, problem is this. It is hard to believe in my caring, or even to take my assertion that I care literally, when we know that I don't believe in the reality of Jago, his friends and enemies, and the events they are caught up in.[2] This is what I am going to call *the problem of belief*. More precisely, the problem is that there is a straightforward inconsistency in the conjunction of the following three propositions:

1. I care about Jago.
2. To care about someone I have to believe in him or her.
3. I don't believe in Jago.

The conjunction of any two of these propositions entails the negation of the remaining one; no one of them alone entails the negation of any other. So the inconsistency is resolved by giving up any one of the three propositions. Note that the problem cannot be solved merely by *adding* something to the three; to resolve an inconsistency you have to get rid of something, so at least one of the propositions must go.

The other problem I shall call *the problem of personality*. I noted above the peculiarity that I seem to want Jago to be elected, when everything I know about the situation suggests that he would be a disastrous Master—and leave aside the difficulty that I don't believe in Jago's existence. If I really do care about this election, as I would about some important election in my own university, why does my caring manifest itself in support for a seemingly worthless candidate? That is an example of the problem of personality. There are many others. We frequently like and take the part of people in fiction whom we would not like or take the part of in real life. The desires we seem to have concerning fictional things can be very unlike the desires we have concerning real life—so dissimilar, indeed, that it is hard to see how such disparate desires could exist within any reasonably integrated human mental economy. Why the disparity? And what does it say about our integrity as persons?

So the problem of belief arises because I seem to care for people I don't believe in, and the problem of personality arises because the way I care often seems at odds with the kind of person I am.

The problem of personality is not solved automatically once we solve the problem of belief. But an adequate solution to the problem of belief should have some bearing on the problem of personality. I will argue that once we have a solution to the problem of belief, we can provide a natural extension of that solution to cover the problem of personality as well.

Before we can solve the problems of belief and personality, we need, strictly speaking, to solve another problem that I shall call the *referential* problem. I have apparently been referring to Jago, saying things about him, and suggesting that it is difficult to see how we can care about him. But if Jago doesn't exist, how can he be referred to, in thought or in speech, and if he can't be referred to, how can I frame the thoughts and sentences that generate the puzzle I am dealing with? My own view, elaborated elsewhere, is that expressions like "Paul Jago," which purport to be names referring to nonexistents, are actually abbreviated descriptions. As such, they make a contribution to the truth conditions of the sentences in which they occur irrespective of whether they denote anything. Because, in fact, they don't denote anything, most of the sentences in which they occur are simply false; it is false, for example, that Paul Jago was a

Cambridge academic. So I say that we don't literally refer to, or think about, Jago. But much of what we call "referring to or thinking about Jago" can be reconstructed within a descriptive theory of fictional names. So it will do no harm, and it will avoid longwinded formulations, if I here allow myself talk of referring to and thinking about Jago.[3]

II. Solving the Problem of Belief

One approach to the problem of belief has it that our first proposition, (1), is false: I don't, after all, care about Jago's future. For example, some writers have suggested that our caring is genuine enough, but they have denied that it is really a case of caring for a fictional character. Rather, it is caring for the real people whose plights the fictional character reminds us of. But the idea that fictional characters serve simply as pointers to the real people about whom we care is not very plausible. For one thing, it is in some cases not clear who those real people are, especially when the character's fate is a very exotic one. For another, the phenomenology of fiction-related caring seems not to bear the suggestion out. The sort of caring I experience while reading *The Masters* is not the generalized and rather vague caring appropriate to having thoughts about people in general whose ambitions are frustrated. Nor is it a caring appropriate to the specific situations of ambitious but frustrated real people I might actually know. The caring induced in me by reading *The Masters* is subtly keyed to the particularity of Jago's fate: the content of my thoughts and the character of my feelings as I read depend in precise ways on what is happening to Jago at that time (or rather, what is reported as happening to him at that time). And as a final objection to this proposal, I note again the peculiarly *unrealistic* nature of my caring about Jago. The Jagos of the real world, if there are any, are not likely to engage my sympathy much—a point that is obscured by concentration on examples like that of Anna Karenina, where our horror at her fate is easily thought of as of a piece with our reaction to desperation-induced suicides in the real world. If my reaction to Jago's fate were really a reaction to like-situated people in the real world, it would most probably be a reaction of indifference.

While this specific suggestion seems to me to have no merit, the general idea on which it is based is surely sound: that the key to understanding our response to fictional characters is our responses to real people. I want to look briefly at the case of *empathetic* response, where I "put myself in the other's shoes," coming to feel as he does. This is a familiar description of a familiar situation. But what, exactly, is going on?

One answer is suggested by a recent development in cognitive psychology, called "simulation theory."[4] According to the simulationists, putting yourself in the shoes of another means putting your own mind into the same state as that other mind, or into a relevantly similar state. Suppose Smith has suffered a grievous loss; the relevant aspect of his psychological state is that he desires X and believes that X is irretrievably gone. Further, his so desiring and believing have certain kinds of internal effects upon him; he experiences those disturbed feelings that go with the perception of loss. Knowing of X's loss, I might come to empathize with him. That is, I do not merely feel saddened *by* his loss; I come to feel *as* he does, as if the loss were to some degree my own. And I do that, according to the simulation theorists, by coming to have the beliefs and desires that he has, and to feel, in consequence, the disturbed visceral and mental sensations that he feels.

But wait. I don't really have his beliefs and desires, do I? If I did, I would act as he does, which I (usually) don't. If empathy gave me beliefs and desires appropriate to someone else's situation, it would be a dangerous thing to engage in. For beliefs and desires are the sources of action, and *another's* beliefs and desires will cause me to act inappropriately. In this situation it is tempting to reach for the idea of imagination. But we must be careful. For example, saying that the empathizer *imagines* himself in the other's situation, and imagines having beliefs and desires appropriate to that situation, suggests that he has a propositional attitude with a peculiarly nested structure. It suggests, in particular, that he imagines that he believes (desires) something or other. Such nested attitudes occur, as when I desire that I believe in God. But that is not what is happening in the present case. To see this, contrast two models of the situation. One goes like this. Albert believes P and desires Q, and I, in empathizing with him, come to imagine that I believe P and desire Q. That's the model I reject. The other has it that while Albert believes P and desires Q, I, in empathizing with him, come to believe^I P and desire^I Q, where "believing^I" and "desiring^I" denote states that bear systematic resemblances to believing and desiring ("I" for "imagining").[5] These states act as substitutes for belief and desire; and imagining being in someone else's shoes is a matter of having substitute versions of the states he possesses. In imagining yourself in someone else's situation, you are doing something like what the child who rides a hobby horse does: the hobby horse stands to the real horse much as belief^I stands to belief. The hobby horse is a real thing, really sat on by the child,[6] but its role is understood only in relation to the object it stands in for. And my I-states (beliefs^I and desires^I) are real states really possessed by me, but my possession of them is to be explained in terms of their relation to your beliefs and desires.

In what ways are the empathizer's I-states like real beliefs and desires? In two ways. First, they are like real beliefs and desires in respect of content, and it is a condition of successful empathy that this should be so. In empathizing with Smith I have a belief^I that X is irretrievably gone, and a desire^I that it not be. These contents are exactly the contents of Smith's (real) belief and desire. If my act of empathizing had resulted in my having I-states with other contents (if it had resulted in my having the belief^I that, say, X was merely on loan), then that act would have missed its goal. The second way in which I-states are like beliefs and desires is more complex, because it is also a way in which they are *unlike* beliefs and desires. I am thinking here of likeness in respect of causal role. Specifically, they are like real beliefs and desires in terms of internal causal role, but unlike them in terms of external causal role. Having a desire^I for beer might, if my imagining is vivid enough, cause those familiar sensations of beer-deprivation, and might trigger a decision to get a beer. But

I won't actually go and get one. I-states are blocked off from behavior. They are, as people sometimes say, "off line."

I shall say from time to time that the empathizer imagines being in the same state as the person he empathizes with. But the whole content of such a claim is that the empathizer is in I-states that bear the kinds of systematic relations I have just described to the beliefs and desires of the person he empathizes with. Notice that this is not being offered as a definition of empathy. As I use it, "empathy" means "the process, whatever it is, that enables us to put ourselves into another's shoes." That we do this by having what I have called I-states is then a hypothesis about what that process is. That hypothesis is the simulation hypothesis, and having I-states is what is (partly) definitive of simulation.[7] Thus, the claim that empathy is simulation (a claim I am making here) is similar to the claim that Jack the Ripper was the Prince of Wales.[8]

I have spoken of empathizing. I could have called it "imaginative role-taking." In empathizing with Smith, I take on, in imagination, the role he occupies, or one of them. But role-taking suggests something more general than empathy. I empathize with real people's real situations; I can take on roles that are merely imagined. I can imagine (in the sense just explained) being in the situation of the suffering Smith, but I can imagine also being in a situation no one is actually in: the situation of someone who is learning about the activities of an ambitious but not very talented academic called "Paul Jago" who is seeking to get himself elected to a Mastership. I can imagine learning about them in a particular way, by reading an account of these events, told by one who knows about them from first-hand experience and whose name is "Lewis Elliott." Imagining all this—putting myself in the shoes of one who is learning these things—would be no easy task if I did not have in front of me a certain text by C. P. Snow called *The Masters* which purports to be just such an account. Armed with that text, the task is a relatively easy one, for the text is replete with (implicit) instructions about what I-states I should have. It tells me what to imagine was said by whom to whom on what occasion, and when it does not tell me directly what happened, it often makes it fairly easy for me to work it out. Whether we call this empathy or role-taking is of little importance. What *is* of importance is that the psychological processes involved in this case are of a piece with those involved in genuine cases of empathy like the one involving me and the loss-suffering Smith. The fiction reader, like the empathizer, is someone who is simulating.

Now we strike a difficulty. Our task was to explain how I respond as I do to the fate of Jago, when I know him to be unreal. I have suggested two things; that in general we feel for people by simulating their mental states, and that readers of fiction simulate the state of a hypothetical reader of fact. But these two propositions look very unpromising as a solution to our problem; given the first proposition, I ought to say that my feeling for Jago arises from my simulating him. But the second proposition requires me to be simulating someone else: a hypothetical reader of fact.

We need to put these two ideas together. As a reader of fiction, I simulate (put myself into the shoes of) someone who is reading a factual account of the adventures of a Cambridge academic called Jago, someone who is moved by Jago's fate, and who comes to feel for him by simulating him. In other words, I simulate someone who is simulating Jago. How does that constitute my simulating Jago? In other words, what guarantee have we that A's simulation of B's simulation of C constitutes A's simulation of C? Is simulation transitive?

It is. Suppose that, according to the story, Jago desires the Mastership and believes, with growing conviction, that he will not get it; the result is an intense feeling of disappointment and inner turmoil. The hypothetical reader who learns about the decline of Jago's fortunes simulates Jago; he comes to have off-line versions of Jago's (relevant) beliefs and desires, and comes thereby to feel some of that disappointment and turmoil. Now I enter the picture; I simulate that hypothetical reader, and acquire off-line versions of his (relevant) beliefs and desires. But how do I also simulate his I-states—the off-line beliefs and desires he got as a result of simulating Jago? Easy: I do that by having exactly those I-states myself. Simulating someone's I-states is different from simulating his beliefs and desires. I simulate someone's belief that P by having a belief^I that P; I simulate someone's belief^I that P by having exactly that state of belief^I that P.

Why this difference between simulating a belief and simulating a belief^I? Recall that simulation is the attempt to mirror someone else's mental state within your own mind. Simulation aims to get me as close as possible to someone else's mental state while stopping short of giving me beliefs and desires on which it would be inappropriate to act. The solution is to give me I-states: states like beliefs and desires in some ways but unlike them in being disconnected from action. But if the state I seek to mirror is itself an off-line one (an I-state), there is no danger to me in having that very state itself, so my mirroring might as well consist in having that state.

To sum up a slightly complex line of thought: reading *The Masters*, I simulate, empathize with, or take on the role of (it's all the same to me) a reader of fact who is learning about, and at some points empathizing with, a Cambridge academic called "Jago." In empathizing with that reader of fact, I come to have off-line versions of his mental states, including those he has in virtue of empathizing with Jago. Those I-states of his become I-states of mine, and constitute my empathizing with Jago. Of course, neither Jago nor the reader of fact are real people, and I know that very well. The effect of the fiction on me does not derive from its creating in me an illusion as to the reality of either that reader or of Jago. My feeling for Jago does not depend on my having false beliefs about his situation—that he exists, for example. My feeling for him is not the product of my beliefs and desires but of my belief^I and desires^I, or what I have generally called my I-states.[9] The novel works by persuading me to engage in a certain piece of imaginative role-play, not by getting me to have false beliefs.

The paradox of caring arose out of the impossibility of holding all of propositions (1) through (3). Which of those propositions should we abandon? The solution I have offered says that I don't really have beliefs and desires concerning Jago. Instead, I have beliefs^I and desires^I about him, and it is the having of these I-states, together with the feelings they cause me to have, that constitute what I call "caring for Jago." So (3) is affirmed. Which of propositions (1) and (2) should we reject? That question is not yet settled. Reject

1. I care about Jago

if you think that

2. To care about someone I have to believe in him or her.

Alternatively, reject (2) if you think that states of caring can be based on beliefs[1] as well as on beliefs.

So—which? Personally, I don't care. I don't know how to settle the question whether caring requires belief or whether it can be based on belief[1] as well. I don't even know whether this is a factual matter rather than something that could be resolved only by some further decision on our part about how to use the word "caring." The great thing is to realize that we have already resolved the paradox of caring, and don't need to ask these further questions.

Distinguishing the substantive dispute from mere differences of verbal style will help us avoid other inviting paths of argument that lead nowhere. For example, I began this essay with the opinion of Hume that "The sentiments of others can never affect us, but by becoming, in some measure, our own." But is that right on my account? My story has it that your mental state does not literally become my mental state when I sympathize with you; rather, your mental state bears a similarity (but not an identity) relation to the state I'm in when I simulate your state. Your beliefs and desires are reflected in my beliefs[1] and desires[1], which are no more beliefs and desires than wooden horses are horses. So it looks as if I disagree with Hume.

But this argument assumes that there is one uniquely correct way to type-identify mental states: if you and I believe P, then we are in the same (type of) mental state; but if you believe P and I simulate believing it, then we are not. Who says? Any type-identification of mental states factors out some causally relevant differences between them; regarding your belief and mine as type-identical merely signals our presumption that they have significant things in common and can, for certain purposes, be treated in the same way. But then your belief and my belief[1] also have (other) significant things in common and can, for certain (other) purposes, be treated in the same way. So Hume's formulation is fine by me. Depending on our purpose, we can regard your sentiments and my simulation of them as type-identical and say in good conscience: your sentiments become my own.[10]

That, anyway, is my solution to the problem of belief. That solution does some substantial redrawing of boundaries within the domain of the emotions. Reading and being absorbed in fiction and empathizing with those you care about turn out to be mental acts of the same natural kind. In putting myself in the shoes of my friend, I imagine myself facing his loss. These imaginings have in me some of the effects that his beliefs and desires have in him; I come to feel a (probably pale) version of the agony of mind that he feels. As a reader of The Masters, I put myself in the shoes of a hypothetical other, imagining myself to be learning about the struggle of Jago for the Mastership. I do not believe in Jago, and I have no desires concerning him; but I do have some beliefs[1] and desires[1] about him, and these states can have in me the effects, or some of them, that beliefs and desires about Jago would have. Among these effects are the relatively mild but still noticeable feelings of anxiety and suspense I have concerning his fate, and the feelings of disappointment I have when I come to learn that he has failed. As a reader, then, I am not a believer in Jago, nor am I a desirer of his success. Instead I am a simulator of such a believer/desirer.

It's this redrawing of boundaries that enables my solution to satisfy what I have called the Moran constraint. Moran warns against solutions to the paradox of caring that contrast our apparently anomalous responses to fictional situations with the apparently rational emotions of real life, as when I am sorry because *I* didn't get the Mastership. As Moran points out, there is a large class of cases of emotional responses not accommodated here. And when we start to consider these other cases, the assumption that our emotional responses to fiction are problematic while our emotional responses to other things are not starts to look very questionable. A great deal of our emotional repertoire is exercised in response to situations that are not fictional, but are also non-actual, or at least currently so. Moran reminds us of our concern for things that might have happened but didn't, or that (like first dates) did occur but are now long gone, or that are happening to someone else (wincing at someone else's pain). All these other cases look rather like the fictional cases and seem to raise the same sort of problems. If it's problematic that I should feel for Jago, whom I don't believe in, isn't it also problematic that I should be upset at the thought of an event that I know didn't happen to my child, or that did happen to me long ago, or to wince at an injury I know isn't my own? So much of our emotional life is dedicated to exploring these possible, past, or other-involving situations that they, along with the fictional cases they so resemble, start to look like the central cases.[11]

My theory can easily accommodate Moran's point. By treating our responses to fictional characters and situations as a matter of off-line simulation, we can unify our response to fiction with our empathetic responses to the situations of others, our earlier selves, or people of our own imagining. Sorrowing for Jago, worrying about my child's future, and shuddering over the disaster that was my first date all get an explanation in terms of a single mental mechanism with respectable psychological credentials: simulation.

III. The Problem of Personality

I just said that the idea of simulation is a respectable one, and so it is. But it is hypothesis rather than established fact, and anyone skeptical of simulation will reject my solution to the problem of belief. The skeptic might point to a number of arguments that have been advanced against the idea of simulation. But most of them are objections to simulation theory as a theory about how we understand other minds; they range from the claim that simulation could not give us knowledge of other minds, to the claim that as a matter of fact it does not.[12] Such objections, whatever their force, need not be objections to simulation theory as a theory of our imaginative relation to fiction. But we must be careful not to attempt a complete separation of simulation-in-fiction from simulation-in-other-matters. If we have the capacity to simulate, that must be because we have acquired it during our evolutionary history. It is natural to suppose, then, that we acquired it because it was in some way useful. But its use could not have its basis in our predilection for reading fiction! That simulation gave us the capacity to read the minds of others and thereby to be better social creatures is one plausible story about how such a capacity evolved.[13] If we are going to reject that idea we had better find another one to fill out the evolutionary Just-So Story about how we came to be simulators. This issue takes us well beyond the scope of this paper, and I shall say merely that other Just-So Stories are possible: simulation might be important for strategy planning, for example.[14]

Assume, then, that the hypothesis that we have the capacity to simulate is a respectable option within naturalistic psychology. Even so, there remain objections to my solution to the paradox of caring. One of them concerns the problem of personality, and that is the subject of this section. Recall: If it really is the case that, in reading *The Masters*, I am playing the role of one who is reading a factual account of the fate of an ambitious academic, then my responses to the fiction ought to be like the responses I would have were I actually (and knowingly) reading nonfiction. The trouble is that this does not seem to be the case, since my reaction to a real-life Jago would probably be one of indifference, rather than the sympathetic reaction I actually experience.

To solve this problem, we need to complicate an already complicated story. Empathetic role-taking, as I have explained it, involves making some adjustments to your own mental economy. In taking on the role of the (real or hypothetical) other, you acquire pretend or imagined versions of some beliefs and desires possessed by the other. In other ways, your mental "set" remains constant; role-taking does not, and probably could not, involve temporarily trading in your whole personality for another. Still, it is plausible that there are degrees of mental accommodation involved in role-play, and some role-playing might involve quite substantial alterations. In particular, coming to play the role of a certain hypothetical reader might involve more than merely taking on pretend versions of beliefs about Jago and his colleagues. It might also involve coming to have pretend versions of *relatively long-term, stable, and personality-fixing preferences.* Think of *The Masters* as implicitly inviting me to imagine myself, not merely as someone reading a factual account of Jago's bid for the Mastership, but as someone whose general outlook is rather like that of the narrator, Lewis Elliott. Elliott tells the story (or, more precisely, it is fictional, in *The Masters*, that he does), and he does so from his own perspective; I learn about Jago and the events he is caught up in, but I also and at the same time learn a good deal about Elliott and his response to those events.[15] As I learn, I am persuaded, through some largely unconscious process, to take on the role of one whose attitudes are not unlike those of Elliott himself, as revealed through his account of the story.[16]

This suggestion is in line with an idea of Wayne Booth, who has argued that the moral experience of fiction is primarily the product of our accepting or rejecting the invitation to become a certain kind of person: the person the novel seems to be intended for. In the case of *The Masters*, the intended reader seems very much to be someone who shares Lewis's outlook, an outlook close to that of the "implied" author, and very probably to that of the real author, C. P. Snow himself.[17]

So it's true that I respond to the fictional fate of Jago in a way rather different from the way I would respond to the fate of someone like Jago in real life. But this is no reason for rejecting the view that the reader of fiction plays the role of one learning from a factual account of Jago's career. Rather, it is a reason for supposing that the role-playing involves a substantial departure from my normal, real-life mental set; I imagine myself not merely to be reading fact, but to be someone with an outlook different from my own real one.

A problem remains. Why should I be willing to imagine myself taking on this different outlook, one that involves valuing in imagination things I don't value in actuality?[18] Various answers are possible, though it is hard to say which of them, or what combination of them, is correct. We might point, first of all, to the natural tendency we observe in people to adjust their own mental set to the mental set of another with whom they are in close communication. Simulation theorists have already pointed to an insightful passage from Hume on this subject; it will do no harm to repeat it:

> So close and intimate is the correspondence of human souls, that no sooner any person approaches me, than he diffuses on me all his opinions, and draws along my judgements in a greater or lesser degree. And tho', on many occasions, my sympathy with him goes not so far as entirely to change my sentiments, and way of thinking; yet it seldom is so weak as not to disturb the easy course of my thought, and give an authority to that opinion, which is recommended to me by his assent and approbation.[19]

But Hume's "agreement of souls" is easily confused with another phenomenon subtly different from it, which is also relevant to explaining our susceptibility to narratorial direction. We have a tendency to "try on" the views, values, and general outlook of others, to imitate, in a playful way, other perspectives on the world. Indeed, it might be functional for us to do so, as long as this mimesis is confined to the imagination. Few of us have an outlook that is undistorted, wholly reliable, and maximally designed to achieve our own flourishing and the flourishing of those we care about.[20] To be critical of our own outlooks and to be willing to see advantages in the outlooks of others might be a useful thing. But to appreciate those advantages we might need to try on for size the perspectives from which they derive. Indeed, we might need to be willing to try on perspectives we don't initially find very attractive. And there certainly are cases in literature, film, and other forms of fiction in which we adopt a perspective quite radically different from our own, and in which the success of the work depends on our doing so. The lovers in *The Postman Always Rings Twice* are not very appealing examples of humankind, but most of us manage some sort of identification with their murderous project.[21]

Another explanation, perhaps merely supplementary to the last one, might be that we are naturally subject to an innocence-by-association fallacy. In the novel, Elliott is presented in a generally attractive light (though the author does not attempt the self-defeating strategy of having Elliott lavish praise on himself). He comes across as judicious, intelligent, firm of purpose, and loyal. Something of an outsider in the College, he is nonetheless liked and admired, and his support is sought by both sides. For some of us, that combination of attractive-seeming qualities might be enough to start us down the road of imagining ourselves to be similar in outlook to him. And by degrees, we come to value, in imagination, the things this apparently admirable character values, even though we would not, on reflection, value them ourselves in reality.

IV. The Problem of Experience

I want to discuss one last difficulty that was put to me by Carolien Rieffe. There seems to be a difference between the ways that different people experience emotions in connection with fiction, a difference not easily accounted for on a simulation model. If A and B are absorbed in a fictional representation of the death of a character's parent, and A has recently lost a parent and B has never experienced any such loss, we would expect, other things being equal, for A to experience a stronger emotion than B will. In general, our emotional response to a fiction depends partly on our experience. But if that response is wholly a matter of simulation, there does not seem to be any room for experience to play a determining role.

There are two kinds of responses to this problem from within a simulationist's position. The first, conciliatory, response is to say that our emotional responses to fiction are not, after all, entirely a matter of simulation. Simulation might be the primary or triggering factor, but other factors may play a role. On the simulationist account I gave above, how I experience a fictional situation depends on how the simulation of belief and desire causes feeling in me. But other things might cause feeling as well—memory, for instance. The recently bereaved reader has memories the other reader lacks, and those memories, being stirred by the fiction, may lead to a more intense experience of feeling than would be caused by the simulation alone.

I have spoken here of memory as if it were something different from simulation. But that is not obvious. Isn't it plausible to think of memory, in the sense of "remembering an experience," as a form of simulation? On that view, recalling the death of your parent might be a case of simulating the experience you had when your parent died.[22] Perhaps the difference between A and B is not that A is doing something other than simulating, but that A is doing *more* simulating than B is. B is simulating the role of one who learns of another's experience of the death of a parent; A, in addition, simulates a role occupied by his own younger self: the role of one who experiences the loss of a parent. It would not then be surprising from a simulationist's position that A's experience was, overall, more emotionally charged than B's.

The thought that memory might be simulation effectively turns a conciliatory response to the objection into a hard-line one, by giving the simulationist a way to explain the difference in affect between A and B as due entirely to simulative differences between them. My second hard-line response is even more unyielding. It insists that the difference between A and B is due entirely to differences between their simulation of a single role: the role of the person who reads about someone's suffering. This response claims that a subject's experience of a situation affects his or her ability to simulate the role of one learning about someone in that situation. Why should this be so? Here is one fairly straightforward reason. Fictions seldom, if ever, guide our imaginings completely; they instruct us to imagine various things only against a background of unstated assumptions about what is true in the fiction and therefore to be imagined.[23] For example, stories rarely tell us that the characters are human beings, even when it is evident on a moment's reflection that they are and that we as readers or viewers have been imagining them as human beings all the while. Now suppose that the fiction tells us of the untimely and tragic death of a character's parent. It is very unlikely to tell us everything relevant to this situation; in fact, even the most vividly described or depicted fictions tell us very little that is relevant. They rely on the readers and viewers to fill in the missing parts. No doubt we do succeed in filling in some of the missing parts, but our simulation is likely to be very much an incomplete one. Perhaps one way in which simulations can be more or less affect-inducing is for them to be more or less specific about what is to be put into the simulation. And it might be that people who have actually experienced a situation relevantly like that depicted in the fiction will have a richer and more quickly accessible stock of relevant background information to assist their simulation and make it more affect-inducing.

These, anyway, are some suggested answers to Rieffe's objection.[24]

V. Conclusion

In this essay I have tried to approach a very familiar philosopher's problem from a novel point of view. I have tried to show how we can resolve the paradox of caring, not merely by showing that there is a way to restore consistency in our beliefs, but also by making our beliefs on this subject cohere with a viable psychological theory: simulation theory. So I am attempting to break out of the philosopher's ghetto within which the aesthetician so often finds herself imprisoned. More and more, cognitive science is questioning the distinction between philosophy and psychology. Aestheticians, who are so concerned with our *responses* to things, should welcome this.

NOTES

1. See my *The Nature of Fiction* (1990), chap. 5. See also Kendall Walton, *Mimesis as Make-Believe* (1990). I am indebted to Walton's work in this area, though our solutions to the paradox differ in various ways.

2. It doesn't help to point out that Jago, like a lot of characters of fiction, is based on a real person, Canon Charles Raven (whose bid for the Mastership of Christ's College was successful). Characters based on existents are rarely identical with those existents, and Jago, I think, is not Raven, though I have no precisely quantified theory of the circumstances under which characters and their originals are the same. Anyway, when I read the book I knew nothing of Raven, and my caring about Jago certainly had nothing, psychologically speaking, to do with the connection.

3. For more on the referential problem, see my *The Nature of Fiction*, chap. 4.

4. See Morton 1980, Heal 1986, and Gordon 1986. A recent book on emotion by Keith Oatley emphasizes the phenomenon of emotional responses to fictions, and refers briefly to simulation. At one point Oatley says that "[a]ny theory of emotions without a postulate about being able to simulate other minds . . . seems unable to deal in a principled way with understanding stories or the emotional effects that stories can have" (1992, 109). But Oatley says little about what simulation is—about how absorption in narrative is simulation (at one point he says "narrative is simulation," 245)—and seems to be agnostic on the question of whether we understand stories by simulation or by having a theory of mind (109).

5. This way of putting it is rather rough, but it will do for present purposes. See my 1995a.

6. Kendall Walton (1990) has emphasized how imagining doing something often involves "props" with which one actually does something like what one imagines. Sometimes the props can be more real than the things they are substitutes for, as Bee well knew: "Ant wished he could play on the rainbow. Bee said no one could play on a real rainbow. So Ant said they must find a make-believe rainbow that they could play on . . . Ant said he would make half the rubber tyre into a make-believe rainbow!" (Angela Banner, *Ant and Bee* [1962], 9). I owe this reference to Gabriel Christopher Currie.

7. For a more general characterization of off-line simulation theory, see my 1995d.

8. See David Lewis 1980.

9. I discuss the problem in a slightly different setting in my 1995a. See also remarks by John Barnden 1995, about the transitivity of simulation.

10. See also note 18 below.

11. Richard Moran 1994.

12. See the essays by Stich and Nichols, Perner and Howes, and Gopnik and Wellman, in Davies and Stone 1995a.

13. See Nicholas Humphrey 1983.

14. See my 1995c.

15. I ignore, for the sake of simplicity, the fact that Elliott himself is an active participant in those events. This does not affect the present argument.

16. Vladimir Popescu pointed out that the problem of desire can arise with respect to fictions where there is no narrator. I agree. So it cannot be only through the influence of the personality of the narrator that we explain the shifts our desires undergo when we are reading fiction. A more general solution to this problem would appeal also to the personality of the implied author, but that is beyond the scope of this paper. See also the final sentence of the next paragraph in the text above.

17. As Vladimir Popescu pointed out to me, the reader need not be thought of as imagining himself to be someone other than the person he is. He may instead imagine himself to be different in various ways from the way he actually is. That may not involve an imagined change of identity.

18. Or valuing things more in imagination than in reality. Elliott values Jago's "heart," and I suppose I value that sort of thing too—but not as much.

19. A *Treatise on Human Nature* [1888] 1978, 592. The quotation at the head of this paper is from the same place. Perhaps I disagree with Hume in one way. I say that it is the faculty of imagination that enables us to share the mental states of others, while Hume says that the sentiments of others could not affect us "so long as they went no further than the imagination" (592). But perhaps the way I conceive the imagination is so different from the way that Hume conceives it that we should be counted as speaking of different things rather than as speaking about the same thing and disagreeing about it.

20. For more on fiction and the plurality of points of view, see my 1993.

21. Peter Kivy suggested this example in discussion.

22. Such a simulation would seem to involve imagery. For the view that visual imagery is itself a simulative process, see my 1995d.

23. For a hypothesis about how this background is constructed, see my *The Nature of Fiction* (1990), chap. 2.

24. For a fuller treatment of this issue, which requires an examination of the relation between simulation and the language of thought hypothesis, see my "Simulation and Cognitive Architecture," in preparation.

5

The Paradox of Fiction

The Report versus the Perceptual Model

DEREK MATRAVERS

I

I am going to assume, in what follows, that when we engage with a fiction we are participating in a game of make-believe; that is (if you prefer), that we are engaging in an imaginative effort. In this paper I shall attempt to identify the kind of game we are playing.[1] I begin with two words of caution. First, identifying the kind of game will be a matter of finding a game whose structure best reflects the facts about our engagement with fiction. The fit, however, will not be exact. In a game of mud pies, the fact that the cardboard box holds a maximum of six globs of mud may make it true in the game that the oven holds a maximum of six pies, but the fact that the box has "Fyffes bananas" written on the side of it will probably not make it true in the game that the oven has the same. Second, the variety of works of fiction makes it unwise to assume that one kind of game will cover all cases. These two provisos might be thought to vitiate my project before it begins. In the face of an objection to my first proviso, namely, that the kind of make-believe I maintain we play with fiction does not mirror the facts of our relations with fiction, I can reply that the structure is not isomorphic in that particular respect. In reply to the claim that in some particular instance we do not play the game of make-believe that I suggest we do, I can simply agree and count it as one of the many exceptions to the rule.

What makes the project worth undertaking is, first, that investigating the nature of make-believe illuminates several aspects of our relations to fiction that are thought problematic; and, second, that my account does offer some resistance to counterexamples. There is a judgment to be made: how accommodating can an account be before it ceases to be interesting? Its explanatory power and the range of cases it covers suggests, to me at least, that my account is worth giving.

I shall simplify matters by focusing, for the moment, on literary fictions, in particular on novels. My claim is that in reading a novel, a reader makes-believe he is being given a report of actual events. In other words, he makes-believe the content of the novel is being reported to him as known fact by a narrator. I shall refer to this as "the report model." There are two types of make-believe involved: make-believing doing something and make-believing that something. The reader makes-believe he is doing something other than what he is actually doing; he is actually reading a fiction and make-believing he is reading a true report. He then has a certain propositional attitude, that of make-believing (or imagining), toward the content of that report.

The question of which kind of make-believe we play with fiction is related to another question: what we should count as the content of a given fiction. It is fictional that Hardy's Mrs. Yeobright has a liver, even if this is not explicitly stated in The Return of the Native. It might look, initially, as if we can get a systematic way of specifying the content of a given fiction from the report model: namely, assume that the narrator is correct in everything he says and accept both what he says explicitly and, in addition, what it would be reasonable to assume he believes (Currie 1990). On this account, it is reasonable to assume that the narrator of The Return of the Native believes that Mrs. Yeobright has a liver even if he never actually says so. This will not do, however, for the simple reason that there are fictions in which narrators are unreliable: what they say is not always true in the story. We could try to define the content of the fiction in terms of what it would be reasonable for a listener (with the relevant qualifications) to believe were he to be told the story as known fact. I think this is an advance, although it would need to be expanded to cope with the following problem. It would be reasonable for a listener to conclude, were he told a supernatural tale such as The Master and Margarita, that the narrator was completely off his head and none of what he said was true; we all know that cats do not smoke cigars, neither are they dead shots with Mauser automatics.[2] The relation between the question of the kind of make-believe we play and the question of content is that we make-believe we are reading (that is, finding out the content of) a report. Hence, something about the make-believe we play should give us the content. The question is too large to be settled here, however, and I shall not discuss it further.

One kind of argument for the report model starts from facts about the stories themselves. The first such is that, in the words of Kendall Walton, "the words of many or most literary works contain hints of feelings or attitudes or inclinations or impressions concerning the events of the story that are best attributed to a narrator."[3] For example, in Mansfield Park, it is not only Fanny who disapproves of the amateur dramatics; the way the tale is told makes it clear that the narrator does so as well. The narrator contrasts the integrity of the position taken by Fanny and Edmund (before he capitulates) with the mean, ignoble motives that drive the players. He also uses terms such as "fortunately," "sadly," "apparently," and so on to convey an attitude. So the fact that fiction is read as a report of actual events gives the author the opportunity to ascribe to the narrator an opinion on the events in the book. This provides a further dimension with which the author can work that greatly adds to the complexity of the result. A great deal more could be said about this argument. Narrative commentary in fiction is not always as explicit as it is in this example; it can take many different forms and, it has been argued by Wayne Booth, is almost ubiquitous (Booth 1991). If Booth is right, this argument would show that a narrator is included in all the appropriate games of make-believe we play with fiction.

Walton has a second argument along similar lines. It specifies a distinctive kind of narrative commentary, namely, commentary that does not give information, but rather makes affirmations:

> Sometimes in "real life" it is important to us that certain things be said or certain attitudes expressed, even if everyone involved fully realizes the truth of what is said or shares the attitudes expressed. . . . So one would expect it to be important, sometimes, that it be fictional that things be said and that it be fictional in our games that we hear them said, quite apart from our learning that they are fictional and/or our fictionally learning or knowing that they are true. It is not enough to suppose merely that the words of the text make it fictional that the propositions expressed are true or the attitudes appropriate. (1990, 366–67)

Both arguments take the following form: within the story, a view is being expressed; there must, therefore, be someone (in the game) to express that view. In some works this is blatant. For example, *Gulliver's Travels* was originally published (anonymously) with the title *Travels into Several Remote Nations of the World in Four Parts by Lemuel Gulliver,* and is written in the form of the reminiscences of one Lemuel Gulliver (complete with a family background by one Richard Sympson). The book mandates that the reader make-believe both that he is reading a journal written by Gulliver and that Gulliver did all these things. *Mansfield Park* is different, but only in degree.

David Conter has objected to the report model on the grounds that, for many fictions (his example is *Macbeth*) there is no evidence of a narrating character within the work (1991, 324). If we broaden our view from novels to include drama and other forms of fiction, it certainly seems difficult to sustain the claim that evidence for a narrator will always be found within the text. There are, however, other arguments for the report model that do not rest on evidence being found within the text, but on characteristics of the make-believe itself. Walton presents one such argument as follows:

> [W]e are so used to declarative sentences being employed to report events and describe people and situations that, when we experience a literary work, we almost inevitably imagine someone's using or having used its sentences thus. And

it is scarcely a strain to regard these nearly unavoidable imaginings to be pre-scribed. (1990, 365–66)

In other words, the situation we are in when reading a novel is sufficiently similar to the situation we are in when reading a report of actual events (made by someone or other) that it is entirely natural for us to imagine that the novel is just that, a report of actual events (made by someone or other).

This argument can, I think, be taken further. I shall assume that the usual experience of reading a novel does not involve the reader in competing experiences. From this assumption it follows that whatever is involved in playing the game of make-believe must be compatible with what the real world is causing the reader to experience at the time. A silly example will make the point: the game of make-believe should not mandate that the reader act out what he or she reads in the novel. That would probably be incompatible with reading a novel and, obviously, is an entirely inaccurate description of the common experience of reading a novel. The actual experience of a reader is of, say, sitting in a chair and reading sentences in a book. What he imagines must not involve him in experiences that are phenomenologically in competition with this. The report model, which mandates him to imagine he is sitting in a chair reading sentences in a book, fits his actual experience perfectly. Indeed, it is difficult to see how any make-believe could fit it better.

For example, Walton has suggested that there might be cases in which the sentences in a paperback do not play themselves, but rather should be thought of as issuing instructions for constructing a make-believe. It is as if someone has said "Let's imagine that," and given us the story (1990, 365). Walton excuses himself from providing an account of the imagination; the term, he says, "can, if nothing else, serve as a placeholder for a notion yet to be fully clarified" (1990, 21). There is, then, no account of what it is that someone who plays such a game will be experiencing. However, if this make-believe project is going to be different from that prescribed by the report model, it would appear to involve the reader in experiences that do not form a phenomenological unity with his actual experiences. For example, if we read "Emma groomed and dressed herself with the meticulous care of an actress about to make her debut," the report model mandates us to imagine reading this sentence as a reported fact. What does the second model mandate us to do? Imagine seeing Emma do this? If that were the case, such an imaginative project would surely interfere with our continued reading.[4]

II

Although he considers other options, Walton accepts that the report model applies to all (or nearly all) literary works (1990, section 9.5, "Absent and Effaced Narrators"). It is a different matter when we consider visual depictions, such as plays or the cinema. Here he favors what I shall call "the perceptual model." If, in a film, Mrs. Yeobright is bitten by a snake, it is fictional that the viewer sees Mrs. Yeobright bitten by a snake. The report model, by contrast, would hold that it is fictional that the viewer sees *a report of* Mrs. Yeobright bitten by a snake. (Notice that the nature of what the appreciator imagines doing varies between media; the viewer does not imagine *reading* a report of Mrs. Yeobright bitten by a snake, but *viewing* a report of Mrs. Yeobright bitten by a snake.)

There is an obvious consideration that favors the perceptual model. Recall the argument above that our situation when reading a novel is sufficiently similar to our situation when reading a report of actual events for it to be entirely natural for us to imagine that the novel is just that, a report of actual events. Or, to put the point the other way around, it is the fact that our situation when reading a novel is sufficiently dissimilar to our situation when we (for instance) see the actual events that makes it difficult for us to imagine seeing the events while reading the novel. However, the experience of seeing a film of Mrs. Yeobright bitten by a snake seems more similar to seeing Mrs. Yeobright bitten by a snake than it is to seeing a report of Mrs. Yeobright being bitten by a snake. Applied to this case, therefore, the argument seems to support the perceptual rather than the report model.

This argument has an initial intuitive appeal. It does seem plausible, when sitting in the cinema, that we imagine seeing Mrs. Yeobright bitten by a snake. Such appeal does not survive further reflection, however. On a very simple level, if we are to imagine seeing Mrs. Yeobright bitten by a snake, what are we to make of those parts of our experience that tell us we are in a comfortable seat in an air-conditioned room? Our total experience bears little resemblance to seeing someone suffering in a hovel. Gregory Currie has gone a stage further and provided an account of how a visual presentation can be made compatible with the report model, on the grounds that it can naturally be taken as part of the telling of a story:

> Imagine the ways in which a storyteller might tell his story. He might describe the events in words. But instead (or in addition) he might act out a shadow play with his hands. Going further, he might use glove puppets and then marionettes. Extending his resources still further, he might rope in others to assist, telling them what movements and sounds to make. From there it is a short step to the conventions of theatre and cinema. Through the successive extensions the teller tells his tale — he simply uses more and more elaborate means to tell it. (1990, 95)

I shall argue that the nature of the game of make-believe played with visual fictions conforms to the report model, rather than the perceptual model. The nature of the interaction we have with the content of visual fictions is explained by the former, rather than the latter. I shall look at two instances of this interaction, and then dismiss one apparent argument in favor of the perceptual model. For simplicity's sake, I will concentrate on examples from the cinema.

First, let us assume that the perceptual model is correct, and that the viewer is mandated to imagine seeing Mrs. Yeobright bitten by a snake. It is fictional, therefore, that he is seeing her bitten by a snake. If it is fictional that he can see her, it would also seem to be fictional that he can help her. Walton allows that it is fictional that the viewer *can* help her, but that it cannot be fictional that he *does* (1990, 241). Furthermore, as Walton remarks, "in appreciators' games psychological participation tends to outrun and overshadow physical participation" (1990, 240). Despite the fact that there is nothing a viewer can do that would make it fictional that there is physical interaction between himself and the character on the screen, it is common for him to make certain psychological claims: "I feel sorry for Mrs. Yeobright"; "I worry for Emma Bovary"; and so on. It is controversial whether or not what the viewer feels should count as an emotion. In order not to beg the question, I shall refer to these apparently emotional states that are directed at fictional characters and situations as "q-emotions" and leave open for the moment the question of whether or not q-emotions are emotions.

What can be said about these apparent anomalies? How can it be fictional that I can help someone, but not fictional that I do? Why is it that physical interaction is impossible, but psychological interaction is not? According to Walton, it is because there is no understanding within the game of make-believe whereby anything the viewer does would count as making it true in the fiction that he physically interacts with the character (1990, 194). This is a brute fact about the make-believe; it is just the way the game is played. An advantage the report model has over the perceptual model is that it has an explanation of why it is played this way. The range of things the viewer is able to make true in the game of make-believe played with the film corresponds to the range of things the viewer would be able to make true were he faced with a documentary report.

Take as a comparison a documentary film of a man struggling with his luggage. If in a game of make-believe it is fictional that the viewer is viewing a report, the limits on what the viewer is fictionally able to do should correspond to what a viewer is actually able to do in viewing this documentary. The correspondence is exact. Because there is nothing he can do to help the man, nothing he does will count as helping the man. He is, however, able to pity, admire, or get angry with the man. The report model describes exactly the limits of the make-believe we play with visual fiction, which is a strong argument in its favor.

What about the question as to whether q-emotions are emotions? What I feel toward the man struggling with his luggage in the documentary may well be anger because I *believe* the man is being culpably incompetent. Q-emotions do not, however, involve beliefs: I do not believe Mrs. Yeobright is suffering; rather, I make-believe it. If we subscribe to the claim that to be an emotion, a mental state must embody a belief, we are forced to conclude that q-emotions are not emotions. This is Walton's view. Make-believing that Mrs. Yeobright is suffering might, according to Walton, cause a state that has the phenomenological and physiological properties of pity. He calls such a state "quasi-pity." What makes such a state quasi-pity (as opposed to quasi-joy, for example) is not simply a matter of the way it feels; it is largely a matter of being caused by make-believing Mrs. Yeobright is suffering (as opposed to throwing a party). It is a principle of the game, claims Walton, that if the viewer actually feels quasi-pity, it is fictional that (make-believe the case that) he feels pity. In the actual world, what he feels is not an emotion; but what he feels in the actual world makes it fictional that what he feels is an emotion.

I am unhappy with the implication of Walton's account that we do not feel emotions toward fictional characters. After all, we commonly claim that we do. Walton dismisses such concerns, pointing out that we would not take a cinema-goer literally if he said " 'There was a ferocious slime on the loose. I saw it coming,' " so why should we take him literally when he says " 'Boy, was I scared!'" (1990, 197)? There is good reason for Walton's desire to rid himself of the burden of proof. If there were two adequate accounts of the viewer's behavior, one of which attributed fear to him while the other attributed quasi-fear, the fact that the viewer describes himself as scared would be a reason to favor the former. Because we are usually right about which mental states we are in, Walton's account is open to being trumped by another account that takes the viewer at his word. Furthermore, Walton's attempt to shift the burden of proof does not stand up to scrutiny. There is no reason for the viewer to endorse a literal interpretation of his first claim. He knows as well as anyone that there is not a dangerous slime on the loose. The problem arises in that he *would* endorse a literal interpretation of the second; we *do* believe we feel the real-world response of the emotions to the other world of fiction. Walton's theory does, therefore, seem to be vulnerable.

III

What I want to show next, and this is perhaps the most intriguing aspect of this whole discussion, is that the report model provides an elegant solution to the much-discussed issue of our psychological relations to fictional characters. The argument given above is that emotions necessarily embody beliefs and that, since q-emotions do not, q-emotions are not emotions. Patricia Greenspan is one of a number of philosophers who have recently attempted to undermine the claim that emotions necessarily embody beliefs. She begins with a simple example of "phobic response"—an agent who, ever since being bitten by a rabid dog, has felt fear in the presence of all dogs (1988, 17–20). This includes Fido, a harmless old hound, well-known to the agent. In Fido's presence, the agent feels fear. This "feeling" comprises not merely the physiological and phenomenological aspects of fear; it also includes a cognitive content. The agent does not, however, *believe* the cognitive content. Instead, he might (for example) "feel as though" Fido is likely to injure him. The absence of belief is clear from the fact that the agent feels no inclination to perform actions such as warning others against Fido. Greenspan concludes:

> Instead of supposing that his beliefs come into momentary conflict whenever Fido comes near, it seems simpler, and preferable from the standpoint of rational explanation, to take this as a case where emotion parts from judgment. It exhibits the tendency of emotions, in contrast to a rational agent's beliefs, to spill over to

and to fix on objects resembling their appropriate objects in incidental ways. (1988, 18)

Even if Greenspan's example is accepted, and q-emotions are not disqualified from being emotions because of the lack of a belief component, they could still be disqualified through failure to exhibit the requisite connection to action.[5] The phobic's fear of Fido connects with his motivational structure; that is, it disposes him to avoid Fido. If it had no influence on his actions *at all*, then, the argument goes, it could not be fear. The general argument is put by Walton as follows:

> To allow that mere fictions are objects of our psychological attitudes while disallowing the possibility of physical interaction severs the normal links between the physical and the psychological. What is pity or anger which is never to be acted on? What is love that cannot be expressed to its object and is logically or metaphysically incapable of consummation? We cannot even try to rescue Robinson Crusoe from his island, no matter how deep our concern for him. (1990, 196)

Walton adds later that "Fear emasculated by subtracting its distinctive motivational force is not fear at all (1990, 201-202). The claim is that we can have emotional attitudes to objects only if the possibility exists of our physically interacting with them. The definitional problem arises from the fact that since a q-emotion occurs within the game of make-believe, it lacks an essential property of emotions—namely, the link to action. However, assuming the report model is correct, the q-emotion, to be an emotion, should exhibit all the essential properties of emotions *aroused as a result of reading (or viewing) documentary representations*. As should be evident from the discussion above, such emotions *do not* generally have a link to action. Hence, the fact that q-emotions do not have a link to action does not disqualify them from being emotions; it is, rather, exactly what we should expect if the report model were true. There is no problem here.

In writing *Robinson Crusoe*, Defoe drew heavily on the journal of the real-life castaway, Alexander Selkirk. A reader of Selkirk's journal could surely be moved to an emotion at his suffering. However, the fact that Selkirk was marooned in 1704 (and died in 1721) makes it impossible[6] that the reader could help him: as with the fictional Robinson Crusoe, "We cannot even try to rescue Alexander Selkirk from his island, no matter how deep our concern for him." Hence, readers' emotions will have no connection to action. If, in general, emotions aroused by documentary representations have no connection to action, the absence of a connection between q-emotions and action is no reason to deny that q-emotions are emotions. Emotions felt for Crusoe do not differ in this respect from emotions felt for Selkirk. We have resolved our standoff. Walton and others maintain that as emotions necessarily have a connection to action, q-emotions are not emotions. This is wrong; we have no reason to expect q-emotions to have a connection to action.

Unfortunately, matters are not that simple. Consider Walton's now notorious example:

Charles is watching a horror movie about a terrible green slime. He cringes in his seat as the slime oozes slowly but relentlessly over the earth, destroying everything in its path. Soon a greasy head emerges from the undulating mass, and two beady eyes fix on the camera. The slime, picking up speed, oozes on a new course straight toward the viewers. Charles emits a shriek and clutches desperately at his chair. Afterwards, still shaken, he confesses he was "terrified" of the slime. (1990, 196)

In nonfictional cases, fear for oneself necessarily involves the belief that one is threatened. I would claim that a state of q-fear that involved imagining one was threatened would also be fear for oneself. Nobody, I take it, would maintain that Charles believes he is threatened. The problem is that, on the report model, Charles cannot make-believe he is threatened either. I have claimed that when Charles sees the film, he imagines seeing a documentary representation. Thus, it is fictional that what Charles is seeing is a report. In the same way that it is true that Charles cannot be threatened by the machete-wielding maniac he sees on the evening news, it is fictional that he cannot be threatened by the slime that he sees in the report he is watching. The same unbridgeable gulf that exists between Charles and the news in the real world exists between Charles and the report in the fictional world. Because of this, Charles cannot make-believe that he is threatened.[7] If he does not believe he is threatened and does not make-believe he is threatened, what he feels cannot be fear for himself.

It is not only Charles's reaction that cannot easily be accommodated within the report model, for neither can the behavior of the slime. Within the make-believe, the slime appears in a report, not (so to speak) in person. Hence, it is fictional that it cannot threaten Charles. So why does it behave as if it can? Charles's terror is a result of an "aside" from the slime: "[a] greasy head emerges from the undulating mass, and two beady eyes fix on the camera. The slime, picking up speed, oozes on a new course straight toward the viewers" (1990, 196).

One option would be to abandon the claim that Charles feels fear, and to describe his reaction in terms of nonemotional states such as shock and alarm (Neill 1993, 5). Consider an undersea photographer in a shark cage, in which he has complete confidence, which is being attacked by sharks. It might be plausible to describe the photographer's reaction as shock, even if he might describe it as terror. This does not, however, do justice to the complexity of Charles's reaction. We need an explanation of at least the following: first, why is it that, in comparison with emotions felt for other people, emotions felt for oneself are so unusual in fiction; second, what is the connection between reactions such as Charles's and asides; and third, why does the frequency of such emotions vary between media. Charles's reaction is unusual in the cinema; it is unknown in the library.[8]

On the perceptual model, there is no problem accounting for interaction between Charles and the slime. In the game of make-believe that Charles is playing, he and the slime occupy the same fictional world. Embracing this model would mean embracing a theory with many flaws, some of which I have already discussed and some of which I will go on to discuss. If Charles and the slime occupy the same fictional world, what accounts for the limits on interaction? Why are asides and, therefore, emotions felt for oneself so unusual? Does Charles, sitting in the cinema at Cambridge watching the screen, really imagine that he lives in New York in the 1950s and is being chased around the streets by a monster? This seems to me a consequence best avoided.

For the structure of a more adequate reply, compatible with the report model, recall Edgar Allen Poe's tale, "The Fall of the House of Usher." The tawdry romance Roderick reads seems to be being played out around him; whenever a loud noise is reported as happening in the novel, that noise resounds around the house. Roderick's friend knows he is hearing a fiction, yet the fiction is not behaving itself. The listener is understandably concerned: "Oppressed, as I certainly was, upon the extraordinary coincidence, by a thousand conflicting sensations, in which wonder and extreme terror were predominant . . ." (275). The vivacity of the surroundings makes it easy for the subject to dwell on the grounds of the belief that he is safe, a belief in which, in cooler moments, he would have complete confidence. The fact that the House of Usher is a gloomy mansion, that Roderick is going mad, that there is a storm outside, and that Lady Madeline has just been buried in the vault downstairs, does nothing to calm the listener's nerves. He believes he is hearing a tale (he thinks the noises an "extraordinary coincidence"), but the bizarre situation forces him to imagine something he knows to be false, namely, that the fiction is coming true around him. He does not believe this; he has "a thousand conflicting sensations." But it does worry him and inspires feelings "in which wonder and extreme terror were predominant."

This might all sound a little fanciful, but it does mirror the problem quite well. It is no part of any account, least of all mine, that Charles doubts that what he is watching is fiction; that belief is completely secure. Recall, however, that Charles is imagining he is being shown a (true) report. Within the make-believe, the report starts misbehaving itself in a vivid and overwhelming fashion. There is a terrifying slime which, to all appearance, seems to be bearing down on him. The report has had Charles on the edge of his seat (both in the game and in real life) and (in the game) his confidence that he is seeing a report is thrown into a maelstrom. Like Poe's listener, he is forced to review all the things he knows to be "true"—such as, for example, that because this is a report, the slime cannot be trying to get him. If the reaction of Poe's listener is credible, so is this construal of Charles's state. Within the fiction, it is not true that the slime can get him, but it is true that the behavior of the slime undermines his confidence that he is safe in a particularly vivid fashion.

At no time need Charles imagine that he is threatened by the slime. The account gives us none of the implausible consequences or needs for special explanations of the perceptual model. It also explains why reactions such as Charles's are unusual compared to feeling emotions *for* characters. Unlike those reactions, Charles's reaction is not part of the usual game. It explains, moreover, the role of asides, for they are essential to causing the peculiar reaction in the first place.

Finally, it explains why Charles's reaction happens in the cinema and not in the library. Charles has to be manipulated into it; he has to be put in a state of heightened expectation so that his reaction is out of order, even in the make-believe. This is much easier in an immediate, vivid medium such as a film or a play than in the detached, cognitive world of a book.

As I said above, Charles's reaction is as seldom encountered in our dealings with fiction as Poe's listener's is in our dealings with life. Indeed, if it were not for the fact that fear for oneself as a reaction to fiction is the central example in the best known work in this area, Kendall Walton's "Fearing Fictions," I doubt whether it would receive much attention. Walton has remarked (in conversation) that he took the example of fear for oneself because it was the most difficult. The danger is, then, to underestimate its peculiarity and distort one's general account of fiction.

IV

In addition to providing a natural account of our interaction with fiction, the report model is also better able to account for action in films presented from a certain point of view. I shall use Walton's own example. In Fritz Lang's *You Only Live Once*, the final shot shows Eddie's last visual experience before he dies. (An earlier shot in the film shows the world from the point of view of a frog.) How is the viewer to cope with this on the perceptual model? It seems as if he must imagine being the person, the sole person, who has these visual experiences. The argument against this has been advanced by Currie:

> [I]n film . . . a single scene may be divided into many shots from different perspectives. As shots succeed one another we don't have any sense of changing our perspective on the action. Those familiar with the conventions of cinema hardly notice the cutting as the camera moves from one face to another. Many camera perspectives would be difficult or downright impossible to achieve; viewing the earth from deep space one minute, hanging from the ceiling in a drawing room the next. In some films what we would have to make believe in order to make sense of our being observers of the scene would be wildly at variance with the conventions of the story. For example, in *The Lady in the Lake*, a film of Raymond Chandler's detective story, the action is depicted through the eyes of Philip Marlowe. If we are to make believe that we are literally seeing events through Marlowe's eyes, the story would seem to have become a science fiction fantasy. This is not the impression created in the viewer's mind while watching the film. (1990, 93–94)

Walton is aware of the danger of boxing himself into this dangerous corner. He suggests the viewer can either imagine himself to be Eddie (to return to his example) having his final visual experience, or imagine he is having a token of the same type of experience Eddie is having (1990, 344). I agree with Currie that the first option ought to be rejected: this is not the impression created in the viewer's mind while watching the film. I am not impressed by the second option Walton offers us, at least not for the examples we have been given. In what way is imagining having a token of the type experience of the last visual impression Eddie has before his death not imagining that one is Eddie having this experience? Unlike (for instance) the experience of tooth-ache, this experience cannot be specified except as *Eddie's* experience. Simi-larly, with Currie's example, it is not enough to imagine a token experience of looking at a drowned woman in a lake; one has to imagine one is having the experience of *Philip Marlowe* looking at a drowned woman (or perhaps even looking at a drowned woman one believes to be Muriel) in a lake. I cannot see how to do this without, at that moment, imagining one is Eddie or Philip Marlowe.

None of these examples pose problems for the report model. The viewer need only play a game in which he is seeing a report of events, including a report of what Eddie or Philip Marlowe experience. This is perfectly compati-ble with the experience of sitting in the cinema watching a visual presentation. Once again, the difference is that in the make-believe the report is true, while in the real world it is a fiction. Indeed, as Currie implies, seeing the action from the point of view of a character is only one of a number of problems for the perceptual model. There is also the point of view provided by a camera, the fact that days can pass in minutes, that locations can be changed almost instantly, and so on. The explanation for all of this can be found within the report model.

Now to the apparent problem for the report model. The following exchange occurs in *Romeo and Juliet:*[9]

> *Rom.* So shalt thou show me friendship. Take thou that;
> Live and be prosperous, and farewell, good fellow.
> *Bal. [aside]* For all this same, I'll hide me hereabout.
> His looks I fear, and his intents I doubt.
>
> (V.3.41–44)

The apparent problem is that it appears as if Balthazar is addressing the audi-ence directly. The report model mandates the viewer to imagine that the con-tent of the play is a report of events that have happened (or are happening) elsewhere. It cannot, therefore, be part of the content of the play that Balthazar addresses a member of the audience when and where the play is performed. No such problem arises for the perceptual model. It is compatible with the game of make-believe in which the viewer imagines watching Romeo and Balthazar that, within the game, the viewer is addressed by them (Walton 1990, 232). It is no problem for the report model if the aside is spoken by the narra-tor; one of the functions of the narrator, as we have seen, is to make statements to the reader.

This criticism—that the report model cannot make sense of characters ad-dressing the audience—is a two-edged sword. Being addressed by a character in fiction is, in common experience, disconcerting, and it would count against an account of fiction that it did not make it so. The fact that the report model has problems accounting for such asides might even be a point in its favor. With this in mind, let us look at a possible reply. The argument is, once again, due to Currie:

> In these cases I think the members of the audience come to play a dual role. They are both spectators of, and actors (or sometimes merely props in), the production. They play characters participating in the action and it becomes make-believedly true that they are those characters. But they are still members of the audience, and as such they observe themselves playing these roles. As members of the audience they are to make believe that they are taking part in a *representation* of actually occurring events, not that they are participants in those very events. (1990, 96)

It is as if the narrator has encouraged one of the people helping him present the story to seek out recruits among the audience when appropriate. When addressed, the audience occupies a dual role as both spectator of and participant in the narration. This duality is uncomfortable, a fact that accounts for the audience's feeling disconcerted.

An alternative defense would take the disconcerting nature of asides seriously and regard them as straightforward violations of the make-believe. The character, in addressing the audience, does not abide by the "rules." Games, and not just games of make-believe, can absorb violations, provided the violations do not become prevalent. For example, if you are beating me at chess, I might even up the sides—-and make a better game of it—by pocketing your queen or swapping a pawn for a knight. Such events are in no way part of the game, although they can only happen within the context of a game. Some asides to the audience can only be construed as violations of this sort. In Tom Stoppard's *Rosencrantz and Guildenstern are Dead*, Rosencrantz bellows "Fire!" at the audience, and then remarks (while looking in their direction): "Not a move. They should burn to death in their shoes." This can be accounted for on neither the report nor the perceptual model; in neither case can it be fictional that the action is taking place in medieval Denmark and a contemporary theater. Indeed, this play derives much of its humor from not allowing the audience to play a consistent game of make-believe. Balthazar's aside is perhaps a "cheating" way to communicate his inner thoughts.

Finally, I want to turn this point back onto the perceptual model. If it is fictional that we are looking at the characters in a drama, why is it so seldom fictional that they are looking at us? What accounts for it being disconcerting when they do? Walton's answer to the first question is the same as that which he gives to account for the differences between physical and psychological interaction—it is conventional within the game that no such interactions occur: "[T]he question is out of place, silly. The appreciator does not ask why fictionally no one pays any attention to him. And it is not fictional that he wonders why no one does or that he tries to come up with an explanation" (1990, 236). There is nothing to be said against this answer as such: Walton has every right to appeal to the conventions that he takes, as a matter of fact, to be operative. However, the fact that the report model requires no additional hypotheses to describe the games of make-believe must be a point in its favor. We can see a report, but people who are being reported on cannot see us.

Walton's explanation of why asides happen less often than the perceptual model would lead us to expect is comparatively weak:

[D]ifferent appreciators will behave differently in front of the work; what fiction-ally they say and do, what they choose to attend to and how, what they mutter under their breath will vary greatly, and some will behave in ways the artist did not foresee. So the artist cannot fit her characters' responses to what, fictionally, the appreciator says or does . . . If fictionally Papageno, in Bergman's rendition of Mozart's opera, appeals to the appreciator for sympathy, it may be fictional that the appreciator willingly complies, or that he brushes off the request with disdain, or that he ignores it. (1990, 235)

Walton exaggerates the problem. It is not as if the appreciator has carte blanche on how to react; there will be an *appropriate* reaction determined by the content of the piece. It is just not an option, if one is seriously engaged in a game of make-believe generated by a pantomime (for instance), to boo the dame and cheer the villain. The artist *can* fit his characters' responses to what, fictionally, the appreciator says or does if the appreciator responds appropri-ately. Of course, the appreciator does not have to react appropriately. He *can* play whatever game of make-believe he likes. But, obviously, if he is to get out of the work what the artist intended him to (and this must, in general, be a consideration), he must respond in the way the work dictates (even if it dictates him to suspend judgment). It seems, then, that the report model has a better account of audience/character interaction when it occurs, and of why it does not occur more often.

NOTES

I am grateful to the editors of this volume, Mette Hjort and Sue Laver, for their careful reading of and helpful comments on an earlier draft of this paper.

1. I shall not be looking at all the candidates on the market; in particular, I will not be considering those proposed in Currie 1991 and Levinson 1994.

2. Perhaps we imagine that the narrator of *The Master and Margarita* is relating events that happened in a place similar to the real world except in certain respects. This does not remove all normativity from the report model; once we have decided the nature of the place from which the narrator is reporting, we can be more sure about what to infer from what he says. I agree with Walton (1990) that there are no hard-and-fast rules for deciding the nature of the place (chap. 4).

3. *Mimesis as Make-Believe* (1990), 366. Further references to this work will be made by page number in parentheses.

4. There is some evidence to suggest that Walton does take this to be mandated; see, for example, 295.

5. In fact, since beliefs are required to be a component of emotions because of their connection to action, the following argument would solve the definitional problem even if Greenspan's claim were not accepted. For simplicity's sake, I will attack the connection to action directly. My own worries about Greenspan's claim stem from skepticism that being phobic about dogs involves fearing them.

6. That is, at least as impossible as time travel. The argument does not require that the impossibility of our relations to past events be equally strong as the impossibility of our relations to fictions. All that is required is that both be strong enough to fulfill

Walton's claim that there is a separation of the psychological and the physical, which, I take it, they are.

7. The particular difficulty is brought out in Neill 1993.

8. An instructive example to think about is the scene in which Mr. Wilson looks up "Pooka" in the film, *Harvey*.

9. This and several of the other examples are Walton's own.

PART II

EMOTION
AND ITS
EXPRESSION
THROUGH ART

6

Contra the Hypothetical Persona in Music

STEPHEN DAVIES

The listener's phenomenal experience of music's expressiveness is more like a face-to-face encounter with someone who publicly and vividly displays his feeling than it is like hearing a dispassionate description of an emotional state. The expressiveness is immediate and direct, not filtered through an arbitrary symbol system. It is immanent in the music, rather than something beyond the music's boundaries to which its sound refers. But if the experience of the expressiveness is as of an occurrent emotion, whose emotion could that be? Given that the music is nonsentient, it appears that an owner of the emotions expressed in it must be found.

Traditional accounts have identified the emoter as the composer or performer on the one side, or the listener on the other, but such theories encounter well-rehearsed difficulties. Serious objections apply to the expression theory, according to which the composer (or performer) discharges his feeling by composing in a fashion such that the resulting musical product discernibly bears the marks of his experience. Some composers sometimes convey their feelings to the music they write, but they do so by matching the inherent expressive potential of their materials to their moods, not by infecting the music with their emotions. No less problematic is arousalism or emotivism, according to which the music's expressiveness consists in a dispositional property or power by which it awakens an emotional response in the listener. Listeners do sometimes respond to music by feeling sad, for example, but the music is sad not because it calls forth that reaction. Rather, it is because the music is expressive that it invites the response. I do not find these theories appealing as explanations of the nature of music's expressiveness, though they have their adherents.[1]

Another possibility is this one: it may be that the emotions heard in music are those of characters designated in the work; are those, for instance, of Rodolfo, Mimi, Musetta, Marcello, and the others in Puccini's *La Bohème*. Against this, it can be noted that we often distinguish what is expressed in the work from what is experienced by a character in it; that is, we talk of what the work expresses in addition to considering how the feelings of those individuals it represents are conveyed. Moreover, in purely instrumental works, no characters are indicated, though such pieces can be redolent with feeling.

By elimination, as it were, we come to this possibility: that the listener imagines or make-believes a person who undergoes the emotions expressed in the music. If the emotions expressed in music must be experienced by someone who is not the composer, performer, listener, or a character represented in the work, then that someone must be entertained by the listener. In hearing sound as emotionally expressive, we animate the music through an imaginative engagement that leads us to hypothesize an abstract or virtual persona. The movements, tensions, and resolutions then heard in the music embody her actions and sensations. As a result, the music comes to life in our experience of it. Call this view "hypothetical emotionalism."

Wait a minute! Is it respectable to treat purely instrumental works as if they are program music? Perhaps not—not, anyway, if the music is used to kick-start the imagination, which then pursues a course individual to the listener who uses the music merely as the occasion for a private reverie. That reaction is a common one, so evocative is music of private associations. But free association leads to inattention, not to a better understanding of the music.

Hypothetical emotionalism does not, however, recommend this kind of listening. The listener is to hypothesize the existence of a persona, but otherwise must carefully follow the unfolding progression of the music, for it is in this that the vicissitudes undergone by this persona are revealed. The "dramatic narrative" of which the listener becomes aware must be uncovered in the music and be responsive to every subtle articulation of its structure. The "story" developed by the listener should map directly onto all the work's parts; it is the "story" of the piece's formal and expressive progress, these two being intimately and inextricably connected. The listener's hypothesizing, rather than leading away from the music, provides entry to the fullest comprehension of the piece's individual characteristics and, if it has them, to overall unity and closure.

I

In acknowledging the importance of music's expressive dimension, hypothetical emotionalism is superior to crude formalism, which would dismiss such matters as irrelevant or impossible. The familiar difficulties of explaining the music's expressiveness in terms of the composer's, performer's, or listener's feelings are dodged. And the theory accords with the common phenomenology locating the expressiveness directly, unmediated, within the sound of the music itself.

How, though, does hypothetical emotionalism fare by contrast with what I take to be its main rival—let us call it "appearance emotionalism"—which is the view that musical materials can be literally expressive as a result of presenting to audition sounds with emotion-characteristics?[2] This alternative denies that music expresses occurrent emotions involving sensation or sentience, so it rejects the motivation given above for seeking an "owner" of the feelings expressed in music. It maintains, rather, that music presents sounds that are expressive without regard to experienced emotions. Music is sad-sounding in much the way that basset hounds or the mask conventionally denoting tragedy are sad-looking. If it takes imagination to hear music's expressiveness, it does not take more than is needed to see face masks as wearing human expressions or willow trees as downcast. (For that matter, it does not require more imagination than is needed to view fellow humans as alive and intelligently aware rather than as androids.) Music would not be heard as expressive unless it were approached in terms of a certain attitude, called by Peter Kivy an "animating tendency," but that attitude is our natural mode of experiencing the world in all its aspects. Its adoption requires no special kind of imaginative hypothesizing.

In comparing these two accounts of music's expressiveness, four points are worth considering, but only the last is decisive:

1. Hypothetical emotionalists emphasize the extent to which the listener's impression of overall structure depends as much on awareness of the pattern of the musical work's expressive character and development as on knowledge of formal features, narrowly construed. This is an important observation, but it does not presuppose hypothetical emotionalism as such. It can be endorsed no less readily by an advocate of appearance emotionalism.

2. Music's expressiveness frequently summons an emotional reaction from the listener. It is easy to understand why we would react to the feelings of a person, albeit one whose existence is hypothesized, but why would we react to expressive appearances that pay no regard to occurrent emotions? The advocate of appearance emotionalism could answer as follows: expressive appearances are evocative of the kinds of responses that music elicits from the listener.[3] We can find such appearances moving, especially when they are contrived or appropriated in the service of artistic communication. The responses to which they give rise typically lack the force of the reactions provoked by the felt-emotions of others (or fictions), because the beliefs (or make-beliefs) and desires (or make-desires) relevant in the latter context are absent from the former. This is consistent, though, with the manner in which listeners react to music's expressiveness and with their continuing interest in works that induce the negative reaction of sadness.

3. Musical works often express emotions, sometimes contrasting markedly, in series. In listening, we expect development, connection, and integration within the music. Hypothetical emotionalism explains how we realize this expectation in following the course of the music's expressiveness. The listener is

to seek pattern and order, such as one might find in the succession of a person's actions or feelings, within the work's expressive features. Just as, when a person acts in character through time, one anticipates continuity in the progress of his emotional states, so, too, the auditor who imagines a persona in the music listens for, and can reasonably hope to uncover, a narrative thread tying together and clarifying the sequence of emotions expressed in the music. Hypothetical emotionalism invites the listener to regard the various emotions expressed within a single musical span as unified with respect to the emotional life and experiences of the imagined persona.

Because expressive appearances typically are fallen into, not adopted, their sequence usually is of no special significance. How, then, does the proponent of appearance emotionalism avoid treating changes in the work's mood merely as a procession of unconnected expressions? Two answers are available, depending on the case. Where the expressive progress of the work is central to its character, the unity and closure achieved within it can be explained as resulting from the composer's control of the material. Even if expressive appearances are not normally deliberately created, within the musical context they are shaped and ordered by the composer. This alone, without appeal to a narrative concerning a fictional persona, makes it appropriate to look for a connection between them and for the possibility of reference through them to the world of human feeling. Alternatively, attention to the work's formal features is likely to be sufficient to explain its coherence and integrity if the work is one in which expressiveness is not the prime concern.

4. Only emotions with distinctive behavioral expressions can be presented in appearances. Those depending on a specific kind of cognitive content or sensation cannot be, for such things are absent from mere appearances. Sadness and happiness may be of the former type, whereas patriotism, shame, pride, embarrassment, envy, and hope are of the latter. Accordingly, appearance emotionalism countenances the expression of only a limited range of emotions within music. Purely instrumental works might be expressive of happiness or sadness but could not be expressive of shame.[4]

Appearance emotionalism can allow that a few works express or hint at the expression of higher emotions, doing so by presenting expressive contexts in which such emotions naturally find their homes.[5] If, however, such expressions are achieved mainly through the musical presentation or invocation of the cognitive contents and attitudes usually presupposed for occurrences of the higher emotions, then hypothetical emotionalism is better placed to explain how this occurs. To make-believe someone personified in the music is to imagine that person as possessing beliefs, desires, intentions, and attitudes, even if the contents or objects of these are not transparently conveyed. To entertain that such a person is present in the work is also to make-believe a context in which cognitively complex emotions might be musically expressed. If it is appropriate to hear music as expressing not solely happiness and sadness but also the more subtle, cognitively rich emotions, hypothetical emotionalism provides for this possibility. If instrumental music often is expressive of the "higher" emotions, this can be explained by hypothetical emotionalism as it cannot be by appearance emotionalism.

What one makes of these two theories is likely to hinge on one's judgment concerning the frequency and musical constitution of expressions of "higher" emotions. For my part, I am skeptical of the claims made by hypothetical emotionalists for the centrality and objectivity of the musical expression of these complex, sophisticated emotional states.

II

Before going further, it is appropriate to examine the claims that might be made in the name of hypothetical emotionalism as it applies to instrumental music. The first is a descriptive one: we can listen to music as conveying a story concerning the emotional life of a persona hypothesized by the listener on the basis of her auditory experience. This is undoubtedly true, but it is also trivial. Equally weak is the insistence that some auditors do, indeed, approach music in this fashion. (Advocates of hypothetical emotionalism are presumed to be among this group.) A stronger thesis holds that listeners typically or characteristically hear music as the expression of a persona. (I believe this empirical claim to be false.) More interesting is this prescription: we should hypothesize a persona in listening to music. The normative force of this latest proposal is backed by the claim that this approach to the listening experience leads to a proper understanding of the music for what it is. Notice that, in this formulation, it is not denied that other styles or methods of listening are viable and might lead equally to a sympathetic appreciation of the works involved. A yet stronger version of the thesis is not so concessive. It maintains that we *must* listen to music in the specified fashion, for this provides the *only* route to its fullest comprehension. Those who hold that music expresses the higher emotions, and that these require the invocation of cognitive elements such as can be attributed to a person, are likely to advocate this last position.

A further matter to be considered is that of scope. Are the previous claims made on behalf of all instrumental works or only some? And if the latter, will an advocate of hypothetical emotionalism insist on the stronger prescription for all the relevant works or only for those that are especially expressive and dramatic?

Those who promote hypothetical emotionalism might have different versions in mind, or differ about the theory's scope. They work from several backgrounds, perspectives, and motivations. Indeed, it is for this reason that I have so far outlined the theory without reference to its proponents.

The vogue for hypothetical emotionalism, for describing works of pure music in terms of narratives presenting episodes in the life of a fictional or virtual persona, is comparatively recent. The position has been presented variously by musicologists[6] and philosophers.[7] It may be that not all these authors share the same goals. The musicologists are keen to counter sterile formalism and undue focus on technicalities within their own discipline. Their aim is to humanize music criticism and theory. Accordingly, they stress the close relation between formal and expressive elements.[8] The philosophers, on the other hand, are perhaps more conscious of opposing appearance emotionalism in developing accounts that acknowledge a central place for the expression of higher emotions in music.[9]

III

"Hypotheticism" has become so popular in the philosophy of art that it is worth distinguishing the variety under consideration from its confrères, especially since some of the philosophers already cited are also "hypotheticists" concerning literature.[10] For the case of literary works, it might be held that, in interpreting their meanings or appreciating their styles, we speculate not about the actual author's intentions and personality but about those of an implied, apparent, or hypothetical author. A similar move could be involved with respect to the work's expressiveness. It might be, that is, that we move from the way the work appears to the emotions that someone might have experienced and expressed in producing it.[11]

The point I wish to make is this: whereas hypothetical emotionalism, as described earlier, imagines a persona *in* the work, the theories just mentioned speculate about a person who stands *outside* the work, as its imagined creator.[12] Hypothetical emotionalism concerns the work's world rather than a possible version of the actual world. The importance of the distinction is apparent from the following case. Suppose that, in reading a novel, we consider the narrator's personality, attitudes, feelings, and so on.[13] Suppose also that we speculate about the intentions of the story's apparent author who, unlike the narrator, is external to the work's world. Now, what can reasonably be inferred about the former cannot be applied necessarily to the latter and vice versa. It may be apparent that the narrator is mistaken about what is true in the work's world, but the apparent author is not. Moreover, the work might convey an aesthetic and moral vision that is attributable to the implied author but of which the narrator patently is oblivious.[14] In developing his version of hypothetical emotionalism in music, Fred Maus (1988) is clearly aware of the distinction. Some musical qualities that might be hypothesized of the persona in the music, such as surprise, could not reasonably be attributed to the work's composer (whether actual or hypothesized). Moreover, what is presented in the music has an indefiniteness that imaginings about the composer could not have. In entertaining thoughts about the work's composer we consider a single individual whose actions give rise to the entire musical structure, but in following the music, we might not be licensed to hypothesize a definite number of musical personas or to regard any as generating through their actions all aspects of the work's detail and structure.

I raise this topic not because I think the philosophers who support hypotheticism in aesthetic/artistic appreciation across several artistic arenas are confused about the differences.[15] My goal is to mark the distinction for the sake of overall clarity, for it would be easy for the reader who browses the relevant literature to come away with the mistaken impression that all versions of hypotheticism are of a piece.

IV

I turn now to criticism. Of the possibilities sketched above, my interest lies in the strongest version of hypothetical emotionalism as it might apply to some, if not all, expressive works of absolute music. I review, that is, the position maintaining that, to understand and appreciate some musical works fully, the listener *must* hypothesize a persona and hear the unfolding of the formal and expressive elements of the music as actions and feelings of, or events affecting, that persona. I take this position to amount to the claim that the musical works in question must be heard as being about the emotional life of the persona whose presence in the work should be imagined.

What might one mean by the assertion that a musical work is about so-and-so? Four possibilities recommend themselves. A musical work is about so-and-so where (a) the composer intends it to be so; (b) it is conventional within the practice of artistic appreciation that such works are to be approached thus; (c) a sufficient number of suitably acculturated listeners would appreciate so-and-so upon reflection on the music; or (d) one cannot understand the music (fully) without invoking the presence of so-and-so within it.[16]

I intend to concentrate on the last of the proposed conditions for musical "aboutness," so I will be brief with the first three. I doubt that there is much evidence to indicate that composers have intended the listener to hypothesize the presence of a persona in their instrumental works. In any event, the fate of (a) will depend on the viability of (b) or (c). Condition (a) must involve a robust notion of intention, I think. The composer could have such an intention only if she could give it public expression, that is, embody it in the music, so that it might be acknowledged by the listener. It is not enough that a composer merely entertain the thought of her works being about a persona and fondly hope this will be recognized. The achievement (and, hence, the possession) of the relevant intention presupposes the existence of public conventions allowing for its communication via the musical work or, at least, for the widespread recognition of the intention. This is to say, (a) presupposes the possibility of (b), practices or conventions calling on the listener to hypothesize a persona in the music, or of (c), general agreement among listeners that such a persona is to be imagined and coincidence in the descriptions then offered of the persona's emotional life. But, again, it seems straightforwardly false that there are public conventions or consensus regarding such matters.[17] Mostly, proponents of hypothetical emotionalism offer their musical analyses as new and as revealing expressive subtleties that generally have been overlooked.

The crucial condition is (d). In relation to hypothetical emotionalism it amounts to this: to comprehend the music fully, the listener must imagine the presence of a persona within it, and to follow the course of the music with understanding, must hear in it the actions, experiences, and sensations of that persona. Obviously, this condition corresponds to what I identified above as the strong version of hypothetical emotionalism—that one must hypothesize the presence of a persona in order to grasp the subtle expressiveness of at least some musical works. And, as already noted, it is plausible to suggest that (d) can be met if many musical works express higher emotions, because their doing so depends on a cognitively rich context that might be supplied only by making believe that the unfolding of the music corresponds to the emotional life of an agent with beliefs, attitudes, and desires. The issue, as indicated previously, is not whether the listener might invent a story about the actions of, or events affecting, a persona, a story that matches the articulation of the music. That can be done easily enough.[18] Rather, the question is whether this mode of listening provides access to an understanding that is both truly of the music and unobtainable by any other kind of listening. To show that (d) is satisfied, it must be argued that the invocation of a persona is essentially implicated in an understanding reaction to the music. Doing so involves establishing that what is imagined is not idiosyncratic or irrelevant to musical understanding; it involves demonstrating that the work invites, controls, and limits what might be hypothesized, so that this approach leads to a revelatory experience of the music as no alternative can.

In discussing (d), I concentrate on recent work by Jenefer Robinson. She outlines a version of hypothetical emotionalism in a paper coauthored with Gregory Karl (1995). They argue "that the expressive structure of some pieces of music can be interpreted as an unfolding of the psychological experience of [a] musical persona over time. . . . [The] formal coherence of the music often consists precisely in its embodying a coherent unfolding of psychological states in a musical persona" (405). The theme is developed in a detailed discussion of Shostakovitch's Tenth Symphony, which they believe to express false hope: "The plot archetype to which Shostakovitch's Tenth Symphony conforms is conventionally interpreted as a progression from dark to light or struggle to victory (adversity to salvation, illness to health, etc.)" (406). The authors continue:

> [V]ery often the formal and expressive threads of a work's structure are so finely interwoven as to be inextricable. Thus, in establishing our case for the musical expression of hope, we had to discuss not only the contours and conventional associations of our focal passage, but also its role in patterns of thematic transformation and quotation spanning the entire symphony. To demonstrate that our focal passage expresses hope we had to engage in a *formal* analysis of the work as a whole. Conversely, we suggest that in a complexly integrated work like Shostakovitch's Tenth, formal and expressive elements of musical structure are so thoroughly interdependent that the formal function of particular passages can often only be accurately described in *expressive* terms. Thus there is no "strictly formal" or purely musical explanation for why our focal passage unfolds as it does in the central section of the third movement; its formal function just is to express the cognitively complex emotion of hope. (412–13)

So far the account is familiar, though it combines the philosopher's preoccupation with the higher emotions and the musicologist's concern with the intimate relation between the work's expressive character and its large-scale structure. Attention to the structure of an entire work, interpreted as the emotional experience of a persona through time, provides access to sufficient cognitive content to allow for the musical expression of complex emotions, such as false hope. Formal coherence in music, it is recommended, often consists precisely in the work's embodying a succession of connected psychological states that are to be attributed to a persona.

Now, hypothetical emotionalism faces the problem of establishing that the listener's making believe a persona, and a cognitive context along with the presence of that persona, stems directly from an appropriate experience of the work's properties. If this cannot be done, the listener's imaginative contribution is gratuitous (and likely to be idiosyncratic). In "The Expression and Arousal of Emotion in Music" (1994), Robinson proposes a solution to this challenge. She argues for an intimate connection between primitive, largely noncognitive, responses aroused in the listener by the music and the process of imaginative engagement that leads the listener to construct a narrative about the experiences of a persona he hypothesizes to reside in the music. While she allows that sad music might lead the listener to feel sadness, Robinson does not believe that music's expression of cognitively complex emotions is explained by its power to call forth such responses. She does maintain, however, that some "primitive" feelings are predicable of music because they are evoked by it. She also holds that the thoughtless reactions kindled by music feed and direct the hypothesizing that reveals in the music a persona who experiences cognitively complex emotions (such as "cheerful confidence turning to despair," to use her own example).

In Robinson's view, the qualities attributed to music in virtue of its power to arouse the listener to a corresponding feeling include tension, nervousness, uncertainty, relief, disturbance, unease, surprise, reassurance, and relaxation. Music is tense just in case it tends to awaken that response in a listener who is familiar with the musical idiom. Whereas emotions usually are rich in cognitive content, involving beliefs, desires, and attitudes, the evocation of unease or relief by music requires little by way of cognitive involvement from the listener, so the response is triggered more or less automatically. The auditor must listen with expectations tailored to the style of the piece, but these usually are not explicitly called to mind. The response that concerns Robinson typically is an unthinking reaction, a somatic feeling. She writes:

> Music that disturbs and unsettles us is disturbing, unsettling music. Modulations that surprise us are surprising. Melodies that soothe us are soothing. . . . [I]t seems to me that the expression of a feeling by music can sometimes be explained straightforwardly in terms of the arousal of that feeling. However, the feelings aroused "directly" by music are not stabs of pain or feelings of unrequited passion, but more "primitive" feelings of tension, relaxation, surprise, and so on. (1994, 19)

What interests her, Robinson notes, is

> the way in which the simple feelings "directly" aroused by music can contribute to the imaginative expression of more complex emotions. . . . Now, just as the

formal structure of a piece of music can be understood in terms of the arousal of such feelings as uncertainty, uneasiness, relaxation, tension, relief, etc., so too can we understand the expressiveness of that piece of music in terms of the arousal of those and similar feelings. . . . If a piece of music is heard as successively disturbing and reassuring, or as meandering uncertainly before moving forward confidently, or as full of obstacles, this is at least in part because of the way the music makes us feel. Disturbing passages disturb us; reassuring ones reassure. Passages that meander uncertainly make us feel uneasy: it is not clear where the music is going. Passages that move forward confidently make us feel satisfied: we know what is happening and seem to be able to predict what will happen next. Passages that are full of obstacles make us feel tense and when the obstacles are overcome, we feel relieved. It is important to notice that the feeling *expressed* is not always the feeling *aroused*: an uncertain, diffident passage may make me uneasy; a confident passage may make me feel reassured or relaxed. . . . As I listen to a piece which expresses serenity tinged with doubt, I myself do not have to feel serenity tinged with doubt, but the feelings I do experience, such as relaxation or reassurance, interspersed with uneasiness, alert me to the nature of the overall emotional expressiveness in the piece of music as a whole. . . . [T]he emotional experience aroused by the music is essential to the detection of the emotional expressiveness in the music itself. At the same time, the emotions aroused in me are not the emotions expressed by the music. (1994, 19–20)

Robinson plainly realizes that, if one is made aware of no more than the unfolding of a pattern (of tensings and relaxings) while listening to an extended piece, then hers is no advance on Kivy's "contour" theory, which is a version of appearance emotionalism. In her view, that theory cannot account for the expression of cognitively complex emotions, since none of these has a distinctively articulated contour. Her criticisms of Jerrold Levinson (1982 and 1990a) and Kendall L. Walton (1988) reveal her view of what more is needed for an adequate account of such expressions. She complains that these authors (who agree that music is capable of expressing cognitively complex emotions) do not adequately explain how music could contain or convey the cognitive content required for the expression (and imaginative evocation) of such emotions. Robinson believes, apparently, that the largely noncognitive feelings aroused by music, or, rather, the accumulation and interrelation of these as generated by the detail of the work's extended form, suggest cognitive complexes and contents that are to be attributed to a persona hypothesized as subject to this musical narrative. It is the succession of thoughtlessly automatic reactions that first animates, then controls, the imaginative involvement revealing to the listener the higher forms of musical expression.

I begin my criticism of Robinson's position by reviewing her suggestion that the tension, and so forth, of music consists in its power to arouse a corresponding, automatic response in the listener. It can be argued that the relevant properties are possessed not as causal powers but intrinsically. The succession of discords and concords in music is the pattern of harmonically generated tensings and relaxings. The *initial* predication to music of such terms as "tense," "uncertain," and "relaxed" might have been suggested by the sensational character of our reactions, but I doubt that the current use of such terms presupposes those responses. If the relevant properties are of the music, we might expect that they could be observed and recognized without also being undergone. Indeed, this seems to be the case. Often one can correctly attribute a pattern of tension and relaxation to the music without having an experience echoing that pattern. I hear discordant major thirds in medieval music functioning as high points of tension, but I doubt that I feel tense in attaining that awareness. Also, where a style of music is boringly predictable, I might be quite indifferent while being aware of the tension of, say, a prolonged dominant seventh leading eventually to a triad on the tonic. And when I listen for the umpteenth time to a piece I know well, I might come to a better understanding than before of the pattern of tensing and relaxing it generates without experiencing feelings that mirror this. I accept that we must observe the flux of tensings and releasings present in its musical fabric if we are to recognize a work's expressive and formal character. I reject, however, Robinson's stronger claims, such as: "[T]he emotional experience aroused by the music is essential to the detection of the emotional expressiveness in the music itself" (1994, 20) and, again, "[T]he expressiveness of the piece as a whole can only be grasped if the listener's feelings are aroused in such a way that they provide a clue to both the formal and the expressive structure of the piece as it develops through time" (1994, 21).

Moving on, I turn to the connection Robinson finds between the arousal of primitive, automatic reactions in the listener and his perception of the higher emotions expressed in the music. As I listed earlier, Robinson writes of our feeling nervousness, relief, disturbance, and reassurance, as well as tension, relaxation, and surprise, as unthinking responses to music. By its power to produce such reactions, music is properly to be described as tense, surprising, disturbing, reassuring, unnerving, and so on. Hearing an appropriate succession of these qualities in music leads us to find, for instance, bold progress checked by obstacles. As a result of hypothesizing a persona, we recognize in all this the expression of, for example, cheerful confidence turning to despair.

I think that nervousness, relief, disturbance, and reassurance typically come surrounded by an atmosphere of propositional attitudes, even where they are initiated automatically. An overdose of caffeine might put me on edge, but, if my state is one of nervousness, this is because my sensations become located within a wider cognitive context, one in which I contemplate some future state or action with apprehension. Now, if music triggers reactions of nervousness, relief, disturbance, and reassurance—and thereby is unnerving, relieving, disturbing, and reassuring—it is far from evident that these qualities *connect* with a cognitive content delivered or directed by the music, as opposed to one created by and *imported* from the listener. Because I think the listener interjects, instead of uncovering, the ideas that fuel her imagination, I doubt that Robinson shows that the music (via the automatic reactions she says it arouses) controls the listener's imaginative involvement with the work. But even if I am mistaken in this final claim, the move from a succession of musical qualities such as nervousness, hesitation, and reassurance to the expression of higher emotions, and, further, to the unfolding life of a persona, requires more imaginative input than is required in following music with understanding. The given pattern of musical qualities is likely to be consistent with many states of affairs in which higher emotions are not expressed, as well as with expressions of many different higher emotions.

As I see it, Robinson is no nearer than her rivals to establishing that higher emotions are expressed in musical works as a result of their possessing features both requiring the listener to make-believe a persona and also controlling the cognitive contents to be fed into the narrative constructed about this persona's experiences. If this is correct, she does not establish the strong version of hypothetical emotionalism, according to which some pieces cannot be understood and appreciated except via such make-believing.

V

My comments on Robinson's view are, of necessity, rather particular. I conclude by raising a more general objection to hypothetical emotionalism.

So far I have implied that, according to hypothetical emotionalism, the listener is to entertain the existence of *a* persona whose tale is revealed in the music's progress. But the advocates of the theory often suggest that many personas might be identified within a piece. Cone (1974) sometimes talks of different instruments and individual themes as distinct personas within a single work. Newcomb (1984b) discusses thematic units in Schumann's Second Symphony as distinguishable personas. Callen (1982) suggests that a work should be thought of as presenting the emotional life of a single organism — or perhaps of several agents. Now, this would present no problem for the theory if the relevant distinctions of number could be preserved in musical works; a story can contain more than one character. Things are not so simple, though. Maus (1988) allows that there is no basis for hearing different agents, as against hearing various parts or elements of the music as the different limbs of a single agent. He concludes that, in respect of the number of personas involved (whether one, several, or many), music is irredeemably indefinite.[19] I believe he is correct in this. Walton (1994) makes a point like Maus's and plainly regards it as raising a problem for hypothetical emotionalism.

The difficulty is this. If the invocation of a persona is essentially implicated in understanding a work, this is likely to be for the reason indicated by Robinson and Karl: the tale told will explain the structure and coherence of the work where a purely technical account will be inadequate. But if any number of personas can be imagined, then (at least) that number of tales can be told, each matching the music.[20] And if these stories differ markedly in their content and form, it must be doubtful that any one of them accounts for the work's coherence (unless all do so, which is extremely unlikely). A work that might be heard as laying out the developing gloom of a depressed persona could be experienced no less convincingly as indicating the unconnected moods of a series of personas, each of whom (independently) is more depressed than the last. The music's structure and coherence cannot be explained by reference to one narrative if others, neither more nor less consistent with what can be heard in the music, misfire in this regard.

A reply to this point suggests that the hypothesizing strategy should be regarded as a form of inference to the best explanation. Where evidence underdetermines theory, we may still prefer some theories over others, discriminating among them in terms of predictive power, economy of elements, elegance of structure, and the like. Similarly, while more than one narrative might be hypothesized in accounting for a work's expressiveness, not all are equally acceptable. If one narrative provides for the unity and closure we experience in the music, whereas another does not, the former is to be preferred. The indefiniteness of the music, as mentioned above, need be no barrier to our judging between competing narratives or to our comparing those that introduce several personas to those that rely on only one. The preferred narrative, as well as matching the music's structure, also encompasses other of its artistically significant properties, such as its unity and closure.

This view of things would be appropriate if the credentials of hypothetical emotionalism were established, but I doubt that it can be used in the theory's defense. In the first place, the "evidence" is disputed. It is not agreed that music commonly expresses higher emotions or, for those cases where it might do so, that it is necessary to hypothesize a persona before this can be understood and appreciated. Secondly, hypothesizing comes after the recognition of musical unity and the like and, therefore, does not account for that experience. We can explain why we would prefer one narrative to another—for instance, one displays the kind of form and unity that also is presented in the work, whereas another does not, despite matching the articulation of elements at the local level—but the features of the preferred narrative do not themselves justify the experience of the music. The integration of disparate elements achieved in the work and experienced by the listener is independent of what is hypothesized. If the work strikes us as episodic and disjointed, it is not plain that we should prefer a coherent narrative over another that is less so. Our preferring one narrative to another presupposes, without explaining, a high level of musical understanding.

If the strong version of hypothetical emotionalism is to justify the force of the prescription that we must listen to (some) works as presenting dramatic narratives, it must show the formation of such narratives to be essentially implicated in the listener's understanding and appreciation of relevant works. I doubt that this has been demonstrated. If the listener's narrative is to be importantly revealing of the music, not just of herself, we should be able to explain why others who wish to understand and appreciate the music must listen in terms of that narrative. Music is too indefinite to constrain the contents of such narratives to the required extent. And while there are grounds for discriminating among various narratives all of which match the music in their detail, these criteria are not of a type that supports strong hypothetical emotionalism. They presume the possibility of the listener's grasping the music's nature, of her recognizing its unity, integrity, symmetry, and so forth, independently of the hypothesizing process. This runs counter to the claim that it is

only in developing a narrative concerning the actions, experiences, and feelings of a hypothesized persona that she can come to the fullest appreciation of
the music in question. It is not the case, I claim, that the hypothetical invocation of a persona is essentially implicated in understanding musical works displaying formal and expressive interrelation.

NOTES

For their comments I thank Robert Stecker, Kendall Walton, and Tom Wartenberg.

1. I criticize these views in detail in *Musical Meaning and Expression* (1994), chap.
4.
2. The best known statement of "appearance emotionalism," also known as the "contour theory," is presented by Peter Kivy 1980. I defend a version of this position in
Musical Meaning and Expression (1994).
3. I develop this view in *Musical Meaning and Expression* (1994), chap. 6.
4. Note, though, that appearance emotionalism can allow that the *manner* of expression is no less particular to each work than are the notes generating its expressive
content, even if the range of emotion-types that can be expressed is restricted.
5. See my "The Expression of Emotion in Music" (1980), and *Musical Meaning
and Expression* (1994), 262–64, where I argue that the pattern of expressiveness within
the entire work can be relevant to assessing the local significance of elements and to
the musical expression of higher emotions.
6. See Edward T. Cone 1974; Anthony Newcomb 1984a and 1984b; and Fred Maus
1988. For a discussion, see Marion Guck 1994.
7. See Donald Callen 1982; Jerrold Levinson, "Music and Negative Emotion" (1982)
and "Hope in 'The Hebrides,' " in *Music, Art, and Metaphysics* (1990b), and "Musical
Expressiveness" in *The Pleasures of Aesthetics* (1996); Bruce Vermazen 1986; Jenefer
Robinson 1994; Aaron Ridley 1995, chap. 8; and Malcolm Budd 1995.
   A philosopher and a musicologist, Jenefer Robinson and Gregory Karl, have collabo-
rated on one paper: "Shostakovitch's Tenth Symphony and the Musical Expression of
Cognitively Complex Emotions" (1995).
8. This is explicit in Maus's and Newcomb's articles. Notice that, in "Those Images
That Yet Fresh Images Beget" (1983), Newcomb voices the same concern without tying
it to hypothetical emotionalism as such. This is no mistake. The projects outlined above
do not commit their proponents to full-blown hypothetical emotionalism (although the
musicologists cited take their accounts in that direction).
9. Callen, Levinson, and Robinson make this clear in outlining their versions of
hypothetical emotionalism. For my consideration of Levinson's position, see *Musical
Meaning and Expression* (1994), 211–16, 263.
10. See Jenefer Robinson 1985 and Jerrold Levinson 1992.
11. See Ismay Barwell 1986.
12. Kendall L. Walton emphasizes the distinction (in discussing literature and painting) and appreciates its significance. He is one who analyzes style in terms of the
actions of the work's apparent creator—see "Points of View in Narrative and Depictive
Representation" (1976), "Style and the Products and Processes of Art" (1979, 1987), and
Mimesis as Make-Believe (1990). But he does not subscribe to hypothetical emotionalism as applied to music, although he thinks that much make-believing goes into the
listener's awareness of and response to music's expressiveness—see "What is Abstract

About the Art of Music?" (1988), and "Listening with Imagination: Is Music Representational?" (1994).

13. Perhaps we entertain the existence of this narrator if none is explicitly introduced in the story. Gregory Currie 1990 holds that all novels are to be approached in this fashion.

14. Currie's (1990) account does not clearly separate the work's fictional narrator from its implied author. He is criticized on this score by Robert Stecker along the lines I have indicated—see Stecker 1996, chap. 11. For Stecker's more general criticisms of hypothetical intentionalism as applied to literature, see also 1987, 1994a, and 1994b.

15. But, in fact, I think Vermazen (1986) is sometimes careless of the distinction, and I note that Robinson (1985) occasionally slides from talk of implied authors to talk of narrators internal to the work. Of course, there is likely to be allowable slippage between the two realms in cases in which there is good reason to suppose that the persona in the work acts or speaks for the work's (imagined) creator.

16. I adapt this last condition from the account of literature provided by Peter Lamarque and Stein Haugom Olsen 1994.

17. Newcomb (1984a) argues that critics of Schumann's day heard his Second Symphony as involving struggle and conforming to a "plot archetype" shared with Beethoven's Fifth Symphony—"suffering finding its way to strength and health." If this is correct, it does not yet show that there was consensus concerning the nature of a hypothesized persona. For a critique of the philosophical assumptions of this approach, see Peter Kivy 1990b.

18. As a child I was given a record of a waltz from Tchaikovsky's *Nutcracker*. A "voice-over" presented a story about mice endangered by a cat. To escape its attentions, the mice disguised themselves as flowers and danced by it. The story matched the music exactly.

19. Obviously, he does not regard this as an objection to his version of hypothetical emotionalism. In that case, it cannot be the strong form of the theory he means to espouse.

7

Emotion in Music

ROM HARRÉ

I. Emotion as It Is Currently Understood

Though the word "emotion" is a late entrant into the English language, nevertheless it is already multivocal in its uses, not least among psychologists. Broadly speaking, there are two main ways of using the word, and so two main fields of studies of the emotional life of people and animals. Particularly in the United States, in both lay and professional discourse, "emotion" is taken to be a bodily condition, either a feeling (for example an abdominal tension), or— for some biologically oriented psychologists—a physiological state (for example a rise in the state of excitation of some part of the nervous system) (Izard 1977). However, this way of locating emotion sidelines most of what is important in the emotionality of human beings and animals, namely, the expressive function of the displays and feelings we label with such phrases as "being angry," "feeling elated," "raging at someone," "envious of someone's success," and so on. From this point of view, an emotion display is an expression of a complex judgment, and, at the same time, is often the performance of a social act (Stearns and Stearns 1988). Both the biological and the discursive points of view allow that emotions can be both inherited and learned, though the biologically oriented students of emotion tend to pay little attention to the huge cultural variations in the repertoires and occasioned uses of emotion displays observed by anthropologists. For example, the great variety of emotion repertoires has been surveyed by Wierzbicka (1992).

As the expression of a judgment, a display of emotion, whether it be public as overt behavior or private as covert feeling, involves several cognitive components:

1. There must be intentionality, that is, the feeling or display must be taken by the person displaying the emotion—and by others who are aware of what is going on if that display is public—to be about something. There is a vast range of "somethings" that emotions can be about. For instance, grief is oriented to a loss, anger to a person who has committed an offence, chagrin to a sequence of events (first the boast or claim to competence and then the failure to come through with the required performance) and so on.
2. There must be an assessment of the value of that to which the emotion is directed. For example, one is envious of someone who possesses something one values; in the malign version, the possession of that good is taken by the envious person as a slight or personal devaluation. One is proud of actions that one regards as worthwhile, and so forth.
3. Closely connected to the dimension of valuation is the way in which those involved in an emotional episode are positioned in the local moral order, the taken-for-granted structure of rights, obligations, and duties that obtains in some corner of the social world. Jealousy is typically displayed by someone who believes that his or her rights in or to some good have been violated or usurped.

A display of emotion, be it public as a performance visible and audible to others or private to oneself in the form of a feeling, expresses a very complex judgment. Unlike many other cognitive processes, the judgments expressed by displays of emotion are usually premiseless, in that they rarely involve reflection. The old word "passion," used for some of those phenomena we now lump together as emotions, reflected the fact that the emotional response to some state of affairs is habitual, unreflective, almost, it seems, caused. We must concede that there is a whole pattern of cognition, extremely important in the management of daily affairs, that is not the realization in psychological reality of the normative discourses of logic. Of course, after the event, we can retrospectively disentangle the bits and pieces of evidence, of interpretation, of reasoning that would have taken place or been relevant had the judgment expressed been the result of prior discursive "work."

But a system of "rapid reaction" to current and (by virtue of our capacity for imaginatively recreating the past and anticipating the future) to nonexistent conditions is not all that is involved in displays of emotion. There is also the performative aspect, the expression of a social act. The performative theory of language use goes back to J. L. Austin (1962), who realized that much of what we say to one another in everyday life is not reporting facts but getting things done verbally. Words can be used not only to describe but also to order, apologize, insult, plead, condemn, and so forth. This aspect of language use is very evident in analyzing emotion displays by analogy with speech acts. A display of jealousy not only expresses a complex judgment about rights and their violations, but also expresses a condemnation of or protest against that violation. A display of grief not only expresses the judgment that a valued being has been lost, but expresses regret that it should be so.

To explore the emotional aspects of music as it is performed, whether in the imagination or in the concert hall, one must keep in mind the full panoply of what we now see as the structure and functions of the acts and feelings of the emotional life.

II. Siting Emotion in Music

Starting with a rough-and-ready distinction, we can contrast music as a medium for the expression of emotion and music as a source or cause of emotional states in listeners. In the former context, musical performance is a public, cognitive/performative act into which the audience enters as interpreter; in the latter context, it is the cause of a bodily feeling in which the members of the audience enter as sensitive organisms. In the former context, it is not only a public phenomenon, but also, insofar as the audience comprises members of one musical culture, a collective phenomenon; in the latter context, it is individual. It goes without saying that each aspect can affect the other, but the lack of a necessary connection between them allows the analyst to seek for an independent account of each.

But this is too simple a categorization. There are also composers and performers who are or may be engaged in this enterprise. The parallel with the psychology of everyday life breaks down at this point, since it is rare indeed, though not wholly unknown, for someone who is bereaved, insulted, or successful, for example, to manifest his or her complex cognitive/performative acts by the use of someone else's body. The employment of professional mourners in the Middle East strikes us as very strange. I know of no culture where there are professionals hired to express the joy of those well off enough to employ them. Occasionally, composers are performers of their own works, but these days, with the exception of jazz improvisation, this is rare. In general, someone other than the composer manifests the public and overt expression of the composer's intentions in the music. Here two familiar aesthetic puzzles appear: how far can the performance by musicians other than the composer be constrained by instructions in the score to manifest a form in which the composer's intentions are surely presented?; and how far should the performance— whether carried out by the composer or by hired hands—be judged a success or failure by reference to the audience's evaluation of whether or not the performance realizes the composer's intentions? Consideration of the role of the orchestra leads one to ask whether there is a site for emotions in the very act of performing? By the looks on the faces of some solo violinists and pianists one might think so; but Jack Brymer, that most lyrical of clarinetists, might be preparing lunch for all his features betray during a performance of the Mozart Clarinet Quintet. One is inclined to dismiss the grimaces and postures of soloists as part of the conventions of musical expression rather than as the overt manifestation of an excruciating bodily state.

Let us change the image. For a person to express emotion in an everyday context, he or she must make use of eyes, lips, hands, and so on as semantic instruments. So too might we regard the orchestral players who bring a work to expressive existence as extensions of the bodily organs of the composer. But it is the music, not the facial expressions or bodily postures of the performers, that expresses whatever judgment and performative act the composer intends to express.

So far, I have been assuming that a composer may be writing music to express a deeply felt emotion, as if all composers were people like Gustav Mahler. But we know that Mozart scribbled down all that "divine" music to pay the bills, and to keep his wife in the state she thought appropriate. He tossed off the adagio of the Clarinet Concerto while mocking and teasing the very performer who was to play it. The composer's derisive comments are still to be seen on the surviving holograph. Peter Shaffer's play (Amadeus) exaggerated the point, no doubt, but there was an essential truth in it.

Yet just as an actor can make use of the local repertoire of grimaces and postures to present him- or herself as someone expressing an emotion, so too can the composer make use of, and indeed even enlarge, the local lexicon of expression.

Even though the orchestra is analytically nothing but an extension of the composer's and conductor's *means* of expression, there is a range of emotions proper to performers, qua executors of whatever is required both by the score and by the conductor, the latter being the dominant influence on how the expressive performance itself is executed. As one who plays a modest role in an amateur orchestra, I can report that "getting it right" is the prime source of satisfaction. What is more, it sometimes comes as a surprise to hear what a particular work sounds like from an audience standpoint. For example, in the second movement of the Bruch Violin Concerto in G Minor (Opus 26), the clarinetist has a seemingly very exposed couple of bars in which he or she inherits the tune. But to the audience listening to the work, the clarinet part is lost in the general goings-on of the whole orchestra. Neither emotion as an overt expression of a judgment, nor emotion as a bodily feeling expressing that judgment for oneself alone, seems to play any essential role in the experience of the players. Of course, the technical requirements of expressing a particular emotional tone through dynamics and phrasing are indeed of paramount interest to performers. The satisfaction of "doing it right" may be the pleasurable accompaniment of a performance in which the elegiac emotional tone of the slow movement of Mozart 41 is the objective.

Where does this leave us? It seems clear that the contemporary understanding of public emotion displays as complexes of judgments and social acts, and of bodily feelings as having essentially the same role, does have application to music. However, in applying the idea, a variety of complications must be noticed. If a musical performance is a public display expressing complexes of judgments and social acts similar to those expressed by the usual bodily repertoire, then we should be able to provide criteria for recognizing them and a system of categories for classifying them. And that, I think, has yet to be done.

III. The Georgetown Experiments

The results of the experiments to be reported below have not been previously published.[1] The investigation was undertaken to test out ideas for presenting empirical psychological studies in video form. However, the results of the experiments do have relevance to this discussion. Music has sometimes been used by experimenters to induce a mood or shorter-term emotional state in participants in various experimental procedures. Our experiments were designed to test how reliable various musical performances were as instruments of mood (emotion) induction. Sixteen volunteers took part. We ascertained that none had any serious interest in or knowledge of any music more sophisticated than rock and contemporary ballads. Eight substantial excerpts of music intended by their composers to express quite specific emotions were presented to the participants. Four were from Mozart's *Magic Flute* and four from performances of the Dalai Lama's choir. The Mozart excerpts expressed happiness (Papageno's song), passion (The Queen of the Night), romantic love (Tamino), and disappointment (Pamina). The excerpts from Tibetan religious music expressed joy, sadness, optimism, and despair, so we were informed by someone familiar with the genre. Our participants were asked to record what emotion they thought the music expressed, and whether they themselves felt anything that could be classified as an emotional reaction to the music.

The emotions expressed (that is, the emotions we can reasonably suppose Mozart intended to express) by the first two Mozart excerpts were correctly identified by everyone. The other two Mozart examples were judged rightly with respect to level of excitation, but not with respect to the specific emotion required by the plot of the opera. No one had any idea at all what the Dalai Lama's choir was trying to express, and the results of that part of the experiment were not significantly different from chance. But on the second point, "Did you feel anything in yourself?" the participants agreed closely. All reported a good feeling on hearing Papageno's song, but few were personally moved in any way by the other three Mozart arias. All reported a feeling of distinct unease while listening to the Tibetan music.

What do these results show? It seems that there is a Western tradition of expressive devices through which music manifests judgments such as "all is right with the world," since even those acquainted only with contemporary popular music (which probably makes use of a lexicon similar to that drawn on by Mozart) were able to read it. Cross-cultural identification failed utterly. The experiment is clearly incomplete, since it should have been repeated with young Tibetans, with no experience of Western music. Would all human beings be able to read the expressive lexicon of Mozart? We have no idea and are not aware of any systematic study that explores this matter. For example, Davies (1978) acknowledges in the first chapter of his book that music is a cultural rather than a biophysical phenomenon. He offers one interesting example of the universal in the particular. In two widely different cultures, classical India and Pygmy, complex interplays of rhythms distinguishable by Western musicologists may yet defy, as a whole, a definite time signature. The same is true of the interplay of key. But he reports no studies of the comparative lexicon. The mood induction aspect of the experiment shows that at least in some cases there is a causal phenomenon, or perhaps a pseudo-causal phenomenon, brought about by early training. Davies (1978) points out that the many examples of simple conditioning by which a tune evokes a feeling show that almost any tune can be evocative of almost any feeling, since it is context rather than musical lexicon that is the effective agent.

The distinctions drawn in the analyses in sections I and II are vindicated; although these experiments do not conclusively prove the finer analysis of the cognitive aspects of emotions as expressed in music, they incline toward the analysis proposed above.

IV. Interpretation

As Berenson (1993) has pointed out, all of the above takes for granted that those who are able to recognize the emotional content of music must have interpreted the patterns of sounds they heard as the musical expressions from the lexicon of Western music. In this respect, the conditions for "getting the emotion" in the first movement of Mendelssohn's Violin Concerto in the change of tempo at the end of the cadenza are no different from those for "getting the storm" in the Pastoral Symphony. Apart from the auditory requirements in each case, there must be interpretation. Again Berenson usefully points out that there are those like Susanne K. Langer who offer a formal account of the emotionality of music. In her case it was the famous theory that a "stretch" of music and an emotional experience are structurally isomorphic. And there are those who propose a "sympathetic" account; who believe, to quote Berenson, that "sad music makes us feel sad." The Georgetown experiments show the general falsity of that thesis, though it is based upon a misunderstood half-truth. That some music is sad is a reading of the cognitive/performative expression of the music, while the sadness we feel (if we do) is induced by some feature of the music qua ordered sound. That which induces sadness may also be the expression of the judgment, for example, by Alfredo in the last act of *La Traviata*, that the death of Violetta is a sad event. But there is nothing necessary about this relationship, any more than there are necessary relations between judgments musically expressed and pictures conjured up in the glosses on "programme" music. The sadness actually experienced by an audience may be mediated cognitively by the interpretation of the expressed judgment.

Berenson offers a defense of the thesis that music is essentially an expression of emotion in sound. He has several arguments, which run as follows:

1. The first argument is inductive. The fascination of Mahler's music, and its very wide appeal, is explicable only in terms of the successful expression of a wide range of "modern" emotions somehow to be encountered *in the music itself*, rather than evoked in the listener by association, or by state-specific memory, as psychologists call it.

2. The second argument is also inductive and related to the first. It points to the known intentions of the composer to use musical devices to express

certain emotions. The Georgetown experiments certainly support this observation as a matter of fact.

3. Berenson's third argument is analytical rather than inductive. Rejecting the naive idea that music's emotionality is to be understood as its power to induce an emotion in a listener, he turns to a deep philosophical argument. It would be generally conceded that emotions are intentional, that is, that they are directed at something. We are despairing *of* something, angry *with* someone, chagrined *about* something, and so on. But since music is allegedly devoid of intentional content of that degree of specificity, it cannot be an instrument for the expression of emotions. Berenson's reply depends on a distinction between music invoking specific references to events in my life (a tune reminding me of a past event whose recollection is still rich in feeling), and involvement in a performance as an integral part of my whole life experience. There is intentionality, but it is not specific to events or objects in my life. The former Berenson calls "reference to self" and the latter "reference to music." Of course, were I not the person I am, the music would offer less or more than it does, or indeed, if it is the Dalai Lama's choir, it would offer me nothing.

But this argument must be protected from the formalists who, like Hanslich (who so influenced Arnold Schönberg and the young Wittgenstein with his conception of what marked out the boundary between music and nonmusic), look to adherence to coherent patterns of rules of composition as the distinguishing mark of what is music. The aesthetics of music, on this view, explores the possibilities of the beauty of formal patterns, setting aside as irrelevant (or worse, vulgar) the emotions for which the music is an expression.

V. The Formalist Case Briefly Examined

Writers such as R. A. Sharpe (1986), who endorse Hanslich's formalist conception of the nature of music and so endorse an aesthetic based on the dry appreciation of the beauty of form, commit the same sort of error as those linguists who think that the essence of language is to be found in syntax. Language is an instrument for action that is possible only if we acknowledge that its meaningfulness arises in the manner of its use rather than in its formal structural properties. When reminded of this, some formalists have even tried to extend the formalist approach to semantics. This is to confuse the nature of the instrument, qua entity, with its role in some human activity. Wittgenstein (1953) provided, once and for all, in the first thirty paragraphs of the *Philosophical Investigations*, a potent array of counter-examples to the idea that form (language) *determines* function (speech). Conventions become established by which certain forms are typical of certain functions, but there is no necessary connection. In speech, one can and does use the question format to issue an invitation ("Why don't we go to the match?" "Please come to the match."), or the indicative to issue an order ("I think I can feel a draft." "Shut the door!"), and so forth. Mahler's use of the minor key to ironize a sentimental country dance motif in his Second Symphony has to be heard as an instrument for a certain task, within the emotional framework of the whole work, the skull behind the flesh, a pessimism to be resolved into hope in the last movement.

A complementary and subtle criticism of the Hanslich account of what music is, namely, "ordered sound," can be found in Margolis (1993). Behind Hanslich's thesis lies a rejection of a particular account of the intentionality of music: that it is representational, that is, that certain patterns of sound reliably refer to something, for example, the *Dies Irae* to funerals. The fate of pro-gramme music in its inevitable detachment from the composers' pictorial glosses shows that representation is not a good account of the intentionality of music. Margolis offers the well-known distinction between representation and expression (which could be linked to Wittgenstein's distinction between de-scriptions of mental states and avowals of "how it is with me"). He uses it to defend an account of the emotionality of music that is very similar to Beren-son's, and against the Hanslich view, by pointing out that there are culturally emergent "incarnate" properties, that is, properties that could exist only in ordered sound, but that are not the mere ordering of the sound. These are the properties upon which the expressive power of music depends. As yet, we lack any systematic account of these "incarnate" properties, and of how "ordered sound" could be their material substrate. But that they exist is phenomenologi-cally secure. In playing in a gamelan, there comes a moment when the me-chanical work of creating the sound (in my case, on the *sarom*) suddenly dis-plays a Margolisian property. It is much like the moment at which a Chinese ideograph or a Hungarian word suddenly makes sense. Wittgenstein struggled with the problem of characterizing the phenomenon. "What makes a portrait a portrait of *him?*" he asked. He explored various avenues toward an under-standing of the phenomenon, such as his studies of the perceptual phenome-non of "seeing an aspect," but all remained inconclusive. The problem is ubiq-uitous, emerging in all those contexts in which the kind of properties Margolis calls "incarnate" are the bearers of meaning.

VI. Conclusion

From the point of view of the audience, an emotion display, whether it be in the expression of a face or in the architecture of a musical phrase, is expres-sively effective whether or not it induces an emotion in the listener. A display of jealousy directed toward me is legible by me whether or not I am induced to feel anything by virtue of my interpretation of the public acts of my rival. In the light of the contemporary understanding of emotion in general, at least one of the seeming problems of the philosophy and psychology of music sim-ply evaporates. Those who argue that students of the aesthetics of music need pay no attention to emotion because one can appreciate music without en-joying gut feelings oneself have simply misunderstood the nature of emotion as a social phenomenon. And it is surely as a social phenomenon that the emotion displays and expressions of musical performances must be examined. The fact that formally differentiated means are required to express emotion does not show that we should build our aesthetics only on the appreciation of form. On the other hand, the emotionality of music, construed within the contemporary framework of our general understanding of emotion, does not reduce that emotionality to the level of "Darling! They are playing our song!"

NOTE

1. The experiments on mood induction by music were conducted by W. G. Parrott and myself during the spring semester, 1991.

8

Emotion and Emotions
in Theatre Dance

FRANCIS SPARSHOTT

Theatre dance is an art of the theatre, and there is a common aesthetic of theatre arts. Drama, dance, opera, mime, theatrical displays, and performance arts generally share a common space, the stage, and a common destiny, presentation to an audience. The arts overlap and blend: whatever shares that space and that destiny belongs to a powerfully unifying reality, theatricality. What is specific to dance (on some interpretations, in some ideologies) is submerged in and may be overwhelmed by the unifying culture of the theatre. That is the first thing to bear in mind.

The topic of emotion in theatre arts sends us back to Plato's supposed thesis in Book X of his *Republic*, that theatre threatens morality by putting emotion where rationality should be. But Plato was referring to the specific genre of tragedy, and the use of that genre as a medium for moral instruction, and his contention was that the conditions of presentation make the audience respond emotionally to what is before them—rather than think about the psychological and social realities involved—and portray the characters as behaving emotionally rather than dealing with the realities of their situation. The objection is not to emotion, in the sense of strong feeling about one's situation, but to emotionality, in the sense of indulging one's inner feelings without close relation to the situation in which one acts. If one wants to consider Plato's views on emotion in theatre arts, one should not ignore the extended discussion in his *Laws*, where civic ceremonies involving dance movement symbolize and inculcate the order of the city in peace and war. In terms of that discussion, which has been enormously influential in thinking about dance, the arts of dance use the movements in which human feelings about actions and situations find expression as the basis of art forms in which these and like movements are clarified, made more visible, and reduced to order. In such a dance, the contrast between emotionality and rationality is not in place.

In his analysis of the basis of animal action in *On the Soul*, Aristotle argued that an animal would not move without both motivation (desire or aversion) and cognition (recognition of a situation as occasioning desire or aversion); and motivation, when generalized and considered without its immediate occasion, may be what that rather elusive term "emotion" means. Descartes, in a more modern continuation of Aristotle's enterprise, identified what the principal types of such action-grounding feelings must be: the "passions of the soul," the main "emotions" which must govern the behavior and attitudes of *any* entity such as a human being is, one in which a thinking substance is welded to a material substance, a social animal in communion with its fellows that support and threaten its identity, and in a body sustained by and at risk from its physical surroundings. It is clear, and was already clear to Aristotle, that these emotions must have manifestations in action, because that is what they are about; must have characteristic physiological mechanisms, because it is the body that moves; and must have cognitive and social grounding, because what they pertain to is the life of an intelligent, social animal. The anger of Achilles is something like "a desire for revenge," stemming from Achilles' wounded self-esteem; it is also something like "a boiling of the blood around the heart," or whatever we may discover about adrenalin and such; and it is also the course of conduct that forms the central plot of the *Iliad*. Insofar as theatre dance consists of human movements recognizable as things being done by humans, emotion in theatre dance will be some variation on the contemporary version of this threefold complexity. And that is the most important thing an essay on this topic has to say.

The foregoing remarks have focused not on emotion or emotions as such, but rather on archaic attempts to articulate the underlying psychic and social realities—attempts that are still worth considering because they aspire to a comprehensive overview of human life. Contemporary speculation and research tend to function as correction to or elaboration on these early attempts. The concept of emotion itself is extremely obscure. The fact that the word is in common use does not guarantee that there is an identifiable entity or topic that could ground discussion. Latinate trisyllables are always to be suspected of being hangovers from forgotten repertoires of rhetorical commonplaces. But what do we mean by "emotion," exactly? There are books on the subject which I have not read, dictionaries I have not consulted.[1] What is emotion, that a book should be devoted to it in the first place? Well, an emotional response or person is one that *overemphasizes* (the term is clearly judgmental, not descriptive) an agent's subjective side, at the expense of the objective grounds for action or attitude; perhaps "emotion" is a generic term for free-floating subjective feeling. But individuated emotions, we just saw, are distinct types of action-guiding subjectivity. All is not clear, however. In the three-part analysis from Plato's *Republic*, no term that translates as "emotion" plays any part. The three-way contrast is among reason—action motivated by attention to situations and what they actually require; "spirit" or "temper"—action motivated by the requirements of the organism as a single embattled entity; and "desire"—action focused on a particular object of appetition or aversion in isolation, without regard either for the agent's own long-term interests or for the objective situation. The objection to using theatre dance as a medium of public education would be that only the third kind of motivation could be effectively present: ideological dance would be a fraud, dancers as such having no means of getting beyond appearances in what they actually perform.

By contrast with Plato, the Cartesian "passions" are not conceived in terms of degree and manner of integration but in terms of the range and nature of involvement of the embodied agent; and a dance, we said, could clearly be (and has often been) organized and articulated by such passions and their actual or symbolic embodiments. Now that the arts are not constrained by conventions, nothing can be said a priori about what kinds of articulation and symbolization are possible: obviously, dance vocabularies could in principle be developed in which the "passions" were extrapolated from ranges of mundane experience (the most cherished contemporary dances in fact do just this) or in which the dance order negated (in postmodern fashion) such preemptive systems of motivation as Plato's *Laws* envisaged.

In addition to the foregoing, a third view of something that could be called "emotions" has long been popular. A passionate response, I said, is, on the Cartesian understanding, presumed to have a physiological underpinning, such as glandular secretions, changes in muscular tension, patterns of neural discharge, and the like. A certain habit of mind now takes an identifiable physiological complex of this sort as actually being the reality to which the name of an emotion refers; and, in principle, the name properly refers to that, whether or not there is any practical involvement or psychological phenomenon to which it was originally applied. Such a proposed change in linguistic habits cannot be carried out, of course, because we continue to have to live our lives with each other. Besides, the physiological complexes were investigated and identified in the first place only as what underlay the observed psychosocial phenomena. But never mind that. For some theoretical purposes, one may choose to identify an emotion with an identifiable psychophysical complex separate both from conscious control and from integration into the course of human life. Jenefer Robinson, in a striking article, has pushed this viewpoint to what must be the limit.[2] She takes as the paradigm of an emotion the "startle response," the reflex reaction that typically occurs in people subjected to a sudden loud sound: an involuntary response, usually taking less than half a second, involving closing of the eyes and widening of the mouth, raising of the shoulders, bending of the elbows, contraction of the abdomen, and the like. The point is, as Robinson sees it, that this response is universal in humans (and many other mammals), involuntary and often unconscious, and a nonjudgmental response to the organism's environment, and that is just what other emotions (such as love) are.

Why Robinson wants to include the startle response among emotions never becomes clear, let alone why she takes it as a paradigm. But let us suppose that we equate emotions with these invariant and easily recognized modifications of the organism. It may then appear that emotions have no special interest for theatre dance or any other art, because they cannot be assimilated to social or formal contexts. Such an "emotion" cannot be expressed, it can only be induced or simulated. But then one may reflect that the simulation could take the form of a stylistically malleable symbolization; and if the startle response is the appropriate model, there can be only a finite (and perhaps rather small) number of human emotional responses that could form the basis of a scientifically warranted version of the sort of vocabulary of legible gestures that traditions of narrative dance have often proposed.[3]

The identification of emotions with a set of involuntary configurations of the physiological apparatus is a far cry from the emotional expressiveness of José Limón's *The Moor's Pavane*. But we may remind ourselves of Sartre's treatment of the emotions, according to which being in the grip of an emotion is an alternative to engagement with the actualities of one's situation, one's love or hatred blinding one to the actual nature of the loved or hated object.[4] He allows no place to emotional or emotion-tinged involvements with the world as one understands it, or to the (quasi-Aristotelian) position that, for a social being acting in a world on which it depends and by which it is threatened, there is no cognition without affect and no emotion without cognition.

As with emotions conceived on the "startle" model, one is tempted to say that emotions on the Sartrien understanding have no place in theatre dance. A dance based on undiscriminating love or hate could have no articulation and no clear content, and hence could have no interest. But then one may reflect that, within the dance, neither choreographer nor dancer is engaged as agent in the world; that a dancer's hate or love is danced out in relation to an imagined objectivity that is present only as projected by the dance itself. One may then prefer to say that the content of any dance is nothing but emotion, and that theatre dance differs from drama precisely in this, that the stuff of drama is actual social and material engagements, whereas in dance the movements really symbolize nothing but the emotions that lie behind such engagements.

Let us try a fresh start. Dance is, if anything is, a culturally emergent entity. Even if there is dance in every society, and even if there are physical and social and psychological constants in human life that account for the universality of dance, what dance is in any culture or historical epoch is always something unique to its time and place, historically determined, conceptualized in ways inseparable from the ways and views of the dancers and their reference groups, and assigned meanings peculiar to the society and culture. So it is not to be expected that one could fruitfully generalize about emotion in theatre dance. Emotions also are culturally emergent entities. No matter what the constancies of response in the human animal, and no matter what the constancies of recurrence in human predicaments, different societies will surely have different concepts to cover the saliences in emotional life and will allow different emphases and values to the emotions they recognize; and, because the concept of emotion is itself elusive, different societies will differ as to what they recognize the different emotions as. The bulk of everyday discussion of the emotions in art and life, valuable as it may be, is bedevilled by the assumption that an emotion is somehow an ontologically established entity. One supposes that there must be true things to be said about what emotions are, and what emotions there are, just as one supposes that there must be true things to be said about what dance is. But both suppositions are ill grounded. They work well enough, and discussions based on them can be profitable. But the whole business is unstable and provisional, and attempts to anchor it in some indisputable reality necessarily fail because the relation of the practices and conceptualizations to the way of life in which they are integral must be primary. (That being said, we must concede that the search for foundations, whatever form it may take, is itself a practice indispensably embedded in the way of life of which it forms a part, as also are the claims made on behalf of such searches.)

Let us try yet another tack. Thus far, we have considered a contrast between the emotional and irrational, on the one hand, and the rational and unemotional, on the other, without perhaps considering whether these are separate factors inherent in every attitude and action, or alternative and perversely extreme modes of coping with the world. And we have considered the possibility of compiling lists of "emotions," discrete or salient modes of subjectivity, differentiated either physiologically or in terms of basic relationships among embodied organisms in an environment. But we have not considered what such interacting organisms are, and hence what dancers are and must be seen as. We cannot sensibly proceed without at least some tentative remarks about that.

I would suppose that any social animal—any animal belonging to a society, normally living in a flock or herd or structured group of beings of its own kind—can be expected to do all of the following with its fellow members: communicate information, express attitudes evoking a response from individuals threatening or threatened, express needs of aid (being lost, hunger, injury), show (and act on) sexual readiness and unreadiness, and establish relationships (fellow membership, place in hierarchy) with members of its group. In humans, language complicates these forms of behavior by facilitating elaboration, simulation, indirection, and so on, in ways that create a new sort of social reality and new constructions of life contexts, but these language-based structures are superimposed on the basic set of relationships. The fundamental consideration is that in all social animals there is a constant and indefinitely complex awareness of the vital manifestations of fellow members of the society as being of vital concern to oneself. It is to this flexible awareness (which may extend to aversion or empathy as well as to a more generalized concern) that our awareness of and response to art as a human phenomenon belongs. Most current discussions of expression and emotion in music and dance are carried out without regard to this all-pervasive aspect of our lives, and accordingly (as it seems to me) are merely foolish.[5] The special phenomena of emotion and the emotions are variably and uncertainly related to this continuum of affective cognition.

Whether or not I am right in thinking that the terms of current discourse on emotion in all the arts call for radical reorientation on the lines I have suggested, it seems undeniable that in dance the artist is present in the art, so that our experience of dance has a sort of complex depth that we cannot eliminate, even if we want to. Theatre dancing is always a display of the dancer's own skill, strength, and control, whatever else it may be, so we are always aware of dancers as beings in their own right, not merely as materials or medium for a work of dance art. Our awareness of dance, accordingly, has several levels. In a formalized or stylized dance, such as classical ballet, the connoisseur may concentrate on the dancing as such, but even there the other levels cannot be excluded from consciousness without stultification; and in contemporary dance performances, we seldom know beforehand what codes or methods of codification the dance will employ, so must remain open to whatever may come. And at a minimum, a dance will normally confront us with, and may derive its value from, all of the following:

1. A formal beauty of visible movement, of abstract form
2. A dynamic display of physical bodies in motion, an inertial pattern of forces
3. A system of animal movement, with the grace and energy of life
4. The movement of human bodies, with their moral intentionality
5. The interplay of human bodies as centers of sexuality and power (In this respect even more than in others, a dance appears differently to different spectators, depending on their age, gender, sexual orientation, and other basic features of their human engagement with the social world.)
6. A dance as a system of specific dance movements and stillnesses, exercises of dancerly skill performed with various stylistic and technical variations
7. The dancers as embodying in their dancing specifically human qualities of personality and character
8. Dancers as identified characters in a danced action
9. The dance as a unified work, a creation embodied in various ways and in various degrees in all of the foregoing.[6]

Any theatre dance performance can be referred to multiple codes and codifications based on any of these nine, even if the dance as a whole cannot be successfully construed in accordance with any or all of them. After all, there is no guarantee beforehand that the dance constitutes a whole susceptible to any single construction or system of constructions, and it is a common experience that contemporary dance often plays on the ambiguity between its many levels, or teases its audience by making it unclear whether a movement is (for example) a dancer's failure to perform a step correctly or an instance of choreographed clumsiness.

To any viewer of any dance, it is likely that some parts or aspects of the performance will be simply null or blank—or rather, perhaps, of meaning so indeterminate as to be indecipherable. Any emotion found to be expressed will be referred to the parts that the viewer was able to construe. And, as we have just seen, it is not possible to make a dance univocal, because human move-ment (including a dancer's movements) is readable throughout, is as it were all signifier. In this it is unlike the enormously elaborate codifications of lan-guage, its semantics and syntactics phonemically rather than phonetically based, which for all practical purposes preclude intercode ambiguities in any but very short texts.[7] Even a highly stylized and tightly structured dance in a well-established genre could not prevent an extrastylistic reading from attaining prominence in the construction of this or that uninstructed or recalcitrant viewer.

A recent work on performance arts has usefully explored the conditions of existence of works intended for a public audience, the coinciding and encoun-tering receptivities of dancemakers and audiences creating a cognitively open space in which dance multiply occurs.[8] An audience member is appropriately ready to be attentive to any aspect of what is going on as prima facie part of the performance and of its context, and the designers and performers are prop-erly attentive to such contingencies. But, in addition to these proper open-nesses, every member of an audience brings to the performance everything that he or she as a person happens to be; and every member of the dancemak-ing collective, whether hierarchically or democratically organized, will contrib-ute to the making of the dance all the perspectives and prejudices that make them what they are. The dance exists only as the resultant of all these inputs from both sides of (what used to be) the footlights.

There are, of course, restrictions on the opennesses just hinted at, and it is these restrictions that form the substance of critical discourse. (Critical dis-course is itself characterized by a similar openness, as I have argued else-where,[9] and that openness is subject to comparable, though less stringent, re-strictions.) In the first place, the continued existence of the theatre, with its heavy investment of material resources and personal commitments, impera-tively requires the maintenance of a working tradition of training, production, and presentation, as well as a continuing public able and willing to manifest itself as audiences. There need be no continuing common character on either side; but some powerful pragmatic continuity there must be.

Recognition of theatre as a continuing institution does nothing to mitigate the openness of specific performances. Such mitigation calls for discrimina-tions between what is relevant and what is irrelevant, what is appropriate and what is inappropriate. The conceptual tools commonly used by critics and theorists for this purpose are such concepts as art or dance. "You're not think-ing of it as art," we say, or "Try to see it as dance"; or a particular work may be dismissed as not being art, or not really being dance. The authority of such recommendations or assertions is never clear; they can be supported only by appealing to a consensus that cannot be shown to obtain, or to an authority that cannot be shown to be authoritative, or to a theory that cannot be demon-strated even if it can be understood. But the underlying position is defensible: it is that those engaged in the performance are doing something serious that is to be taken seriously. The concept of dance calls on us to take seriously the trained skills and sensibilities of the performers, and not to neglect them at the expense of what lies outside that training. The concept of art calls on us to take seriously the level of human endeavor at which the performers intelligently aspire to function.

The relevance of the foregoing to our topic, emotion and emotions in theatre dance, is as follows. The institution of theatre precludes no emotion from expression or recognition; anything at all can be seen or shown, with the qualification that the emotion observed or manifested or responded to automatically becomes stage emotion, with the status of part of what is there for attention, even if we identify it as part of the performer's personality or personal life. Sore feet and bleeding hearts lose their privacy as soon as they are detected or inferred. But the concepts of art and dance serve to rule out any unstructured or unassimilated aspects of subjectivity. Neither dancers nor artists as such can be emotional. Any emotions they may feel or have felt are to be ignored; only the emotions they express in their art and dance (that is, give a form that is a proper part or aspect of their work) can be relevant. So, when we see the dancers performing a choreographic work of art, we discriminate within the humanity we see and share something that by form or context we single out as proper object of our attention.

The judgment of propriety whereby we single out the preferred object need not take any one form, of course. The viewer may simply note that something is no proper part of the work without much caring whether it is or not; or may be irritated by the intrusion of something alien; or may find the intrusion (or absence of refinement) itself a matter of interest—in any number of ways. The essential point is that we do all know what it is to be trying to do something, to be engaged in something, to be concentrating on something, and to be distracted from that, or to be interrupted in it, or to lose one's concentration; and this important branch of understanding does not desert us when we attend a dance performance, in which the performers are clearly up to something, whether or not we think we know what it is. So some of what we identify as emotion may be part of the dance, and some may not. This, however, has no specific consequences, for it is part of our understanding of artistic skill and dance art that artists may incorporate their own personalities into their skill, without limit—and we have seen that dance is distinctive among arts, including theatre arts, for the way in which the artist cannot but be directly present in the art.[10]

Sartre has a useful thought in this connection.[11] In a marble statue, the marble from which the statue was made is still present, the underlying stuff of the statue, with its own physical and perceptible properties. But in a successful statue the marble is not an alien or resisting presence on which the sculptural form has been imposed; it is the stuff of the statue itself. Similarly, a performer's personality is present as the basis of the performer of the performance, not as an alternative and irrelevant configuration, but as the human substance of the performer; and, in just the same way, the audience member's personality is present as the underlying substance of what is here and now pure spectator. Sartre embeds this in a lot of phenomenologizing. For present purposes, though, I would say that it is an idealization. It envisages the work of art as a pure aesthetic object, with its own autonomous unity as object of criticism. But I have been saying that the artist and the spectator are still there in their real selves, and that the transaction between them inescapably involves their humanity as well as their performance and appreciation, respectively, of the work that is being performed. Theorists cause themselves and each other much unnecessary grief by trying to fix on some describably determinate way in which these variable relationships should be resolved. But why should there be? It is rather the variability of the dynamics themselves, which we understand as we understand our families more than as we understand a recipe, that constitutes what we know as dance or as art.

Sartre offers us one way of fixing the emotional tone of a dance as encountered in the theatre, a way that accommodates as much as possible of the traditional aesthetics that postulates an invariant "aesthetic object." An alternative possibility is suggested by the "rasa" theory of classical Indian dance-drama.[12] "Rasa" means something like "flavor," and the doctrine requires that every dance be characterized by the flavor of one of the nine major human emotions (rage, jealousy, tranquillity, and so on). The chosen flavor must permeate every aspect of the dance—movement, music, decor, costume, imagery, color—and the tradition specifies the ways in which this is to be done. The connoisseur is not affected psychologically by the emotion in question, but responds affectively to the way it is worked into the specific dance: the response is aesthetic, but not colourless like a Kantian "aesthetic judgment." The humanity of the connoisseur is engaged not in sympathy, but in recognition of the humanly affective character in the work.

It is not clear to me how the list of nine basic emotions is arrived at. It could, of course, rest on some long-forgotten analysis of necessary relationships comparable to the one essayed by Descartes; but it seems to me more likely to be based on the stock characters in the dance-drama forms current when the theory was originally formulated.[13] But, on reflection, one wonders whether the metaphysical basis of Descartes's own "analysis" was not contaminated by the cultural and literary stereotypes of his own day; I doubt whether anyone now living would come up with anything much like it.

In talking about dance, the term "emotional" is generally applied to gestures and performances rather than to dance works as wholes. But it would make sense to call Jooss's *The Green Table* an "emotional" dance, by contrast with one of which the interest derived from the formal properties of its movement. I suspect that we would use that word only when the work or performance insistently suggested an origin in some visceral disturbance such as Robinson exemplified by the "startle" response. If so, then she is right in pointing to such phenomena as central to emotion and the emotions. I suspect, further, that we would call a work or performance emotional only to the extent that we are inclined to refer it to one of the *named* emotions—after all, both the Cartesian list and the Indian list are of emotions that already have names before any theoretical analysis is performed. If that is so, then the conceptual scheme employed and embedded in the language no doubt mediates the physiological data that we actually recognize. The conceptual apparatus enables us to acknowledge our recognitions, to identify what it is that we are recognizing (the range of phenomena that we are taking to be mutually linked), and to determine what we have recognized it as—and, hence, how it is to be systematically related to the general ways in which we take our lives to be structured.

That every dance inevitably has an indefinitely complex and many-layered affective and emotional import, I have been urging. That there must, in any artistic dance, be a single pervasive emotional tone is a questionable contention derived from more general notions about unity as the basis of artistic value (such as have abounded in theories about the aesthetics of music). That such a single pervasive tone must be identified with a named or nameable emotion, especially one taken from a predetermined list, can hardly be more than the stylistic preference of a historical tradition, however widespread and durable that tradition may be—unless that relation to a nameable list can be shown to open up a unique depth of aesthetic significance, something I have never seen argued.

Consideration of the rasa aesthetic may move us to conjecture that, although we may find a dance moving and engrossing in the depth of the humanity that appears in the performance, we do not normally think of a specific nameable emotion as being expressed, or as characterizing the performance itself, otherwise than by relating it, in the light of our experience, to some stereotype derived from existing artistic forms. What the rasa theory does, in relation to a highly stylized practice, is prescribe narrow codes and conventions for what our own multicultural and insistently variable artistic practice does in an unsystematic and unchartable way.

In addition to this strict codification, the rasa theory does two things. First, it locates the emotion flavor in the performance itself, and insists that it permeate every aspect of it; and second, it requires that a unified work have a single flavor, not a succession or pattern of flavors. One can imagine an alternative aesthetic that used the same devices and relied on the same refined connoisseurship but used them in a "postmodern" way, sometimes straight, sometimes allusively, sometimes satirically, sometimes contrasting one flavor with another (as in a Shakespearian tragedy); but my sense is that such variations are resisted, perhaps in the mood that makes one cringe when a straight razor is used to sharpen a pencil.

In our own rough world of art, certainly, the use of feeling-tone as the predominant unifying force in composition is only one possibility: an aesthetic resource, not an imperative.[14] The *Nātyaśāstra*, which is taken as authoritative, gives no grounds for its basic positions, which claim the status of divine revelations; but, no doubt, the cultural community in question is one committed to the notion of a classical art, deliberately confined to exploiting the possibilities of a culture accepted as definitive, not inherently subject to variation and change as Western civilization has taken itself to be throughout the period in which modern dance has existed. The Indian classical tradition is an invaluable foil against which our own assumptions and practices can be understood, but is not easy to incorporate into the Western world of thought and action.

The connoisseurs of rasa relish the emotional character of the beauty that moves them, but are not affected or infected by the emotion. Since Plato and Aristotle, by contrast, the convention of Western thought has been that spectators are somehow themselves moved, as if one were gladdened by a dance of joy or saddened by a threnody. But, of course, one is not really saddened, or one would not pay to see the show—if one is really saddened, it is presumably by something in one's own life, or in the world as one experiences it, the recollection of which is stirred up by something onstage to which one responds. There is no agreement as to quite what one is to say about this, probably because theorists, like other folk, differ widely among themselves in how they handle their own emotional lives and in how they represent those strategies to themselves from time to time. The underlying fact, I have said, is undoubtedly the flexible responsiveness with which social animals necessarily take account of the actions and fortunes of their fellow animals. But the contrast between Indian classical methods and our own suggests that this flexibility of response is itself a major resource of art, and especially of the theatre arts in which the medium is the selves of some of our conspecifics. The best exposition of this theme is Edward Bullough's article on "Psychical Distance," once widely quoted but seldom seriously studied and almost never understood.[15] What Bullough points out is that the manipulation of aesthetic distance is a major resource of artistic practices: the nature, degree, and manner of the audience's involvement with the emotional material presented is something that artists systematically work on. The interesting question is not what makes artists able to do this—the variability of vital involvement is a pervasive feature of our lives—but the ways in which they do it. What Bullough rather left out of account is the variability of audience members, who are sure to vary in their degree of responsiveness overall, in their susceptibility to different emotional zones and presentational devices, and in their personal experiences and interpretive skills. But that is of no consequence; the condition of the public practice of the arts is that every work is meaningful in many ways for many kinds of viewers, and functions variably in experience rather than as an invariant object for uniform perceivers.

One of the things that makes the arts possible is that there is not and cannot be any sharp difference between the ways we process truth and deception, fact and fiction. If I hear a group of people talking about some other people and what they have done, there is no way in which I can tell whether they are discussing real people or fictional characters, unless and until they move to another mode of discourse in which (for instance) the speakers describe their own interactions with the people they were discussing, or allude to the construction of the fiction in which they figured. (They could, of course, be lying about that, deceiving me as to the reality status of what they had been saying; but that would be a deception, and deceptions are possible only because they can evade immediate detection.) Theorists sometimes write as if there were a world of reality to the whole of which we have immediate access, or access mediated only by the filtering of our systems for codifying experience, and fictional worlds as to which we suspend belief and disbelief and rule out the question of access altogether. But little of what we know of the real world comes to us firsthand, and little of what we have been told is verifiable; much of the time, over much of our experience, our emotional responses to what might move us are in suspense, hypothetical, subject to rescinding or revision. We come to a dance or a dramatic performance already armed with a system for processing information and for responding to it appropriately without relating it to the real world in a determinate way, a system that does not originate in artistic imagination but is already involved in our engagement with a world of which we know even what may directly concern us largely by hearsay.

In commenting on the rasa theory, I remarked that the insistence on the expression of a single named emotion could be no more than a stylistic preference. But we may have second thoughts about that when we reflect that J. L. Hanna, a highly sophisticated observer, investigated an international dance season by asking audience members and performing groups what they had, respectively, thought was being expressed and intended to express.[16] Granted, what is said to be "expressed" is not necessarily an emotion or emotional state, but may be an opinion or an attitude; but in the present context the respondents (who received no explanation of what exactly the question meant) presumably thought they were being asked about the subjective ground of the meaningfulness of the whole, what it was that made the dance a unified enterprise worth undertaking and worth attending to. The significant thing, for my present purpose, is that Hanna thought it made sense, and expected her respondents to find it sensible, to assume that the animating principle of the dance performance as a whole must be something that could be concisely and accurately stated. And it does make sense. If I am to attend a performance by a group from an unfamiliar tradition, surely it makes sense for me to seek a preliminary orientation by asking what is going on, what I am supposed to get out of it, what they think they are up to, how to be sure I am not the victim of some radical misunderstanding. It is useless to say "just look and see" or "relax and enjoy it" because there is no antecedent reason to suppose that the most meaningful, moving, and important aspects of the performance are something that a person like me could appreciate — could see just by looking.[17] Hanna's assumption must be that performers must have some general idea of what they hope or expect audiences to get out of what they are doing, and that *something* must be sayable about this, even if the work has no statable meaning and no precisely describable emotional tone; and that there may be better or worse matches between such a general idea and the ideas that audience members infer as intended on the basis of what they see and know.[18]

The foregoing material is the most important, but must now be set aside while we say something more specific about modern dance. The historic mission of modern dance was to displace ballet as the paradigm of dance as a "fine" or "high" art. The first thing that needs to be said here, very relevant to our discussion of Hanna, is that aesthetics in the late nineteenth and early twentieth centuries was dominated by two versions of the idea that art (and, accordingly, dance as art) is essentially the expression of emotion. In the first version, derived from eighteenth-century romantic ideas about the origin of language, a true work of art is the bringing to conscious expression of an inchoate mental content, an intuition that defies analysis. Such intuitions (or "emotions" as Collingwood thought they were more appropriately called[19]) are the basis of all epistemic structures. As a work of art, an art dance, though it might be made up of distinct steps within a learned tradition, would be an indivisible cognitive/affective unity—each of its parts would have its meaning only within the unity of the whole. In the second version, a true artist has a feeling that he or she wants to express, and the work of art succeeds or fails (only the artist can say which) in giving adequate expression to this. This version seems especially attractive in connection with dance, which can be thought of as made up from the dancer's autonomous body movements and giving direct expression to the mover's feelings. The former version dignifies art as epistemically fundamental, a level of clarity to be attained; the latter makes art autobiographical and psychological, and is favored by teachers democratically seeking a space for self-expression in a school system. Both versions encourage a view of dance as inherently emancipated from set forms and traditions and able to find a cognitive or vital space of its own within the culture of a developing civilization.[20]

In general, the idea of art is obfuscatory: it is used to make a number of distinctions in addition to those just mentioned, and hence to imply indiscriminately a variety of restrictions, not all of which are in place in all discussions. But its use does indicate a set of powerful though often vague aspirations, without which the enterprises of modern dance are unintelligible. The general idea of dance is obfuscatory in much the same way, implying indiscriminately a variety of discriminations among practices, some of which are supposed to count as *really* dance while others do not. Pioneers of modern dance identified their own practice in various ways in relation to various existing practices; to say that they were all dance is in a sense obviously true, but it is not at all clear what it means, except that in each case there was some way in which they could be plausibly integrated into a history that could as reasonably be called a history of dance as of anything else.[21]

The origins of all modern dance lie in the general idea of art as essentially the expression of emotion. This made it possible for the pioneers to be accepted as artists by the artistic community generally, without regard to their acceptance or rejection by the custodians of institutionalized artistic dance. In fact, they operated in milieus independent of that establishment. I will conclude with a few remarks on some modern dance practices and practitioners.

The mystique of non-balletic art dance centers on the figure of Isadora Duncan (1878–1927).[22] Her rejection of what she knew of ballet represented the ideology of the progressive American professional classes, opposing the mass squalor of industrialized cities in the name of hygiene and human autonomy as symbolized by Hellenic civilization.[23] In a way, Duncan's dance expressed a single emotion: the sense of freedom of the unconstrained female body in natural movement. The specific emotions expressed in particular dances tended to come from the accompanying music, the sensed emotive meaning and movement of which the dance was felt to embody; but she had no theory as to how this was to be done. The technique she developed had little to do with specific emotions, but served rather to organize and liberate the central energies of the female body. The lesson of her career was that one could become recognized as a great artist by doing this; reactions of the balletic world were mixed, many being contemptuous of her lack of visible method, and it seems that when her body lost some of its tone in her later years she had no expressive resource to fall back on.

In Europe, too, the art inspiration of modern dance tended to draw on resources outside the traditions of dance art. A central figure is that of Émile Jaques-Dalcroze (1865–1950). Dalcroze began as a music teacher who concentrated on rhythm; the problem, as he saw it, was to free the performer's movements from body habits and make them subject to conscious control. He devised a method of training ("eurhythmics") in which students danced out what they felt to be the meaning of a musical piece. There was no system for identifying that meaning, that being left to the dancer's feeling for the movement in the piece. Dalcroze's school at Hellerau became vastly influential as a center of dance teaching, but became a source of specifically dance art largely through the work of his student Mary Wigman (1886–1973).

Wigman left Dalcroze for Rudolf Laban (1879–1958), who was working out a general system of body movements and dance movement in particular—a general system of dynamics that lies behind much modern dance but was conceived in terms unrelated to emotional expression as such. The aim in dance was to "tame the freed and wild-growing movement, to lead the overflowing waters into the controllable channel of a consciously limited harmony—so it might become a speakable, legible and imitable language of its own."[24] Wigman, under Laban's inspiration, went away and set about converting her body into "a rhythmic instrument rather than a mere physical torso" (83); and on this basis she "created dances which to me seemed expressive of the joys, the sorrows, the conflicts of mankind" (51). Apparently the seeming is enough: once one has transformed one's body into an instrument and mastered a comprehensive language of controlled movement, one's feelings and imagined feelings are sufficient guide. Not everyone can become a dance artist, but "everyone can profitably engage in dancing and thereby articulate stifled, half-formed emotions, and literally find a form of speech through the body" (53), because "there is something alive in everyone enabling him to make outwardly visible what stirs within him, by means of physical motions" (142). In their reliance on the artist's own understanding of feeling and their way of focusing artistry on the technical means of transforming subjective states into artistically viable forms, these thoughts answer closely to the eighteenth-century German music theory loosely called *Affektenlehre* and exemplified by Johann Mattheson. Wigman's dance equivalent, under the name of *Ausdruckstanz*, became hugely influential in Europe until it was effectively destroyed by the Hitlerian regime; most of its leading exponents fled to America and helped to shape modern dance there, but a certain amorphousness diffused its effect.

An alternative source for the expression of emotion in modern dance is the work of François Delsarte (1811–71). Delsarte's concern was not with dance but with drama, the training of voice and gesture. A lifetime of observation gave him the confidence to work out a system of expressive gesture, determining the expressive possibilities of the torso and limbs and assigning specific meanings to their possible positions—all in connection with an idiosyncratic anthroposophical system of his own devising. Delsarte's methods were systematized and promoted in America by his disciples and played an important part in the physical education of women at the beginning of the present century; their importance as a resource for dance was emphasized by Ted Shawn.[25] Whatever one thinks of Delsarte's schematism in detail, the underlying idea is surely important in relation to the indeterminacies of Duncan and Wigman: that the body parts have specific physical properties and relationships to the organism, and that the relative movements and positions of these parts cannot but control the emotive meaning of the visible body and must accordingly receive specific attention from a choreographer.

The dance of Ruth St. Denis (1879–1968), whose colleague in the Denishawn company Ted Shawn was, differs from the others I have named in being centered in theatre and show business, designed to attract and impress a public. The distinctive emotional effects of her work tended to stem from the evocation of exotic scenes and practices—"oriental mysticism" and the like, dependent on preexisting stereotypes and associations to add affective color to her artistry. This has been a stock resource of ballet throughout its history, but has mostly been repudiated by modern dance, presumably as unauthentic and meretricious.

Martha Graham (1894–1991) was a principal dancer and teacher with Denishawn, which she left in 1926.[26] She built on Delsartian and Dalcrozian principles, and on the insistence on the primacy of breathing which formed part of the orientalism of Denishawn, but developed a powerful and comprehensive new technique of movement which was incorporated in a rigid system of training. What was distinctive in her dance, apart from her overpowering genius, was the range and power of this technique itself; but its most striking features (contraction and release; use of the floor; use of the curved foot) lent themselves to a new and characteristic range of emotion, predominantly dark, but above all inward-turning and isolating rather than outgoing. A Graham dancer does not grieve, but suffers. In later years she turned to mythology in connection with "depth psychology" (especially Jungian), in which relationships between vaguely named characters stood as metaphor for the supposed components of the human personality. Jung and Freud have retained their popularity in the culture at large, whatever science may say, and are a standing temptation to choreographers, though it seems to be hard to make them add either subtlety or power to the emotional content of a dance. In Graham, however, myth and depth psychology enabled her to make group dances without compromising the inwardness of meaning.

Ironically, for all its powerful emphasis on individual isolation, Graham's dance imposed an iron discipline on its dancers. Merce Cunningham, for one, found the technique constraining, and broke away to found a company in which all movements should be created equal.[27] His methods involved the repudiation of specifically emotive or expressive movements, though his dances have often been found profoundly moving, as if by accident; and the movements he employed were inescapably those of a superbly trained and skilled dancer. Audiences reported "an overwhelming experience," but (I would suggest) an overwhelming experience *of dance.*

Whatever has a recognizable dance character, as Cunningham's work had, must inevitably, for reasons I explained earlier, have a complex and many-layered emotional character. In the palmy days of the avant-garde, attempts were made to eliminate even these vestiges of humanism, along with the elitism that singled out some movements and skills as more dancelike than others. A group of dancers working out of the Judson Dance Theater in 1962–64 sought to show, roughly, that anything that could be performed could be performed as dance, and anything that could be seen could be seen as dance.[28] But what it is to see something "as dance" cannot be explained otherwise than as "seeing" it (in some sense or other) in some relation to some practice or institution that one for some reason identifies as dancelike. The requirement is too indeterminate to sustain a practice, and any emotion found by someone to be expressed or instigated must be quite adventitious. People whose taste and judgment I trust assure me that interesting dance was danced, but the source of the interest is obscure.

In a way, this must be the end of the line. Dance nowadays tends to be eclectic and often multimedia and (in accordance with the postmodern aesthetic) quizzically or equivocally related to established systems of meaning and expression. Immeasurable new areas are thus opened up to the arts of dance, at the expense of those effects, still valued by a large and exacting public, that depend on a reliable language in which elaborate things can be definitely said. The story of the postmodern is a set of narratives of methods and manners that, in principle, defy generalization.

The line that seems thus to be ended is not, however, the only line there is. In Pina Bausch's dance theatre, for example, a blatantly erotic or violent scene may be simultaneously heightened by the eloquence of the dance action and neutralized by its stylization, in a way that some audiences find deeply disturbing. A full account of emotion in modern dance would need to take account of the range of feeling that such methods open up. And, more significantly for the future of dance, a whole new genre of dance has been developed in Japan that in a unique way symbolizes the human condition, by refinement of gesture and an extreme deceleration contriving to open up a range of feelings germane to the course of life, the suffering and survival of the human "forked animal." The implications and possibilities of these methods are being explored by a variety of dancers in the west—notably, if my experience can be trusted, in Montréal.

Dances of which the feeling tone, if not the content, seems to depend on their symbolization of the human condition itself come close to the phenomenological dance that some critics have postulated, in which what is danced out is the actual basis of the relationship of consciousness to the world. But that is really a different study, because the concern of phenomenology must be with universal and necessary forms, and the specific phenomena of emotion are contingent and variable.

NOTES

1. The entry under "emotion" in the *Oxford English Dictionary* (first edition) is instructive. First, the entry is rather short. Second, the sense that concerns us here comes fourth in order, and is labeled "figurative." (It reads: "Any agitation or disturbance of mind, feeling, passion; any vehement or excited mental state.") The entry goes on to identify a secondary sense of the word, crucial for our discussions here, in which emotion is contradistinguished from cognition and volition. The source (and, even more, the authority) of this three-part schema is obscure. Is it a misunderstood version of Plato's tripartite soul, alluded to in my text? Is it an analysis of subjective phenomena (and innervation) into input (emotion), output (volition), and processing (cognition)? In any case, it obviously represents somebody's old theory, from which I suspect that the concept of "emotion" has never really disentangled itself in the century since that *OED* entry was compiled.

2. Jenefer Robinson 1995b.

3. See, for example, the scenario to John Weaver's *Loves of Mars and Venus* [1717] (1985).

4. Jean-Paul Sartre 1948.

5. See my "Music and Feeling" (1994).

6. These and other possibilities are explored and explained at length in my *Off the Ground* (1988), chap. 8, and *A Measured Pace* (1995).

7. A friend has related to me his disappointment in discovering that a volume on a French bookseller's shelves entitled *Harmonie des Seins* was not what the title had led him to expect but a German work of metaphysics, and I almost believe him. But I do not believe that (for instance) a book that could be read as an English detective novel could also be read as a manual on botany in some extraterrestrial language.

8. Paul Thom 1993.

9. Francis Sparshott 1981.

10. See my *The Theory of the Arts* (1982), 48–55.

11. Jean-Paul Sartre 1971, 785–90. Cf. my *A Measured Pace* (1995), 347–49.

12. For the definitive doctrine as formulated in the *Nātyaśāstra*, perhaps in the second century CE, see J. L. Masson and M. V. Patwardhan 1970; for a contemporary statement see Sushil Kumar Saxena 1991.

13. Compare Theophrastus's *Characters*, which has the appearance of a typology of personality traits but is now suspected of being a description of stereotypical characters in the fourth-century "new comedy" of Athens. Javanese dancing, it appears, recognizes five basic character types, each with its own identifiable costume, movements, music, and so on; and these seem to be based not on any sociological or psychological analysis, but on the preferred narrative forms—see Judith Lynne Hanna 1988, 82.

14. Johan Mattheson in *Der vollkommene Capellmeister* (1739) appears to argue that in a humanistic music, melody (not harmony, certainly not counterpoint) must be primary, that melodic effectiveness depends on affective expression, and that artistic unity in a composition depends on the unity of the affect predominantly expressed. But I do not know how carefully this was thought out, or how seriously it was taken.

15. Edward Bullough, "Psychical Distance as a Factor in Art and as an Aesthetic Principle" in his *Aesthetics* (1957). The article was first published in 1912 and has been much anthologized.

16. Judith Lynne Hanna 1983.

17. An article entitled "Don't Be Afraid of Contemporary Dance," by Paula Citron (1995), incorporates three quotations from respected choreographers: (a) "Reacting to body language is part of our everyday lives, so why not just sit back and enjoy the body language of superbly trained dancers? Don't struggle to find meaning, but let the images stimulate you visually, emotionally and spiritually" (Christopher House); (b) "Accept choreography as someone's personal language which expresses, through movement, what a composer is expressing through his music" (Danny Grossman); (c) "Cultivate your curiosity. . . . you can't understand a book without learning to read; therefore, first discover the physical language of dance, and with each new experience, your vocabulary will grow" (Serge Bennathan). It is, to say the least, not obvious that these recommendations are mutually compatible; so it is not absurd for someone unacquainted with a choreographer's work to seek guidance as to how, in broad terms, the work is to be approached.

18. Some years ago, an Inuk drum dancer was demonstrating his art to a Toronto audience. After a while, he stopped, turned to his audience, and said: "You know, this is actually very difficult to do." He surmised, correctly, that none of us had the least idea of the significant variations in steps and drum movements, and he wanted to make sure that we knew he was doing something worth seeing if we knew how to see it.

19. R. G. Collingwood 1938.

20. The connections and ramifications of these two versions are explored in my *The Theory of the Arts* (1982), chaps. 3 and 11–12.

21. But see further what is said below about the Judson Dance Theater. The perplexities hinted at here preoccupy (and are explained by) my *Off the Ground* (1988) and *A Measured Pace* (1995)—and, more pointedly, my article "How Can I Know What Dancing Is?" (1993).

22. For Duncan's career and significance, see Frederika Blair 1986.

23. See Nancy Lee Chalfa Ruyter 1979.

24. Walter Sorrell, *The Mary Wigman Book* (1975), 32. Further page references in the text are to this book.

25. Ted Shawn 1968. For Shawn and his connection with Ruth St. Denis, see Suzanne Shelton 1981.

26. Graham's death in 1991 coincided with the appearance of three notable books on her work: Graham's own *Blood Memory* (1991); Agnes de Mille, *Martha: The Life and Work of Martha Graham* (1991); and, perhaps most usefully for our purposes, Marian Horosko, ed., *Martha Graham: The Evolution of Her Dance Theory and Training* (1991). These do not replace such earlier studies as Ernestine Stodelle's *Deep Song: The Dance Story of Martha Graham* (1984).

27. See Merce Cunningham and Jacqueline Lesschaeve 1985.

28. See Sally Banes 1983.

PART III

THE
RATIONALITY
ᵒF EMOTIONAL
RESPONSES
TO ART

———

9

On Looking into Titian's *Assumption*

WILLIAM LYONS

1. Titian's *Assumption*, James, and the English Couple

In volume 2, chapter 25, of his *capolavoro*, *The Principles of Psychology*, William James discourses on the nature of emotion. He begins with a comparison between emotions and instincts. While every object that excites an instinct can also excite an emotion, the reverse is not the case. Some objects might strike us as hilarious or worthy of deep admiration, to take just two examples, but would not thereby excite in us any of those reflex actions or reactions we call instinctive. In addition, emotional reactions are more internal and physiological than behavioral and practical. They primarily exhibit themselves as a rigidity of this muscle or a relaxation of that one, a constriction of arteries here or a dilation of them there, a quickening of the pulse or a slowing, and so on. These patterns of physiological changes associated with emotion are, of course, also personal and idiosyncratic to a certain extent, like everything else to do with individual humans.

James then goes on to distinguish the coarser emotions (such as grief, fear, rage, love), which are characterized by coarse or strong physiological reactions, from the subtle emotions (such as the moral, intellectual, and aesthetic ones), in which the physiological reactions are of a more delicate kind. With the coarser emotions, James claims, it should be quite clear by now that the emotions as such are the feelings of the strong physiological reactions. That is, the emotion proper, in every case of a coarse emotion, is the subjective registering in our consciousness of our bodily perturbations, caused more or less reflexively by the stimulation of one or more of our senses by some object or event. Indeed, says James, what could grief be without the tears, the sobs, the suffocation of the heart, and the constriction in the area of the breastbone? It would be, he assures us, nothing but an empty, cold judgment to the effect that certain circumstances are deplorable. Such "a purely disembodied human emotion is a nonentity." [1]

The subtler emotions—the moral, intellectual, and aesthetic ones—are not so much the mirror image in our consciousness of our physiological perturbations; these latter are slight, as the direct effect (registered as either pleasure or displeasure) on our consciousness of the immediate stimulation of one or more of our senses. The subtler emotions are the enjoyment (or the opposite) of the very form or structure of our immediate perceptions of some object or event.

My interest here is in James's account of aesthetic emotions. So let us hear James himself, with some more details, on this matter:

> Aesthetic emotion, *pure and simple*, the pleasure given us by certain lines and masses, and combinations of colors and sounds, is an absolutely sensational experience, an optical or aural feeling that is primary, and not due to the repercussion backwards [to the physiological level] of other sensations elsewhere consecutively aroused. To this simple primary and immediate pleasure in certain pure sensations and harmonious combinations of them, there may, it is true, be *added* secondary, pleasures. . . .[2]

James then goes on to make a distinction between a "classic taste," in which the pleasure is almost entirely in terms of this primary and immediate enjoyment attendant upon perception of the lines and masses, and of combinations of colors and sounds, and a "romantic taste" in which the pleasure or other affective responses are almost entirely of a secondary sort, that is, in the form of a physiological "repercussion" set up by an aesthetic emotion pure and simple. By "secondary pleasure," it seems that James means that the pleasure is attendant upon someone's reaction going beyond the initial pure or classical enjoyment of the raw perceptual qualities of, for example, a painting, and extending in a pronounced way to the physiological level by the raw perception having caused, for example, an increase in our heartbeat and pulse rate, or some constriction around the heart and rib cage. In turn, these physiological reactions are clearly felt, even if not as strongly as the feelings associated with the coarser emotions, as an overlay upon the pure feelings of the initial, purely perceptual response. Thus, someone with a romantic taste will view a painting as gloomy or mysterious or haunting, but will not sob with grief or quake with fear. In consequence, the romantic will maintain that this richer "repercussive" reaction is the proper reaction and believe that the thinner "purer" reaction is simply aesthetically anemic.[3]

William James assures us that he is not "discussing which view [the classic or romantic] is right, but only showing that the discrimination between the primary feeling of beauty, as a pure incoming sensible quality, and the secondary emotions which are grafted thereupon, is one that must be made."[4] What is to be regretted is a third approach, namely that approach to painting which eschews, or at least is unable to register, either of the two sorts of approved feelings, and takes refuge in the thinnest and driest of intellectual "emotions." Such a response is almost purely intellectual or cognitive and is the preserve of the dry critic, sated and blunted by overfamiliarity with great works of art. So, in short, what is condemned here is the substitution of an intellectual judgment, no matter how clever and informed, for an aesthetic feeling.

However, there is another response that is to be condemned without reserve or qualification. Indeed James reserves the full flowering of his outrage and contempt for this response alone. This response is the preserve of the self-righteous sentimental philistine smugly wallowing in a mélange of coarse emotions. What sentiments the philistine can evoke are neither a result of a classic taste nor of a romantic one, nor are they a form of pure intellectual response; rather, they comprise a coarse affective response of an entirely irrelevant and spurious kind. Such a response is built upon associating, say, a painting— either its colors, or forms, or artist, or style, or context, or anything else—with something that evokes emotion, coarse emotion, in the viewer. The woman dressed in black in the corner of the picture reminds the viewer of his mother's funeral and so makes him sad. The white swan on the river evokes in the viewer the memory of a consummately pleasurable picnic that she had with her parents when she was young, and she is overcome by nostalgic pleasure. The depiction of the soldier interrogating the child unnerves the viewer. The smile on the *Mona Lisa's* face makes the viewer indignant. So a fourth category, encompassing the coarse "sentimental and spurious" emotional reaction, is necessary for a complete logical geography of James's position on emotion in relation to fine art.

It is into this fourth and last category that William James places the response of the "English couple" described in his account in *The Principles* of his visit to the Accademia in Venice:

> I remember seeing an English couple sit for more than an hour on a piercing February day in the Academy at Venice before the celebrated "Assumption" by Titian; and when I, after being chased from room to room by the cold, concluded to get into the sunshine as fast as possible and let the pictures go, but before leaving drew reverently near to them to learn with what superior forms of susceptibility they might be endowed, all I overheard was the woman's voice murmuring: "What a *deprecatory* expression her face wears! What self-abnegation! How *unworthy* she feels of the honor she is receiving!" Their honest hearts had been kept warm all the time by a glow of spurious sentiment that would have fairly made old Titian sick.[5]

Let me say a little about the painting in question, Titian's *Assumption*. For, at the end of this essay, I want to discuss in more detail James's reaction to the English couple's response to that painting. While Titian (Tiziano Vecellio) painted two *Assumptions*, from the above passage it is clear that William James is referring to the *Assumption* that was painted for the Chiesa dei Frari (more accurately called the *Chiesa di Santa Maria Gloriosa dei Frati Minori* in Ven-ice.[6] It was erected in that church, as an altarpiece, in 1518. However, this painting was removed from the church and brought to the Accademia in Ven-ice for restoration in 1817, and not returned to its original location till after the First World War. During the latter years of its stay in the Accademia, it was on show to the public. It must have been at this time, but before 1890 when *The Principles* was published, that both James and the English couple viewed the picture.

The painting itself is large, almost seven meters in height and some three and a half meters in width. If such categories might be permitted, it was painted by Titian in his "reddish-brown mode" rather than in his "blue mode." The upper center of the painting depicts a slightly apprehensive Virgin Mary being borne upwards by a cloud of putti with a little help from some more regular cumulonimbus clouds. Above Mary's head is God the Father, who appears less than welcoming. Below, earthbound, is a rather scruffy-looking band of apostles and disciples, looking a little disoriented by the sudden levita-tion. All are suffused by a rich golden and reddish-brown light emanating from a sun placed directly behind God the Father's midriff.

Before moving on, let me recapitulate. There are, according to James, only two sorts of legitimate response to works of art. Both of these involve feelings or emotion. The first of these legitimate responses is the response that he called pure and "classic," in which one responds directly and immediately with a feeling of pleasure (or the opposite) to the basic sensations. In the context of paintings, this means responding to the perceptual harmonies of color, shape, and arrangement. Secondly, there is the response that he called "romantic," which involves an emotional response evoked by physiological "repercussions" from the more immediate and purer response. James mentions another two kinds of response to a painting. Both of these he finds inadequate. The first of these inadequate responses is that of the dry and dispassionate critic who, able only to evoke thin and intellectual "feelings," readily passes informed but desic-cated judgment. The second is that of "the English couple" and their kind who, unable to respond in either a "classical" or a "romantic" way, and too ignorant to call up even the etiolated delights of the intellectual's substitute for feelings, under the sway of memory and imagination pass complacently philis-tine remarks and so evoke whatever coarse, and so spurious, sentiments might accompany them.

In the next four sections of this essay, I want to sketch a different, richer view of the interplay between emotions and paintings, and then discuss the categories outlined by this sketch. As I think this interplay is most revealingly recorded in a step-by-step, layered way, I will begin at the beginning, namely, with emotion in the painter. Then I will move along the spectrum from the artist to the painting itself, and finally to the viewer of the painting, such as "the English couple." Though this will only become clear in the final section of this essay, I want to employ this richer panoramic or "spectrum" account as the backdrop for a more liberal and less censorious account of what we should allow as a legitimate emotional response to a painting.

II. A Richer Panoramic Account of the Emotions
in Relation to Paintings

I will start with a rather bald description of the whole spectrum from the artist's emotions to the viewer's. Then I will backtrack in order to discuss each division or category one by one. The spectrum involves a division into seven categories:

1. Emotion *in* the Painter. The painter may paint out of emotion. It is his (or her) emotion that moves him to paint.
2. Emotion *transferred from* the Painter. While the painter does not set out to paint because of some emotional episode, nevertheless any concomitant emotion in the painter while painting, even if fleeting, may have some effect on the resulting painting.
3. Emotion *depicted by* the Painting. The painter, whether in an emotional state or not, may set out to depict or express some emotion or emotions in his painting.
4. Emotion *generated through* the Painting. The painter may set out, via his painting, but not via the depiction or expression in it of some emotion, to generate a particular emotion or emotions in a viewer.
5. Emotion *discovered in* the Painting. Whether or not the artist intended it, a viewer might discover, or believe she discovers in the painting, a depiction of some emotion.
6. Emotion *provoked by* the Painting. Whether or not the artist intended it, a viewer finds that the painting, through what is depicted in it (though this does not involve the actual or imagined depiction of emotion), directly provokes emotion in her.
7. Emotion *connected with* the Painting. A viewer indirectly, and sometimes idiosyncratically, through memory or imagination or association, makes a connection between the painting and some other object or event, which connection evokes emotion in her.

Of course, this spectrum, and its divisions into categories, is highly artificial. All such divisions, generated for philosophical purposes, are. For our emotions, in the context of paintings as in most contexts, do not come uniformed and step by step in single file. On the other hand, like some analytical chemist of the affections, I am trying to break things down into their elements in order to show that, when built up again, matters are much more complex and complicated than they might previously have appeared. However, in the next three sections, I intend to breathe some life into these rather cold and morbid categories by discussing them through the medium of examples.

III. Emotion *In* and *Transferred from* the Painter

A closer look at the divisions of the foregoing panoramic account of emotion in relation to painting will reveal that the seven divisions or categories could be said to fall under three meta-groupings. The first of these meta-groups is carved out by the painter's own emotion in relation to what he is painting; the second by emotion as depicted in the painting; and the third by the viewer's emotion in relation to the painting.

In this section, I shall discuss the first meta-group, that is, divisions or categories (1) and (2) of the panoramic account. Category (1), "emotion in the painter," concentrates on emotion as the cause of the painter's taking up his (or her) brush and painting. Category (2), "emotion transferred from the painter," considers those cases in which the emotional state of the painter spills over into the painting.

First, then, I shall consider in more detail the case of the painter being led by his (or her) emotion into taking up his palette and brushes and attacking the canvas. Of course, "attacking the canvas" is misleading, for it assumes that a painter, who has been moved to paint some picture because of some emotion, must ipso facto have been moved by some strong or perturbatory emotion. But there are calm emotions that dampen down our reactions rather than get the adrenaline going. It may have been the case that Picasso was led into painting his *Guernica* out of consuming anger and sadness at the bombing of the Spanish city of Guernica by the Falangist forces. In fact, as he did several versions of the painting, the final version is more likely to have been the result of a cool head and steady hand than the immediate result of deep passion. On the other hand, the very first drawing or oil sketch may well have been done in a flurry of deep emotion. Again, although he took an enormously long time to complete the painting, Titian may have been led into painting his *Assumption* by a quiet but deep mood of religious devotion, or in a state of deep depression about his own fading religious belief.[7]

Whether or not Picasso was moved to paint his *Guernica* or Titian his Venetian *Assumption* while under the sway of some emotion, any motivating emotional state will not necessarily be detectable in the resulting painting. It all depends on what the artist wants to achieve. The emotion that led Titian into wanting to paint a certain subject and perhaps to begin the process of painting, may not spill over into the painting. This will be especially true of a painting that, like the *Assumption*, takes years to complete. For practical reasons, it is probably also true of any painting that is painted in a style that requires a cool head and steady hand. Even if on Tuesday, Titian, while in a rapture of religious feeling, was moved to begin painting the Virgin's features, on Wednesday and Thursday he would probably go back over what he painted on Tuesday and correct any hasty or impulsive lines and daubs. But a painter may want her emotion to "spill over" into the painting. She may want just that sort of effect. However, the painter does not have to be in an emotional state to produce a painting that looks as if it was the result of an emotional state. Delacroix seems to have taken days or weeks and even months, presumably of careful and cool craftsmanship, to achieve pictures of swirling, passionate painterliness.

In discussing emotion as a motive for painting, I do not want to imply either that it is the only motive for painting or a fortiori that it is the only legitimate motive for painting. One critic says of Bridget Riley's "optical art" that it "seems to parallel scientific analytical procedure."[8] If this is also a true account of her motivation, it may be fair to say that emotions have little or nothing to do with the production of many of her paintings. This would certainly seem to be true of a painting like *Hidden Squares 1961*, which, as the title indicates, involves cleverly "hiding" a series of black and white chequer-board squares inside a larger square of black dots on a white background. To take another case, it is hard to imagine emotion entering into the creative process of some minimalist artist who, rather short of some paintings for his upcoming exhibition, exhibits a pure white, untouched canvas, entitled *Canvas, 1995*. In such a case, emotion could enter in, but it might not show. The artist might have a perfervid obsession with "purity of materials" or a deep fury with "academic painting." A clearer case of paintings where the artist deliberately insulates her emotion from the canvas would be those painted according to some "aleatory method."[9]

On the other hand, as my category (2), "emotion transferred from the painter," describes, sometimes it may be all too obvious that the painting was the result of some burst of emotional energy or the consequence of some deeper seated and longer lasting mood. Derek Jarman's painting, *Drop Dead*, in which the words "drop dead" are crudely scrawled over a slap-dash background of Jackson-Pollock-like dribbles and splashes of primary colors, must be a prime candidate here. It was painted, with the help of some friends, by Derek Jarman as he lay dying of AIDS. It is so swift and blunt in its execution that it bears the direct impress of emotion. Whether this emotion was one of anger or sadness or anxiety or confusion, or some admixture, I do not know. Perhaps Jarman himself did not know.

I once saw a documentary about a painter who said that he could paint only when driven by emotion. And "driven" was probably the right word here. For his technique involved, first, placing a large canvas on the floor and then pouring paint from large tubes and tins onto the canvas. Then, stripping himself naked, he would pause in trance-like fashion for a minute or so. Finally, as if possessed by the Eumenides (perhaps bent on wreaking confusion upon his critics), he would spring forward and roll around upon the canvas, all the while flailing his arms and legs. There was, certainly, an immediacy to his work. I have not heard of him since that time. Perhaps he suffered some sort of emotional burnout.

In general, I expect that such clear and unambiguous evidence, on the canvas, of an artist's emotion while the canvas was being painted is comparatively rare and only possible for paintings that take a short time to execute and do not require drafting of an intricate sort. Even then, it will be quite difficult to discern and describe what particular emotion was the driving force. Is a white canvas, criss-crossed with two broad swathes of black, crudely superimposed with the French word "merde," and finished in an overheated, ten-minute session, the result of hate or anger or self-contempt?

IV. Emotion *Depicted by* or *Generated Through* the Painting

In this section, I will discuss the second meta-group, namely that comprising my divisions (3) and (4). This meta-group concerns itself with how the painter might use a painting as a vehicle, first, for depicting emotion, and second, for generating emotion in a viewer. Both of these effects should be distinguished from the effect, which I have already discussed, whereby the painting is made to look as if it had been painted in a flurry of passion. When discussing the use of a painting to depict emotion or to generate emotion in a viewer, I am also prescinding from the question of whether the painter is undergoing any emotion.

Under category (3), "emotion depicted by the painting," I want to draw attention to those cases in which the painter's avowed aim is to depict some emotion. The painter must do this in some conventional way, at least if he wants to communicate with those who view his painting. But he need not do this in a representational way.

The archetype of this sort of painting is, I suspect, Edvard Munch's *The Scream*. Here we have a depiction, in a deliberately exaggerated expressionist way, of a person who is screaming hysterically while running away in fear along a jetty. Scream is "written all over her face," and the pear-shaped contorted contours of her face are echoed by the tortuous curves of the sky and fjord in the immediate background and underlined by the blood red of the clouds. However, as examples of emotion clearly depicted in a painting, Munch's companion pieces, *Anxiety*, *Despair*, and *Melancholy*, are less conventional and so less "successful." Another archetype would be Van Gogh's *Old Man in Sorrow*. The old man, with his head in his hands, could serve as an illustration, in a textbook of social anthropology, of a typical sorrowful position for a person in Western culture. In addition, Van Gogh chooses what is, for him at any rate, a restrained, pastel color, or conventionally "watery" palette for this painting.[10]

Under (4), "emotion generated through a painting," I want to consider those paintings that have been quite clearly designed as a medium for eliciting emotions in the viewer. The archetypes here are the genre paintings of the Victorian era in England and Scotland. Think of all those paintings of poor peasants being evicted from their tenant cottages by cruel landlords, or foreign fields littered with the carnage of brave cavalrymen, or those acres of beds with wan figures gasping their last breaths surrounded by their stricken families. My own favourite is Sir John Everett Millais's *The Blind Girl*. Nothing is left to the imagination. The sky has not one rainbow but two. And the blind girl has her back to them while her younger sister turns and, presumably, exclaims with delight at the sight which her poor sister is incapable of enjoying. To rub it in, Millais has the blind girl's right hand plucking at a wildflower, a harebell, while a beautiful butterfly lodges on her right shoulder. In case there might still have been a dry eye in the house, Millais depicts the blind girl as having a concertina on her knees. This, together with the sign around her neck saying "Pity the Blind," indicates that she is reduced to busking for her livelihood. I expect that it was only a deep sensitivity to the technological limitations of book publishing in his time that stopped him placing in the girl's left hand a book entitled "Great Paintings of the World in Full Color."

Of course, those painters who wish to stir up emotions in the viewer *through* the painting, realize that one sure way of doing so is to depict emotions *in* the painting. The Victorians certainly knew this—take, for example, Alexander Farmer's *An Anxious Hour,* which depicts an anxious mother at her daughter's bedside, or William Windus's *Too Late,* which depicts the almost grotesque despair of a lover who returns to find his beloved dying of consumption. But the Dutch and Italian and Spanish painters of the seventeenth and eighteenth century, particularly the religious painters, were equally alive to this. Think of all those crucifixions with grieving apostles and disciples strewn about, and all those "Last Judgments" depicting the fears and agonies of the damned. Through fear and anxiety and sorrow and guilt and remorse the faithful were to be led on by these paintings to more faithful service.

Periods of more or less complete retreat from representation in painting are also, I suspect, periods of retreat from any crude desire on the part of an artist to generate emotions in a viewer. More generally, they are probably periods in which the artist remains aloof from the task of eliciting any particular response from the viewer. One part of the largely unspoken program of abstract art is that interpretation is not to be forced upon the viewer. Like free love and free verse, as regards its interpretation, abstract art is saying "feel free." By and large, it is left up to the viewer what response, if any, she makes. Certainly there is no obvious desire or demand for an emotional response. Abstracting from representation necessarily involves taking some steps back from any clearly articulated communication with the viewer. There is no story being told and no emotion being depicted. Of course, this does not mean that no emotion is being elicited. It could be that the artist desires irritation or frustration from the viewer, or perhaps some nirvana-like state of tranquillity. On the other hand, a Mondrian caption to a painting, such as *Composition with Red, Yellow and Blue,* or a painting with no caption, seems designed to make it clear that no particular response is expected or overtly sought.

Leaving aside the question of what emotion might have been sought by the artist, it is clear that even abstract art can and does elicit emotion. I know of people who find some of Franz Kline's works deeply unsettling and, given that they could afford them, would not wish to have them in their house. But this is a case of someone discovering emotion in a painting rather than the artist depicting it or painting in such a way as deliberately to elicit it, and strictly speaking falls under our discussion of the next section.

V. Emotions *Discovered in, Provoked by,* or *Connected with* a Painting

Under this meta-group, I want to consider emotions solely from the point of view of the viewer. That is, I want to consider the different ways in which the person who looks at paintings might become emotionally involved with them.

Let me take category (5), "emotion discovered in the painting," first. I have deliberately described this category as "discovered in a painting." For the implication is that the viewer can and often will discover emotions depicted in a painting where there has been no intention on the part of the artist to depict any emotions. The viewer can see something in a painting as depicting emotion in the same way as I can see the cloud formation at sunset as depicting a red hen.

I suppose that the clearest case of seeing emotion as depicted, though it has not been deliberately depicted or intended by the artist, is the cross-cultural case. A Japanese person, viewing Claude Monet's *Turkeys at Montgeron*, might see it as symbolic of death. For white is the color of mourning for the Japanese, and the all-white turkeys seem to be gathering, in their slow and studied way, as if for a funeral.

But a painter-viewer gap, or rather a viewer-painter gap, in regard to the discovery of emotion in a painting can just as easily occur within the same culture. Quite simply, the viewer might be attuned to something to which the artist is not. For example, I myself find many of Gwen John's portraits to be of rather sad and lonely people. Whether or not Gwen John intended this I do not know. Somehow I doubt that she did, as she not infrequently depicts her sitters with a smile on their faces. But nevertheless, to me, it is a sad and wistful smile, especially when seen in the context of the whole painting. For her portraits, such as *Mère Poussepin, Young Woman in a Shawl,* and *The Convalescent,* invariably depict the sitter in a convent-girl posture, with straight back, and hands clasped neatly and defensively on her lap. Furthermore, John almost always paints them seated on chairs that lack any ornamentation and in rooms with bare or almost bare walls. In short, there is often more in a picture, including more emotion, than meets the painter's eye. But why should this surprise anyone? The viewer, after all, has a different eye from the painter's.

Category (6), "emotion provoked by the painting," must be distinguished carefully from the two other categories of this meta-group. In category (5) cases, emotion is found depicted in the painting (even if not deliberately so depicted by the painter) or is deliberately generated via the iconography of the painting. In category (7) cases, as we shall see, emotion is generated by a painting solely because of its relation to external events that are the ultimate source of the emotion. Category (6) is in between. It carves out those cases in which the painting itself does generate the emotional response in a direct manner, but it does so neither because of any emotion depicted in the painting nor because of any indirect relation to external events past or present. What generates the emotion is the immediate confrontation between the painting's contents and the viewer's values. Let us take the paintings of Allen Jones as the paradigm here. The ones I have in mind are his Pop Art paintings of women in erotic fetish clothing. They tend to excite a strong negative emotional response, such as outrage or disgust or both, in some viewers. Sometimes this is because the viewer simply finds them obscene (and so believes they should be *ab-scaena*), sometimes because the viewer sees them as "politically incorrect" insofar as they lead to the "objectification of women's sexuality." It is the content's prickly relation with conventional morality or good taste or some such canon of the acceptable that generates the emotion in the viewer, not its power to invoke memories or produce personal associations or provoke the subconscious.

Sometimes, of course, an artist may deliberately set out to outrage or disgust or, in general, to provoke the viewer. The Dadaists spring to mind. But that sort of provocation, being deliberate, properly falls under category (4), "emotion generated [by the artist] through the painting."

This brings me, then, to the final category, (7), "emotion connected with a painting." Under this category fall those cases in which the painting stirs something in the viewer's memory or imagination, and thereby generates an emotional response. This category encompasses the most tenuous of the connections between a painting and an emotion. For what generates the emotion in the viewer is some quite circumstantial and contingent relation between the painter or the painting and some event. This event might be an event or supposed event in the painter's life, or in the life of the painting, or in the life of what is contained in the painting, or in the viewer's life, or simply in history. Furthermore, sometimes this external emotion-generating relation between painting and event, while real and generating emotion in the viewer, might nevertheless remain hidden from the viewer.

Let us take this last, rather unusual, case first. I might feel unsettled by Feininger's Bauhaus cubist architectural paintings but not know why. It might be because they are so cold and austere, with no humans about. It might be because of their fractured cut-crystal cubist style. Or it may turn out that it is neither of these things but something much less patent, or even latent, that nevertheless triggers something in me. Perhaps my record of some traumatic event has been, until now, buried in my subconscious world. Yet, while the painting stirs the memory traces in me of these traumatic events, it does not stir them enough for me to be able to pull the event back into consciousness and so articulate these events. So, what Feininger's paintings do to me is leave me unsettled but not knowing why.

More often the reason why a painting evokes an emotion in a viewer will be patent, at least to the viewer, but often to the painter as well. Many paintings can be connected fairly readily with some emotive event in the life of the viewer or in the life of the painter or in recent history. Sometimes this connection will have been invited by the artist, sometimes not. The paintings of an official war artist are commissioned as chronicles of war, including the boring and banal episodes as well as the horrendously traumatic ones. When they are of traumatic events, it will be no surprise if, by reminding a viewer of those events, they frequently disturb people emotionally.

But there are more interesting cases where more or less completely fortuitous information can endow a painting with deep emotional significance. For chronological reasons, such information (or much of it) may not have been available either to the painter at the time he painted the picture or to viewers for many years afterwards. Let me take an example. To anyone who saw Dresden at the end of the Second World War, Kokoschka's *The Elbe near Dresden* (painted c. 1921) must stir the emotions appropriate to witnessing the destruction of both people and an architectural heritage. Add to that before-and-after contrast another layer of information, to the effect that Kokoschka made his home in Dresden, and a new set of emotions enter in. Then add still another layer, namely that in 1937, the National Socialists confiscated and destroyed (as being "degenerate") a large number of Kokoschka's works. A viewer with all that information is likely to find an otherwise straightforward landscape deeply moving.

Sometimes these fortuitous reasons that imbue a painting with deep emotional significance will be extremely personal and so not information open to anyone else. A Chardin still life (his *Silver Goblet*) becomes an intensely sad painting for Jacqueline, not because it depicts sadness nor because it is associated in the life of the painter or in recent history with sad events, but for a very personal, contingent, biographical reason associated with her, the viewer. It was when viewing this painting for the first time with her lover that he told her that he had been unfaithful to her and must leave her for another woman. Ever since that moment, in her mind, the *Silver Goblet* of Chardin has been a symbol of deep and devastating loss and, when again viewed, even as a reproduction, an occasion of renewed sadness. What is more, over the intervening years, her sadness has reflected itself back upon the details of the painting, and in so doing has subtly changed the nature and focus of her sadness. The mellow, suffused, red-gold coloring of the painting has become for her, now, in her old age, a wistful autumnal light that reminds her both of summers past and of that winter from which no spring emerges.

VI. James and the Legitimacy of Emotional Responses to Art

It is time to return to where we began, with William James and the English couple. What, with the hindsight of our discussion, should we think of the emotional reaction of the English couple sitting before Titian's *Assumption* in the Accademia in Venice on a cold winter's day?

William James was quite clear in his mind as to what we should think of them. James accused them of being able to summon up only coarse, and so spurious and philistine, feelings in response to Titian's incomparable masterpiece, a response which "would have fairly made old Titian sick." For not merely did the couple not exclaim with wonder or admiration or delight at the immediate painterly perceptual qualities of the painting, but they also seemed incapable of the "repercussive" romantic feelings which might follow on and deepen the immediate perceptual delight in beauty. As James put it, all that warmed their hearts was the "glow of spurious sentiment" which accompanied their vulgar interpretation of the Virgin's expression and state of mind. "What a *deprecatory* expression her face wears! What self-abnegation! How *unworthy* she feels of the honour she is receiving!"

In effect, James censures the English couple on two counts: first, for their failure to register either of the two kinds of approved emotional response, and then, because of their embrace of spurious sentiment. Let me take their failure first. Why should we accept that the only legitimate sorts of emotional response to a work of art are what James called the "classical" and "romantic"? The former, recall, is an immediate gestalt response to the basic perceptual or painterly qualities of the painting, the latter a "repercussive" sequel that engenders richer, more diffused feelings by engaging deeper and more widespread physiological responses. But why cannot we hold that, in regard to our emotional response to paintings, there are many categories of legitimate response? To refer back to the categories discussed in the body of this essay, it seems perfectly possible to respond, in simpatico harmony, with some emotion *discovered* by the viewer *in* the painting. The English couple might, for example, believe that they discern feelings of confusion and fear on the faces of the apostles and disciples. Why would it be spurious if, through an exercise of imagination on their part, and because of their possessing sympathetic natures, the English couple after viewing the painting came to feel some of that confusion and fear? And what would be inauthentic or even inappropriate about an emotion that was *provoked by* the painting's clashing with their moral or religious or political attitudes? For example, it would seem to be both a perfectly reasonable and appropriate reaction if it turned out that the English couple, because of their piety, were rather shocked by the painting. Perhaps they are taken aback by a painting that they think depicts the Virgin with a burden of rather too obviously human frailties, such as those of self-doubt and lack of confidence. And what would be spurious or even inappropriate about an emotional reaction that was only marginally and fortuitously *connected with* the painting? It makes them sad because they associate it with the last time they saw this painting. At that time, the very next day after seeing it, they were summoned back to England to their dying daughter's bedside.

In effect, William James has ruled out of court, as not merely irregular or nonstandard, but as spurious and sentimental and coarse and philistine, the whole meta-grouping of emotional responses I described as being *discovered in* a painting, or *provoked by* a painting, or *connected with* a painting. It is curious that William James should describe such emotional responses as deeply unacceptable, as one result of studying the history of art is to widen our aesthetic responses in just these ways. The more you know about a painter and the conventions of painting in his or her time and the history of that time and the provenance of the painting from that time till now, the more you create layers of interest and so of the possibility of affective response. I respond with such complex emotions to Kokoschka's *The Elbe near Dresden* because I have come to know certain things about Kokoschka, Dresden, National Socialism, and the Second World War.

What could be wrong with emotions generated by my learning about such things? Just because they are mediated by such knowledge, and so not immediate and gestalt-like, seems irrelevant to the appropriateness or acceptability of such responses. I suspect that James, because he was so intent on expressing outrage at the emotional response of the naive and "Philistine" English couple, was blind to the fact that in his outrage he had dismissed from the aesthetic playing field almost all of our emotional responses based on the study of some painting or its painter or its period or its provenance. Better to rule out all "tertiary" emotional responses (to build on James's categories of primary and secondary), that is, all emotional responses resulting from memory or association or imagination or learning applied to our perception of the painting, than to allow "the English couple" into the band of the "aesthetically correct."

I also suspect that James was influenced by a reasonably widespread view of the time to the effect that ordinary emotional responses (his "coarse emotions"), being so unsubtle, were quite out of keeping with the aesthetic context. *Fine* art merits *fine* or subtle responses from *refined* people. The viewer required by fine art is the connoisseur. However, James's view is more austere than this. For the connoisseur's response would be the response that results from an intimate knowledge of the period in which the work was executed, of the school from which the painter was drawn, of the conventions that the painter employed, of the provenance of the work itself, and so on. But all that is something over and above any gestalt-like response to the immediate painterly qualities of a painting or to any immediate "repercussive" effects.

VII. Knowing Versus Naive Emotional Responses

In this section I want to extend the discussion even further, and in so doing to go somewhat beyond my dissenting position in regard to William James's views on acceptable emotional responses to works of art. I want to argue, positively, for the rather laissez-faire view that even an emotional response based on a lack of connoisseurship can nevertheless be an acceptable response to a painting and is, in many contexts, to be applauded rather than condemned.

Put more combatively, we respond, emotionally, as we are able. A child might view the *Assumption* and be struck with amazement at the levitation that is taking place. Or the child's emotions might be woven around a story, which her imagination weaves for her, and which has nothing to do with the religious story of the miraculous bodily assumption of the Virgin into heaven. She might think that the Virgin is some sort of parachutist, like the one she saw recently at the air display. Sometimes a child will see things in a painting that we adults cannot see. We have been ruined by too much reading about what we *ought* to think about a painting. Sometimes we are too "enculturated," if I might be excused such a rebarbative word. The emotions of a member of the Ifaluk tribe from the Western Caroline Islands will also, and inevitably, be very different from those of William James or Bernard or Mary Berenson. But that is it. They are just different. Our responses, just as much as those of the child or the tribesman, are shaped by our capacities and our circumstances.

James's emotional responses to Western art, being those of a well-read, well-heeled, and well-traveled person brought up in a Western cultural milieu, and also of someone who has discussed aesthetics and come to hold decided views on it, will be generated in a very different and much more informed way from those of the child or the tribesman. These responses may also be close, or even identical, to the ones that Titian would have liked a viewer to have, though, as we shall see, I doubt it. But even if that were so, it does not rule out or lessen the acceptability of other responses from different people with different backgrounds and different capacities and in different times. Once a painting is in the public domain, the painter has no more right to dictate the viewer's emotional responses than you or I or William James have.

I should make it clear at this point that I am not claiming that we cannot criticize, in a normative way, responses, including emotional responses, to art. For example, our emotional responses can exhibit failures of understanding, such as failures to understand conventions. The backwoodsman who climbs on to the stage to "save" Desdemona misses the point of the drama. The child who thinks that the Blessed Virgin in Titian's *Assumption* is a free-fall parachutist coming down rather than a saint miraculously going up also exhibits a failure to understand a convention.

However, I am claiming that we cannot criticize the emotional response of the backwoodsman or the child as "incorrect" or "spurious" or "coarse," and so as inadmissible or unacceptable. For we are not all conversant with, nor need to be conversant with, say, the conventions of drama in Western culture. Or should I say, the conventions of *watching* drama in *modern* Western culture? For it is arguable that Shakespeare, or his theater manager, while instructing his squad of hired bouncers to keep the lid on things, would have been pleased at such audience participation from the pit as was exhibited by our backwoodsman. Likewise, we are not all conversant with the dogmas of one branch of Christianity and with the pictorial conventions of sixteenth-century Italian altarpieces. The child responds emotionally as she is able. So did the middle-class English couple who had never studied art history. Titian should (and would?) have been pleased at their response, not sickened.

In clearer terms, I am first distinguishing the acceptable-unacceptable spectrum from the knowing-naive one. Then I am suggesting that to be ignorant of an artist's intention or the conventions of a period or art history or aesthetics or even a whole culture, is indeed a privation of sorts. But to say that is thereby to place someone on some point of the knowing-naive spectrum in regard to art, not on the unacceptable end of some other spectrum.

Indeed, a warning is in order. To conflate these two spectra is likely to lead to the temptation of conflating "a true connoisseur's response" to some work of art with "the acceptable response" to a work of art. It is likely to result in most responses falling short of that of "the true connoisseur" and meriting a guilty verdict implying some degree of unacceptability.

Let me put this another way. Even to be tempted to link "proper understanding of a painting" to "acceptable response to a painting" is to ride down a pot-holed road on a rickety bicycle. For once you take that road, someone can ask, "What sort of knowledge is the acceptable knowledge in this case?" Is it what the artist intended or the art historian indicates or the semioticist deconstructs or the aesthetician decrees or the connoisseur "sees" with his more sensitive eye? To legislate in favor of one or more sorts of background knowledge as de rigueur for an acceptable response, including an acceptable emotional response, is ipso facto to rule out other sorts of knowledge and other kinds of approaches to a work of art. To see with a naive eye or with the eye of *Les Fauves* can give you a perspective and so a platform for responding emotionally upon which a Bernard Berenson and a Peggy Guggenheim are probably incapable of stepping. More bluntly, what sort of argument *could* clinch the conclusion that it is *better* to be in Bernard Berenson's emotional shoes than in those of the English couple?

Of course, if my interpretation of James's position is correct, it seems he would say that it is better to be neither! For, strictly speaking, *neither* response is what he would call a "primary" or "classical" response or a "secondary" or "romantic" response. They are both what I have called "tertiary" responses.[11]

VIII. A Just-So Story

But let us return, one last time, to the response that the English couple did in fact make: "What a *deprecatory* expression her face wears! What self-*abnegation!* How *unworthy* she feels of the honor she is receiving." It seems plausible, given that the period in question was likely to be around 1850 to 1885, that the English couple would have been familiar with the current styles of Victorian painting. One could say that, insofar as they had an interest in painting, they had been "brought up" on those styles. At that time, for example, there would have been a number of exhibitions of Victorian genre paintings and such paintings would have been popular items in dealers' galleries in most cities in Britain. They would also be beginning to be purchased for the city galleries of at least some of the larger provincial cities. At any rate, let us suppose that the English couple were attracted to Victorian genre paintings. If that were so, they would naturally have been prompted to interpret the *Assumption* in a narrative way. For that would have been the informed way of interpreting paintings at that time. Sitting before the painting, it would have been quite natural for them to wonder what the Virgin Mary was thinking about or what the Virgin was feeling. Indeed it would have been more natural for them to think along those lines rather than to try to fix their gaze, in a Jamesean manner, upon the harmony of colors or, in the manner of a Berenson, to discern the wealth of conventions relating to sixteenth-century Italian religious art that were incorporated into the painting. Their comments to the effect that the Virgin has a deprecatory, humble, and uncertain expression on her face seem to me quite perceptive. More interestingly, such comments would have been considered perceptive by a sixteenth-century critic as well. For such a critic would have approved of comments upon the "narrative" of the painting just as much as the Victorians would have.

I have before me the catalogue of the 1990 Titian exhibition in the Palazzo Ducale in Venice (which travelled subsequently to the National Gallery in Washington in the same year). The editor of that catalogue, Susanna Biadene, wrote the notes for the entry on the Venice *Assumption*. In those notes she quotes a contemporary sixteenth-century critic, Lodovico Dolce: "Truly she [the Virgin] appears to ascend with humility written all over her face."[12] Just so!

NOTES

I should like to acknowledge, very warmly, the help I obtained from the most perceptive and informed comments on an earlier draft of this essay by the editors of this volume, Mette Hjort and Sue Laver, and by Catherine Marshall of the History of Art Department at Trinity College, Dublin. In addition, Dr. David Novitz of the University of Canterbury at Christchurch and Peter Lamarque of the University of Hull, have saved me from certain philosophical excesses. Those that remain are entirely my own doing.

1. *The Principles of Psychology* [1890] (1950), 452. For general background reading on James, I recommend very highly Gerald E. Myers, *William James: His Life and Thought* (1986). My own view of emotion, spelled out at length in *Emotion* (1980), is that they are much more than just feelings. In that book I put forward a robustly cognitive view of the emotions, namely that emotions involve beliefs, especially evaluative ones, and desires, as well as physiological changes and consequent feelings, expressions, actions and reactions. On the other hand, this difference, between my view and that of "the feeling theorist" will play little or no part in this essay.

2. *The Principles of Psychology* [1890] (1950), 468.

3. As regards James's views on aesthetics, and the influence of those views, Catherine Marshall pointed out to me, in correspondence, that William James had a connection with Mary Berenson and that, in consequence, there may have been a "possible influence on Bernard Berenson whose role in the development of Art History and theory this century is significant."

4. *The Principles of Psychology* [1890] (1950), 470. I myself have doubts that James's distinction between the two sorts of "approved" emotional responses in the aesthetic context, the "classical" and "romantic," can be made. For I have doubts that we can see in a "pure" or "classical" way. A month-old infant might be able to have such "pure" or "classic" gestalt-like perceptions, but then she could not have any deeper "romantic" ones, for the simple reason that, because an infant cannot have any concepts, she cannot have any conception of the mysterious or the gloomy or the haunting. An adult can clearly have the latter, but there are doubts that he or she can have the former. For adults, "seeing" always seems inevitably to be "seeing as." So there may be no one who can have both. But I'll leave the matter there, as this debate is not my concern in this essay.

5. *The Principles of Psychology* [1890] (1950), 471–72.

6. That is, the "Church of the Holy and Glorious Mary of the Friars Minor," which in turn means a church under the care of the Franciscans.

7. Though I do not want to argue the case here, I am taking it that moods are affective states on a continuum with emotions. They differ from emotions in a number of ways, such as, for example, in their tendency to have greater independence from any describable object or target. A very good discussion of the contrast between moods and emotions is to be found in Claire Armon-Jones 1991, esp. chap. 3.

As regards Titian's religious belief, my reference to his "fading religious belief" at the time he was painting the Venetian *Assumption* is entirely hypothetical. I simply do not know in what state his religious belief was.

8. Maurice de Sausmarez 1970.

9. Catherine Marshall was particularly informative about these matters.

10. His early, more or less pre-Impressionist, palette was also limited. However, in that period, it was dark rather than light, and dark in a way that was reminiscent of earlier, seventeenth-century, Dutch landscapes and interiors.

11. Famously, of course, in the Introduction to *The Story of Art* (1966), Ernest Gombrich wrote that "I do not think that there are any wrong reasons for liking a statue or a picture. Someone may like a landscape painting because it reminds him of home, or a portrait because it reminds him of a friend. There is nothing wrong with that. All of us, when we see a painting, are bound to be reminded of a hundred-and-one things which influence our likes and dislikes" (5). One aspect of this present essay is to endorse this liberalism of Gombrich in the particular context of a viewer's emotional response to paintings.

12. Susanna Biadene 1990, 170.

Evaluating Emotional Responses to Fiction

PAISLEY LIVINGSTON & ALFRED R. MELE

Philosophical discussion of emotional responses to fiction has been dominated by work on the paradox of fiction, which is often construed as asking whether and how we can experience genuine emotions in reaction to fiction. One may also ask more generally how we *ought* to respond to fictional works, a question that has to do both with what we should *do* when reacting to fiction and with what we should and should not *let happen* to us. Is it possible to delineate any principles regarding the rationality, and more generally, the appropriateness of emotional responses to fiction?

We begin with some background on the paradox of fiction and on emotion. In section II, we investigate the topic of norms relative to aesthetic and artistic responses to fictional works, beginning with Gregory Currie's thought-provoking remarks on the matter. In section III, we move on to a proposal of our own on this topic.

In the sphere of emotions, as elsewhere, ordinary linguistic practices often leave it open whether types or tokens are at issue. Our concern here is with emotion-tokens, particular instances of pity, fear, joy, and the like. Unless we indicate otherwise, our use of emotion-terms is intended to designate tokens. Even among pertinent tokens, there is a difference between a long-standing condition of a given type and particular episodic states of the same type that are partially derivative from, or "activations of," the prolonged condition. Contrast, for example, a man's long-standing fear of snakes with the episodic fear occasioned by his spotting a snake in his garden now. We will focus on episodic emotions.

I. Background

Peter Lamarque summarizes the paradox of fiction as follows:

> On the one hand, it is assumed that as reasonably sophisticated adults, we are not *taken in* by fiction; that is, we do not believe or come to believe, when knowingly watching a fictional performance, that the depicted sufferings or dangers involve any real suffering or danger. No one is in fact murdered in the performance of *Othello*, just as no one is in fact jealous or innocent. And we know that. On the other hand, we respond often enough with a range of emotions, including fear and pity, that seem to be explicable only on the assumption that we do after all believe there to be real suffering or real danger. For how can we feel fear when we do not believe there to be any danger? How can we feel pity when we do not believe there to be any suffering?[1]

Bijoy Boruah offers commentary on this passage:

> The apparent tension between the beliefs we hold about the nature of fiction and the beliefs needed to explain our being moved by fictional characters and situations can, presumably, leave us with two broadly conceived options. The first is that we somehow look for alternative ways of construing the phenomenon of an emotional response to fiction which would depict such an emotion as *not* involving a set of inconsistent beliefs as delineated above. The second option is to concede that it is not possible to give a veridical description of [such] emotions that does not include reference to a set of inconsistent beliefs, which means admitting that [such] emotions exist as a rationally inexplicable category of mental phenomena.[2]

Boruah's commentary highlights a puzzle about the *rationality* of emotional responses to fiction. On an alternative reading, the paradox of fiction is about the very *existence* of emotional responses toward fictional characters and situations. Robert Yanal, in an instructive paper, formulates the paradox as follows:

(1) We feel emotions towards the characters and situations of some works of fiction.

(2) We feel these emotions even though we believe that such characters and situations are fictional and not real.

(3) We feel emotions towards characters or situations only when we believe them to be real and not fictional.[3]

This collection of propositions obviously is internally inconsistent. If (1) and (3) are true, (2) is false. If (1) and (2) are true, (3) is false. To the extent that this collection of propositions is paradoxical, it is so because each of its members is plausible. And notice that no member of the set asserts anything about rationality.

We start with the puzzle about rationality. Suppose a friend watching a performance of *Othello* with us says that he pities Desdemona. We ask why and he replies, "Because she is suffering dreadfully." We then ask our friend whether Desdemona exists, and he says, "Of course not! She's a fictional character." Does our friend hold inconsistent beliefs? Is his belief that Desdemona is suffering inconsistent with his belief that Desdemona, being a fictional character, does not exist? Not necessarily. His belief that Desdemona is suffering might have been underdescribed. Perhaps what he believes, more fully, is that, *in the pertinent fiction*, Desdemona is suffering. And he may also believe that, *in the pertinent fiction*, Desdemona exists. These beliefs are consistent with the belief that Desdemona does not exist (though they are inconsistent, obviously, with the belief that she does not exist in the pertinent fiction).

Of course, we are still left with the question of how someone can rationally pity Desdemona, recognizing that she is a fictional character. Inconsistent beliefs might not be the only obstacle to rationally pitying her.

Before asking how a person can have a rational emotional response to a fictional situation or character, it will prove salutary to inquire about the conditions under which emotional responses to real-world, nonfictional situations are rational. This is a difficult issue. One way to approach it is to begin by defending a particular analysis of emotion. However, that task would require an essay of its own. Fortunately, for our purposes, there is no need to embroil ourselves in the lively and important debate over what, exactly, emotions are.[4] The position we defend in this paper is compatible with a range of competing analyses of emotion.

Tests for the rationality or irrationality of an emotion can be conducted from various perspectives. A brief look at belief will prove useful in this connection. When people say that a belief is warranted and rationally held, they typically have in mind what may be termed *evidential warrant*. On a popular view, belief aims at truth, and evidence is the best guide. However, even false and evidentially unwarranted beliefs may have *practical* advantages. This goes part of the way toward explaining occurrences of self-deception. One's belief that one's spouse is faithful, or that one's troubled child is just experiencing growing pains, may enable one to function normally, even if the belief flies in the face of the evidence. It seems possible, at least in principle, that a belief that it is best *on the whole* — and most rational — for a person to hold sometimes lacks sufficient evidential warrant.[5]

When people speak of a warranted *emotion*, they typically have in mind an emotion that is an appropriate response to the evoking stimuli.[6] Crudely put, this appropriateness is a function of normal standards relating emotion-responses to stimuli. Fear may be an appropriate response in this sense to certain threats, but not to others. When an armed thug is demanding one's money, fear normally is appropriate; when a small child threatens to tickle one's toes, fear would typically be a bizarre response. However, in addition to having the virtue of appropriateness, emotions sometimes have *prudential* value. Our fear of the thug may motivate us to take life-preserving measures, for example. Furthermore, people attribute *moral* value to many emotions. It is morally proper to feel sympathetic in some circumstances and outraged in others, or so it is often said.[7] Often, considerations of appropriateness, prudential value, and morality pull in the same direction. But things are not always so neat. Although anger and resentment may be appropriate responses to one's spouse's extramarital fling, they may also be imprudent ones. The man who hopes to save his marriage may find that his hostile feelings toward his wife make this impossible. Are anger and resentment *rational* responses in that case, however appropriate they may be?

Sometimes attributions of rationality or irrationality to a person are sensitive to hypotheses about the control that the person had over the relevant episode. If a woman fears a harmless garden snake because of a posthypnotic sugges-tion, does she irrationally or simply nonrationally fear the snake? If any charge of irrationality, by its very nature, carries criticism of the person at whom the charge is leveled, it would be difficult to sustain the claim that the woman irrationally fears the snake. How can she be blamed for fearing it, given the etiology of her fear? Then again, "phobia" is standardly defined as "an irratio-nal fear," even though some phobic persons may be in no way responsible for their phobias (including the generation and the retention of the phobia).[8]

Whatever position one favors on this issue, it is clear that people have some control over what they feel and over the intensity of their emotions.[9] Movie-goers sometimes stem a discomforting flow of sympathy for a character in a film by reminding themselves that he is only a fictional being.[10] The woman who regards her anger at her child as destructive may dissolve or attenuate it by forcing herself to focus her attention on a cherished moment with the child. The timid employee who believes that he can muster the courage to demand a raise only if he becomes angry at his boss may deliberately make himself angry by vividly representing the injustices that he has suffered at the office.[11] These are instances of what we term *internal* control.

Many emotions are subject to *external* control as well—control through the individual's overt behavior. Jane knows that if, for some reason, she wants to be angry, a phone call to her mother will turn the trick. John defeats mild depression by calling his sister. Notice that in each of our illustrations of inter-nal and external control, *means* are taken to alter one's emotional condition. In the case of feelings, as in the case of beliefs, control should not be confused with *direct* control, or the capacity to *x at will.*

We return to the issue of the rationality of emotional responses to fiction in section II. Turning now to the puzzle about the *existence* of emotions toward fictional characters and situations, we believe that the weakest member of the inconsistent set is (3): "We feel emotions towards characters or situations only when we believe them to be real and not fictional." The first and second members of the set give voice to what seems to be a common experience: the experience of one's own emotional response toward a character or situ-ation that one knows to be "fictional and not real." This seeming experience speaks directly against (3). And (3), of course, can be supported only on theo-retical grounds: a proponent of (3) must appeal to a supporting theory of emo-tions. Why shouldn't the apparently common experience simply be viewed as providing a counterexample to any theory of the emotions that includes or entails (3)?

Kendall Walton writes: "It is not implausible that pity involves a belief (or judgment, or attitude) that what one pities actually suffers misfortune, and admiration a belief that the admired object is admirable, but the normal appreciator does not think it is actually the case that Willy [Loman] suffers or that Superman is admirable."[12] However, someone viewing *Death of a Salesman* may well believe that, in that fiction, Willy Loman suffers misfortune. Why should one need a different belief than this one to pity Willy? If pity involves a belief that the object of one's pity actually suffers misfortune, why shouldn't the belief required in some cases simply be the belief that *in the pertinent fiction*, so-and-so actually suffers misfortune? There is even work for the word "actually" to do here. For in some fictions, characters who appear to suffer misfortune do not actually do so. In Ingmar Bergman's *Smiles of a Summer Night*, it seems for a moment that Fredrik Egerman has killed himself while playing Russian roulette, but it turns out that unbeknownst to him and to most of the other characters, the gun was loaded with blanks. So Fredrik only apparently suffers a terrible misfortune, while Desdemona and Willy Loman actually do—in their respective fictions. Discerning viewers appreciate the difference: They believe that Fredrik does not actually suffer a great misfortune in the relevant fiction and that Desdemona and Willy Loman do suffer in *Othello* and *Death of a Salesman*.

Obviously, it has not been our aim in this section to solve theoretical problems about the nature of emotion or about the assessment of particular emotions as rational or irrational. Rather, we have tried to convey a sense of a portion of the difficult theoretical terrain on which the paradox of fiction lies. Against this background, we pursue our main concern here: understanding the conditions under which an emotional response toward a fictional character or situation is artistically justified. Obviously, if there were no emotional responses to such things (not even "quasi-emotional" responses, in Walton's sense), our project would be pointless. But we are confident that any theory of the emotions that entails that there are no emotional responses of this kind will prove to be unacceptable.

II. Currie and the Sophisticated Reader

John is reading a novel in bed late one night. His mirth is appropriate to the work's comic story, inappropriate because his laughter keeps his wife awake, yet valuable to him because it chases away some morbid thoughts. Reading the novel makes John feel jealous, though, because an old rival of his wrote it and he is envious of the man's talent and success. But since John owns the publishing house and the novel is a best-seller, he is also pleased with the book for making big profits. It is clear, then, that emotional reactions to a fiction can be evaluated from a number of strikingly different perspectives. Whether a given emotion is appropriate or warranted depends on the specific interests or values in question.

One kind of appropriateness corresponds to our interest in responding to works of art qua works of art, that is, in ways that are artistically or aesthetically relevant to the work at hand. Providing analyses of artistic and aesthetic relevance is beyond the scope of this essay, but we can easily identify some paradigm cases of responses that are artistically or aesthetically relevant, as well as of some that are neither.[13] John's financial interest in the novel is not a specifically artistic or aesthetic interest, but his mirthful experience of the work's comic structures is. In thinking about the author's skillful and innovative application of certain generic patterns, John is attuned to artistically relevant features of the work. An essential element in the paradigmatic cases of an aesthetically relevant response is the contemplation of the work's stylistic features, and it is often thought that this experience must be of intrinsic value to the agent if it is to be an aesthetic experience.[14] A particular response that is highly appropriate to a work in an aesthetic or artistic sense could be useless or even harmful in other respects, just as it is possible for unsophisticated reactions to junk fiction to have worthwhile consequences. In what follows we focus on the kind of appropriateness corresponding to a specifically literary type of expertise, the ability to recognize and respond to a work's artistically and aesthetically relevant features. This expertise comes in degrees. In many cases, there is no single best performance with regard to a particular task. But there are clear-cut cases of incompetence, just as there are often good reasons for holding one reading better than another.

We begin with Gregory Currie's discussion of the matter, for much can be learned from his brief but far-reaching remarks.[15] Having proposed a solution to the paradox of fiction, Currie adds that "There are other questions one can ask about our responses to fiction" (213), and then explores some issues pertaining to the appropriateness of emotional reactions to fiction. Evoking the possibility of comic treatments of events that are normally the object of a serious attitude, Currie asserts that it is not possible to derive a standard of appropriateness of response uniquely from an examination of the work's fictional events. Even if we believe that death and suffering are serious matters, we must recognize that they can be portrayed in fiction as fit occasions for laughter. Currie proposes, then, to analyze an emotion's appropriateness to a work in terms of what he calls *congruence*, a relation between the reader's (or viewer's) response and the emotion(s) *expressed in the work*. A work is expressive of an emotion, Currie states, "just in case it provides evidence that the fictional author experienced that emotion" (214).

To grasp this idea, we must understand that according to Currie, when reading a work of fiction, we make believe that someone tells the story as known fact. This someone is not the narrator, but a personage whose attitudes and beliefs we imagine, basing our make-believe both on the textual evidence and on facts about the real author's context. A work is expressive of an emotion when there is good evidence that the fictional author experienced the emotion. The sensitive reader of a work, then, is capable of understanding which emotions are expressed by the work and experienced by the work's fictional (or implied) author. Such a reader is said to be capable of experiencing an emotion of the same type as the fictional author's emotion, the only difference being that the reader's emotion is based on make-believe (and make-desire):

The implied author's state and the reader's state are not the same state; they are congruent in that they differ only by the substitution of make-belief for belief and make-desire for desire. If they differ more radically—if, for example, the implied author's state is one of cynical amusement whereas the reader's state is one of (quasi-) fear for the character concerned—then the reader's response is incongruent. (215)

Responding as a sensitive reader, however, does not suffice to make one's emotional reactions *sophisticated*. Sophisticated readers must be both sensitive and refined. The sensitive reader knows which emotions are congruent, but the *refined* reader "responds congruently only to works that have a certain kind of merit" (214). The refined reader may laugh rather than weep at the heroine's suffering because the work is too hackneyed to be taken seriously. Sophisticated readers know which works are worthy of response, and they know which responses are congruent to those works.

Although Currie does not explicitly argue for the following thesis, his remarks do bring it to mind: (1) a response is sophisticated—and more generally, aesthetically or artistically justified—just in case it is both sensitive (i.e., congruent) and refined (i.e., arising in reaction to a work correctly recognized as having sufficient merit). This thesis is, of course, the conjunction of two weaker ones: (2) if a response is both sensitive and refined, it is sophisticated; and (3) if a response is sophisticated, it is both sensitive and refined. Are any of these theses right? We think not, but some of Currie's insights are carried forward in the proposal advanced in the final section.

Thesis (3) looks problematic. Consider the case of Oswaldo, a student of literature who rightly thinks that Theodore Dreiser's *The Financier* is on the whole a pretty bad novel, just as the *Trilogy of Desire* of which it is a part is an artistic disaster. Oswaldo is attuned to the many flaws of Dreiser's inconsistent and often coarse style; he thinks Dreiser's imagination is rather limited; he finds the novel's portrait of the "financier-artist" uninsightful, inconsistent, and badly marred by the writer's tendency to linger over his character's boring romantic problems. Even so, Oswaldo finds one scene in the story quite moving. Must this be an error of artistic or aesthetic appreciation on Oswaldo's part? What is more, Oswaldo responds emotionally, sometimes in ways that are not congruent, to aspects of the fiction that he finds badly flawed.

It would seem, then, that some sophisticated and congruent responses are not reactions to works of merit. And some responses are sophisticated but neither congruent nor refined in Currie's sense. Part of the reader's literary expertise is an ability to respond appropriately to flawed and inferior literary works, and such responses are not always a matter of refraining from any form of congruent emotional engagement in the fiction. An adequate model of the reader's competence would account for diverse appropriate reactions to artistically inferior aspects of works.

Thesis (2) is false if there is a case in which a response is sensitive and refined, but unsophisticated. Consider the following example. Given Currie's account of congruence, it is uncontroversial that Charles Baudelaire's "A Celle qui est trop gaie" expresses what Erich Auerbach called the "destructive frenzy" and "gruesome hopelessness" of a frustrated misogynist.[16] The speaker (the fictional author, if you like) is a man whose passion for the woman to whom he addresses the poem is a terrible mixture of lust, envy, and hatred, culminating in a sadistic desire to "punish her joyous flesh":

> I would like to [. . .] bruise your pardoned breasts,
> and cleave into your astounded side
> a wide, deep wound,
> And with vertiginous sweetness
> through those more vivid and beautiful new lips,
> infuse my poison into you, my sister![17]

One looks in vain in this poem for evidence of any authorial attitudes of distance or disapproval.

It is also uncontroversial that expert readers such as Auerbach recognize the remarkable artistry of this poem, which expresses these morbid and aggressive feelings in an inventive and vivid way.[18] Yet are we to hold as well that the correct response to this poem is to experience a make-believe and make-desire analog of the ugly feelings that it expresses? We think not. The competent reader must in some sense be able to understand these terrible sentiments, and must also appreciate Baudelaire's skill at expressing them, but assuming that *comprendre, ce n'est pas tout pardonner*, disgust and horror are wholly appropriate reactions to the poet's emotions, and complicity would be revolting.[19]

One might reply that having the congruent emotion in response to the poem is *aesthetically* or *artistically* sophisticated independently of moral considerations. Yet it seems wrong to hold that the moral content of fiction is irrelevant to an appreciation of the art of literature. Attempts to define the specificity of the artistic and aesthetic responses to works of fiction along purely formalist lines have been notoriously problematic, and any defense of (2) along these lines will depend upon the development of a successful doctrine of this ilk.[20] Although we cannot prove that no sound doctrine of this sort can be developed, we think the burden of proof lies on the shoulders of those who hope to do so. They must explain why an adequate contemplation of a fictional work's features must never include a careful thinking through of the moral implications of the events and attitudes the writer has proposed for our make-believe. If, on the contrary, moral and political ideas are an intrinsic part of many literary works of art, their assessment would seem directly relevant to an evaluation of the works' overall merits.

One might try to protect thesis (2) by suggesting that the "certain kind of merit" that refined readers require of a work can include a moral component. If Baudelaire's poem lacks this sort of merit, then refined readers should not respond congruently. But could there not be a work which, although *globally* acceptable with regard to its artistic merit, *locally* expresses emotions that are unacceptable to the refined reader? Many examples could be proposed. Virginia Woolf's otherwise wonderful novel, *The Waves*, arguably contains such a passage. Bernard, who in many ways functions as the novelist's *porte-parole*, praises Perceval's soldiering in India, and in so doing conveys a British colonial-

ent to those fictional truths, is an unreliable narrator, behind whom stands the ever-reliable fictional author. But how, within such a framework, does one accommodate intuitions about failed expressive intentions?

Suppose that the first half of a story very obviously encourages a comic response by describing a variety of outlandish and transgressive events having no harmful consequences for the inane and unimportant creatures who populate the fiction. Suppose as well that at a certain point in the text, gruesome details about the consequences of one comic mishap are suddenly presented. But immediately after this unsettling moment, the farcical and harmless antics continue as before. It is likely that in some such cases, the reader should detect an unintended shift in tone or loss of control on the part of the author, who, while intending to promote a comic attitude throughout the work, mistakenly included gruesome details that warrant a different kind of response. "I am meant to keep on laughing here," the reader thinks, "but the joke has been carried too far and this is not really funny." But we cannot say that the *fictional* author erred, and given the textual evidence, we must attribute to the fictional author both the comic and serious attitudes that we found congruent to the fictional events. So it is clearly our grasp of the fictional events that determines our sense of congruence, and the fictional author is just a name for an imaginary repository where we imaginatively "locate" the attitudes we have decided are congruent to the fictional events. It is unclear, however, what is gained by thinking in terms of such a repository. If the reader is to understand the sudden shift in tone as a flaw in the work resulting from a loss of artistic control, she must think in terms of the real author's attitudes and activities. The real author, one can of course add, failed to create the kind of fictional author he wanted to create; but is it not simpler to say that the real author failed to realize his intentions in the text? We suggest, then, that readers need not and should not make assessments about a work's expressive features by means of speculations about a fictional author's attitudes. Instead, they should assess the textual evidence directly, making inferences about the real author's expressive aims.

Currie's idea that part of a reader's aesthetic competence is a matter of being sensitive to the work is, we think, correct. But if our arguments are sound, the autonomy of fictional events thesis is false, and the concept of sensitivity we require is not equivalent to emotional congruence vis-à-vis the fictional author's emotions. We require a better understanding of sensitivity, then, just as we need a principle to replace Currie's concept of refinement, for we agree with him that responses that are sensitive to the work are not always sophisticated or justified. We turn now to the articulation of such an account.

III. Artistically or Aesthetically Justified Emotions, Congruent and Contrary

Part of what renders the question of the justification of emotional responses to works of fiction so difficult to answer is that the issue embraces a number of other, notoriously difficult, questions, each of which requires a solution if the larger problem is to be solved. Two questions in particular may be isolated:

Q1. Given a work of fiction, what determines what is true in that fiction (i.e., what happens in the story)?

Q2. How do pragmatic factors influence the assessment of emotional responses to nonfictional and fictional works?

In what follows, we propose some broad solutions to these problems so as to be in a position to offer an analysis of artistically or aesthetically justified emotion.

Q1. Given a Work of Fiction, What Determines Fictional Truth?

David Lewis has proposed that statements about what is true in a fiction, such as "Sherlock Holmes met Gladstone," should be analyzed as abbreviations of longer sentences beginning with an operator, "In the fiction f . . ."[24] A prefixed sentence to the effect that in a particular fiction, Sherlock Holmes met with Gladstone does not entail the non-prefixed sentence that the actual Gladstone met Holmes, but it does entail a prefixed sentence to that effect. From mixtures of prefixed and unprefixed sentences nothing follows.

Lewis mentions a provisional analysis in which propositions true in a given fiction are all and only those explicitly stated in the text in question, plus any other propositions entailed by them. Propositions explicitly stated in a text are those yielded when the text is interpreted standardly in the writer's language. Such an approach is inadequate, Lewis notes, because we require additional premises if we are to reach adequate conclusions about what is the case in a fictional story. For example, our background knowledge of basic facts about time, space, and human anatomy are relevant to the Sherlock Holmes stories. With the need for background propositions in view, Lewis proposes two different analyses of truth in fiction, both of which give readers a broader base for making inferences about the content of a story. In both cases, statements about truth in fiction are treated as counterfactuals. The prefixed, fictional premises are taken as suppositions contrary to fact, and in reasoning about them, we are supposed to rely on unprefixed premises as well, departing from actuality only as far as we must to reach some possible world or worlds where the antecedent and consequent of the counterfactual supposition are true.

The first analysis is a matter of assuming that what happens in fictional stories is as close as possible to what we know the real world to be. The second analysis takes into account the fact that the implicit premises required for reasoning competently about fictions do not all derive from the competent reader's storehouse of knowledge—or even beliefs—about what is the case in the actual world. Lewis's second proposal, then, is that truth in fiction be taken as the joint product of the text's content and a background of beliefs overtly held in the community in which the fiction originates. So if a supernatural belief figures in the network of reciprocally held consensual beliefs in the author's community, a reader who does not share that belief should nonetheless adopt it as a premise in reasoning about what goes on in a fiction in which that belief is operative or in force.

Lewis does not argue for the superiority of either of the two principles he discusses. As Currie and others have shown, neither principle on its own underwrites a competent manner of determining the content of a fiction, because each warrants too many inappropriate inferences and fails to yield other, crucial ones.[25] An alternative is the idea that the appropriate choice of background beliefs is underwritten by a complex intentionalist principle. Competent readers and spectators do not make inferences about the implicit truths in a story by importing all of their beliefs about the real world or by activating what they take to be the belief systems of bygone or alien communities. Instead, they do so by paying attention to the text's features and by reasoning about the aims and attitudes of the actual author. Storytelling is not always a matter of the author sincerely expressing his or her convictions and feelings, so many of an author's actual emotions and beliefs do not determine story content and thus are not appropriate premises for inferences about fictional truth. Even so, in writing a story or making a film, an author has attitudes about the story he or she aims to tell, as well as attitudes concerning how readers or viewers should make sense of the text. An author may be fairly open-minded or even confused about what happens in the story, but to invent and tell a story at all, one must make some hard and fast decisions about what is and is not the case in the story, including decisions about basic premises—sometimes moral premises— that may remain unstated in the text. And authors usually have settled on at least some broad outlines with regard to the kinds of emotions they want to produce in a target audience; for example, they usually have taken a stance with regard to the broad distinction between comic and serious attitudes. So what we are after are not the attitudes of a fictional author who tells a story as known fact and feels certain emotions about those facts; rather, we are interested in what the actual author decided was to be the case in the story he or she was inventing and trying to communicate, as well as the emotions that author meant to arouse in a target audience, provided, of course, the ensuing text is in fact compatible with such intentions.

Very generally, then, we propose the following breakdown with regard to story content or fictional truth. Some fictional truths are explicit in the text (provided that the text is interpreted standardly in the language in which the author wrote it). Other fictional truths are not explicit in the text. Some of these are entailed by propositions representing truths explicit in the text. Others are based on the author's effective, communicative storytelling intentions. With regard to the emotions that are congruent to the work, some are based on truths explicit in the text, but most can only be determined by reference to the author's implicit aims.

What about contradictory fictional truths? Authors can successfully communicate a story in which some proposition and its negation are both true. Authors also inadvertently tell stories in which there are inconsistencies. Although readers speak of an incoherent story in the latter cases, they tend to think of them as mistakes in the work and they strive to eliminate the story's inconsistencies. It is not true, readers think, that in the fiction the donkey was and was not present at the inn. But intentional inconsistencies have a different status. In such cases, one must acknowledge that the storyteller wants the story to contain an inconsistency. It does not follow that the author intends for every other arbitrarily chosen proposition to follow from an intended inconsistency, so readers should not hold all such consequences to be fictionally true.[26]

Here, then, are some central ingredients of an analysis of fictional truth according to the form of intentionalism we find attractive[27]:

1. If a proposition, p, is explicit in a text, T, or is entailed by a proposition or propositions explicit in T, p is fictionally true in the work's story.
2. If a proposition, p, is consistent with all propositions satisfying (1)'s antecedent, and either
2a. the work's author had a reasonable and effective communicative intention that p be imagined and accepted for the purposes of the fiction by members of the work's audience (i.e., the author had the intention and had good and sufficient reason to believe that the proposition would be imagined and accepted for the purposes of the fiction, on the basis of available evidence, by members of the target audience), or
2b. p is entailed by other propositions so intended, then p is fictionally true in the work's story.
3. Unintended contradictions are not fictionally true in the work's story, and intended ones are fictionally true in the story if and only if they satisfy (1)'s antecedent. Warranted contradictions in a fictional work do not entail all other propositions. Obviously, developing a full-blown analysis of fictional truth would require a separate paper.

Q2. How Do Pragmatic Factors Influence the Assessment of Emotional Responses to Works of Nonfiction and Fiction?

We agree with Currie and others that what makes a work fiction is not its semantic or other properties, but the kind of (illocutionary) action that produces it. Very roughly, an utterance (in a broad, Gricean sense) is fiction just in case the agent or agents who produce it communicatively intended for some target audience to adopt an attitude of imagination or make-believe with regard to (relevant features of) the contents of the utterance.[28] Given this pragmatic approach to the fiction/nonfiction distinction, we want to draw a schematic contrast between two different kinds of situations: (a) situations in which someone describes some events, asserting that the description is true (i.e., that the events happened as described); and (b) situations in which someone describes some events, proposing that we imagine or make believe that the events have happened.

Pragmatic factors affecting our response to a situation of type (a) include the speaker's sincerity, reliability, intent, and motives, as well as the appropriateness (e.g., propriety) of making the assertion in the context. In a situation of type (b), the relevant factors are not all the same: sincerity and reliability do not have the same significance, but the fiction-maker's intent and motives are still relevant. In artistic contexts, factors related to the speaker's skill and the aesthetic or artistic value of the text, come to the fore. Factors having to do with propriety apply, but may operate differently because there are contexts where it is appropriate to assert something, but not to propose that it be "imagined," and vice versa.

Expert readers are attuned to the pragmatic dimensions of storytelling. Sometimes it is crucial to know that the author intended members of one target audience to recognize a work as fiction, but that this act of fiction-making was linked to the goal of getting a second target audience to understand the work as referring to actual agents and events. Such intentions can make a big difference to the kind of response that is warranted. Suppose, for example, that readers learn that the author's intent was to cause someone harm by revealing damaging information via the fiction. In such a case, it could be wrong to respond congruently. Here we endorse Felicia Ackermann's perceptive analysis of ways in which basing fictions on real persons can be morally wrong; we would also extend this analysis to cases where the harmful intent is directed at groups or types of persons, and not particular individuals.[29] Judgments of strict liability may even be appropriate in some cases, for it could be true that the author's intentions were not malicious, but that the author should have foreseen the harmful consequences of a work. For shorthand, we refer to an assessment of all of these kinds of factors below as *the pragmatic criterion*.

We turn now to an analysis of emotional congruence. Fictional truth, we contend, is the key to emotional congruence. Our basic claim is that some emotion, *e*, is a congruent response to some feature of a work just in case either (1) *e* is warranted by the work's fictional truths, or (2) *e* is intended by the author to be the appropriate response of the target audience, provided that the author's intentions are compatible with the textual evidence. We recognize that mixed feelings can be congruent to some aspect of a work, but this does not entail the appropriateness of any and every emotional response to the same work or to other aspects of the same work.

The basic idea behind this claim is very simple: if people are capable of responding appropriately to events in the world, the same capacity allows them to respond appropriately to events in fiction, provided that they recognize what is fictionally true in a work. If anger is the appropriate response to a certain kind of unjustified aggression in actuality, anger (though not necessarily of the same intensity) is also the congruent response to such events in fiction.[30] But one may ask whether there is not a gap between emotional appropriateness in actuality and emotional congruence to fiction. Suppose, for example, that it is true in the fiction that the members of each of two competing teams justifiably hope to win a fair contest. When the match is over, the winners are understandably joyful, while the losers rightly feel disappointment and some measure of sorrow. But what should *we*, the readers, feel? It could seem that we cannot determine congruence in the absence of some indication concerning which agent's (or agents') situation is to provide the readers' affective focus. Is the choice of such a focus as arbitrary as the idle television viewer's decision to root for an arbitrarily chosen team when watching a basketball game about which he is otherwise indifferent?

Most often, fictional truths explicitly presented in the text provide the indications required for a nonarbitrary choice of congruence. For example, viewers of Sergei Eisenstein's *Alexander Nevsky* know that it is true in the fiction that the German knights are machinelike invaders who viciously burn babies, while the Russians are good, fun-loving folk justifiably driven into a righteous war of self-defense. The audience's knowledge of the author's intentions and pragmatic circumstances are also relevant and provide additional guidance. When the members of the target audience are themselves Russians who also know that the director is a comrade who wants the work to bolster their sense of opposition to a common enemy, congruence is not hard to establish. In works lacking a clear protagonist/antagonist distinction, congruence may not be so simple and straightforward, and it may be appropriate for the reader to feel the opposing emotions in alternation, or perhaps a third emotion arising from attention to the conflict between the contrasting perspectives. Sometimes we are not meant to take sides, but to experience sorrow over the plight of armies fighting to the death over plots too small to bury them in.

Emotional congruence to a work, we have claimed, is contingent upon fictional truth. Yet we agree with Currie that congruence does not suffice to make an emotional response an artistically justified one, because other features of the work, including facts about context, are also relevant. Currie focuses on artistic merit, and we return to this matter below. Moral factors, we claimed above, are also directly relevant to an artistic appreciation of a work of fiction. This is the case because people can skillfully devise fictions that we have good reason to deem immoral, in which case we should not want, for a variety of reasons, to be the kind of people who experience the congruent emotions. Although the objectionable emotions are congruent to the fiction, they are *not* congruent to the kind of life we value and want to lead.

For example, when we read the Brothers Grimm fairy tale, "The Jew Among Thorns," we know that it is true *in the fiction* that the Jew is a rogue and a thief whose suffering is meant to be a source of comic delight and Schadenfreude.[31] These emotions are not only congruent, but central, to the work, provided that we recognize the fictional events as described and interpret them in terms of the authors' anti-Semitic attitudes. Any competent reader of the story, we contend, must know this, but we see no good reason why the reader's literary expertise would entail any experience of such evil and prejudicial feelings, which flagrantly contradict the reader's values and self-conception.[32]

Congruent emotions, we claim, are artistically justified only when they are also morally acceptable. Readers should filter congruent emotions in terms of a morality criterion, the application of which is a matter of overruling objectionable moral premises while respecting as much of the textual evidence about fictional events as possible. Congruence, then, is determined by the story as told by the author, while refinement is in part a matter of responding to the story within one's own justified moral framework.[33] In the case of "The Jew

Among Thorns," we accept the text's explicit indication that the Jew sincerely confesses to theft; but the death sentence passed on him by the judge is no longer a matter of joy and relief. Nor is the fiddler's initial attack on the Jew retroactively justified by the confession, but is instead recognized as an unjustified and prejudicial act of brutality. Applying this moral criterion is often a matter of refusing to work with intended authorial premises that one recognizes but is loath to accept.

Does satisfaction of the morality and pragmatic criteria suffice to make all surviving congruent responses sophisticated ones? We agree with Currie that it is an aesthetic error to weep over the goings-on in sentimental trash, just as it is a mistake to howl in delight at the supposed ironies in what is in fact a botched melodrama. A difficult question concerns where we should set the bar with regard to this kind of merit. Does competence or expertise require us to respond congruently only to works of very great originality and skill? A severe evaluative stance may have the advantage of promoting sharp attention to works' artistic structures, as opposed to the emotional pleasures they may occasion. Yet it remains to be shown that such austerity is the only means, or even a good means, to that end, so we are inclined to place the bar lower. If the aspect of a work to which one responds is of at least moderate artistic quality, one is justified in responding congruently, other things being equal. This criterion of artistic quality is indexed only to the facet of the work to which one is responding, and not to a global evaluation of the work's artistic merit. If the aspect of the work is unacceptably bad, the congruent response is not justified, even if it is morally acceptable.

When a congruent response is not justified, some *contrary* response may be. With regard to the nature of justified contrary responses, we note that there is probably no one-to-one function mapping works' defects onto appropriate responses. We do, however, believe it possible to make a broad distinction between two varieties of contrary emotional response. When the relevant feature of the work fails to satisfy either the pragmatic or morality criteria, some proportionate feeling of moral disapproval (outrage, shock, anger, irritation) is warranted. Other kinds of artistic flaws warrant any item from a collection of responses that includes boredom, laughter, and whatever feelings accompany the winces and groans people manifest in response to fictional howlers. There are also mixed cases. When one is angry at the author for having produced and sold an inferior work, one's disapproval is partly moral. And when one finds the moral flaws in a work tedious and ugly, one's reaction is in part a sentiment of artistic disapproval.

In light of our previous comments, we are ready to present the broad outlines of an analysis. Artistically justified responses to aspects of works of fiction are either congruent or contrary. Congruent responses are those based on fictional truths. Contrary responses are reactions to what one views as a work's artistic or moral defects. Congruent responses are appropriate only when the feature of the work to which they are reactions satisfies the morality, pragmatic, and artistic criteria. Gathering these schematic factors up, we have the following analysis. An emotional response to a feature of a work is artistically justified if and only if: either (1) it is congruent and proportionate to the feature of the work to which it is a response (where congruence is a matter of justification by fictional truth); and it is a response to a feature of the work that satisfies the morality, pragmatic, and artistic criteria; or (2) either the emotion (i) is a response to a feature of the work that fails to satisfy either the morality or pragmatic criteria, and the response is a proportionate instance of moral disapproval; or (ii) it is a response to a feature of the work that fails to satisfy the artistic criterion, and is a proportionate instance of artistic disapproval.

NOTES

Parts of section I derive from Mele, *Autonomous Agents* (1995). Thanks to Stephen Davies, Jerrold Levinson, David Novitz, Greg Currie, and Robert Stecker for comments on a draft of this paper.

1. Peter Lamarque 1981, 291.

2. Bijoy H. Boruah 1988, 28–29. By "rationally inexplicable," Boruah means not explicable in a way that treats the emotion as a rational response. Incidentally, our bracketed "such" replaces the word "fiction." We take Boruah's expression "fictional emotion" to be misleading in this context.

3. Robert J. Yanal 1994, 54–55.

4. For discussion of this issue, see, for example, Ronald de Sousa 1987; Allan Gibbard 1990; Robert M. Gordon 1987; Patricia S. Greenspan 1988; and Justin Oakley 1992.

5. See Alfred R. Mele 1995, chap. 5.

6. See, for example, Greenspan 1988 and de Sousa 1987. For detailed discussion of the appropriateness of emotions, see Greenspan 1980. A precise, successful account of the appropriateness and inappropriateness of emotions will depend on what, exactly, emotions are. The more relevant dimensions an emotion has, the more ways it can be appropriate and inappropriate. Intensity is a case in point. If emotions come in varying degrees of intensity, then an emotion's appropriateness may involve its having a degree of intensity proportionate to its object. An emotion could be appropriate in kind, but disproportionate in intensity, and hence inappropriate.

7. For a recent defense of the justifiability of moral assessments of individuals for their emotions, see Oakley 1992, chap. 5. In chapter 4, Oakley offers telling objections to various arguments designed to show that people cannot be morally responsible for their emotions.

8. Incidentally, many phobic people realize both that certain of their episodic fears are inappropriate responses to the evoking stimuli and that they would be better off without them. See Aaron T. Beck 1976, 158–65, and Isaac M. Marks 1969, 3. Often, phobic individuals regard some of their own fears as irrational. Some, wanting not to be saddled with fears that they deem irrational, seek treatment. Such treatment, of course, is not always successful.

9. A growing body of empirical work supports this claim. For useful, documented discussion of the literature, see Nico H. Frijda 1986, chap. 8, and Eric Klinger 1993. Also, see Gordon 1987, chap. 6.

10. Asher Koriat, et al. 1972, especially 613, 617.

11. B. F. Skinner 1953, 236; Dianne Tice and Roy Baumeister 1993.

12. Kendall L. Walton 1990, 203.

13. For some background on this topic, see David Novitz 1990; Carolyn Korsmeyer 1977; and Noël Carroll 1986. An aesthetician who makes a sophisticated and convincing use of the distinction between artistic and aesthetic attributes is Jerrold Levinson. See his 1990b, especially 182–84.

14. For background on intrinsic value, see Mele 1995, chap. 5. To develop the line of thought evoked, one may add that an aesthetic experience of a work of art need not involve a wholly positive assessment of that work. But if we find the work so awful that our experience of it has no intrinsic value, our experience of the work is not an aesthetic one. Thanks to Stephen Davies for his query on this topic.

15. Gregory Currie 1990. Page numbers given in the text refer to this edition.

16. Erich Auerbach 1959.

17. This is Paisley Livingston's literal translation. In the original, the quoted lines read: "Ainsi je voudrais . . . meurtrir ton sein pardonné \Et faire à ton flanc étonné \Une blessure large et creuse, \Et, vertigineuse douceur! \A travers ces lèvres nouvelles, \Plus éclatantes et plus belles, \T'infuser mon venin, ma soeur!" Charles Baudelaire, 1924, 171–72.

18. For more detailed remarks on the poem's formal artistry, see Graham Chesters 1988, 36, 48, 60.

19. In his helpful comments on a draft of this paper, Jerrold Levinson suggests that a full appreciation of the poem requires that the reader first experience the objectionable target feelings before moving on, as a result of moral reflection, to an attitude of retrenchment or disgust. Yet, like Hume (1757, 246), we doubt that proper appreciation requires that the necessary recognition of the poem's target feelings be accompanied by any emotional complicity. Why should one have to give rein to objectionable and ugly feelings in order to understand and appreciate a work of fiction? One's inability or refusal to experience such feelings does not make one incapable of *recognizing* the work's artistic qualities, and can indeed serve to facilitate an awareness of both its merits and shortcomings.

20. Given a traditional view of the aesthetic, many *artistically* relevant features of a work of art are not *aesthetic* features of the work, and a work's moral merit would not be relevant to an aesthetic evaluation. We do not endorse such a narrow conception of the aesthetic, but cannot pursue this argument here. What we do claim is that the larger category of *artistic* relevance includes the moral relevance of some of a work's features.

21. Virginia Woolf [1931] 1990, 88–89.

22. For incisive surveys of the arguments, see Gérard Genette 1988; Robert Stecker 1987; and Jerrold Levinson 1992.

23. For similar reasons, psychologists often distinguish between actual events and subjects' "appraisals" of them. See, for example, Ira J. Roseman 1991.

24. David K. Lewis 1983.

25. See Currie 1990, 63–81; George M. Wilson 1991; and Alex Byrne 1993.

26. For more on inconsistency in fictions, see Currie's useful remarks in 1990, 68–70 and 87–89.

27. For background on intentionalism, see Paisley Livingston and Alfred R. Mele 1992, and Alfred R. Mele and Paisley Livingston 1992.

28. See Currie 1990, 31–35.

29. Felicia Ackerman 1991. We do not contend that Ackermann's analysis is complete; little is said, for example, about how the notion of "harm" is to be construed.

30. Anger is not an appropriate response to instances of harmless and inconsequen-

tial mock "aggression" in many comic works, precisely because the laughable events are not genuinely violent in these fictions.

31. "Der Jude im Dorn" in Heinz Rölleke, ed., 1985. For background, see Maria Tatar 1987.

32. But could not one reasonably want to have objectionable feelings in response to fiction, not for their own sake, but in order to "cathart" or otherwise rid oneself of them? It can reasonably be doubted whether such a strategy is (a) really known to be effective as a mode of self-modification or control; or (b) a good way to relate to artworks qua artworks. What is more, one can give reasons why one's preferred self-concept ought not to include being the kind of person who engages with objectionable attitudes or impulses in this manner.

33. We wish to remain neutral on a variety of metaethical claims about the status of justified moral assertions. For background, see, for example, David O. Brink 1989, and Jonathan Dancy 1993.

Fetishism and Objectivity
in Aesthetic Emotion

RONALD DE SOUSA

I. One of Plato's Mad Ideas

My problem starts, as do so many, with one of Plato's mad ideas: the thought
that we don't *really* love the people that we think we love, but only something
else, beauty itself, of which our lovers merely occasioned the recollection.
Thus, progress in love consists in extending our love from the original individual to all those of the same type, and from there to the Type itself:

> And if, my dear Socrates, . . . man's life is ever worth the living, it is when he
> has attained this vision of the very soul of beauty. . . . [O]nce you have seen it,
> you will never be seduced again by the charm of . . . comely boys, or lads just
> ripening to manhood; you will care nothing for the beauties that used to take
> your breath away and kindle such a longing in you.[1]

In addition, Plato taught that since art merely copies life, and life is already
one step away from the ideal, art is worse than useless. But when he urged us
to spurn the products of art as imperfect copies, was it their *imperfection* that
most warranted contempt or their being *copies*? The question seems more ur-
gent now that we have *actually* become capable of making copies to an arbitrary degree of perfection, and that we are able to envisage at least a *theoretical*
possibility of copying persons too, whether by cloning or teleportation.[2]

Whatever the answer, the common sense of our age would say that Plato was definitely wrong about the appropriate objects of love: true love is of individuals, not types, and one may consistently love a person without loving her doppelgänger. About art, the question is not so easily answered. For at least one plausible tradition regards art as important because of the *experience* it affords, so that all objects capable of causing the same experience should be valued equally. This idea is closely linked to that of art as *disinterested*, as an island secluded from the tyranny of purpose. Art, after all, is among a small number of human activities that one would prefer to think can figure only as the premise of a justification, not (unless one is attempting to impress a banker) as its conclusion. If art needs no justification beyond itself, it had better stand apart from the range of things that do. Such is the attraction of the idea of pure aesthetic response.

Even if there is such a thing as a purely aesthetic response, however, we are unlikely often—or ever—to experience it unmixed. It is doubtless a safe axiom that no emotion is unmixed, and aesthetic emotions are all the more mixed for aspiring to purity. Suppose, however, that it were possible to isolate a pure strain, it is not obvious how we could know it for what it is.

These musings introduce three questions:

1. Should our attitude to art be essentially different from our attitude to people?
2. What is the role of the particular in aesthetic experience? More specifically, is the particularity of the target ever an essential part of what makes the aesthetic experience what it is?
3. Can we isolate components of our experience in such a way as to separate the aesthetic element from other interests?

My tentative answers to these questions will emerge indirectly, by way of a question that lies on the margins of the issue of disinterestedness. I'll begin by considering what we might call "weakness of taste," or aesthetic akrasia. This will lead me to ask to what extent we can single out the several qualities that constitute the focus of our aesthetic attention, and isolate a "purely" aesthetic emotion. It will also lead me to ask in what sense and to what extent the focus of aesthetic attention is properly taken to be a particular, and to what extent it is, or should be, logically *general*. This will amount, for reasons that will become clear, to the question of whether *fetishism* is a legitimate part of aesthetic emotion, and if not, whether it is avoidable.

II. Aesthetic Akrasia

Just as ordinary akrasia is a failure to act on what one knows to be the best counsel, so aesthetic akrasia is a failure to react with what one knows to be the appropriate emotion: the inability to respond as one "knows one should" to some aesthetic stimulus. Typically (though not exclusively) it is a failure of *enjoyment*, and it can go both ways: one can like what one knows to be trash, or one can fail to respond to what one knows to be great art. The "knowledge" involved here must not, of course, be mere hearsay: it isn't aesthetic akrasia if

I've read in reliable art books that this is a great work, but am myself quite unable to see the slightest merit in it. Assuming that the reliable art book is right, and (note the presupposition) that there is something to be right or wrong about, this experience is more like blindness or wickedness than it is like akrasia.

Not everyone will agree that there is such a thing as aesthetic akrasia; but then, not everyone is disposed to admit that ordinary motivational akrasia really exists either. Socrates argued that it is logically impossible *really* to think one course of action best and choose another: on this view, all cases of akrasia are similar to my "mere book knowledge" of aesthetic value. It isn't really akrasia, because there's no real conflict. Socrates was surely wrong about ordinary akrasia. As to the aesthetic kind, on the other hand, I fear our efforts to justify its existence may be vain. But I anticipate.

The best available account of ordinary akrasia is based on Donald Davidson's (1970). Both the problem and the solution to it are best described in terms of the fact that the conclusions of practical arguments are not automatically *detachable*. What this means is that the argument's correctness is judged relative to a set of considerations, but the conclusion might be preempted by another argument based on a more inclusive set of considerations. The crucial element in this account for my purposes here is this: akrasia is the plugging into the motor system of a conclusion based on *less than the most comprehensive set of available considerations*.[3] Thus our akratic acts have the structure of intentional, rational actions, since they are determined by practical arguments and based on relevant considerations. On the other hand, we can also see what makes them irrational, since they are not based on the most comprehensive set of relevant considerations and are therefore in the literal sense *partial*.

But this is just where there seems to be a crucial formal difference between regular akrasia and the aesthetic kind. For while the fault in the ordinary case consists in the fact that we respond to too *small* a range of considerations, the fault in most cases of aesthetic akrasia is that we seem to be responding to too *large* a range of considerations: typically, we fail to isolate the range of considerations that are, properly speaking, relevant to the aesthetic question. The failure of *judgment*, unlike the failure of *action*, may lie in responding to what is irrelevant rather than failing to respond to everything that is relevant. *Judgment* here needn't refer exclusively to aesthetic judgment, since, in the sort of judgments made in courts of law, juries are often admonished to disregard what they have just heard. Thus, if cheap music is potent, this may be due to our emotional cowardice in the face of personal, or merely sentimental, or even political associations that by some standards *ought not* to figure in our enjoyment of music.

Some properties of the targets of aesthetic contemplation, then, are generally regarded as *unworthy* of consideration when aesthetic judgments are made. Typical of these sorts of unworthy properties is *monetary value*. One may concede that much of what goes on in the real world of art appreciation instantiates this kind of aesthetic akrasia. But inextricably bound up with it is the one that especially interests me here, namely the weight placed on *associations with particular persons.* Those who would pay high prices for artifacts touched by Elvis Presley or Madonna might not claim that their former owner's magic touch enhances their *beauty*; but then why should Salvador Dali's signature on a print make that more *aesthetically* valuable?

Most people would concede the possibility of self-deception in such cases. To quote Mary Mothersill (1993), I may "think it is your handsomely outfitted house that I admire whereas in fact I am flattered by being invited to visit your handsomely outfitted house." One might add: I am flattered by the very fact that I know how much all this costs: thus making explicit the link between individuality and money. But it is this association with particulars in itself that warrants suspicion. I suggest that it constitutes a special case of aesthetic akrasia, which I propose to call "fetishism." This claim requires clarification of two terms: the relevant notion of "particularity," and my use of the word fetishism.

Particularity is best explained by contrast with a second term that also stands as the opposite of "generality," for generality has two antonyms, each defining a different sense of that word. The first is "specificity": in this sense, the more general is the less specific. The concept therefore admits of degrees: a concept can be more or less general, in the sense of less or more specific. "Particular" is the other opposite of "general." Generality in this sense is compatible with any degree of specificity. Particularity does not admit of degrees and is a logical category rather than a category of experience: for while we no doubt experience particulars, their particularity is part of our experience only insofar as we take stock of the fact that our awareness of them is occurring at a particular moment in space and time. Particularity is not a *feature* of an experience, but a logical category that applies both to it and to its target.

Fetishism, in my sense, owes something to its use in anthropology and something to its psychoanalytic usage, but is different from both. In the original anthropological sense, a fetish is something that is held in awe because of its putative relation to something else for which it stands, particularly a deity or supernatural being. In psychoanalysis, a fetishist is someone for whom a part of the body, or a physical object of a nonsexual nature, arouses sexual excitement because of its (causal or associative) relation with something more commonly regarded as sexually significant. My special sense of fetishism abstracts from both the supernatural and the sexual connotations of the two other uses, but retains the central idea of borrowed power vested in an object the intrinsic qualities of which are unimportant: fetishism is the valuing of a particular object for the sake of its causal link to some other particular, which is held to be of intrinsic (or at least prior) value.

Now, the assumption I shall develop in a moment is that qualitative experience, as such, cannot relate essentially to a particular as such. An experience's closest relation to a particular is as its contingent cause. This raises directly the second of the questions posed above, about the role of particulars in aesthetic experience.

III. Aesthetic Experience and the Particular

We prize individual works of art. These are often said to be *unique*. This means not necessarily that there are no others just like this one, which would exclude "original prints" or bronze statues cast in several copies, but that each copy counts as an original in virtue of having been produced by some physical process that relates it causally to the artist in specific ways. What criteria must be satisfied for something to "count" as original, however, is not easy to say. An original signature is expected on an "original print," but not on a bronze cast; Henry Moore's own hands molded the plaster maquettes now in the Art Gallery of Ontario, but someone else did the casting for the bronze that stands outside: that bronze, nevertheless, is no less "authentic" than the plaster. All this seems to have less to do with aesthetics than with the conventions and the sociology of art. Moreover, there are media in which uniqueness seems irrelevant: the aesthetic appreciation one may feel for a movie, for example, or for the purely abstract object that is a piece of software, or a fortiori a mathematical theorem, is not tied to any particular even where the work cannot be enjoyed in isolation from its embodiment in some particular hunk of matter. For a somewhat transitional case, consider the criteria that individuate a live performance, or, worse, a recording of a live performance—which might in turn be taped from a later broadcast: these criteria seem to have a lot more to do with the protection of commercial interests and with issues of copyright, than with issues that have any intrinsic aesthetic significance.

Here is one more complication. Many people feel that the beauty of what they are contemplating depends in part on the (nonperceptual) knowledge of how *common* the object is: if something exists in many copies, then perhaps it can be no more than pretty, and it loses not only monetary but also, it is felt, aesthetic value.[4] The frisson provoked by extreme rarity is familiar to collectors, and drove Leibniz to the wonderful and lunatic idea that God couldn't possibly have created two of anything. And that seems to have some sort of aesthetic flavor to it, on God's part at least. (But wouldn't God miss the pleasure of pairs? the titillation of triplets?) Rarity is clearly a general property, in the sense that it can logically be true of more than one thing. Yet its applicability depends on its not having many instances. At the limit, it becomes equivalent to uniqueness. But the odd twist is that it still doesn't amount to particularity, for on the standard (Fregean) view, uniqueness, like number or existence, is a property of (general) concepts, not of (particular) individuals. So the requirement of rarity can't be automatically dismissed as akratic on logical grounds, along with the requirement of particularity. Nor can it be assimilated to fetishism on the ground of not being connected to experience: for, while the nonuniqueness of the object of contemplation can't be something directly perceived (unless the copies are simultaneously presented, like a multiple Warhol image), it might still be something that one experiences in memory: and surely it would be an absurd constraint on aesthetic experience to exclude from it anything that depends on what one remembers.

One might think to settle the question by reference to the meaning of "aesthetic." Aesthetic experience has, in the classic and etymological sense of the word *aesthesis*, an essential connection with the sensory. It is first about perception. I shall make as much of this as I can in a moment; but I must acknowledge right away that this may not amount to as much as we might hope, for two reasons.

First, confining aesthetic response to the perceptible leaves unexplained the aesthetic pleasure we take in abstract objects, from mathematical theorems to conceptual art. The insistence on art's perceptual aspects may reflect no more than the historical fact that art was first plastic craft. Second, "etymology," though it etymologically means "true meaning," is not truly meaning. In any case, there is no standard answer to the question of what are the proper objects of perception. Is the relevant sense of "aesthesis" sensation, in a purely qualitative sense, before interpretative understanding? Or is it interpreted perception? If the former, it is certainly qualitative rather than referential. But even if it is perception of ordinary objects, the focus of the aesthetic qua experience may still be in the object's quality as represented rather than in its particularity. Are aesthetic emotions properly directed at particular targets, or do they attach to the focus of acts of perception?[5]

Representations are not necessarily general. They can include particular references: "Ronnie," for example, may function as a representation of this particular, me. But this feat of representation is achieved in the context of a system of representation, a language, in which the tools exist to say what it is to refer to a particular. Strawson (1959) showed that this entails an anchoring in an egocentric space of particulars in which other things can take their place; and the externalist literature of the recent couple of decades has stressed that meaning can sometimes be anchored in some particular individual or kind.

Yet in spite of all this, there is a good deal of plausibility to the idea that we should think of representation, in the sense in which it is relevant to aesthetic experience, as purely qualitative or general (in the sense that allows it, you will recall, to be as specific as you like, indeed, specific enough to guarantee uniqueness in practice). I don't know how to prove this, but here are two arguments for it.

The first is rooted in the assumption that Strawson was right (which I won't attempt to argue here). If the aesthetic is supposed to be disinterested, then this means that we have no motive to manipulate its objects (which doesn't mean that we can't manipulate various particulars in the service of aesthetic experience).[6] Strawson's demonstration suggests a reason for aesthetic objects to be general: if we are able to identify particulars, it is because we are able to *act* upon them. We typically act on objects for a purpose. So, if aesthetic experience is essentially purposeless, it should be accessible in abstraction from any particulars as such. Hence, we seem justified in calling an aesthetic experience fetishistic if it is essentially tied to the apprehension of properties by a given individual and no other.

I'll come in a moment to a second argument for the thesis that the proper objects of aesthetic experience are qualities, not particulars. But it's worth noting in passing that if this is correct, then Plato was indeed wrong in supposing that Beauty is the true object of love. For fetishism, in my special sense, is not a perversion where the object of an attitude or emotion is a *person*: on the contrary, it would seem more than odd to value a person solely according to the universal properties that he or she exemplifies. Beauty (as the object of aesthetic experience) is logically general, whereas the object of love is logically singular. The logic of aesthetic experience is such that there is some inconsistency in deriving pleasure from a certain object, and not deriving pleasure from another that is indistinguishable from it. Love, by contrast, is generally held to be irreducibly historical: its object is its target, not the focus of any specific experience. When Alcmene was deceived by Zeus, who took the shape of her husband Amphitryon, Zeus could not reasonably have deflected her complaint by merely pointing out that he had made himself indistinguishable in her experience from Amphitryon. For that is precisely how she was deceived.

In practice, the art world is highly fetishistic, as if it were modeled on the logic of love rather than on the logic of beauty. We care tremendously about whether a certain work is authentic or fake, where being "authentic" means that it is made by a specific individual, or at least that it is causally linked in the right way to that individual. Thus, some might have paid millions for the pleasure of contemplating a van Meegeren while under the impression that it was a Vermeer, but would have felt cheated in the discovery because the pleasure of contemplating a van Meegeren knowing that it is a van Meegeren is worth only hundreds (or thousands, since after all van Meegeren is *famous*). What's more, most art lovers will defend this as obviously sensible. Yet it violates the equally plausible principle that aesthetic pleasure, or the appreciation of beauty, relates to a certain range of aesthetic properties that are capable of being experienced, not merely known. This is the second reason for thinking of the proper objects of aesthetic emotion as general, and the one that takes the etymological argument as seriously as it can be taken. It is embodied in Mary Mothersill's suggested definition of what it is to take something to be beautiful:

> Definition 1. *Someone takes an individual to be beautiful if and only if the individual pleases him and he believes that it pleases him in virtue of its aesthetic properties.* (Mothersill 1984, 342)

To make this more precise, Mothersill adopts a suggestion of Sue Larson's about what is to count as an aesthetic property:

> [Larson's Law] "F is an aesthetic property" means that for any x, if F of x, then for any y, F of y if and only if y is indistinguishable from x. An aesthetic property, in effect, is a property common and peculiar to individuals that are indistinguishable from one another. (344)

Now, there are notorious problems about what counts as indistinguishability: how long and with what instruments one might be allowed to look, and so forth.[7] But the key idea, which I propose to pass unchallenged here so that we can look at some different problems, is that aesthetic properties are apprehended in experience (typically, but not exclusively, in perceptual experience), not by extraneous knowledge of the particular in question. This doesn't mean, of course, that one's perception isn't influenced by all kinds of general knowledge, but it raises the theoretical possibility of sorting through those influences to isolate the purely aesthetic. For it seems to licence the crucial conclusion that aesthetic experience is based on *properties* that *can logically belong to any number of particulars.*

Mothersill and Larson's ideas go back to Arnold Isenberg (1949), who addressed the problem of how critical discourse might refer to objective qualities even though generalizations from critical remarks never seem to be supportable. Thus, for example, Isenberg (followed by Mothersill) quotes a critic on El Greco's *The Burial of Count Orgaz:*

> Like the contour of a violently rising and falling wave is the outline of the four illuminated figures in the foreground: steeply upwards and downwards about the grey monk on the left, in mutually inclined curves about the yellow of the two saints. (162)[8]

But while there is indeed a wavelike contour in the picture, and while one might well agree that it contributes crucially to the pleasure of the picture (to its beauty, if you like) it seems preposterous to suggest that the same contour would make a similar contribution to any other picture. Its contribution is not generalizable, but if not generalizable, how can it genuinely be said to contribute to this picture at all? Isenberg's solution is this:

> It seems reasonable to suppose that the critic is thinking of another quality, no idea of which is transmitted to us by his language, which he *sees* and which by his language he gets *us to see.* This quality is, of course, a wavelike contour; but it is not the quality designated by the expression "wavelike contour." Any object which has this quality will have a wavelike contour, but it is not true that any object which has a wavelike contour will have this quality.[9] (162)

Now, Mothersill goes on to describe the situation as involving a "particular quality" (336). But that is a confusing expression: qualities are by definition not particulars, but universals. She must mean that we are dealing with a maximally *determinate* quality, in the sense that any two determinates of it would be indistinguishable under normal observation conditions. With this clarification, it's possible to understand how the aesthetic properties in question are both genuine properties and *apparently* generalization-proof: generalizations involving them are logically correct, but are bound to have an air of triviality, since nothing short of indistinguishability will count as yielding the same quality.

I conclude that a reasonable case can be made for insisting that the objects of aesthetic experience are indeed essentially general. Nevertheless, our responses to artworks and other objects of aesthetic interest are frequently affected by the identity of the particular target that gives rise to them. This suggests that our responses are not merely aesthetic, but compounds of aesthetic response and other sorts of response. Insofar as they are experienced as aesthetic responses, yet are tied to a particular individual, they instantiate fetishism. But if fetishism is indeed a form of aesthetic akrasia, then should we not be able to pick out the thread that belongs to the authentic response, and separate it from the irrelevant factors?

IV. *Change of Taste and Objectivity*

If we take to heart Larson's law, above, then we must insist that whatever knowledge we acquire about a particular must be ruled out-of-bounds in terms of strictly aesthetic appraisal, unless it is acquired by direct perception. As I've already indicated, determining whether some piece of knowledge has been so acquired is a far-from-straightforward task. Luckily, there is an argument that may excuse us from having to try. This connects to the closely related case of trying to separate out different factors in phenomenological experience. Mary Mothersill describes the case in question as follows:

> One's taste changes over time, and in retrospect it may come to seem that some earlier enthusiasm, though admittedly genuine, involved a species of misperception. . . . Of course, I may be mistaken or self-deceived, dwelling fondly on my supposed superior powers when in fact my taste has progressively deteriorated. (1984, 264)

Now this talk of improvement or deterioration of taste implies that there are no fewer than two matters of objective fact about which one might be right or wrong. The first is the fact of *what my taste is* and whether it has changed; the second concerns whether my taste is or was *correct*.

In a moment I'll focus on the first type of fact, ignoring the second. First, though, it's worth stopping to notice that the interplay of these two "facts" leads to an intriguing puzzle, which is the appearance of a kind of hyperobjectivity of aesthetic judgment. It leads to the pleasing thought that in matters of aesthetics, as in matters of logic or mathematics, *you can't both understand me and disagree with me*—except by virtue of aesthetic akrasia.

The idea that one might tax someone with a failure to understand simply because he or she disagrees, is, at first blush, preposterous. "If you don't agree, this shows you don't understand," is just too easy an argumentative gambit to be generally valid. Yet the example of logic or mathematics shows that it can sometimes be right. We would indeed reject the claim of someone who said: "I certainly understand what you are saying when you insist that the square root of 9 is 3, *but I just don't agree.*"

In more sophisticated cases the claim makes better sense, as in "I certainly understand what you mean when you say that if the universe is unbounded then it must be infinite, but I don't agree." In cases such as this, however, it is still true that one of the parties is able to claim a more comprehensive understanding. (In this last example, the one who makes a distinction between boundedness and finitude can understand what it is to confuse them.) This tight connection between understanding and knowledge signals objectivity in the subject matter. As we go to "softer" subjects, however, it seems to be of the essence of meaning that it is distinguishable from truth, that it is the mere possibility rather than the actuality of truth. Hence, most ordinary contexts allow a gap between meaning and truth, understanding and knowledge; and when disagreements become particularly difficult to settle, as in ethics, we may be tempted to infer that the domain in question does not admit of objectivity at all. Now aesthetics is the "softest" and reputedly most "subjective" domain of all. Yet the situation seems to flip back again, as if this were once more a domain of perfect objectivity. For it can again seem plausible to insist that if one's interlocutor does not agree with one's aesthetic judgment, then that judgment hasn't been properly understood: that the experience on which it is based has not properly been shared. If you are to understand me, then you must have an experience qualitatively identical with mine. But if you and I have just the same experience, then how can you not love it or hate it as I do? Wouldn't that show that our experiences weren't the same after all? In these cases, it seems that it is the very extremity of subjectivity that licenses us to insist on the ability to universalize. For we saw that the appropriate determinant of aesthetic emotion is not its target, but the experience it affords: a focus on a motivating aspect of the target. And pleasure (or its absence) is part and parcel of my experience; so, *ex hypothesi*, if you experience no pleasure you can't be having my experience.

The problem is that there is not and cannot be any independent criterion for the identity of two experiences. This fact threatens the intelligibility of aesthetic akrasia. For that concept requires that we can pick out an illegitimate thread (perhaps a fetishistic one) among the components of a reactive emotion. If we cannot, then there remains nothing more to aesthetic akrasia than a vague guilt feeling about one's own aesthetic preferences. Worse, it seems that there can be no systematic basis for making a difference between those of our emotions that are targeted to people and those that are targeted to art. Let us take a closer look at how this comes about.

V. *The Case of Chase and Sanborn*

In the context of a discussion of the problem of qualia, Daniel Dennett (1990) has both sharpened the description of the case of changing taste, and shown that it turns out, in the end, to involve a distinction without a difference.

Dennett envisages two coffee tasters, Mr. Chase and Mr. Sanborn, who have been tasting coffee for Maxwell House for many years. Mr. Chase confesses that he no longer likes the taste of Maxwell House coffee, although that taste is exactly the same as it was. Mr. Sanborn avows that he too, has ceased to like the taste of Maxwell House coffee, but not because his taste has changed—he still likes the way the coffee used to taste, but perhaps his taste buds don't work right any more, for it doesn't taste the same to him. (Chemical tests establish to the satisfaction of both that the change isn't traceable to any change in the coffee itself.)

Now we could simply take them both at their word: since they are, after all, reporting on their own qualia, who is to second-guess them? Even if we believe that we have some kind of privileged or even incorrigible access to our own qualia, however, what is here being reported is about how and why they have *changed*. And that is a causal hypothesis, not a simple report of a quale. We can envisage different cases for each man. In the case of Chase, for example,

a) Chase's coffee-taste-qualia have stayed constant, while his reactive attitudes to those qualia, devolving on his canons of aesthetic judgment, etc., have shifted . . .

b) Chase is simply wrong about the constancy of his qualia; they have shifted gradually and imperceptibly over the years while his standards of taste haven't budged. . . . [H]e is in the state Sanborn claims to be in, but just lacks Sanborn's self-knowledge. (527)

As for Sanborn, he could in principle be in corresponding states of correct or incorrect belief. Or—what makes it worse—either could be in any of an indefinite number of intermediate states.

Could there be scientific tests to settle the matter? As Dennett points out, defenders of qualia who grant that (b) is possible will surely be willing to countenance such empirical tests. But the experiments will not decide the issue. For whatever the results of the physiological tests, the phenomena available to scrutiny—the subject's reports—would be the product of two factors, "roughly, dispositions to generate or produce qualia and dispositions to react to the qualia once they are produced" (1990, 530). And that is just a new form of the very problem we've been facing: how to gauge the proportional contribution of different components of one's own experience. Even supposing we devise a physiological test, it won't tell us whether the subject has made any psychological compensations for the change in perception, or on the contrary whether the adjustment is made in memory:

There are *still* two stories that might be told:
I   Chase's current qualia are still abnormal, but thanks to the revision in his memory-accessing process, he has in effect adjusted his memories of how things used to taste, so he no longer notices any anomaly.
II   The memory-comparison step occurs just prior to the qualia phase in taste perception; thanks to the revision, it now *yields* the same old qualia for the same stimulation.

And Dennett points out that we can't rely on the subject to just tell us which is right. For in order to calibrate the corresponding brain events, one would have to have a clear case in which one knows which is which. And it is precisely "in order to confirm or disconfirm Chase's opinion that we turned to the neurophysiological evidence in the first place" (1990, 531).

VI. *The Prospects for Objectivity*

Our inability to make the distinctions needed to adjudicate between the various possible interpretations of Chase and Sanborn's claims has dire consequences for our ability to detect aesthetic akrasia. For Dennett's phrase, just quoted—"dispositions to generate or produce qualia and dispositions to react to the qualia once they are produced"—identifies precisely the factors that we need to distinguish if we are to determine whether a certain emotional response is a case of aesthetic akrasia. Thus we can always claim, without fear of refutation, that if our interlocutor does not share our evaluative opinion (our "dispositions to react") it is because they do not share our *experience* (our "dispositions to . . . generate . . . qualia"). We can say it, but it will be wholly devoid of content because we will never be able to say about ourselves, let alone about others, what influenced our evaluation. Thus, we can never know whether our disagreements relate to a difference in the relevant focus, in our perception of it, or to a separable component of evaluation that applies to that perception or focus or supervenes upon it. There will be no reliable way of comparing the components of those experiences; only the global judgment will be accessible. In turn, this has the further consequence that one won't be able to exclude the possibility that the price of a painting, or the individual origins of a manuscript, are what actually determine the dominant feeling of that global "aesthetic" judgment.

It may have been optimistic, therefore, to hope for a clear-cut distinction between love, which is properly focused on a particular, and aesthetic experience, which is disinterested, general even where it is unique, and tied only to the quality of the experiences on which it supervenes. While it seemed at first that love of persons would turn out to be properly "fetishistic," while love of art would not be, it now turns out that the distinction is harder, indeed impossible, to make out.

Maybe it's proper that there should be no such thing as pure aesthetic experience. It fits well enough with the likely fact that there is no perception without action;[10] and since there is no action without a setting in a space and time occupied by individuals, including ourselves, it may well be that the roots of what I have called fetishism are deeper than the merely crass weight of association, unnaturally grafted upon the purity of aesthetic emotion. It may be, in other words, that there is no such thing as aesthetic emotion.

Perhaps this is just as well, if it means we can import our aesthetic sense into life as freely as we can import the rest of life into our aesthetic emotions.

NOTES

1. *Symposium.* In Hamilton and Cairns 1961, 211.

2. Insofar as imperfection could be considered a consequence of copying, it is ironic that Plato is the grandfather of *digitality*, the technique that affords us, in the computer age, the possibility of endless reproduction to arbitrary degrees of perfection. For that technique rests on treating resemblance between two things as a three-place relation: instead of copying an object, we copy the paradigm of which the "original" was a copy: thus, in an indefinitely long chain of further copying, the last is always really just two steps away from the first.

3. Note that this "plugging in" must be done by some factor that is neither a brute mechanism (for then akrasia would cease to be something for which anyone could be held responsible), nor a strictly rational process (for then there would be nothing wrong with it from the point of view of rationality). See de Sousa 1976. I have argued in 1987 that this dilemma constitutes a powerful motive for treating emotions, and their role in rationality, as reducible neither to beliefs or desires, nor to the rules that govern their rational exercise.

4. That isn't the only possible reaction. Walter Benjamin's celebrated essay on the implications for art of the "age of mechanical reproduction" stresses that while mass-produced objects will not have the "aura" of uniquely crafted ones, what is most likely to follow is a change in the conception and function of art, not necessarily a decay of art: "To an ever greater degree the work of art reproduced becomes the work of art designed for reproducibility. From a photographic negative, for example, one can make any number of prints; to ask for the 'authentic' print makes no sense" (1968, 224).

5. Among the many ways in which we speak of the "object" of an emotion, I have argued elsewhere that we should distinguish at least half a dozen different items (1987). For present purposes, we need to attend particularly to the distinction between the emotion's *target* (the actual physical object, if any, toward which that emotion is directed), and the *focus* of attention, which is the apprehension of some (real or illusory) property of the target. Under certain conditions, which define the standard case, the focus (which is an experience) or focal property (which is its content) is also the *motivating aspect* of these emotions, that is, it is the cause of pleasure. In a standard case of aesthetic emotion, the target is a *particular*; the motivating aspect and focus, however, are *general*. In terms of these distinctions, the question I am raising could be rephrased like this: If what matters in an aesthetic experience is indeed the focal property or motivating aspect of a given target, is there any justification for preferring one target over another, providing they afford indistinguishable experiences?

6. In the *Critique of Judgment* [1790] (1952), Kant defines "interest" as "the pleasure we take in the idea of the existence of an object" (I, 1–2). This definition has the same consequence: if no part of my pleasure is due to the idea of the existence of the object, then the particularity of the object doesn't matter to me either.

7. Nelson Goodman (1976) has argued that the potential discovery of perceptual differences justifies the weight given to authenticity in practice. This may be true, but it still affords conceptual space for a thought experiment in which the indistinguishability persists.

8. Cited by Mothersill 1984, 336.

9. Cited by Mothersill 1984, 336.

10. I refer to a rising consensus in cognitive science, that successful modeling of perception will never be possible until we have robots that acquire their perceptual capacities by acting on their environment. Merleau-Ponty (1962) was the great precursor of this point of view; for a sampling of recent exponents, see Johnson 1987, Rosenfield 1992, and Damasio 1994.

I 2

Art, Narrative, and Emotion

NOËL CARROLL

Despite the great interest in the reception of art and media in recent years, little attention has been paid to the way in which narrative fictions, whether high or low, address the emotions of readers, listeners, and viewers. Instead, emphasis is generally placed on hermeneutics. Interpretation of what is loosely called the meaning of the work has preoccupied attention in the humanities. New interpretations, often called symptomatic readings, of what are generically identified as "texts" are still the order of the day in liberal arts journals. And even what some in cultural studies call "recodings," and what some feminists call "readings against the grain," focus on the putative interpretive activities of certain groups of readers, listeners, and viewers. What is not studied in any fine-grained way is how works engage the emotions of the audience. What I wish to deal with in this article is how we might go about doing just that.

It is not my contention that, in principle, hermeneutics is illegitimate. Rather, I think that our research into the arts should be supplemented by considering their relation to the emotions, especially if we are interested in audience reception. Moreover, the present moment is particularly propitious in this respect, since recent research into the emotions over the last two decades in fields like psychology and philosophy have made the possibility of interrogating the relation of art to the emotions feasible with a heretofore unimagined level of precision.[1]

Perhaps it will be felt that I have already misdescribed the situation. One might argue that I have overstated the degree to which scholars in the humanities have ignored the emotions. For a great deal of recent humanistic research is psychoanalytic, and, at least ostensibly, psychoanalysis is concerned with the emotions. And yet I would respond that psychoanalysis of the sort that is popular among scholars in the humanities today is not really concerned with the garden-variety emotions—that is, the emotions marked in ordinary speech, like fear, awe, pity, admiration, anger, and so on—which garden-variety emotions, in fact, are what keep audiences engaged with artworks.

Psychoanalytic critics seem more concerned with certain generic, ill-defined forces like desire and pleasure that they speak of without prepositional modification. For example, they write of Desire with a capital "D," rather than of small d-desires for this or that. Or they seem preoccupied by certain anxieties, like male castration anxiety or anxieties about the dissolution of the unity of the subject whose purchase on the reading, listening, and viewing activities of audiences are highly suspect and controversial. Indeed, one might speculate that psychoanalytic critics pay scant attention to the operation of the garden-variety emotions of readers, listeners, and viewers exactly because psychoanalytic theory itself has little to say about the nature of such emotions, but often merely assumes the definition of emotions, like fear, that are already in operation in ordinary language.[2]

Nevertheless, it seems to me that if we are really concerned with audience reception, we should pay more attention than we do to the dynamics of the audience's emotional involvement with narrative artworks, both high and low, and especially to the way in which such artworks are designed to elicit garden-variety emotional responses from readers, listeners, and viewers. For in large measure, what commands and shapes the audience's attention to the artwork, what enables the audience to follow and to comprehend the artwork, and what energizes our commitment to seeing the narrative artwork through to its conclusion is the emotional address of the narrative artwork. Speaking metaphorically, we might say that to a large extent, emotions are the cement that keeps audiences connected to the artworks, especially to the narrative fictions, that they consume. Moreover, the emotions in question here are generally garden-variety ones—fear, anger, horror, reverence, suspense, pity, admiration, indignation, awe, repugnance, grief, compassion, infatuation, comic amusement, and the like.

One way to suggest partial substantiation for this assertion might be simply to consider the degree to which popular fictions rely so heavily on the activation of specific, garden-variety emotions. So many melodramas, for example, rely upon the audience's concern for protagonists, whom we not only pity for their misfortunes, but whom we also admire for their character, especially as it is manifested in their self-sacrificing behavior, such as Stella Dallas's self-willed separation from her daughter.[3] Horror fictions, of course, require not only that we be thrown into a state of fear toward and repulsion by the monsters that threaten the human race, but that we feel mounting anxiety as the protagonist ventures into the hidden recesses of the old dark house. But, of course, the evidence for the importance of emotional involvement for the reception of narrative art is not simply that it is a recurring feature of the popular arts. For as Aristotle pointed out long ago, essential to the tragic response to high art is the elicitation of pity and fear in the audience.

With much art, especially narrative art, eliciting the appropriate emotional response from the audience is a condition of our comprehending and following the work. For example, if we do not hate certain characters, then the trajectory of a narrative bent upon punishing them will not only be unsatisfying, but even unintelligible. What, we might ask ourselves, is the author's point in detailing their comeuppance? Why is so much time and elaboration being spent on showing us how this vicious character comes into his just deserts? It will not compute, unless we are attending to the story in the emotionally appropriate way.

But the emotions engaged by the plot are generally not only a condition of the intelligibility of the story. They are often typically what keeps us glued, so to say, to the story. The emotions in life and in art have the function of focusing attention. And with narrative fictions, they keep us focused on the plot on a moment-to-moment basis. They organize our attention in terms of what is going on in a scene *and* they also prime our anticipation about the kinds of things to expect in future scenes. To be more specific: our emotional responses to earlier scenes will generally contribute to organizing the way in which we attend to later scenes. If we are indignant about a character's behavior when we first encounter her, then, when she next appears, we will be on the lookout for more evidence of nastiness in her behavior. Emotions organize perception. Emotions shape the way in which we follow character behavior, just as in everyday life they enable us to track the behavior of others.

Moreover, although most of my examples so far have relied on our emotional involvement with characters, clearly what I have said can also apply to situations and events. The horror that we feel about the initial outbreak of vampirism in a novel like *Salem's Lot* emotionally colors the way in which we attend to subsequent scenes. Our emotional involvement alerts us to the potential dangers in situations that we might otherwise overlook. Indeed, it quite frequently alerts us to dangers in situations that the characters overlook. Small animal bites on the neck may mean little to them, but they loom large in our attention.

Though I think that what I have said so far is fairly obvious, there is one line of misunderstanding that I would like to neutralize before it takes root. I do think that we should pay more attention to the role of the emotions in our commerce with artworks, but I am not advocating a reversion to the sorts of expression theories of art that were advanced by theorists like Leo Tolstoy and Robin Collingwood.[4] Tolstoy and Collingwood were in the business of developing universal theories of art. As such, they maintained, in different ways, that the communication or expression of emotion was an essential or defining feature of art. Their theories were universal characterizations of the nature of all art. In contrast, I am not defending a theory about all art, or even all narrative art.[5] I simply wish to talk, albeit theoretically, about the operation of the emotions in art, especially narrative art, where it occurs. And this is logically consistent with eschewing an expression theory of art in general.

I do not want to deny that there may be some art that does not traffic in emotions, especially in what I have called garden-variety emotions. Some paintings may be about the nature of painting—maybe much of Frank Stella's work is about the conventions of framing; and some films, like *Zorn's Lemma* by Hollis Frampton, may be about the nature of film. These works may be articulated in such a way that they address cognition exclusively. Unlike Tolstoy and Collingwood, I would not argue that these works are not art inasmuch as they are not connected to the emotions. For my claim is not that all art is involved in the elicitation of the emotions, but only that some is—indeed, much is—and, furthermore, I contend that it is useful to develop a theory about the relation of art to the emotions for these works, even if the result is not a universalizable theory that pertains to all art, or even all narrative fiction.

There are also other important issues of detail that distinguish my approach from those of Tolstoy and Collingwood. Tolstoy maintained that the relevant emotions requisite for art status were those that were felt by both the author in making the work and the audience in consuming it. That is, he thought it criterial of art status that the emotion experienced by the audience be the same emotion that had been sincerely undergone by the artist. But I am interested in the emotions elicited by artworks whether or not they parallel the emotions felt by the artist in creating the work. As Denis Diderot so forcefully argued, actors typically evoke emotional responses from audiences that they may not have felt; a performer can communicate Othello's jealousy without being jealous.[6]

For Collingwood, art expresses emotion, by which he maintained that the artwork, properly so-called, was an occasion for the artist to work through or clarify some initially vague feeling. This process of clarification is supposed to stand in contrast to the arousal of emotion, which Collingwood thought of as the aim of pseudo-art. It was pseudo-art according to Collingwood because it relied on the deployment of tried-and-true formulas to arrive at preordained effects. And given Collingwood's somewhat Kantian biases in this regard, anything that smacked of rules or formulas could not count as art properly so-called.

But I, in contrast, take it to be an empirical fact that much of what we correctly call art does traffic in arousing emotions; or, if arousal talk strikes you as too strong, much art is involved in promoting, encouraging, or eliciting preordained emotional responses from readers, listeners, and viewers, often by routine techniques and formulas; and it is my purpose in what follows to look at that art with an eye to developing a theoretical framework for discussing some of the structures artists use to elicit such emotional responses from readers, listeners, and viewers.

II. Plato versus the Cognitive Theory of the Emotions

Of course, as Collingwood knew, not all philosophers have been opposed to associating art with the arousal of emotion. The Greeks were not, and, as a result, Collingwood called their view the technical theory of art. Plato articulated this view very elaborately in the *Republic*, although, as is well known, he did it in order to banish the arts from the good city. Nevertheless, Plato does provide us with a coherent picture of the relation of the arts to the emotions and, as such, a quick review of his theory and its shortcomings can still afford us an instructive point of entry through which we can dialectically develop a better theoretical framework for the discussion of the relation of art, specifically narrative fiction, and the emotions.

Plato had a battery of arguments against dramatic art and painting, many of which revolved around the way in which works of that kind addressed the emotions of spectators. His central argument hinged on his conviction that the emotions are irrational in the sense that they undermine the rule of reason both in the individual and, in consequence, in society. Certain emotions, like pity and the fear of death, were of particular concern for Plato, since they would undermine the citizen-soldier's capacity to wage war. That is, Plato thought that these emotions were maladaptive. One did not want troops disposed to pity themselves or the enemy, nor troops who feared death. Plato believed that by using dramatic texts as the Greeks did, reading them aloud in the process of education, people would acquire these untoward emotional dispositions by playing certain roles, that is, by identifying with the characters who vented these emotions.

But Plato was not simply concerned that certain unsavory emotions would be disseminated through the influence of and identification with dramatic poetry. He distrusted the emotional address of poetry and painting irrespective of the specific emotions they elicited, because he believed that the promotion of the emotions in general is problematic. For the emotions, on his view, oppose reason, and any threat to reason constitutes a threat to the community at large. Moreover, Plato thought that drama is bound to promote emotion over reason, because artists would have to pander to the emotions of the untutored masses if they were to have audiences at all. That is, Plato argued, the general audience, knowing little, has to be addressed in terms of its emotions rather than reason. That is why, a latter-day Plato might say, shows like *L.A. Law* are preoccupied with the drama of office romance rather than the drama of legal research. The latter requires a background of legal education in order to be comprehended; the former, merely gut reactions. Thus, Plato, in effect, proposed the first economic theory of art, explaining why consumption dictated the unavoidably emotional address of drama.

Of these Platonic arguments, the most general and the deepest is that art essentially addresses the emotions and thereby undermines reason, presenting a clear and present danger to the community. The presupposition here is that reason and the emotions are in some sense at odds. Reason must dominate the emotions. Left to their own, so to speak, the emotions will gravitate toward the irrational. In Plato's conception of human psychology, reason and emotion appear to occupy different regions. There is no expectation from Plato's point of view that they will converge and even more grounds to anticipate that they will pull in opposite directions.

Plato's tendency is to think that the emotions are irrational or opposed to reason. Thus if art or drama addresses the emotions, it will address the irrational in us and thereby undermine reason's control over us. But the obvious question to ask about this argument is whether in fact the distinction between reason and the emotions is as sharp as Plato maintains. Are the emotions necessarily irrational forces in the way Plato supposes?

The tendency in contemporary psychology and in analytic philosophy is to reject Plato's presupposition that the emotions are irrational. Instead, it is more common to maintain that reason and the emotions are not opposed, inasmuch as reason is an ineliminable constituent of the emotions. Thus, in order to undercut Plato's argument and to set the stage for our own positive account of the relation of the emotions to art, specifically to narrative fiction, it is profitable to look at the picture of the emotions—often called the cognitive theory of emotions[7]—that has been developed by contemporary researchers and that challenges the prejudice that the emotions are by their very nature irrational.

In order to determine whether emotions are irrational, we need some conception of what an emotion is. Perhaps the first answer we might naturally turn to in order to answer this question is that an emotion is a feeling. When we're in an emotional state, our body changes. Our heart rate may alter; we may feel our chest expanding or contracting. Physical changes occur as we move into an emotional state—the adrenal glands produce corticosteroids; and there are psychological or phenomenological changes as well. When we are angry, we may feel "hot under the collar." But are these physical and phenomenological changes in the body the whole story? Supporting this view, we might notice that in English we often do refer to emotions as "feelings."

But proponents of cognitive theories of the emotions deny that emotions are simply feelings—neither merely physical alterations, nor phenomenological feelings, nor a combination thereof. Why not? Because it is easy to imagine chemically inducing the sorts of bodily feeling states that are associated with emotions where there is no question of our being in an emotional state. Suppose we chemically induce the feeling states in you that you exhibited the last time that you were angry. Here you are now alone in a room in exactly the same physical state you were in when your colleague said something sarcastic to you in a faculty meeting last month. Are you angry? Not if there is no one or no thing with whom or with which you are angry. Remember that you are in the same physical state you were in last month. But you are not in the same mental state. You are not thinking about your colleague or anyone else. The chemicals only induce certain changes in your body.

Admittedly, you may be in an unpleasant physical state. But you cannot be said to be in an emotional state of anger unless there is someone who or something that you think has done you or yours some wrong. For emotional states are directed—you are afraid *of* war, or you are in love *with* Mary. Bodily feelings, however, are not directed at anything. They are physical states. They are internal events without external reference.

But what is it that links our internal feeling states to external objects and situations? What's the bridge, so to speak? Cognitive theorists of the emotions say that it is our cognitive states (that's why they are called cognitive theorists). For example, it may be our states of belief that connect our internal feelings to external situations. Suppose that I believe that George took my money and that, in doing so, he has wronged me. This is apt to give rise to anger. That is, taken by this belief—which is directed at George—my sympathetic nervous system is activated, and I begin to feel tension throughout my body. I feel myself tightening up. The reason that I am in this physical state is my belief that George has stolen my money. That's why my blood boils whenever I see him. In short, my belief that George has stolen my money *causes* my blood to boil.

So as an initial approximation, let us say provisionally that an emotion is made up of at least two components: a cognitive component, such as a belief or a thought about some person, place, or thing, real or imagined; and a feeling component (a bodily change and/or a phenomenological experience), where, additionally, the feeling state has been caused by the relevant cognitive state, such as a belief or a belief-like state.[8] Furthermore, a conception of the emotions like this one is bad news for someone like Plato, since it incorporates cognition into the structure of the emotions, thereby denying that reason is totally opposed to the emotions; for if reason/cognition is a constituent of an emotion, emotion cannot be the antithesis of reason/cognition. But in order to make the problem for Plato even more explicit, let's look a bit more closely at the cognitive component of an emotion.

I am angry at George because I believe that he has stolen my money. But theft of my property is only one of many occurrences that might, under suitable circumstances, provide grounds for anger. I could be angry at George for cutting ahead of me in line, or for throttling my little brother. Theft, queue breaking, throttling, and so on are instances of a broader class of things, any of which might warrant anger. What is the relevant broader class of things— that is, what must I believe about someone if I am to be angry with him? I must believe that he has done wrong to me or mine. I think that George has stolen my money, and that falls into this larger class of things. So, in order to be angry with someone, I must believe that the object of my anger has done some wrong to me or mine.

Similarly, other emotions are directed at objects that belong to a specifiable or delimited class of things. In order to be afraid of x, I must think that x is dangerous—that it belongs to the class of harmful things. X might not really be dangerous. But to fear x, I must perceive it to be harmful, even if it is not. In order to pity x, I must think that x has suffered misfortune. I cannot pity someone who I think is on top of the world in every way. In order to envy x, I need to think that x has something that I lack. I cannot envy Quasimodo's good looks, if I believe Quasimodo is grotesque. And so on. In short, what emotional state I am in is determined by my cognitive state—by, for example, beliefs or thoughts about the objects of the emotional state in question.

If I believe that I've been wronged, and this causes a feeling of agitation in me, then, all things being equal, the state I am in is anger; but if I believe that

I'm in danger, and this causes my blood to freeze, then the emotional state I am in is fear. That is, as these examples should indicate, emotional states are governed by *criteria*. But what exactly does that mean?

In order to be angry at x, in the standard case, I must believe that certain criteria have been met, for example, I must believe that x has wronged me or mine. To fear x, I must believe that x is harmful; to pity x, I must believe that x has suffered misfortune; to envy x, I must believe that x has something I have not got. To be in these emotional states, I must be in the relevant cognitive states. These cognitive states are constitutive of the identity of the emotional state in which I am. Having the relevant cognitive states is a necessary condition for being in these emotional states.[9] These cognitive appraisals of the situations in question are criterial for being in just these states. Indeed, the relevant cognitive appraisals are the reasons that I am in these states.

If you ask me why I am angry, my reason is that I think that I or mine have been wronged. If you ask me why I'm afraid, my reason is that I've been threatened. Why do I pity Oedipus? Because he's suffered grievous misfortune. Why do I envy Donald Trump? Because he's got lots of money and I don't.

Now if what I've said so far is persuasive, then it looks as though the emotions are necessarily governed by reasons. Indeed, to say that I am in one of these emotional states, sans the requisite cognitive appraisal, would be virtually self-contradictory, the very height of irrationality. To say that I am afraid of potatoes at the same time that I genuinely believe in my heart of hearts that they are not harmful is sheer nonsense, a logical absurdity—what Gilbert Ryle called a category error. Indeed, if I made such a claim, you would probably either attempt to find some hidden, unacknowledged reason why I think that potatoes are dangerous or suspect that I did not understand the meaning of my own words. These explanations might account for the utter irrationality of my assertion. But the very search for these kinds of accounts shows that, in the standard case, we think that the emotions, contra Plato, naturally possess a kind of rationality.

Perhaps some evidence for the view that emotions possess some sort of rationality—that is, that they are governed by reasons—is that our emotions can be modified or changed by changing our beliefs or reasons. Our emotions are educable. If reasons can be given to show that the object of our fear is not harmful, then the emotion of fear typically evaporates. We try to convince the child not to be afraid of the monster underneath the bed by proving to her that there is no such monster. Furthermore, if I can be shown that an action that I thought was cowardly is courageous, then my emotion standardly will shift from contempt to admiration. Why does this happen? Because inasmuch as emotions are determined by cognitive states, like belief, a change in the relevant cognitive state will change the emotional state, either by transforming it into another emotional state altogether or by sublating it entirely. The relation of emotions to cognitive states, like beliefs, is, of course, the basis for the psychoanalytic talking cure, which, in effect, modifies dysfunctional or inappropriate emotional behaviors by disentangling our sedimented, mistaken, or erroneously associated beliefs and patterns of attention. Thus, though certain emotional episodes may be irrational in the sense that they are based on defective beliefs, the emotions as such are rationally tractable.

Moreover, if emotions are susceptible to being changed by reasons and to being modified by cognitive states, such as belief states, then we must conclude, contra Plato, that the emotions respond to knowledge. They respond to knowledge naturally, since knowledge-like cognitive states, such as beliefs, are components of all emotional states. The consequences of these observations for Plato's view should be straightforward. The emotions are not necessarily irrational. They have rational criteria of appropriateness that are open to logical assessment. They are naturally responsive to reason and knowledge. Thus, addressing the emotions in the manner of drama and narrative need not necessarily undermine reason.

Indeed, the emotions may serve reason in general by effectively guiding our attention to important information. Thus, there are no grounds for worrying that the emotions, such as the emotions elicited by art, will necessarily subvert reason, since, among other things, reason or cognition is an ineliminable constituent, indeed a determining force, of the emotions. Therefore, it is not the case that all representations threaten reason; only those that encourage defective cognitive states, like false beliefs, are affronts to reason—and not because they are emotional states, but only because they are epistemically defective. Or, in short, Plato's most general argument about the relation between art and the emotions must be rejected.

In addition to his general argument about art and the emotions, Plato also claims that the specific emotions—like pity and fear—that are engendered by dramatic poetry are maladaptive. Encouraging these emotions would, he believes, contradict certain reasons of state. Perhaps that is another reason that Plato thinks that these emotions are irrational. Of course, whether these emotions do contravene larger purposes raises at least two kinds of questions that are not of direct interest to us: whether, in fact, these emotions really have the consequences that Plato attributes to them, and whether, in the specific cultural circumstances, these emotions are dysfunctional. However, if Plato fears that the emotions are maladaptive in general, he is surely wrong.

For emotions are part of our biological makeup. This is not to deny that they are culturally modified. To be angered, we must believe that we have been wronged, but, of course, what counts as a wrong is in large measure a matter of cultural determination. Yet, along with the influence of culture, the emotions are also rooted in biology. And as biological phenomena, their persistence can be explained according to the principles of natural selection. That is, in opposition to the suspicion that the emotions are maladaptive, we may argue that we have the emotions because they contribute to the fitness of the human organism. In other words, we have the emotions because they enhance our prospects for survival. Undoubtedly this is connected to the fact that they respond to knowledge and reason. But in any case, the emotions are hardly impediments to adaptation; rather, they are devices in the service of adapting to the environment.

Moreover, we need not base this claim on the abstract supposition that any biological component as entrenched as the emotions must provide some adaptive advantage. I think that we can begin to specify with some precision the evolutionary service that the emotions perform for the human organism. Of course, the most obvious service that the emotions perform for the organism is to motivate behavior, since the emotions are typically made up of desires, as well as cognitive states. Emotional states cognitively organize our perceptions of situations in light of our desires and values, and thereby prepare the organism to act in its perceived interests. Anger and fear, for example, prime the organism to fight or to flee, respectively.

The bodily effects that the emotions induce ready the organism to carry out certain activities effectively. But connected to their role in the preparation of the organism for action, the emotions also shape our perception of situations.[10] And this, of course, rather than their action-motivating potentials, is what should be most interesting for aestheticians.

Perception and the emotions are interrelated in a number of ways. First, it is our attention to certain aspects of a situation—say, the harmful ones—that moves us into certain emotional states in the first instance. But the emotions provide feedback to our processes of attention. Once alerted to the harmful aspects of a situation, our fear will impel us to search the situation—to scan the scene—for further evidence of harmfulness. The emotions focus our attention. They make certain features of situations salient, and they cast those features in a special phenomenological light. The emotions "gestalt," we might say, situations. They organize them. They make certain elements of the situation stand out. They are sensitive to certain aspects of various recurring situations, like danger, and they size up and organize certain situations rapidly. And then they hold our attention on the relevant features of the situation, often compelling us to pick out further aspects of the situation under the criteria that define the emotional state we are in. As Jenefer Robinson puts it: "If I respond emotionally . . ., then my body alerts me to my conception of the situation and registers it as personally significant to me."[11] For example, we might first detect the large wave coming at us, and then our fear further apprises us of its lethal velocity.

Clearly, the attention-guiding function of the emotions is connected to the role the emotions play in determining action. The emotions focus attention on those elements of situations that are relevant for action, given our desires. The emotions are evolutionary devices for identifying the significance—generally the significance for effective action—of the situations in which we find ourselves. And they are very economical devices in this respect, especially when contrasted to other, slower mental processes like deliberation. The emotions are good things to have when the organism has to scope out a situation immediately. Thus, in terms of both their action-guiding potential and their service to attention, the emotions are optimal adaptive mechanisms. This is not to say that particular emotional episodes are not frequently out of place or inappropriate, just as certain logical deductions may be unsound. Nevertheless, the emotions as a general feature of human nature are adaptive.

Thus, Plato is wrong in his suspicion that the emotions are maladaptive. Nor do I think that he can make the case that certain emotions—like pity and fear—are always maladaptive. For example, fear of death may be maladaptive for a soldier in battle, but it is not for someone, like a philosopher king, stepping out of the way of an oncoming chariot.

As you will recall, Plato also has a theory of the way in which the emotions are engaged by drama. His theory is probably the first theory of identification in Western civilization. He thought that when people read plays aloud, a practice that was quite common in Athenian culture, they would take on the emotions of the characters whose parts they were reading. And this was problematic, he thought, because in doing so, not only would they risk contamination by unsavory emotions, but also, in giving vent to the emotions through play-acting, reason would be sent on a holiday. We have already seen why these worries about irrationality were misplaced. But it also pays to note that Plato's theory of how the emotions are communicated by drama is mistaken.

In the standard case, we do not identify emotionally with characters by, so to say, taking on their emotions. When we are happy at the end of the movie because the lovers have finally gotten together, that is not a function of the fact that we are in love with the characters. Which one of the characters would it be, anyway? Both? But if we are in love with both the characters, then we are in an emotional state that neither of the characters is in, since each of them is only in love with one person. And actually, we are in love with neither of them. We are happy that they have gotten together, but we are happy in the way of onlookers, not participants. Our emotions do not duplicate theirs, although our recognition of what their emotions are and that the lovers' desires have been satisfied are ingredients in our rather different emotional states.

Similarly, when we are angered by the behavior of both Antigone and Creon, our anger is based on our assessment that both of them are unyieldingly stubborn, an emotional assessment that neither of them shares with us. And when Creon's son and wife commit suicide, we pity him, whereas his emotional state is one of self-recrimination. In short, in the standard case, there is an asymmetrical relation between the emotional state that characters undergo and those of the audience, whereas identification requires identity (of emotions), which is a symmetrical relation. Therefore, the notion of identification cannot provide us, contra Plato and his contemporary avatars, with a general theory of our emotional involvement with dramas in particular or with narrative fictions in general.

I have spent a great deal of time elaborating the problems with Plato's conception of our emotional involvement with art for heuristic purposes. For in laying out what is wrong in Plato, I have been able to introduce enough information about the emotions to construct a positive account of the way in which our emotions are engaged by narrative fictions. In my criticisms of Plato, I have rejected the possibility that emotional identification characterizes the general mechanism or structure that elicits the audience's emotional response to narrative fiction. Let me begin my positive account of our emotional involvement with fiction by proposing an alternative structure.

II. An Alternative Account of the Relation
of Emotion and Narrative

Emotions are intimately related to attention. It is this feature of the emotions that should be important to art theorists, rather than the action-mobilizing feature of the emotions, since artworks, in the standard case, command attention, not action. I have suggested, furthermore, that the emotions are related to our attention-focalizing mechanisms. They direct our attention to certain details, rather than others; they enable us to organize those details into significant wholes or gestalts, so that, for example, our attention selects out or battens on the concatenation of details in the situation that are, for example, relevant to harm or to misfortune. The emotions operate like a searchlight, foregrounding those details in a special phenomenological glow. And, as well, once we are in the midst of an emotional state, we not only hold to those details, often obsessively, but are prompted to search out more details with similar relevance to our emotional assessment of the situation. The emotions manage our attention when we are in their grip. And that management undergoes changes in the sense that it first alerts our attention to certain gestalts and holds our attention on them, and then encourages further elaboration of our attention, inclining us to search for further elements of the relevant gestalt in the stimulus and leading us to form expectations about the kinds of things we should be on the lookout for as the situation evolves.

Now if this picture of the way in which our emotions and attention mesh is accurate, it should provide us with a useful way in which to think about our emotional involvement with narrative fictions. In life, as opposed to fiction, our emotions have to pick up on the relevant details of a situation out of a welter of unstructured details. We are sitting in a room talking distractedly to some friends; we notice a faint smell of something burning. Our emotions alert us to danger; our attention is riveted on the odor. We begin to look and to sniff about for further evidence of fire, readying ourselves to confront it or to flee.

But in fiction, of course, the situation has already been structured for our attention. The author has already done much of the work of focusing our attention through the way in which she has foregrounded what features of the event are salient. After all, the author has not only chosen, indeed invented, the situations we encounter, but she has also decided what features of those events are worthy of direct comment or implication. Thus, again and again in Uncle Tom's Cabin, Harriet Beecher Stowe confronts us with scenes of families being separated, and, in case after case, she emphasizes the innocence and decency of the slaves whose family ties are being sundered, and the cruelty and callousness with which it is being done. These perhaps none-too-subtle promptings lead us to perceive the scenes under the category of injustice, which, in turn, elicits the affect of indignation from us. And this indignation, in consequence, bonds us to the details of the text as well as preparing us to anticipate and to be on the lookout for further evidence of injustice, which, of course, Stowe's text delivers in abundance.

Or consider the character Fledgeby in Dickens's novel *Our Mutual Friend*. As Fledgeby taunts his factotum Riah, Dickens keeps in the foreground of our attention Fledgeby's viciousness, underscoring his abusiveness and his un-flinching anti-Semitism, which he, Fledgeby, attempts to pass off as humor. Through Dickens's descriptions, Riah is shown to be Fledgeby's moral and human superior in every way. All Fledgeby has is money, which he uses to subordinate everyone else, including Riah. Dickens does not have to come right out and say that Fledgeby is contemptible. Rather, the way in which he has described the situation engenders hatred of and contempt for Fledgeby in us, which primes the way in which we attend to his appearance in other scenes, and which encourages us to hope for his downfall.

Or think about how suspense is engendered in fictions and how it keeps us riveted to the action. Suspense is an emotion, one that in fictions generally involves an event where some outcome that we regard to be morally righteous is improbable. For example: in the recent motion picture *Speed*, it is likely that the bus will explode; in *True Lies*, that the nuclear device will detonate; and in *Outbreak*, that the antidote will be blown away with the rest of the town when the army drops its firebomb. In each of these cases, the outcome that I've mentioned has been depicted as immoral in the relevant fictions, but at the same time, it is the one that is most likely, given the world of the fiction as it has been presented to us. Or, to put it alternatively, the moral outcome is presented as if it were improbable. When confronted with such prospects, we attend to the events onscreen with suspense; the emotion rivets us to the screen and shapes our attention in such a way that our mind is preoccupied with tracking the features of the event that are relevant to the emotional state in which we find ourselves. And with suspense, that means keeping track of the shifting probabilities for the forces of good versus the forces of evil.[12]

I have chosen examples in which the emotions involved are somewhat in-tense and in which their elicitation has a forceful, one might say, an "in-your-face" character. I have opted for such examples because I think that they show the dynamics of our emotional responses to fiction in bold relief. However, there is no reason to think that the elicitation of emotions by narrative fictions is always as aggressive as it is in these examples. The emotional cues in the text may be more recessive or subtle, they may be initially obscured by irony or ambiguity, and it may take them longer to hit the reader than the examples I have mentioned. This may especially be the case as we ascend from examples of popular culture to so-called high art. And yet, even in these cases, I think that we will discern the same regularities in operation.

Whether verbal or visual, the text will be prefocused. Certain features of situations and characters will be made salient through description or depiction. These features will be such that they will be subsumable under the categories or concepts that, as I argued earlier, govern or determine the identity of the emotional states we are in. Let us refer to this attribute of texts by saying that the texts are criterially prefocused.[13]

For example, horror is an emotion that involves fear and revulsion.[14] The criterion of fear is the harmful; the criterion of revulsion is the impure. Events are horrific when they are subsumable under the categories of the harmful and the impure, that is, when they satisfy the criteria for horror by being harmful and impure. Thus, when authors of horror describe or depict events that they intend to elicit horror from us, they will describe or depict events, situations, and characters that are harmful and impure—for instance, slavering, fetid mounds of cankerous flesh with razor sharp claws and cosmic antipathy toward all things human. That is, the author will describe or depict the putative objects of our emotional state so that the *salient* features of that object are apt, for the normal audience member, to be slotted under the categories of the harmful and the impure. This categorization need not be a conscious operation, no more than my recognition that an oncoming car is potentially harmful need be accompanied by my saying it.

So the first step in the elicitation of an emotional response from the audience is a criterially prefocused text—a text structured in such a way that the description or depiction of the object of our attention is such that it will activate our subsumption of the event under the categories that are criterially relevant to certain emotional states. Once we recognize the object under those categories, the relevant emotion is apt, in certain conditions to be discussed below, to be raised in us. We will undergo some physical changes—with horror fictions our flesh may begin, as they say, to crawl; with suspense, we may feel our muscles tense; with melodrama, we may shed a tear; with comedy, we may laugh—and, in addition, our attention becomes emotively charged: the object of the emotion rivets our attention, while our emotionally governed perception casts its object in a special phenomenological light. The emotion glues our attention to those features of the object of the emotion that are apposite to the emotional state we are in; it encourages us to survey the event for further features that may support or sustain the presiding emotional state in which we find ourselves; and, protentively, our emotively charged state shapes our anticipation of what is to come by priming us to be on the lookout for the emergence or appearance of details subsumable under the categories of the reigning emotion. Or, in short, the criterially prefocused text gives rise, in the right circumstances, to emotive focus in the audience, where by "emotive focus" I am referring to the way in which the emotional state of the reader, viewer, or listener both fixes and shapes her attention.

Plato's story of our emotional involvement with the text posits characters, venting certain emotions, with whom we identify in such a way that their emotions are transferred to the audience. In contrast, I maintain that the structure involves a criterially prefocused text that elicits an emotively focused response. That is, a criterially prefocused text brings our attention to certain details, stimulating an emotional response, which quickens our attentiveness and which binds us to the text so that we are ready to assimilate it in the relevant way. Relevant to what? Relevant to the presiding emotion state, which, in the standard case, is the one that the author designed the text to engender in us.

The emotional states of characters may be pertinent to the emotional state we are in; that we perceive a character to be in anguish may be material to our pity for him. But it is the way in which the text is criterially prefocused that is crucially determinant to the audience's emotive response, and not some putative process of character identification. Rather than character identification, it is our own preexisting emotional constitution—with its standing dispositions that the text activates—that accounts for our emotional involvement with narrative fictions.

Of course, simply presenting a reader, viewer, or listener with a criterially prefocused text does not guarantee that the reader, viewer, or listener will respond emotionally. For a criterially prefocused text can be read dispassionately. Something more is required to elicit a passionate response. And what that "something more" is amounts to a concern or a pro attitude on the part of the reader, viewer, or listener of the fiction regarding the way in which the situation depicted in the fiction is or is not going. That is, in addition to being criterially prefocused, the narrative must instill certain concerns about the fictional characters and events in the reader, viewer, or listener. These concerns function like the desires in many everyday emotions, and when added to the mental content or conception derived from the criterially prefocused text, the combination, all things being equal, should elicit an emotional response in accordance with the criterial features of the situation that the text has made pertinent for attention.

The structure of our emotional involvement with a narrative comprises at least a criterially prefocused text plus certain concerns or pro attitudes, and together these are apt to elicit broadly predictable responses in standard audiences. The criterially prefocused text embodies a conception of a situation. But a conception of a situation alone is not sufficient to motivate an emotional response, as is evident from the reactions of certain sociopaths. To prompt such a response requires that audiences be invested with concerns—certain pro and con attitudes—about what is going on in a story.[15]

This suggestion makes the assumption that narrative structures can enlist audiences in preferences about the ways in which a story might go. This is not to say that all stories do this—narrative instructions about how to fix a broken water pipe may not. Nevertheless, I think that it is equally noncontroversial to suppose that many narratives do induce readers, listeners, and viewers to form preferences about how the story should evolve. For example, in Grant Allen's *The Woman Who Did*—called "the bestseller that scandalized Victorian Great Britain"—the implied reader is concerned for Herminia Barton (the woman who believed in sexual relations outside of matrimony). Said readers respect her sincerity and prefer that Herminia be spared from harm. Thus, at the end of the story, when Herminia feels compelled to commit suicide, the reader is moved to sadness, not simply because the story has portrayed her plight melodramatically, but because the story has elicited a pro attitude toward Herminia from the reader as well.

Typically, stories develop in such a way that readers, viewers, and listeners have a structured horizon of expectations about what might and what might not happen. And, in addition to having a sense of the possible outcomes of the ongoing courses of events, one also, generally under the guidance of the author, has convictions about what outcomes one would, in a certain sense, prefer to obtain versus those one would prefer not to obtain. In some cases, the preferred course of events correlates with the express goals and plans of the protagonists of the story; what they want to happen—say, averting nuclear disaster—is what the audience wants to happen. However, in a great many other cases, the story may proffer preferred outcomes independently of the express goals and plans of any of the characters. That is, the story may have its own agenda, as in the cases of all those fictional lovers who find themselves amorously involved in ways they never planned and even might have abhorred antecedently.

But however motivated, audiences develop concerns regarding the situations in stories, and when those concerns are threatened, we tend to react with dysphoric (or discomforting) emotions, whereas, when the concern in question is abetted by narrative developments, our emotions tend to be euphoric.[16] Which particular dysphoric or euphoric emotion is engaged, of course, depends upon the way in which the text is criterially prefocused. For example, considering some dysphoric emotions, if I have a pro attitude toward a character and he is morally wronged in a way that the text makes criterially salient, then, all things being equal, I will feel anger, particularly toward those characters who have wronged him; whereas, if presented with the gross misfortune of a group that has elicited my concern in a criterially prefocused way, I am apt to feel pity for them.

Furthermore, euphoric emotions of different sorts also are likely to evolve in accordance with the way in which the text is criterially prefocused (where our concerns or desires about the direction of courses of events are also satisfied). When a character toward whom we bear a pro attitude overcomes obstacles, saliently posed in the text, we are likely to respond with admiration, whereas the manifestation of virtually limitless power by an agency of which we approve—for instance, nature or a god—will tend to evoke reverence.

Authors of narratives are able, fairly reliably, to induce the emotions they set out to evoke—especially basic emotions (like anger, fear, hatred, and so on)—because of the fact that they share a common background (cultural, but biological as well) with their audiences, both in terms of the criteria relevant to the experience of specific emotions as well as in terms of what it standardly takes to elicit concern for given characters and their goals, and for the alternative directions that situations may take. Inasmuch as authors generally share a common background, cultural and otherwise, with their audiences, they may use themselves as detectors to gauge how audiences are likely to respond to their texts. They can use their own reactions to predict the direction of the standard audience member's concern, as well as the specific emotional states the criterial prefocusing will encourage.

Of course, authors are not infallible in this regard. In his book *American Psycho*, Brett Easton Ellis expected audiences to respond with hilarity—because he intended a postmodern parody—whereas they greeted the book with disgust. Nevertheless, with most narrative fiction, such wild mismatches of intended affect with actual affect are the exception rather than the rule. Most narratives are relatively successful in raising the kind of emotion at which they aim, though not always in the degree to which they aspire (frequently eliciting too much or too little of the intended affect).

The reason for what accuracy there is in this matter is that generally, in sharing a background (an ethos, a moral and emotive repertoire, a cognitive stock, and so on) with audiences, authors are able to conjecture what their confrères' reaction should be in terms of which emotional responses are appropriate to situations depicted in certain ways. Within the boundaries of certain cultures, there are certain criteria concerning which emotional responses are normatively correct—that is, which emotions certain situations are supposed to elicit. Authors, as members of that culture, possessed in common with audiences, use their knowledge of what is normatively correct in terms of emotional responses and compose narrative situations accordingly. Thus, authors can broadly predict how readers will respond to the events they construct because they know the way in which members of their culture are supposed to respond emotionally to situations of various sorts. Where most storytellers fail (when they fail), it seems to me, is usually not in evoking the emotions they intend to evoke, but in evoking them at the wrong level of intensity. And this, I speculate, is very frequently a matter of the failure to elicit the appropriate amount or type of concern for the characters and situations depicted.

But, be that as it may, emotional involvement with a narrative depends upon the combination of a criterially prefocused text with pro and/or con attitudes about the ways in which the narrative situation can develop—that is to say, a combination of a conception of the situation along with some relevant concerns, preferences, and desires. Together, these provide necessary and sufficient conditions for an emotional response to the text to take hold in such a way that the reader, viewer, or listener becomes emotionally focused, that is, in such a way that the abiding emotional state fixes and shapes her attention.

Insofar as audience concern often takes its cue from the goals of characters, it may be tempting to reintroduce the Platonic notion of identification at this point, claiming that audiences take on the goals of characters in fictional narratives by identifying with the characters and deriving their (the audiences') concerns by means of this process. But this brand of identification cannot provide us with a general theory of how concerns are engendered by narratives, since the direction of our concern in many stories runs in different directions from those of the protagonists. So it cannot, across the board, be the case that, in order to form our concerns, we must be identifying with characters and their express goals. Often we form our concerns about how the story should go in a paternalistic rather than an identificatory fashion. Frequently, we do not think that the characters should get what they want. Thus, identification once again fails as a general account of how we are emotionally engaged by narratives.

Contra Plato, the mechanism is not a matter of identification. We do not become the character and acquire her goals. The character's emotion does not transmigrate into us. Rather, our preexisting emotional makeup with its standing recognitional capacities and our preexisting dispositions to certain values and preferences are mobilized by the text's providing an affective cement

that fixes our attention on the text and shapes our attention to the evolving story.

Moreover, it will be recalled that Plato tried to explain the function of the emotions in drama purely in terms of economic necessity. The audience understands little, Plato contends, so the only way to engage it is through the emotions, understood as irrational forces. I reject this account, because I think that the emotions are connected to cognition. Indeed, addressing the emotions may, in fact, provide understanding. Thus the elicitation of emotional responses from audiences is not an alternative to cognition and understanding. Rather, the real function of the emotions for narrative fictions is, on my account, the management of the audience's attention. Of course, successful management of the audience's attention may be economically beneficial. But this may be regarded as a secondary effect and not the primary reason that emotions are virtually indispensable to fictions.

III. Ramifications for Research

If my account of the emotional involvement of the audience with regard to narrative fiction is acceptable, it suggests a certain direction of research. In order to analyze how a text elicits an emotional response, it is of central importance to isolate the way in which the text is criterially prefocused. Using herself as a detector, the critic begins with a global sense of the emotions that the text has elicited in her. Then, using the criteria of the emotion in question as a hypothesis, she may review the way in which the text is articulated to isolate the relevant descriptions or depictions in the text that instantiate the concept of the emotion in question. In following this procedure, one can pith the emotive structure of the text.

What "pithing the emotive structure of the text" amounts to here is finding the aspects of the depictions or descriptions of the object of the emotion that satisfy the necessary conditions for being in whatever emotional state the audience is in. This is what explaining the emotional state of the audience generally comes to (along with identifying the concerns or preferences with which the narrative invests the audience).

For example, I cite the descriptions of the putatively rancid odor of the monster in a horror fiction because it contributes the satisfaction of one of the necessary conditions of one's being horrified (viz., that the object of the emotion be perceived as impure) and thus my citation contributes to explaining why the audience is horrified by the novel. Of course, it is impossible to predict exhaustively every way in which authors will satisfy the necessary conditions of the emotional states that concern them. After all, artists can be original. However, there is room for limited generalization in this area where theorists are able to identify recurring formulas—both in terms of constructing emotive salience and enlisting audience preferences—that are routinely used to secure certain affects.

Admittedly, this order of research may not always be practicable. For example, one may not always be able to articulate with precision one's emotional

response to a text. In that case, one might be better advised to tackle the descriptions and depictions with an eye to seeing what they make salient and then compare those saliencies with the criteria for the better known emotional states. This may lead to a clarification of the emotional address of the text in question. Needless to say, I would not wish to claim that the emotional address of a text is always unambiguous, nor would I deny that some texts may introduce novel emotional timbres. Nevertheless, in these cases the procedure that I have recommended is still valuable, because it will enable us to identify the general contours of the emotional ambiguities and novel emotional timbres in the text.

Of course, in many cases, especially those in which we as ordinary readers are dealing with texts that are remote from us in time and place, we will not be able to depend on our own emotional responses to the text because we do not have the appropriate cultural background. This is exactly where literary history, film history, art history, dance history, and the like have an indispensable role to play. For historians can supply us with the background necessary to make the emotive address of texts from other cultures and other periods in the history of our own culture emotionally accessible to us.

My emphasis on the emotional address of texts may trouble some readers who worry that it makes textual analysis too much like sociology. It may sound as though I am advocating that we must go out into the field and find out how audiences actually respond to texts. And yet, I am not proposing that sort of empirical sociology. For I am concerned with the normatively correct address of the text—the emotive effect that the text is supposed to have, or is designed to have on the normal audience. Some people may find beheadings humorous; but that is not the emotional response that A Man For All Seasons is designed to promote. Throughout this paper, I have been concerned with the normatively correct emotional response to texts and with the structure that encourages that response. This is a matter of textual analysis, albeit against the background of the culture of the emotions in which the text is produced. It is not a matter of sociological polling. This, of course, is not said to deny that the results of sociological polling may be interesting. But in many cases, I suspect that it is redundant, since to a surprising extent, it seems to me, texts tend to elicit actual emotional responses that are normatively appropriate to them.

IV. Fiction and the Emotions

So far, I have been developing a framework for understanding our emotional engagement with fictional narratives. In doing so, I have presumed that such engagement is logically possible. But there are certain theoretical considerations that suggest that the relations I have attempted to unravel simply can't obtain. So for the brief remainder of this essay, let me address those worries in order to allay them.

I have embraced a cognitive theory of the emotions in order to characterize our involvement with fictional narratives. Cognitive theories of the emotions

maintain that a central component of the emotions is a cognitive state, such as a belief. But if the requisite cognitive state that is partly constitutive of an emotion must be a belief, as some cognitive theorists contend, then it is difficult to understand how readers, viewers, and listeners can be emotionally moved by narrative fictions, because such audiences know the narratives in question are fictions, and, therefore, do not believe them. To fear x, under one standard analysis, is, among other things, to believe that x is harmful. But then how can I be in a state of fear with regard to a vampire novel, since I know that the novel is a fiction, that vampires do not exist, and, consequently, that the vampires mentioned in the novel cannot really be harmful? Similarly, insofar as other emotions involve other sorts of beliefs, which, like fear, putatively cannot be sustained for persons, objects, and events we know, and, therefore, believe do not exist, how is any emotional response to fiction possible at all? Perhaps emotional responses to fiction are just impossible.

My answer to this challenge relies on my rejection of the supposition that emotions require beliefs in all cases.[17] The cognitive theory of emotions requires a cognitive component, but, I would argue, the form that component can take is diverse, including not only beliefs, but thoughts and perhaps even patterns of attention.[18] And, furthermore, the form that is most relevant to understanding our emotional responses to fictional narratives is thought, not belief.

But what do I mean by "thought" in this context? In order to answer that question, let me contrast what I am calling thoughts with beliefs. A belief, for my purposes, can be conceived to be a proposition held in the mind as asserted. To believe that there is a table in front of me is to be committed to the truth of the assertion of the proposition "that there is a table in front of me." A thought, on the other hand, is a matter of entertaining a proposition in the mind unasserted, as one does when I ask you to suppose that "Albania has conquered the United States" or to imagine that "Manhattan Island is made of pizza." To imagine is to remain neutral about whether we know or believe whatever it is that we imagine. It is to entertain a thought-content, to entertain a proposition as unasserted, to understand the meaning of the proposition (to grasp its propositional content), but to refrain from taking it as an assertion, and, therefore, to be neutral about its truth value.

Moreover, it seems to be indisputable that emotions can be engendered in the process of holding propositions before the mind unasserted. While cutting vegetables, imagine putting the very sharp knife in your hand into your eye. One suddenly feels a shudder. You need not believe that you are going to put the knife into your eye. Indeed, you know that you are not going to do this. Yet merely entertaining the thought, or the propositional content of the thought (that I am putting this knife into my eye), can be sufficient for playing a role in causing a tremor of terror. For emotions may rest on thoughts and not merely upon beliefs.

We can evoke bodily changes in ourselves by means of thoughts. We do this all the time when we stimulate ourselves sexually in the process of imagining compliant beauties beckoning us to embrace them. Arachnophobes can send a chill of fear down their spine by imagining that a tarantula is on their back, and most of us can make ourselves gag with disgust, if we suppose that the food in our mouth is really someone else's vomit. Thoughts, that is, can play a role in generating emotional states.

Furthermore, this aspect of the emotions is particularly pertinent to our commerce with fictional narratives. For fictions are stories that authors intend readers, listeners, and viewers to imagine.[19] Fictions comprise sentences, or other sense-bearing vehicles, that communicate propositions to audiences, which propositions the author of the fiction intends the audience to imagine or to entertain in the mind unasserted as a result of audience members' recognition of the author's intention that that is what they are meant to do. In making a fiction, an author is creating an assemblage of propositions for prospective readers, viewers, or listeners, which the author intends to be entertained in thought. The author presenting a fiction in effect says to the audience: "hold these propositions before your mind unasserted"—that is, "suppose p" or "imagine p" or "entertain p unasserted."

Thus, if thoughts, as distinct from beliefs, can also support emotional responses, then we may have emotional responses to fictions concerning situations, persons, objects, and things that do not exist. For we can imagine or suppose that they exist, and entertaining unasserted the propositional content of the relevant thoughts can figure in the etiology of an emotional state. Fictions, construed as propositions to be imagined, supply us with the relevant, unasserted propositional content, and in entertaining that content as the author mandates, we can be emotionally moved by fictions. It is not impossible to be moved by fictions. It is quite natural, as we can see by putting together two theses: (1) the thesis that fictions are propositions that authors proffer to us with the intention that they be imagined or entertained as unasserted and (2) the thesis that thoughts, construed as propositions held in mind unasserted, can play the role of the cognitive constituent in the activation of an emotional state.

On my account of our emotional involvement with fictional narratives, authors present readers, listeners, and viewers with propositions to be imagined that depict or describe situations that have been criterially prefocused and that arouse our concern so that we become emotionally focused on the text—that is, our attention (1) becomes riveted to the objects of our emotional state (said objects are lit, in a manner of speaking, in a special phenomenological glow), (2) our attention is inexorably drawn to those features of the object of the emotion that are apposite to the emotional state we are in, (3) we are encouraged to search the situation for more features of the sort that will support and sustain the prevailing emotional state, and (4) we are prompted to anticipate further details of the evolving story that are subsumable under the categories of the presiding emotion. Emotions are a central device that authors have for managing the attention of readers, listeners, and viewers. Not only do authors use our already existing emotional constitution to direct our attention and to fill in the story in a way that makes it intelligible; our emotions keep us locked on the text on a moment-to-moment basis.

NOTES

1. A useful survey of this material in the philosophical literature is John Deigh's 1994. For a discussion of a wide range of research in psychology, see Keith Oatley 1992.

2. Oatley remarks, for example, that Freud has no theory of the emotions as such (1992, 143).

3. Flo Leibowitz 1996.

4. Leo Tolstoy [1898] (1960), and R. G. Collingwood 1938.

5. Some modernist narratives may intentionally suppress emotive address entirely.

6. Denis Diderot 1957.

7. For different versions of this view, see, for example, William Lyons 1980; George Rey 1980; Robert C. Solomon 1976; Irving Thalberg 1964 and 1980. Of course, not everyone accepts the cognitive theory of the emotions as a universal theory of the emotions. However, even if it is not a universal theory of the emotions, I still think its usefulness in discussing the emotions elicited by narratives is defensible, since most of those emotions appear to fall noncontroversially into the class of cognitive emotions.

8. The caveat "at least" here is meant to acknowledge that desires may also be constituents of many everyday emotions. Some theorists argue that desires are constituents of all emotions. See, for example, Jenefer Robinson 1983 and O. H. Green 1992.

9. This is not to say that we always recognize the emotional state that we are in by reference to the necessary criteria for being in that state, nor that everyone can explicitly articulate the necessary criteria for being in a given emotional state. Often, we identify the state we are in by means of what Ronald de Sousa has called "paradigm scenarios"—narrative prototypes that we use to match emotions to certain types of situations. For a discussion of paradigm scenarios, see Ronald de Sousa 1987. For an initial attempt to suggest the relevance of paradigm scenarios for aesthetic research, see Noël Carroll 1990.

10. S. Tomkins 1979, Kent Bach 1994, and Jenefer Robinson 1995b.

11. Robinson 1995b, 65.

12. This theory of suspense is defended in Noël Carroll 1996.

13. I think that it is the fact of criterial prefocusing that Jenefer Robinson leaves out in her essay on the emotions in fiction in her article "Experiencing Art" 1990).

14. This account of horror is defended in Noël Carroll 1990b.

15. As I understand these pro attitudes, they are not themselves emotions; rather, they are like the desires that comprise many everyday emotions.

16. Here, I am extrapolating from what is sometimes called the conflict theory of emotions. Representatives include F. Paulhan 1930, G. Mandler 1984, and Keith Oatley 1992, esp. 107–09 and 174–77.

17. This view is defended at greater length in Noël Carroll 1990b, esp. chap. 2.

18. See Amélie Rorty 1980.

19. This view of fiction is advanced in Gregory Currie 1990, and in Peter Lamarque and Stein Haugom Olsen 1994.

PART IV

THE
VALUE OF
EMOTION

———

Toward a Poetics of Emotion

WILLIE VAN PEER

I. Poetic Texts

Sometime in 1861, Emily Dickinson entered the following poem in one of her handsewn "portfolios": [1]

> I felt a Funeral, in my Brain,
> And Mourners to and fro
> Kept treading—treading—till it seemed
> That Sense was breaking through—
>
> And when they all were seated,
> A service, like a Drum—
> Kept beating—beating—till I thought
> My mind was going numb—
>
> And then I heard them lift a Box
> And creak across my Soul
> With those same Boots of Lead, again,
> Then Space—began to toll,
>
> As all the Heavens were a Bell,
> And Being, but an Ear,
> And I, and Silence, some strange Race
> Wrecked, solitary, here—

And then a Plank in Reason, broke,
And I dropped down, and down—
And hit a World, at every plunge,
And Finished knowing—then—

This is a chilling text, gripping in its sheer frankness about death, arousing the reader's anxiety and drawing attention to its mysterious message. Who is the I-person in the poem? Is she dead, and speaking to us across the boundary of no return? Is she hallucinating, imagining her own death? Where is she, and how (if she be dead) can she be listening to the Mourners? Why do they wear "Boots of Lead"? Why are they beating a drum?

The questions the text raises are not, I think, exceptional in kind. Many, if not most, poetic texts have the capacity to puzzle their readers, to command their attention, or to arouse their curiosity. Yet this cognitive interest—which undoubtedly exists for many readers—is not all there is to the phenomenology of poetic encounter. For many, reading the above poem will be accompanied by strong affective reactions. They may feel sad or tense. They may have an eerie feeling, or a genuine experience of what it is to be utterly alone and deserted. The Medical Humanities Database (on the World Wide Web) calls the poem "a fine description of the experience of depression or melancholia." Is it not strange that a text may do this? Why, one wonders, do words and sentences have this dual effect of raising both our cognitive interest and our emotional involvement?

It could be argued that what has been said so far may be the case for *some* readers only, while others may remain quite stoical vis-à-vis the poem. That, however, is no mystery, and may be explained by invoking the variation among individuals. Even if large groups of people remain unaffected by reading a particular text, that still leaves unaccounted the fact that some *are* affected by it. Also, while some readers may not be drawn to Emily Dickinson's text, most readers will readily acknowledge that they may sometimes be moved by other texts. But how can that be, to be moved by black marks on white paper? How can we be so involved in what is merely a "representation"?

II. Emotions and Literary Theory

The intimate relation between emotions and literature has been observed in literary theory from its onset. In this sense, the relationship of literature and emotion seems a happy and an old one. However, from the very beginning, there was also a serious problem. It will be remembered that Plato condemned literature for its emotional content and effects. As we read in *The Republic*, Plato recognizes the power that literature may exert: "[Y]ou know how even the best of us enjoy it and let ourselves be carried away by our feelings" (1987, 605d). And precisely this ability of poetry to affect us is seen as a source of evil: "We are therefore quite right to refuse to admit him [the poet] to a prop-erly run state, because he wakens and encourages and strengthens the lower elements in the mind to the detriment of reason" (1987, 605b).

Aristotle, his student, praised poetry for partly the same reason. He agreed with his teacher's analysis of the power of literature, but according to him, literature contributes to the elevation of mankind, to *paideia*. Readers and spectators are drawn into the passage of tragic events, "incidents arousing pity and fear, wherewith to accomplish its catharsis of such emotions,"[2] a process that purifies us of megalomania (*hybris*), safeguarding democratic government and protecting us from unrestrained tyranny.[3]

The opposing views of Plato and Aristotle still stand side by side and the issue remains unresolved. Although many Western societies seem to have adopted the Aristotelian perspective on literature and the arts, as I have argued elsewhere (van Peer 1995a), as long as societies have censorship laws, literature is suspect, and the Platonic view prevails. I propose that the source of the problem is located in the opposition between emotions and reason. This opposition forms the core of what could be called the "folk theory" of emotions. It argues that emotions are unimpeded by our reasoned selves. As Nussbaum puts it:

> According to some influential modern views that have left a deep mark on popular stereotypes, emotions like grief, anger, and fear come from an animal irrational side of the personality that is to be sharply distinguished from its capacity for reasoning and for forming beliefs. Emotions are simply bodily reactions. (1994, 79)

According to the folk model, "one can direct one's thoughts but one cannot control one's feelings, which are a natural consequence of events. And feelings can become so strong they prevent clear thinking and lead to irrational action" (D'Andrade 1995, 218).

The view would be innocent, and the debate over the opposition it paints between reason and emotions would be futile, if it were not so deeply entrenched in our culture. Plato is certainly not the only philosopher who propounded the view. It is echoed in Pascal's famous dictum "Le coeur a ses raisons que la raison ne connaît pas," and found a strong defense in Romanticism. Since we are still largely the children of this Romantic world view, as Charles Taylor (1989, 505) has convincingly argued, the view continues to dominate our ways of thinking and our cultural habits. The point is, however, that the folk theory of emotions is wrong; if there is one point on which all emotion psychologists concur, it is the conclusion that reason and feeling are not in fact opposites.[4] If this be so, then we might well ask how the relation between reason and emotion is to be otherwise described.

III. Emotion and Reason

Frijda defines emotions as "modes of relational action readiness, either in the form of tendencies to establish, maintain, or disrupt a relationship with the environment or in the form of mode of relational readiness as such" (1986, 71). Similar accounts of the emotions abound in the literature. D'Andrade (1980), for instance, emphasizes that emotions give us a picture of how the world is, in a vivid way; that they often increase the activations of various action schemas, but permit delay so that planning, goal sequencing, reappraisal, and other complex procedures can occur. . . . They hold information in an active form, so that it doesn't go away, yet does not pre-empt everything else."[5]

Solomon concurs:

> An emotion is a basic judgment about our Selves and our place in our world, the projection of the values and ideals, structures and mythologies, according to which we live and through which we experience our lives.
>
> This is why our emotions are so dependent upon our opinions and beliefs. A change in my beliefs (for example, the refutation of my belief that John stole my car) entails (not causes) a change in my emotion (my being angry that John stole my car). I cannot be angry if I do not believe that someone has wronged or offended me. (1993, 126)

Lazarus affirms that emotions are, in effect, "organized cognitive-motivational-relational configurations whose status changes with changes in the person-environment relationship as this is perceived and evaluated (appraised)" (1991, 38) and concludes that many theorists and researchers "now accept the prem-ise that adult human emotion can best be understood in cognitive terms" (129). Goleman (1995) even gives his book the title *Emotional Intelligence*, a term he borrows from Salovey and Mayer (1990).

IV. Hot Cognition

Emotions, then, are intimately related to cognition. Thus, in assessing the emotional potential of literature, we shall have to take this relation into ac-count. Reading literature is not an activity in which emotions have the upper hand, and readers are not (contrary to what Plato believed) segregated from their more rational concerns. Herbert Simon, one of the pioneers of cognitive science, speaks of "hot cognition" in this respect. Reading literature is, in his view, one such form in which our emotional involvement has clear cognitive overtones. In outlining the role that literature can play in societies at large, he points to the obvious advantages that a literary treatment may have over other, more worldly approaches:

> I could go down a long list of such alternatives: *War and Peace* versus a treatise on military sociology, Proust and Chekhov versus a textbook on personality. If I were in a position where I had to defend the role of the humanities in education, . . . I would argue for them on the grounds that most human beings are able to attend to issues longer, to think harder about them, to receive deeper impressions that last longer, if information is presented in a context of emotion—a sort of hot dressing—than if it is presented wholly without affect. (1983, 32)

Over the past decades, it has become abundantly clear that Simon's hypoth-esis about "hot cognition" is more than a metaphor, supported as it is by a good deal of empirical evidence. Thus, for instance, Dutta and Kanungo (1975) found that emotionally provocative materials were remembered better than emotionally neutral materials. Laird et al. (1982) have similarly shown that emotion influences the quantity and quality of recall. Gilligan and Bower (1984) report several experiments that demonstrate the influence of emotions on cognition. They argue that emotions thus seem to be "inextricably related to how we perceive and think," influencing our thoughts at every turn. Indeed, their results suggest "that emotion is often a central component of cognitive processes in general" (568–69). Similarly, Martins (1982), in an experimental study of story reading, found that intensity of affect was one of the determining factors in the text processing. He concludes that

> the explanations proposed by Robinson (1980) and Packman and Battig (1978) may be accepted, according to whom semantic information associated with a high degree of intensity of affect is processed at greater depth than semantic information of an indifferent nature, provided other factors remain constant. Greater depth of processing is interpreted here as being determined by an increase in the level of arousal, accompanied by a high degree of intensity of affect, all leading to more sustained attention being paid to this type of information. (152)

Thus, it would seem that emotion psychology has not only solved the age-old puzzle concerning the oppostion between feeling and reasoning, but has also provided the grounds for a poetics of emotion. Indeed, the rationale for the existence of literature lies precisely in its ability to work on issues that concern us deeply. And it does so in a way that keeps our motivation at its highest intensity. Literature is fuel for "hot cognition." One may presume that imaginative literature is a property that all human cultures possess and as such may provide humans with an evolutionary advantage.[6] This is also Walton's conclusion; reflecting on the value of psychological participation in games of make-believe (to which literature undoubtedly belongs), he pinpoints a Darwinian explanation: "Probably it has survival value. So evolutionary pressures may be responsible for our being organisms of a kind susceptible to quasi-emotions" (1990, 245).

V. The Paradox of Emotion

Let us go back now to the poem by Emily Dickinson quoted at the beginning of this essay. It will be clear that the text generates a fair amount of "hot cognition." It thematizes an aspect of our existence that transcends our normal powers of reasoning, our goals and plans, namely, our own mortality. Already the thought of our death ("a Funeral, in my Brain") can overwhelm us ("My mind was going numb"), lead to severe tension ("creak across my Soul") and sensory collapse ("Space began to toll"), and ultimately to the feeling of total desolation ("Wrecked, solitary, here"). The final stanza of the poem demonstrates the incapacity of our reasoning ("a Plank in Reason, broke") and the lyrical persona remains, after all rituals and drum beatings, inexorably alone, "And Finished Knowing—then."

The poem's affective appeal derives from its emotionally charged concentration on the helplessness we feel in being confronted with our existential vulnerability. Total vulnerability means the literal absence of any plans, as well as the impossibility of constructing any new plans (Oatley 1992, 303). It is this total na-kedness, in which one's ultimate concerns are torn to shreds, that arouses our emotions when reading the poem. Poets like Emily Dickinson possess the talent and the technique to communicate such ideas in a gripping form.

What the text demonstrates, therefore, is that emotional processes are not limited to everyday interactions: reading literature may also set the processes of "hot cognition" in motion. Of course, the theme of Emily Dickinson's poem is in itself an extremely poignant subject for most of us and, therefore, already a sensitive issue in our lives. It seems, then, that it is mainly in virtue of the formal properties of works of art that the literary and the everyday treatment of such issues must be distinguished. Before we look into this matter, however, it is necessary to clarify an issue that has escaped our attention so far.

If emotions are a form of "hot" cognition in the sense that they draw and guide our attention to important concerns and keep us concentrated and moti-vated for prolonged periods of time and at higher levels of intensity than we usually bring to our dealings with the world, then we inevitably find ourselves in a paradox.[7] Indeed, qua emotions they cannot really come to terms in a pragmatic sense with the concerns that generate them in the first place. Practi-cal action usually demands "cold" reasoning, decisions to be taken, action, planning, and cooperation with others. Emotions are pretty much helpless in this respect. In many cases we observe that strong emotions may even impede the acts necessary for solving the problem at hand. Hence, emotions power-fully focus our psychic energies on a particularly pressing problem, without, however, in any way showing us a solution to that problem. If we eventually come up with one, it is largely *despite* our emotions—though one should add immediately that without the emotions involved, the solution might have looked fundamentally different. All this leads to the insight that emotions are basically *processing devices*. They *trigger* a reevaluation of our goals, plans, and concerns. But they have little control over the processing activities themselves, and thus lack a strategy for reaching a decision; this is why they may start leading a life of their own, why they do not terminate themselves and may lead into paralysis and pathology.

Here is a (literary) example: after Macbeth and his wife have killed Duncan and usurped the throne, they become immersed in feelings of guilt, first Mac-beth himself, who is rebuked for his unmanly behavior by Lady Macbeth. Later, however, she is drawn into similar feelings herself, walking nightly about the castle, in the course of which she has been observed by her attendant to keep washing her hands for a quarter of an hour on end. Act V, scene 1 shows us another such instance, in which her attendant has now called in a physi-cian:

> *Lady M.* Out, damn'd spot! out, I say! One—two—why then 'tis time to do't. Hell is murky. Fie, my lord, fie, a soldier, and afeard? What need we fear who knows it, when none can call our pow'r to accompt? Yet who would have thought the old man to have had so much blood in him?
>
> (V,1,35–40)

Nightmarish thoughts of the murder haunt Lady Macbeth's sleepless nights, while she compulsively keeps washing her hands, which she thinks are still stained with Duncan's blood. There is nothing wrong in itself with washing one's hands; it is the compulsive nature of it that shows us that Lady Macbeth has gone over the brink into pathological behavior. Her emotions are processing devices for the sense of guilt which has come over her, but these emotions now take over and force themselves relentlessly into her mind, paralyzing her thought. Indeed, as the physician observes: "What a sight is there! The heart is sorely charg'd" (V,1,53–54).

VI. The Work of Mourning

Hence, emotions are important mechanisms guiding and sustaining our attention, while at the same time interrupting our actions, concentrating all our energies on the concern involved. In this perspective, literature and the arts seem to be of little value: they monitor and maintain a high level of emotional involvement, but keep us from getting things done. This is part of the critique Plato formulated when he described the emotional content and the affective response created by poetry. It is also, by and large, the commonsense view of literature: that it is fine as entertainment, but that one should draw a sharp distinction between such emotional gratification in leisure time and the more serious business of everyday life.

Yet this negative view of emotions is too limited. Sometimes, our concerns may demand that we not act immediately, but surrender to the impact of events; that we refrain from efficient plans, and instead contemplate and undergo the process of coming to terms with our concerns, at least for a period of time. One clear example of this is the "work" of mourning, as described so incisively by Freud.[8] Already in *Studien über Hysterie* (1895), Freud noticed the peculiar form in which mourning activities keep a person immersed in profound sadness, prolonging suffering by continuous confrontations with memories of the deceased. In "Mourning and Melancholia" (1915), Freud describes the process as absorbing all the ego's energies while opposing the realization that the loved person no longer exists. This opposition is repeatedly defeated by reality, yet continues to resist reality. Here we have an emotion fostering protracted resistance against remedy. It devours all motivation, all interest in other pursuits of life, including any effort to move beyond the realization of the loss. It is obvious that the process is extremely painful to the individual involved. But why is this the case? Why is not the loved one replaced by someone else? That would be a pragmatic "solution" that most of us, however, would naturally abhor. Apparently the loss of a loved one is such a blow to our concerns that cold cognition does not (and would not) work. We have to dwell on and ponder the death of our beloved, to immerse ourselves in our grief, in order to process the immensity of the loss involved. Note how this hot cognition (again) is not without its dangers: the emotional processes may take over the person's functioning and thus lead to pathology.

How the process of mourning (in nonpathological cases) subsides is instructive as to the functionality of the emotions concerned. It appears that humans, when confronted with tragic loss, are unable to cut the ties with the deceased easily. Instead, they will surrender themselves to recurrent memories of the lost person. Although going through these memories is extremely painful, they cannot be avoided. Their final effect, however, after a period of mourning, is recovery from the pain that the loss has caused. Hence, we must conclude, with Freud, that these acts of recall are necessary for coming to terms with the grief that the loss has caused (1915, 265). Each of the memories involves a new confrontation with the difference between what *is* and what *was*. The present state of confusion, of suffering, and of desolation, is mapped onto the memories of a happier state of affairs. The difference is so great that the present cannot (yet) be accepted. The step from the one to the other is simply too great to be taken. It requires repeated efforts of reprocessing, of reorientation, and of reevaluation, and a new sense of positioning oneself in life. This is what Emily Dickinson's first stanza captures so well: that sense breaks through only after prolonged mourning. The aim of mourning can therefore be said "to kill death" (Laplanche and Pontalis 1972, 512). Although the emotions involved initially prevent us from acting, they seem to be a necessary ingredient in overcoming the sense of utter loss and loneliness. In the process, something new is gained: the self emerges with a new awareness, in which the grief is now grounded in a richer sense of belonging. As Oatley so aptly formulates it:

> Adjustments are made. Sadness even has in itself a potentially creative quality, provoking the kind of reflection that fairly drives a person to understanding and working through the causes of a grief (1992, 387).

VII. The Poetics of Emotion

This seems to be the kind of emotional effect sought and created by literature, and it is the view developed by Aristotle, against the condemnation by his teacher. "I felt a Funeral in my Brain" involves the kind of confrontation one witnesses in the work of mourning. It involves the (painful) contemplation of life's vulnerability, of existential loneliness, and of the realization that one may lose one's grip in trying to understand it all. Of course, literature involves other emotions and other themes besides death. It also deals with joy and ecstasy, with passion and sensuality, with commitment and courage. But it does so by drawing us *into* these emotions, momentarily cutting the ties with our environment and our practical concerns. We do not rush to Oedipus's side to help prevent him from committing those tragic crimes. We do not tell Don Quixote that the peasant girl is no Dulcinea. Nor do we provide aid or counsel to poor Emma Bovary. We have learned that by renouncing action, by letting go, and by immersing ourselves in the tragic (or comic) events, we will eventually gain something more precious than immediate intervention might have yielded. The fact that this attitude is acquired early in socialization is significant testimony to its functionality. Reading literature impedes our immediate reactions, so that we may come away from it a richer person, one who has experienced the abyss of despair and the peaks of exaltation. Literature takes us away from our grey everyday experience, but brings us back enriched with new sensibilities.

This possibility of literature is caused (so my hypothesis runs) by the presentation in literature of unusually intense states of affairs, including heightened or acute emotional experiences. We know there is no (literal) Funeral in the Brain; we know there are no Boots of Lead in the world we inhabit. It is, however, precisely in their breaking with the ordinary and expected that literary emotions can have a revelatory effect on readers. The value of literature would then lie not only in drawing and sustaining our attention, as Simon proposes, but also in extending and enriching our sensibilities. This assumption is at the heart of the theory of "foregrounding," as it was first formulated by the Russian Formalists: art exists so that we may regain a sense of our position in the world. A number of hypotheses associated with this theory have been corroborated by empirical research (van Peer 1986, 1992). Its link to emotional experiences has been conceived in van Peer (1994) and established empirically by Miall and Kuiken (1994). Wollheim (1980, 315) has pointed to a connection between emotions like mourning and the literary genre of the autobiography, but one need not restrict this view to particular genres, or indeed to "high" literature. Similar processes are at work in the encounter with more popular genres. Drotner, writing about melodrama, provides a neat characterization of the issue:

> Precisely in its break with the ordinary, the expected, the familiar, melodrama allows for a presentation of the extraordinary, the unexpected and the unfamiliar. This has an obvious revelatory effect which critics often explain in psychoanalytical terms; by evoking fears and desires that are submerged, marginalized or tabooed in modern society, modern melodrama creates a "return to the repressed" in Freudian terminology. (1991, 65)[9]

That literature, through imagined experiences unfolding during the reading process, is able to evoke such powerful emotions, should not surprise us when we reflect for a moment on the powers of the imagination. Lang et al. (1980), for instance, have shown that people who are asked to imagine fearful situations report that they really experience this fear; they also show psychophysiological reactions associated with fear, such as increased heart rate and other somato-visceral activity. Literature, in this view, is a powerful instrument for evoking such strong emotions. By facilitating the process of imaginative engagement, it affords readers the opportunity for emotional experimentation, intense contemplation, self-evaluation, and possible reorientation in the everyday world. Indeed, insofar as literature can present a richer and more profound sense of the world we inhabit, it may provide readers with the occasion to acquire a new sense of self. In this way, the poetics of emotion offers continuous opportunities for hot cognition. As our analysis of its apparent paradox reveals, it is a poetics that is in demand: humans would find it hard to live without.

NOTES

1. Dickinson 1970, 128–29.

2. *Poetics*. In Barnes 1984, 1449b27–28.

3. For more on this opposition between Plato and Aristotle, see Salkever 1986. On the notion of catharsis, see Nussbaum 1986. For the most comprehensive empirical research on catharsis to this day, see Scheff 1979. On Aristotelian psychology and its relation to matters aesthetic, see Belfiore 1985.

4. See, for example, Stich 1983 and Oatley 1992, 132.

5. Quoted in Tsur 1992, 19.

6. See, on this issue, Dissanayake 1988. On literature's potential for cultural adaptation, see van Peer 1995b.

7. This is to be distinguished from (but is not unrelated to) Solomon's "pragmatic paradoxes" (1980, 259).

8. What follows should not be taken as an unqualified subscription to Freud's theory. Oatley, for instance, convincingly shows Freud to have been wrong in his analysis of mourning and melancholia in a number of ways (1992, 301). For further work on emotions and vulnerability, see Fisher and Reason 1988 and Garber and Seligman 1980.

9. This aspect has received further attention in Brooks 1976.

14

In Defense of Sentimentality

ROBERT C. SOLOMON

A sentimentalist is simply one who desires to have the luxury of an emotion without paying for it.

—Oscar Wilde, *De Profundus*

Kitsch causes two tears to flow in quick succession. The first tear says: how nice to see children running on the grass!

The second tear says: how nice to be moved, together with all mankind, by children running on the grass!

It is the second tear that makes kitsch kitsch.

—Milan Kundera, *The Unbearable Lightness of Being*

"What is Wrong with Sentimentality?" That question already indicates a great deal about a century-old prejudice that has been devastating to ethics and literature alike. According to that prejudice, it goes without saying that there is *something* wrong with sentimentality, even if it is difficult to "put one's finger on it." To be called "sentimental" is to be ridiculed, or simply to be dismissed. Sentimentality is a weakness, a personality flaw. It suggests hypocrisy, or, at any rate, an exaggerated, distorted sensibility. Or, perhaps it is the fact that sentimental people are so . . . so embarrassing. (How awkward it is talking or sitting next to someone weeping or gushing, when one is oneself dry-eyed and somber.) Or perhaps it is the well-confirmed fact that sentimentalists have such poor taste. Sentimental literature is, above all, literature that is tasteless, cheap, superficial and manipulative—in other words, verbal *kitsch*. Such mawkish literature jerks tears from otherwise sensible readers, and sentimentalists are those who actually enjoy that humiliating experience. Perhaps that is why Oscar Wilde thought that sentimentalists were really cynics. ("Sentimentality is merely the bank holiday of cynicism.")[1] Or, perhaps what bothers us is what once bothered Michael Tanner, that sentimental people indulge themselves in their feelings instead of doing what should be done (1976, 1). It is often said that the problem is that sentimentality and sentimental literature alike give us a false view of the world, distort our thinking, and substitute a "saccharine" portrait of the world in place of what we all know to be the horrible realities.

Moreover, as Mark Jefferson more than merely suggests, the "simple-minded sympathies" of sentimentality might actually promote fascism and racism.[2] Mary Midgley similarly suggests that sentimentality leads to brutality.[3] But even where sentimentality is a harmless diversion—a Daphne du Maurier novel on a sad Saturday afternoon—it seems to be all but agreed that sentimentality is no virtue, even if it is not, like cruelty and hypocrisy, intrinsically vicious. Something is wrong with sentimentality; the only question is, what is it?

In this essay, I want to argue that there is *nothing* wrong with sentimentality. Of course, like any quasi-ethical category, it admits of unwarranted excesses, hypocritical abuses, and is prone to various pathological distortions. But the prejudice against sentimentality, I want to argue, is ill-founded. It is, I want to suggest, an extension of that all-too-familiar contempt for the passions in Western literature and philosophy. Our disdain for sentimentality is the rationalist's discomfort with any display of emotion, warranted as well as unwarranted, appropriate as well as inappropriate. It is as if the very word, "sentimentality," has been loaded with the connotations of "too much"—too much feeling and too little common sense and rationality, as if these were opposed instead of mutually supportive. It is as if sentimentality and its sentiments are never warranted and are always inappropriate. The word has come to be used as the name of a deficiency or a weakness—if not, as some critics have written, a malaise. But I take sentimentality to be nothing more nor less than the "appeal to tender feelings," and though one can manipulate and abuse such feelings (including one's own), and though they can on occasion be misdirected or excessive, there is nothing wrong with them as such and nothing (in that respect) wrong with literature that provokes us, that "moves" us to abstract affection or weeping. Sentimentality implies no deficiency in one's rational faculties and does not imply any inappropriateness, unwillingness, or lack of readiness to act. Sentimentality need not involve any distortion of the world, and it need not impede but often prepares and motivates us to react in "the real world." It need not be an escape from reality or responsibility; quite to the contrary, it may provide the precondition for ethical engagement, not an obstacle to it.

I. The Sad Decline of the Moral Sentiments

I want to trace the historical fate of sentimentality to the parallel fates of the "sentiments" and their apparently doomed plea for ethical legitimacy in what was once called "moral sentiment theory." My thesis is that the sentiments have had a bad time in Anglo-American moral and social philosophy for well over a century, and sentimentality has been held in contempt for just about the same period of time. During at least some of the eighteenth century, morality was thought to be, first of all, a matter of the proper sentiments (whether "natural" or "artificially" cultivated), and sentimentality, accordingly, was something of a virtue. But, today, the "moral sentiment" theorists—David Hume and Adam Smith in particular—are studied only because of their other virtues, for instance, Hume's dazzling skepticism and Smith's buoyant (if longwinded) defense of the free market. But in their own minds, their theories of human nature and of the "natural" sentiments that are a part of that nature were essential aspects of their respective philosophies. Despite some sophisticated efforts on the continent to keep the moral sentiment tradition alive (e.g., in the work of the German phenomenologist Max Scheler), that tradition is all but dead in moral philosophy. Immanuel Kant did away with "melting compassion" as an ingredient in ethics once and for all before 1800 in a single sarcastic comment in the *Grounding of the Metaphysic of Morals:* "[K]indness done from duty . . . is practical, and not pathological . . . residing in the will and not in the propensions of feeling, in principles of action and not of melting compassion."[4] The other "inclinations" did not fare much better in his philosophy, except perhaps for "respect," "dignity," and "faith," which, because of their importance, were not treated as mere "sentiments" at all.

Most of ethics since Kant has been wholly absorbed in the vicissitudes of reason and the priority of various rational principles and quite suspicious of the sentiments. Indeed, when some feminist psychologists and philosophers argued just a few decades ago that feelings had a place in ethics along with reason, their suggestion was treated as revolutionary, so far from memory had moral sentiment theory drifted. But reason appealed not only to the prejudices of philosophers, but to hard-headed dogmatists in every walk of life. Rational principles are universal. Feelings are too often particular and personal. Rational principles are "objective" and demand argument and demonstration. Mere feelings are wholly "subjective" (which is multiply ambiguous) and (supposedly) not vulnerable to logic. Rational principles are (unlike love) truly forever, while feelings are capricious and come and go. Rationality is by its nature unemotional and "disinterested." The sentiments as emotions are not only "interested" but involved, "caught up" in the circumstances and incapable of unbiased judgment. The Humean humanist emphasis on the sentiments was replaced, accordingly, by the still-current scholastic debates about deontic semantics, and doing right became much more a matter of acting on the right principles (though not necessarily Kantian or "deontological" principles) and much less a matter of feeling the right feelings. Worst of all, on this account of ethics, was to feel the feelings alone and not entertain in some more or less self-understanding way the principles upon which one was bound to act. Mere sentiment—even the most tender sentiments—became an ethical liability.

It should not be surprising, therefore, that sentimentality had an even worse time of it. It indicated not only an unhealthy emphasis on sentiment but a pathological overload of sentiments, and just in those situations in which reason should be in command. Accordingly, sentimentality is not only excluded from most discussions of ethics but, when discussed at all, is condemned as a serious or a laughable ethical defect. To call someone a "sentimentalist" in ethics is to dismiss both the person and his or her views from serious consideration, adding, perhaps, a disdainful chortle and an implicit accusation of frivolousness. And in literature as in ethics, sentimentality is viewed as a serious defect. Sentimentality is kitsch. Sentimentality substitutes cheap manipulation of feeling for careful calculation of form or judicious development of character. But sentimentality as kitsch and sentimentality as an ethical defect are two very different charges, and part of the problem in the general condemnation of sentimentality is that it too readily identifies the two and treats them together. I abstain here from an opinion on kitsch, but I do want to defend sentimentality—and with it the role of emotions in ethics and literature—against the bad reputation it has recently acquired.

It is worth noting that the offensive epithet "sentimentalist" has not long been a term of abuse: just two hundred years ago, when Schiller referred to himself and his poetry as "sentimental" (as opposed to Goethe's "naive" style), he had in mind the elegance of emotion, not saccharine sweetness and the manipulation of mawkish passions. But in 1823, Southey dismissed Rousseau as a writer who "addressed himself to the sentimental classes, persons of ardent and morbid sensibility, who believe themselves to be composed of finer elements than the gross multitude."[5] This charge of elitism was soon to be reversed: soon, a sentimentalist would have distinctively *inferior* feelings. If Rousseau's audience was objectionable early in the century because it believed itself to have "finer" feelings, the object of Oscar Wilde's scorn (the young Lord Alfred Douglas) was attacked as a "sentimentalist" for his fraudulent and contemptible passions. By the end of the century, "sentimentalist" was clearly a term of ridicule.

I suggested that the status of "sentimentality" went into decline about the same time that the sentiments lost their status in moral philosophy, and that the key figure in this philosophical transformation was Immanuel Kant. Perhaps it should also be said that Kant, in his "precritical" period (around 1770) wrote of the sentiment of compassion that it was truly beautiful,—*even if it ultimately had no ethical import.* But fifteen years later, Kant's aesthetic appreciation had turned to contemptuous disdain, and with a sneer he dismissed "melting compassion" as irrelevant even to love. However, Kant's unprecedented attack on sentiment and sentimentalism must be seen, at least in part, as a reaction (perhaps a visceral reaction) not only against the philosophical moral sentiment theorists (whom he at least admired), but against the flood of popular women writers in Europe and America who were then turning out thousands of widely read potboilers and romances that did indeed equate virtue and goodness with gushing sentiment. It is no secret that the charge of sentimentalism has long had sexist implications as a weakness which is both more common (even "natural") and more forgivable in women than in men, and one might plausibly defend the thesis that the moralist's attack on sentimentality cannot be separated from the more general Victorian campaign in pseudoscience and politics against the rising demand for sexual equality. But in the purportedly nonpolitical, genderless world of philosophy, sentimentalism was forced into a confrontation with logic and became the fallacy of appealing to emotion instead of argument (now standard in almost every ethics or logic textbook). In ethics, to be accused of "sentimentalism" meant that one had an unhealthy and most unphilosophical preference for heartfelt feeling over hardheaded reason. Sentimentalism more generally became a matter of moral bad taste, a weakness for easy emotion in place of the hard facts and ambiguities

of human social life; and the literature that provoked and promoted such emotions became itself the object of moral—not only literary—condemnation. Not
surprisingly, a prime target for such a charge were those same women's novels—and the emotions they provoked—which were and still are dismissed as
"trash" by the literary establishment.[6] But though designated "sentimental rubbish" by their detractors, some of these novels achieved unprecedented success, in terms not only of popularity but of moral and political influence as
well. Harriet Beecher Stowe's much demeaned *Uncle Tom's Cabin* was not
only the first American novel to sell a million copies but perhaps the most
politically influential book in postcolonial American history. Sentimentalism
may have been dismissed as mere self-indulgence by its critics (including feminist critics), but it was in fact a sufficiently powerful moral influence to warrant
its status as the target (if not the explicit object) of Kant's renowned attack.

II. Sentimentality in Art: Kitsch

The very notion of "taste" in art necessitates the existence of "bad taste" and,
consequently, bad art. But bad art comes in many varieties and is subject to
different kinds of objections. There is sheer technical incompetence, just to
begin with (although artistic inability as such is much less fatal than it used to
be); there is ignorance of the medium, the tradition and its history, the current
fashions and the tastes of the times. For those outside the bustling art centers,
what seems to be bad art may be just bad timing. There is unimaginative
imitation and straightforward plagiarism. There is such a thing as having "no
eye," the failure to understand color or composition. But there is also an "ethical" dimension to bad art, as in the depiction of the forbidden, the blasphe-
mous, the vulgar expression of the inexpressible, the provocation of the improper and of cruelty. (For example, a bar stool whose legs are actual, stuffed
buffalo legs.) Once upon a time, bad art was, above all, such use of unacceptable subject matter, evoking the wrong emotions and provoking the wrong
reactions (e.g., visceral disgust and nausea), but this too seems to have recently
dropped out of the picture. These days, it is far wiser for an aspiring young
artist to offend or disgust the viewer than to evoke such gentle sentiments as
sympathy and delight.

But this is just what is particularly interesting, from a philosophical point of
view, about that peculiar variety of "bad art" called kitsch, and, in particular,
that variety of kitsch sometimes called "sweet kitsch." Sweet kitsch is art (or, to
hedge our bets, intended art) that appeals unsubtly and unapologetically to the
softer, sweeter sentiments. Familiar examples are the roadside ceramics of
wide-eyed puppies and Kean-type paintings of similarly wide-eyed children.
Saccharine religious art (so long as it is serious and not sarcastic) would be
sweet kitsch, and so, too, perhaps, much of Muzak and Rod McLuen–type
poetry. Examples of sweet kitsch are often mentioned as paradigm instances of
bad art, but the nature of its "badness" is just what makes kitsch philosophically interesting. Sweet kitsch is not always badly done. Indeed, it may be
highly professional, much in vogue, and keenly aware of the artistic and cul-

tural traditions in which it gains its appeal. What makes sweet kitsch kitsch seems to be that it is flawed by its very perfection, its technical virtuosity and its precise execution, its explicit knowledge of the tradition, its timeliness, and the fact that it stimulates the very best emotions—the "soft" sentiments of kindness and sympathy and the calm passions of delight. But the best emotions seem to be the worst emotions where art is concerned, and "better shocking or sour than sweet," has become something of a rule of thumb for artists and a criterion of good taste for connoisseurs. But why is this? What is wrong with sweet kitsch? Its deficiencies appear to be just what we would otherwise think of as virtues: technical proficiency and a well-aimed appeal to the very best of the viewer's emotions.

What is wrong with sweet kitsch, of course, is its sentimentality, its easy evocation of certain "sweet" emotions. (When I speak simply of "kitsch" here, it is to be understood that it is this "sweet" variety alone that I have in mind, though some of my arguments may well also hold where "sour" and "bitter" kitsch is in question.[7]) Sentimental art suffered the same fate as the sentiments in the eighteenth and nineteenth centuries. Just as in popular literature the advent of the "woman's novel" inspired a flood of widely read romances that equated virtue and goodness with gushing sentiment, in French art, the revolutionary moral sentiments evoked by David and exotic fantasies inspired by Delacroix were succeeded by the sentimental mastery of such academic artists as Greuze, Messonier, and Bouguereau.[8] By the end of the last century, artists in Paris who had been praised only a century before as the "geniuses" of Official Art became figures of loathing and ridicule, curators of kitsch who produced paradigms of "bad art" which we keep in our museums only for the sake of the historians and as contrasts to the great art of the "Refused" in the room next door. Kitsch thus serves us well in museums, where it is not only part of the historical record but also flypaper for the Philistines, who in their ignorance flock to the sweet perfection of classical kitsch and leave at least some space in front of the great Impressionists and their successors.

There is a range of quality to sweet kitsch. On the one hand, there are those "cheap" mass-produced K-Mart–style artifacts, disdain for which surely has more to do with economic class distinctions and manufacturing values than with aesthetic evaluation as such. Much of the literature attacking kitsch is political rather than aesthetic, though ironically much of it comes from Marxists and their kin who despise the mass-marketing origins of kitsch at the same time that they would defend the people who are most likely to purchase such objects. But whether kitsch is attacked because it is cheap and "low-class" or because it is the product of a debased economy, what is wrong with kitsch surely cannot be, philosophically speaking, either the rationalization of snobbery or contempt for its manufacturing and marketing. (We should be suspicious about the depth of class prejudices underlying even the most abstract aesthetic argument and the extent to which the charge of "sentimentality" is in fact an attack on unsophisticated taste.) But though much of what is called "kitsch" is disdained because it is "cheap" (a word that often performs multiple functions in discussions of kitsch), because it is mass-produced and "plastic," because it is the sort of item that would (and should) embarrass someone with a proper aesthetic education, there is, on the other hand, some quite expensive and well-produced "high" kitsch, for example, the academic painting of the mid-nineteenth century that I will shortly use as an example. It is this kind of kitsch that focuses our attention on sentimentality as such, that has attracted such critical abuse, and that has been accused of moral as well as artistic degeneracy. And high kitsch, whatever else may be said of it, cannot be openly dismissed as "cheap." It is typically very professional, well-made, and expensive. Of course, this opens up a new argument along class lines, as an attack on the "nouveau riche" who have money but not taste. Recent aesthetic theory would suggest that proper aesthetic appreciation consists of an appreciation of form, presupposing more than a modicum of education and refinement in the viewer. Being moved by the emotional content, by way of contrast, is at best a distraction, if not a dead give-away that one is having a "cheap" emotional experience instead of a cultivated aesthetic response. High-class kitsch may well be "perfect" in its form and composition: the academic painters were often masters of their craft. Thus, the accusation that a work is kitsch is based not on lack of form or aesthetic merit but on the presence of a particularly provocative emotional content. (The best art, by contrast, eschews emotional content altogether.)

The term "kitsch" comes from the nineteenth century. One of several suggested etymologies is that the word is German for "playing with mud,"[9] and, toying with this, we might speculate that the "mud" in question is emotion, and that mucking around with emotions inevitably makes a person "dirty." The standard opinion seems to be that kitsch and immorality go together, and that sentimentality is what is wrong with both of them. Here, for example, is Karsten Harries: "Kitsch has always been considered immoral."[10] Of course, one culture's or one generation's kitsch may be another's avant-garde, and what is obligatory as "compassion" or "sympathy" in one age may be dismissed as mere sentimentality in another. Accordingly, the sentiments that are provoked by and disdained in sweet kitsch may vary as well.[11] But whatever the cause or the context, it is the sentimentality of kitsch that makes kitsch kitsch, and sentimentality that makes kitsch morally suspect, if not immoral. Granted, kitsch may be bad art. Granted, it may show poor taste. But my question here is why it is the sentimentality of kitsch that should be condemned, why it is thought to be an ethical defect and a danger to society.

Let's look at the sentimentality of sweet kitsch. I recently attended an exhibit at the Denver Art Museum that featured, among other nineteenth-century French works, a painting by Adolph Bouguereau (1825–1905) and one by Degas, more or less across from one another in the gallery. The Bouguereau is a classically arranged portrait of two very pretty little girls, in rosy pink and soft pastels, set against an expansive sky. The Degas, by contrast, catches one of his dancers in an awkward back-scratching gesture, her body turned away from us, her face unseen. She is framed in a cramped canvas in pale green, ochre, and burnt orange. The Bouguereau is one of those well-painted pieces of sweet kitsch that gives French academic painting a bad name. At the same time, it is an almost "perfect" painting. John Canaday writes, in his classic textbook on modern art,

> The wonder of a painting by Bouguereau is that it is so completely, so absolutely, all of a piece. Not a single element is out of harmony with the whole; there is not a flaw in the totality of the union between conception and execution. The trouble with Bouguereau's perfection is that the conception and the execution are perfectly false. Yet this is perfection of a kind, even if it is a perverse kind. [12]

The Degas, on the other hand, is anything but "perfect" in this sense. It is one of those tiny discomforting treasures that haunts the viewer for hours afterward. But it is the Bouguereau that turns out to be one of the most popular pieces in the museum. The curators of the exhibit comment, "Most of our visitors readily admit they don't know a whole lot about art. So it's only natural for them to look for works that are pretty and easy to understand." And then they add, "novice viewers rarely speak of the Bouguereau's features and aesthetic qualities. Instead, they use it as a springboard to dreams of the future or nostalgic memories of the past. More advanced viewers are soon bored." [13]

What makes Bouguereau kitsch? What makes it bad art? From an aesthetic point of view, it is the "perverse perfection" that is so offensive and cloying, the absence of any interpretive ambiguity or dissonance on the part of the viewer, but most important (for our purposes), it is the manipulation of emotion, the evocation of "cheap," "false" emotions that makes this otherwise "perfect" painting perverse. Clement Greenberg, for instance, complained (in 1939) that kitsch "is mechanical and operates by formulas. Kitsch is vicarious experience and faked sensations. . . . It is the epitome of all that is spurious in the life of our times. Kitsch pretends to demand nothing of its customers except their money—not even their time." [14] To call a work of (bad) art "kitsch" is not just to condemn the glibness of its technique; it is also to question the motives of the artist and the emotional maturity of the audience. In such cases, sentimentality is the culprit, manipulated by the artist, indulged in by the viewer. It is, we hear from critic after critic, false ("faked") emotion. And so, the sentimentality of kitsch becomes not ultimately aesthetic but ethical, a species of dishonesty. (Karsten Harries: "[T]o isolate aesthetics from ethics [is] to misunderstand what art is all about." [15])

What makes Bouguereau kitsch is the one-dimensional purity of the emotion. These girls don't do any of the nasty things that little children do. They don't whine. They don't tease the cat. They don't hit each other. They don't have any bruises. They aren't going to die. The art itself leaves us without imagination; it wholly determines the images we ought to have. It "manipulates" our feelings. There is no ambiguity. Above all, there is no discomfort, no ugliness or awkwardness, no sense (as in the Degas) of intruding on privacy. Bouguereau himself writes, "I see only the beautiful in art . . . art is the beautiful. Why reproduce what is ugly in nature?" (Cf. Degas: "I show my models deprived of their airs and graces, reduced to the level of animals cleaning themselves.") It is here (though not only here) that ethics meets aesthetics, in the images we are given of human reality, visual theories of human nature, if you like—one a portrait of pure innocence, the other a reminder that we are awkward animals. Sentimentality is "false" because it gives us a picture of ourselves that is too pure, too ethically one-sided. But isn't the Degas portrayal just as "one-sided," as far as its philosophy (its theory of human nature) is concerned? It may be an infinitely better painting (as a painting), but is it better as a moral theory? Even if we were to accept the rejection of kitsch as art, why is the sentimentality of kitsch to be condemned, in other words, not just as art but as ethics?

III. Sentimentality and Social Responsibility

The great philosopher Kant was moved to attack sentimental gush in both morality and art (though he himself was no great connoisseur), and the two—bad art and an overly emotional sense of morals—have been conflated ever since. Together, they suggest not only bad taste but also, despite the false front of compassion, a lack of social responsiveness and social responsibility. Of course, good art, correct morals, and social responsibility had been tied together through the moral sentiments before, notably in Denis Diderot's deservedly famous criticism and in Schiller's positive praise of sentimentality, but for them, sentimentality clearly encouraged honorable ethical impulses. Nevertheless, one of my aims here is to disentangle them. Bad art is one thing, sentimentality another, and while bad literature in particular may try to prove its redeeming value by evoking tender feelings, its sentimentality is not the cause of its badness, and sentimentality is not a species of immorality. Sentimentality in certain circumstances can be in bad taste, of course, but sentimentality as such is not always (or even usually) in bad taste, and bad taste does not always (or even usually) reflect bad character. A decent sense of social responsibility has encountered many obstacles in our times (not least, the "rationality" of "the market" and widespread political cynicism), but sentimentality, I want to argue, is not among them.

But let us consider some famous counter-examples: William James depicts a wealthy society matron who weeps at the plight of the characters on stage while her waiting servants freeze outside. Then there is a story about Rudolph Hess weeping at the opera put on by condemned Jewish prisoners during the Holocaust. Such stories do demonstrate that sentimentality divorced from life may reflect a particularly despicable or dangerous pathology, but it is not sentimentality as such that is at fault in these two famous cases, and just the same charge might be leveled against that use of reason (as in "thinking the unthinkable") that entertained the hypotheses of game theory while deliberating the fate of millions in the calculations of nuclear deterrence. It is not sentimentality (or rationality) that is troublesome but rather its utter inappropriateness in the context in question. Sentimentality is rarely the symptom (much less the cause) of moral deficiency. We can agree that certain sentiments and sentimentality can be inappropriate and excessive without granting that sentiments and sentimentality are immoral or pathological as such, and we can similarly agree that sentimentality in literature can be inappropriate and excessive without granting that sentimentality marks a deficiency in literature or in the reader who responds to it. It is simply not true, as several great cynics have claimed (Oscar Wilde among them), that sentimentality betrays cynicism. It is rather that sentimentality betrays the cynic, for it is the cynic and not the sentimentalist who cannot abide honest emotion.

The history of the moral sentiments in connection with art and literature made it almost inevitable that the turn against the sentiments would be not only paralleled by but identified with a turn against sentimentality in the arts as well. Diderot insisted, in his review of one of Jean-Louis David's more provocative political paintings, that he wanted first of all, that art should "move me, astonish me, break my heart, let me tremble, weep, stare, be enraged." One would be hard put to imagine a similar demand from an art critic today, but Diderot was very much a part of the moral sensibility that made up the moral sentiment movement. That link between emotions, art, and ethics, once forged, would not easily be broken. But whereas the evocation of emotions was once a great virtue in a novel, poem, or painting, it now became something of a vice, a reason not only to disparage the quality of the work but to doubt the sincerity and the integrity of the writer or the artist. Superb technique could always be criticized as "manipulative" and the emotions evoked could always be said to be "false"—for how could a work of fiction be expected to evoke a "true" one?

Sentimental art and literature thus became "bad" art and literature, and this in turn reflected a moral as well as an aesthetic flaw in both art and artist, as well as in the audience. But what this presupposed was that sentimentality itself was somehow blameworthy, cynical, or vicious, and my thesis here, accordingly, is that as there is nothing essentially wrong with sentimentality (though of course there are pathological excesses and inappropriate objects, here as in the use of categorical imperatives), so there is nothing wrong with sentimentality in literature. On the contrary, sentimentality is essential to both ethics and literature, and the real worry is rather those many moralists who think and don't feel; those writers who sell and readers who buy pure narrative or entertainment devoid of tender feelings; and those avant-garde writers who plot the deconstruction of their own writing and leave us with nothing. The excessive manipulation of tender feelings is not the problem of sentimentality; the problem of sentimentality is the lack of them altogether.

Sentimentality is variously conceived (1) in terms of the "tender" emotions (I call this the "minimal" definition), (2) in terms of emotional weakness or "excessive" emotion (the "loaded" definition), and (3) in terms of emotional self-indulgence (the "diagnostic" definition). Sometimes, sentimentality is identified by the "epistemological" definition (4) in terms of its "false" or "fake" emotions, though one must then provide an account of what a "false" or a "fake" emotion (as opposed to a merely pretended emotion) might be. Obviously, the case that can be made for (or against) sentimentality depends upon the neutrality or the bias of the definition. My main concern is the defense of sentimentality in terms of the minimal definition, as an expression of and appeal to the tender emotions. If the tender emotions (pity, sympathy, fondness, adoration, compassion) are thought to be not only ethically irrelevant but ethically undesirable (in contrast to hard-headed practical reason, for example), then it is not sentimentality that should be called into question but rather the conception of ethics that would dictate such an inhuman response. My central argument, which I have pursued elsewhere as well (1989), is that no conception of ethics can be adequate unless it takes into account such emotions, not as mere "inclinations" but as an essential part of the substance of ethics itself. It is thus that I want to defend sentimentality as an ethical virtue and suggest that sentimentality in literature might best be conceived as the cultivation and "practice" of our moral faculties.

On the other hand, if sentimentality is defined or diagnosed as an ethical defect, as weakness or self-indulgence (though it is far from clear that weakness and self-indulgence are, as such, *ethical* defects), that loads the issue against sentimentality and makes it hard to see how a defense of it would be possible. Indeed, the very pronunciation of the term "sentimentalist" as well as the characterization of "sentimentality" indicate deep disdain for emotions as intrusions and for emotionality as vulnerability. For instance, it is difficult to see how strong sentiments could constitute a weakness unless there is already operating some powerful metaphor that views our sentiments as alien and the integral self as a will that is supposed to contain or control them but fails to do so. So, too, sentimentality seems to be self-indulgence if a person is seen to indulge in his emotional weaknesses. One could thus view the reader as the willing victim of the emotionally manipulative author, as an alcoholic is the willing victim of that first drink. Sentimentality is "giving in," and a preference for sentimentality suggests a perverse willingness to make oneself vulnerable. Thus, according to this unflattering picture, the reader indulges in sentiments that are not his own but are rather caused by a more or less skillful storyteller, and the moral flaw is the failure to control and contain these emotions. The author, on the other hand, is something of a seducer, though the fruits of a successful seduction may be only a tear or two. Sentimental literature violates the reader's sense of self by provoking these unwelcome emotional intrusions, at an intensity that cannot be controlled (except, of course, by firmly putting down the book in question). And if one adds to this any one of a familiar set of ideas about aesthetic "detachment" or "appreciation of form," the ethical flaw becomes a failure in aesthetics as well. Whatever else literature is supposed to do to us, it ought not to "manipulate" the reader's emotions, interfering with both autonomy and aesthetic appreciation. Any normal reader will feel some emotion, to be sure, but this is as irrelevant to good literature as it is to doing the right thing in ethics. Or, as Maureen Mullarkey writes in the *Nation* (March 6, 1989), "[Art is irrelevant] as a political act . . . An artistic conscience and a social conscience are not the same, and there's too much at stake to confuse them."

IV. The Ethics of Emotion

The unspoken premise in the attack on sentimentality is the unflattering nature of the sentiments, the emotions themselves. It is emotional engagement as such that is alien to the properly rational and ideally detached self, the substitution of feeling and its expressions for means-ends calculation and reason-directed action. Sentimentality is itself not the problem so much as the emotions to which one makes oneself vulnerable. They are always, except in their mildest forms, "too much"—too self-involved and self-indulgent and too excited to allow for deliberate or reasoned judgment. Any emotion, on such accounts, is excessive, for an emotion or a sentiment as such is a disruption of the life of reason and an obstacle to aesthetic appreciation rather than an essential ingredient in them. Excessive sentimentality may indeed be a vice, but sentimentality and the sentiments as such are not excessive, unless, of course, one thinks that the emotions are intrusions that are always unwarranted and unwelcome, which I suggest is what is behind the whole attack on senti- mentality in the first place. But I reject these loaded characterizations, and I would want to point out that most of the critical literature does not in fact employ them. Arguments by Jefferson, Tanner, and Midgley, for example (as well as those implicit in Oscar Wilde) do not take the word "sentimentality" to mean "too much" but rather charge that the character of sentimentality, even conceived in the minimal sense, leads to self-indulgence and ethical im- propriety or inaction. The charge is not a trivial one, that "sentimentality" (like "vice") already means that something is wrong. Their arguments rather turn on the subtle nature and consequences of sentimentality, the alleged falseness of the component sentiments, the "distortions" that these impose on percep- tion and judgment, and the dangers of what is argued to be the unrealistic simplicity of the sentimental worldview.

The charge of self-indulgence is a serious one, quite apart from the meta- phor of sentiments and emotions as intrusions and the image of sentimentality as a weakness. The insight behind the charge is that we, in fact, enjoy having emotions, sometimes quite apart from what in particular that emotion is about. Thus, one can enjoy a good piece of fiction despite the fact that the story is not, strictly speaking, "about" anything at all, for the characters do not exist and have never existed and the circumstances described are wholly fictitious. One can enjoy "a good cry" quite regardless of what initiates or triggers one's tears; indeed, it is far better if the initiating stimulus is unimportant or inappro- priate, a mawkish novel or a trivial accident, rather than a real-life tragedy that would fully justify such behavior. So, too, it is far preferable for most of us to enjoy the thrills of high adventure, the horrors of nature run amok, and the suspense of a threatened murder quite detached from the circumstances in real life that would inspire such emotions. We enjoy the thrill, the horror, the suspense without ever being in any real danger ourselves. But is such behavior self-indulgent? Is it wrong to enjoy an emotion for its own sake? And isn't it even worse willfully to provoke such feelings through the use of literature and the imagination, instead of paying attention to real-life tragedies and hardships that we can in fact do something about?

I think that the mistake here is the very idea that there is such a thing as "an emotion for its own sake." Every emotion has its context, its implications, its place in our personality, whether or not it has objects that are real or appropriate (as opposed to fictional or merely convenient.) I do not want to argue that sentimentality or emotions in general are "good in themselves." Whether a particular emotion is "appropriate" depends upon the situation, including the object and the nature of the emotion in question, the identity and character of the person having the emotion, and the overall social context. So, too, whether sentimentality is appropriate, good or bad, morally uplifting, self-defeating, or humiliating depends upon the situation, including the object and nature of the sentiment in question, the identity and character of the "sentimentalist," and the overall social context. Weeping at an opera while Jews are being gassed at one's command nearby is grotesque, but weeping at an opera is not. We cultivate and enjoy as well as suffer emotions, but we do not do so wholly apart from context; at a minimum the context is our own self-consciousness. We pride ourselves on our sensitivity, and we enjoy feelings of power as well as, on safe occasions, powerlessness. We may well speculate about why people voluntarily provoke fear and suspense in themselves (e.g., by reading semifictional accounts of impending doom or adventure thrillers that provide something more than Agatha Christie "whodunit" curiosity), but there seems to be little mystery why people would want to cultivate the tender emotions. Whatever else may be going on (and Nietzsche, for one, suggests that a great deal else is "going on"), we feel good about ourselves when we experience the tender emotions, and we feel even better when, reflectively, we perceive ourselves as the sort of people who feel such feelings.

It is in this context that we should read Milan Kundera's now-famous discussion of kitsch and sentimentality in *The Unbearable Lightness of Being*, where he writes:

> Kitsch causes two tears to flow in quick succession. The first tear says: how nice to see children running on the grass!
> The second tear says: How nice to be moved, together with all mankind, by children running on the grass!
> It is the second tear that makes kitsch kitsch.[16]

But notice that this charge (a peculiar kind of "self-indulgence") does not suggest that we have the tender emotions "for their own sake," but rather in order to feel better about ourselves. We might now ask, what's wrong with this (in contrast, for example, to the feeling of self-righteousness that accompanies doing one's moral duty or moralizing in terms of this or that moral principle)? Kundera, of course, is concerned with a particular kind of political propaganda, which intentionally eclipses harsh realities with emotion and uses sweet sentiments to preclude political criticism. To be sure, sentimentalizing fascism is one of the clearest possible examples of the "inappropriate" use of sentimentality, but it does not follow that this is the true nature of sentimentality or that sentimentality is cynical or bad in itself. If the emotion were disgust or fear, would similar reflections (on the shared virtue of recognizing the world's vulgarity or fearsomeness) be similarly sentimental? Why is it only the tender sentiments that come in for such criticism and abuse? More recently, Kundera has written, "Kitsch is the translation of the stupidity of received ideas into the language of beauty and feeling. It moves us to tears for ourselves, for the banality of what we think and feel."[17] Here the charge is not self-indulgence at all, but rather our banal and unoriginal ideas. But why must an honest feeling claim originality, and why, again, are only the tender sentiments (as opposed, for example, to such vulgar negativities as fecal monism) subject to such a test? We can readily share Kundera's concern for the use of kitsch as a cover for totalitarianism; but then it is not sentimentality that is at fault, and there is nothing intrinsically wrong with our being moved by the children playing in the grass and then by our further being moved by our being moved. Is the "second tear" self-indulgence, or is it, in philosophical circles, what would normally be called simply "reflection," the precondition of "the examined life"? Why should reflection be tearless, unless we are wedded to an indefensible divorce between reason and the passions, the latter wholly self-absorbed and without reason, the former a merely "ideal spectator," wholly dispassionate and wholly without feeling?

V. Sentimentality, Appropriate Actions, and False Emotions

Michael Tanner raises a similar but more powerful objection to sentimentality. It is worth noting that Tanner takes sentimentality in music as his paradigm (a starting point that makes his analysis somewhat incoherent to start with, caught between the nonrepresentational nature of music and the intentionality of emotions, the purely aesthetic enjoyment of music and the urge to vigorous action appropriate to emotion). But despite his paradigm, Tanner is concerned only secondarily with sentimentality in art and comes out strongly against sentimentality as such. He echoes Wilde's suggestion that the feelings that constitute sentimentality are "in some important way unearned, being had on the cheap, come by too easily. . . . to be sentimental is to be shallow." But Tanner's real objection to sentimentality is that it "doesn't lead anywhere."[18] It is this gap between sentimentality and action that Tanner rejects. In "emotional generosity," which Tanner contrasts directly with sentimentality, one "acts on [one's] feelings without anxiety about the point and value of doing so . . . feeling and action become fairly closely linked. Sentimental people, by contrast, "avoid following up their responses with *appropriate* actions, or if they do follow them up appropriately, it is adventitious."[19]

If this objection could be sustained, much of what we are arguing here would be fatuous, namely, that sentiment is essential in ethics. But it seems to me that the manipulative sentimentality of a novel such as *Uncle Tom's Cabin* shows quite conclusively that sentimentality is not nearly so ill-directed nor so ineffective as Tanner suggests, and, to the contrary, being deeply moved by some specific (even if fictional) circumstance (for example, the death of little Eva—which Tompkins calls "the epitome of Victorian sentimentalism") would seem to be a much more reliable prod or at least conduit to action (e.g., in raising an outcry against slavery) than a well-rationalized set of categorical imperatives. It is true, of course, that one can do very little about political situations in a foreign country that arouse our indignation or sympathy (in neither instance a case of what is usually called "sentimentality"), but that does not make the emotion "cheap" or "easy to come by." Direct action would be rather costly, to put it mildly, but one can always write a letter or two—or a check. (There is the existentialist proviso: you can always *do something!*)

Does the sentimentalist act (if and when he acts) only with anxiety about doing so? Granted there is always room for hypocrisy, self-deception, and incontinence, but is there any greater danger here than elsewhere in the realm of human behavior? And where the object is fictitious, what sort of action would be appropriate and what would be adventitious? (It is worth noting that some critics of sentimental kitsch, Karsten Harries for instance,[20] object to sentimentality because it lacks that distance to which Tanner objects.) There are people, of course, who become so caught up in their own emotional reactions that they block their access or attention to action, and there are people who are sentimental all of the time, inappropriately responding to situations as "moving" or "sweet" when they would be better viewed as disgusting or dangerous. But such pathological sentimentalists are hardly fair examples of sentimentality as such. The gap between emotion and action is not itself the objection against sentimentality.

The most common charge against sentimentality is that it involves false emotion. But what is it for an emotion to be false? It is not, as I have argued elsewhere,[21] for the emotion to be "vicarious." The fact that an emotion is vicarious (in some sense "second-hand") does not mean that it is not real or that it is not of the morally appropriate type. Sympathy for a fictional character in a novel is nevertheless genuine sympathy. Horror provoked by the grisly view of an apparently decapitated cat on a movie screen is real horror, perhaps accompanied by real disgust and real nausea, no matter that the viewer knows it to be another one of Hollywood's many tricks and the special effects man to be a cat lover. Indignation about the maltreatment of African Americans in *Uncle Tom's Cabin* is rightful indignation, whether or not the character evoking sympathy and the situation provoking indignation are actual or modeled after an actual character and situation. Nor is an emotion "false" if it is divorced from action. It is the nature of some emotions, such as grief, to be cut off entirely from effective action and open only to "adventitious" (though more or less appropriate) expression. Self-indulgence in an emotion may make it "false" in the sense that one exaggerates either its importance or its effects, but it is not the emotion itself that is false. So, too, excessive self-consciousness of one's emotions may well lead to the suspicion that an emotion is overly controlled or "faked," but as I pointed out (with reference to Kundera), emotional self-consciousness is not itself fraudulent but rather an important philosophical virtue, and a thoroughly righteous emotion (such as indignation) may well be self-conscious without in the least undermining its claims to legitimacy.

One prominent suggestion is that sentimentality yields "fake" emotions because the object of the emotion is not what it claims to be. It is *displaced*. A sentimentalist only pretends to be moved by the plight of another; he or she is really reacting to a much more personal plight. A sentimentalist sobs his or her way through a "tear-jerker" novel, but he or she is really weeping for a just-lost lover, a dying aunt, a recent and humiliating reprimand at work. One can imagine Milan Kundera claiming that even the first tear is fake because it is not really about the children but about oneself. We should note that this is different from the charge that the emotions involved in sentimentality are vicarious, that is, based on fictional situations or situations that (though real) are not one's own. Vicarious emotions have (in some complex sense) unreal objects, but the emotion is nevertheless directed toward those objects. Displaced emotions only seem to be directed toward their putative objects but in fact are directed elsewhere. Thus, there is a suggestion of hypocrisy in the displacement charge that is not at all evident in the claim that sentimentality is vicarious. But many emotions are displaced. (Indeed, some extreme Freudians and symbolists would claim that all are.) Displacement has nothing special to do with sentimentality, and does not generically make an emotion false. A man gets angry with his boss at work and comes home and yells at his misbehaving kids. His anger is displaced, but it is nevertheless not the case that "he isn't really angry at his kids," even if it is true that, in a more mellow mood, he would tolerate their screaming without such explosive irritation. A woman is shattered when her lover leaves, but the very next week she falls madly in love with a man who seems remarkably like the one who just made his exit. "Love on the rebound" is a form of displacement, but, again, one cannot hastily conclude that it is therefore false. What is presupposed in such discussions is a kind of quantitative zero-sum or qualitative unidirectional assumption such that an emotion can "really" have but one and one only object. If the man is really angry at his boss, he cannot also be angry at his kids, and if the woman is still in love with the first lover, she cannot also be in love with the second. But there is no reason to accept such monotopical restrictions on our emotional life, and if sentimentality is to a considerable extent a phenomenon of displacement (why else would we respond to some of those novels and movies?), then it should be credited with enriching and enlarging our emotional lives. It would be a nightmare, not a matter of integrity, if we could direct our emotions only at their primary objects, if we could not express and satisfy ourselves with secondary, derivative, and fictional objects as well.

One long-standing argument is that sentimentality is objectionable and its emotions false because it is *distorting*. Mary Midgley, for instance, argues that, "the central offence lies in self-deception, in distorting reality to get a pretext for indulging in *any* feeling." Returning to the much-discussed example of the death of Little Nell in Dickens's *Old Curiosity Shop* (which Wilde insisted could not be read without laughing), she claims,

> Dickens created in little Nell and various other female characters a figure who could not exist and was the product of wish-fulfilment—a subservient, devoted, totally understanding mixture of child and lover, with no wishes of her own. This figure was well-designed to provoke a delicious sense of pity and mastery, and to

set up further fantasies where this feeling could continue. One trouble about this apparently harmless pursuit is that it distorts various expectations; it can make people unable to deal with the real world, and particularly with real girls. Another is that it can so absorb them that they cannot react to what is genuinely pitiful in the world around them.[22]

Sentimentality, she argues, centers around the "flight from, and contempt for, real people." In literature, kitsch characters—Dickens's Nell or Stowe's Eva—are one-dimensional, inspiring an excessive purity of emotion. These girls don't do any of the nasty things that little children do. They don't have any blemishes on their perfect cuteness. They are, accordingly, false characters, and our feelings are distorted. So too, Mark Jefferson argues that "sentimentality involves attachment to a distorted series of beliefs" (526). But the reply to this objection is, first of all, that all emotions are distorting in the sense intended. Anger looks only at the offense and fails to take account of the good humor of its antagonist, jealousy is aware only of the threat and not of the wit and charms of the rival, love celebrates the virtues and not the vices of the beloved, envy seeks only the coveted object and remains indifferent to questions of general utility and the fairness of the desired redistribution. But why call this "distortion" rather than "focus" or "concern"? And what is the alternative— omniscience? Always attending to everything that one knows or remembers about a subject? Reviewing the history of Denmark as well as the literature on step-child relations before one allows oneself to be moved by *Hamlet*? Never having a nice thought without a nasty one as well? What is wrong with sentimentality is not a matter of distortion of reality for the sake of emotion, for all emotions construct a perspective of reality that is specifically suited to their concerns.

There are, of course, ways of carving up the world, ways of selecting the sweet from the surrounding circumstances, that are indeed falsifying and dangerous. We can sentimentalize the situation of the Southern plantation slaves before the Civil War, the virtuous motives of the "freedom fighters" in Nicaragua. We can sentimentalize mischievous children who are bound for reform school (or worse), or all mammals that are on farms or in experimental laboratories. Gwynne Dyer warns us, in his terrifying study of war, against the temptation to "sentimentalize war."[23] It is obvious that in such cases we are already in ethical territory, but what is at stake here is the mode of categorization, not sentimentality. One might (and many do) reach the same results through the affectless application of principles. It is not the nature of the feelings that characterize such problematic cases of so-called "sentimentality" but rather the inappropriate or even dangerous way of misperceiving an ethically loaded situation. So, too, we should react to the example of the Jewish prisoners' opera. It was not Hess's weeping that is damnable but his evil ability to focus on a single, narrow aspect of a situation that ought to inspire horror and revulsion (not sentimental emotions) in any civilized human being.

Mark Jefferson has one example—and I think that it is a very telling example—of how sentimentality can become a danger to morality. In E. M. Forster's *Passage to India*, the English fiancée (Miss Quested) becomes sentimentalized as the symbol of "the purity, bravery and vulnerability of English womanhood." Her alleged attacker (Dr. Aziz) is complementarily cast as "lust-ridden and perfidious" (along with his people). But I would argue that the point made here has much more to do with chauvinism and racism than with sentimentality, and it has little of that innocence of feeling that constitutes sentimentality. There is a confusion here between the alleged innocence of Miss Quested and the innocence of the emotions felt about her. There is also an ambivalence about the relationship of sentimentality and action, for while Tanner and others tend to indict sentimentality for its "distance" from action, here is Jefferson complaining that sentimentality provokes actions of the most violent kind. But it is not sentimentality that provokes (directly or indirectly) the vilification of Aziz and his people, and the "simple-minded sympathies" bestowed upon Quested are hardly an example of sentimentality. Here, again, I think we see the danger of that zero-sum sense of emotion, manifested in a confusion between idealization on the one hand and a dichotomizing conflict on the other. One need not, in celebrating the virtues of an Englishwoman, imply or conclude anything unflattering about the non-English. Competitive winners may entail the possibility of losers and praise may entail the possibility of blame, but there are many forms of idealization that do not entail such contrasts.

So too, Jefferson's examples of World War propaganda, of Germans ("Huns") bayoneting Belgian babies, do not tell us anything about the dangers of sentimentality. They do tell us something about war paranoia and they do presuppose the tender sentiments we all have for babies which make such depictions loathsome. But these sentiments will be degraded as sentimental only if they are perversely demeaned or grotesquely misunderstood, and if caring about babies is sentimentality, then why would Jefferson wonder "What is Wrong with Sentimentality?" This is neither "malaise" nor "a distortion of the way things are" nor is it a "fiction" to be "associated with brutality" (except as we most fear harm to those most vulnerable and most dear to us). There is, I want to argue, nothing wrong with sentimentality, at least not in ethics. Of course, here as elsewhere there is room for excess and pathology, but sentimentality is not itself excessive or pathological. The accusations against it reflect our general uneasiness with emotions, especially "sweet" emotions, and the discomfort of "hard-headed" intellectuals in particular. One might add a sociological-historical hypothesis about the fact that the high class of many societies associate themselves with emotional control and reject sentimentality as an expression of inferior, ill-bred beings, and it is easy to add the now-familiar observation that male society, in particular, has held such a view. Sentimentality is supposed to be undignified (as opposed, for example, to cold-blooded respect, devoid of feeling). But, of course, that depends on what one means by "dignity," and I would suggest that there is more human dignity in rolling around kitsch-like with a baby or a puppy than in the proud arrogance of "being above such things."

VI. Conclusion: In Defense of Sentimentality

What becomes more and more evident, as one pursues the objections to sentimentality, is that the real objection to sentimentality (and kitsch) is the rejection (or fear) of emotion, and of a certain kind of emotion or sentiment in particular, variously designated as "tender" or "sweet" or "nostalgic" (Harries: "cloying sweetness," "sugary stickiness"). We find few similar objections in either art or ethics, we might note, to one-dimensional cynicism, to that gloomy view of the world that commonly co-opts the name "realism." Karsten Harries warns us: "[H]ow easy it is to wax lyrical over despair, to wallow in it, to enjoy it. This too is kitsch, sour kitsch."[24] Mary Midgley points out that "thrillers" have much in common with kitsch and sentimentality, although they distort reality and manipulate emotion to a very different end, "to let the reader feel . . . pleasingly tough and ruthless" (385). But in practice, the charge of sentimentality is almost always aimed at some common tender human sentiment— our reactions to the laughter of a child, or to the death of an infant, for example. It is true that such matters, especially if presented baldly, unambiguously, and without subtlety, are virtually guaranteed to arouse emotion, and they therefore provide a facile vehicle for second- or third-rate painters and novelists. But if such incidents are clichéd, it is because they are such a common and virtually universal concern, and the fact that this may make for some very bad art and literature should not be used to encourage our embarrassment at experiencing these quite natural sentiments or to discourage those sentiments themselves.

It is discomfort with the tender affections, I am convinced, that is the ultimate reason for the stylish attack on sentimentality. Philosophers have long felt uncomfortable with emotions and passion in general (especially those that Hume called "violent"), but the attack on sentimentality, though an obvious symptom of this discomfort, is not an attack on emotion as such (angry indignation and bitter resentment have never gone out of style in Western intellectual life), so much as it is an attack on the "sweet" sentiments that are so easily evoked in all of us and so embarrassing to the hard-headed. It is true that such sentiments "distort" reality, and it is true that they do so in the service of their cautious and obviously self-serving cultivation of certain pleasant emotions. But it is time that we philosophers stop rejecting and start enjoying those emotions, even qua philosophers. Telephone advertisements pressing us to "reach out" to a grandmother or a grandson or a long-absent friend may be annoying because they are so crassly commercial, but it is not the strong, tender feelings evoked that ought to be the target of our disdain. Somewhat similar public service announcements for the Save the Children Foundation and Care provoke similar feelings without the accompanying disdain, and it seems perfectly right and proper for them to do so. How else should one appeal for donations to feed a starving family or to inoculate a stricken village against the ravages of disease? By appealing to our Kantian sense of duty?

Nostalgia is a form of sentimentality, and given the unfortunate fact that most of our experiences are at least tinged with unpleasantness, nostalgia requires considerable effort in selecting, editing, and presenting memories. This does not mean that the memories are false or falsified, however, although that may sometimes be the case. To remember grandpa on what may have been his one healthy and happy day in a decade is not to have a false memory, and to remember together with fondness and laughter the half-dozen tiny tragedies that almost wrecked the wedding and consequently the marriage is not falsification. Nostalgia as sentimentality is the ability to focus on or remember something pleasant in the midst of what may have in fact been tragedy and horror; for example, old soldiers fondly remember the camaraderie of a campaign and forget the terror, bloodshed, and death that surrounded them. But why should this be cause for attack and indignation? If it were used as a defense of war, to "sentimentalize war," such indignation might be justified, but that is not its usual purpose, and a preemptive general strike hardly seems called for.

What I am suggesting is that the attack on sentimentality is wrong-headed and possibly worse, a matter of self-deception or serious self-denial. (That, of course, is just what the critics say about sentimentality.) The usual attack on sentimentality is, I am convinced, too often an attack on innocence and the innocent enjoyment of one's own tender and therefore "soft" emotions. Mark Jefferson makes this point quite convincingly, though he then goes on to join in the attack himself. He argues that sentimentality distorts reality and is "ill-formed," but then he wisely concludes that "it is true that we misrepresent the world in order to indulge in many types of emotion—"soft" and "hard"—but it is not true that every sort of emotional indulgence is equally objectionable."[25] And yet, Jefferson resists extending this concession to sentimentality as such. As it turns out, it is almost always the soft emotions that come most under fire. Jefferson goes on to catalog a number of such "dishonest or self-deceptive appraisals of the world," including "thrill seekers" and people who are by cultivation melodramatic and disdainful. At the end of these (not all of whom seem to me to be either "dishonest or self-deceptive") comes the sentimentalist, whose "trick is to misrepresent the world in order to feel unconditionally warm-hearted about bits of it." But it is not at all clear to me that the usual examples (Little Nell in Dickens) "distort" reality in anything like the damnable sense that Jefferson, supporting Midgley, suggests. Allowing oneself to become teary-eyed about the tragic death of an impossibly idealized girl does not "make us unable to deal with the real world" but rather activates our sensitivity to lesser as well as equal actual tragedies. There is always the aberrant case of the parents who go goo-goo–eyed over the child they physically abuse, but again, it is a grotesque mistake to conflate such inappropriate and (pathologically) inconsistent sentimentality with the brutality that goes with it. The sum-total vision of our emotional economy, according to which we have only so much sympathy to spend, seems to me to be a particularly ill-considered and corrupting doctrine (as it has seemed to several other authors, e.g., Jerome Neu and Ronald de Sousa[26]). It is true that a single trauma can exhaust our emotional resources, but it is unlikely that reading about Little Nell or Little Eva and experiencing "melting compassion" will do that to us. Indeed, that is precisely the virtue of sentimentality, that it stimulates and exercises our sympathies without straining or exhausting them. So considered (as a sort of spiritual exercise), sentimentality is not an emotional vice but a virtue.

NOTES

1. Quoted in Tanner 1976.
2. Mark Jefferson 1983, 519, 527.
3. Mary Midgley, "Brutality and Sentimentality" (1979).
4. *Groundwork of the Metaphysic of Morals* [1785] (1964), 13 (in Paton, 67).
5. Quoted in Mark Jefferson 1983, 519.
6. Jane Tompkins 1985: "[G]iant [male] intellects struggling manfully against a flood of sentimental rubbish" (125).
7. Is there a "salty" kitsch?
8. For example, see Robert Rosenblum, 1967.
9. Karsten Harries 1968, 74, with reference to *Trübners Deutsches Wörterbuch*.
10. Karsten Harries 1968, 77.
11. Kathleen Higgins 1992; Calcineau 1977; Harries 1968, 77.
12. John Canaday, *Mainstreams of Modern Art* (1959), 154.
13. From the catalog of the exhibit.
14. Clement Greenberg, *Art and Culture* (1965), 10.
15. Harries 1968, 77.
16. *The Unbearable Lightness of Being* (1984), 251.
17. "Lecture in Jerusalem" (1985), 5.
18. Michael Tanner 1976, 130, 131. An enormous literature has grown around the question of emotions and music, some of it dating back to Plato's *Republic* and to Confucius, who had a good deal to say about emotions, music, and ethics. More recently, Eduard Hanslick's harsh attack on emotions and sentimentality in music (or, more accurately, in musical listeners), in his *On the Musically Beautiful* in 1854, inspired continuous debate. Some recent contributions include Peter Kivy 1980, Kathleen M. Higgins 1991, and Stephen Davies 1980.
19. Michael Tanner 1976, 139–40.
20. Karsten Harries 1968, 77.
21. "The Philosophy of Horror" (a review of Noël Carroll's book of the same name) in my *Entertaining Ideas* (1992), and in my review (1990) of Bijoy Boruah's *Fiction and Emotion* (1990).
22. Mary Midgley 1979, 1.
23. *War* (1987).
24. Karsten Harries 1968, 253.
25. Mark Jefferson 1983, 523.
26. Jerome Neu 1980 and Ronald de Sousa 1987.

15

The Anaesthetics of Emotion

DAVID NOVITZ

Some things seem so obvious that few people ever question them. Except when I am doing philosophy or being silly, I do not doubt, even for one moment, that the people I speak to are conscious human beings capable of having thoughts and emotions. Nor do I doubt that at least some of the things that I say and write will be understood by them, and that the overwhelming majority of my utterances are meaningful. With almost as much certainty, I believe that it is wrong to torture kittens or puppy dogs, to beat defenseless people, to exploit the innocent, to make love in public, or to betray your spouse of many years. These beliefs and values cannot easily be abandoned–not primarily because of their content but because of the role that they play in my life. They are the beliefs in terms of which I organize my existence and shape my world, and it is precisely because they impart sense and order to my life that I have considerable difficulty with the idea that they are either misleading or false. This is not to say that I cannot ever acknowledge their inadequacy; only that it will cost much to do so. For any challenge to such beliefs tends to undermine the foundations of my world, threatens its stability, and with it my own security and sense of place.

For all of these reasons, any challenge to one's deep convictions is likely to be met with an emotional response. One may be upset, outraged, bewildered, shocked, and sometimes, when it is all too much, one may be irritated beyond words or else reduced to helpless laughter. If a large part of your life is organized around, say, the sanctity of the marriage vows, my public attack on the value of marriage is bound to be met with anger or sorrow, sometimes wry amusement, or else contemptuous dismissal. Again, if I challenge your deeply held political or religious convictions, you will be outraged or deeply angered; if I challenge your beliefs about the stability of the earth's crust, you will either be incredulous, perhaps exasperated, or else convinced and scared.

Now, it is well known that works of art—paintings, plays, novels, films, poems—frequently challenge our everyday understandings, and that, in so doing, they try to make us see and think differently. They give us new ways of looking at and construing the world around us, and in the process they tease and test some of the values and beliefs that we hold most sacred, and to which we are committed in our everyday lives.[1] Subtly, and often without directly confronting our commitments, literary fiction suggests alternative ways of evaluating, construing, and eventually understanding. Think of what *Madame Bovary* does to one's view of marriage and adultery; of what Joseph Heller's *Catch 22* does to one's understanding of patriotism; of what John Irving's *Cider House Rules* does to one's beliefs about the sanctity of life; of what *Middlemarch* does to one's views about scholarship and the scholarly life. None of these works suggest definitive answers to the questions and doubts that they raise, but all challenge certain deeply held views that some people have of the world and their place within it. The interesting fact that I wish to explore is that when art does this, it frequently manages to prevent the sorts of emotional responses that normally accompany challenges to our deeply entrenched beliefs and values. My initial question is why this should be so. When once I have answered this question, I ask why this is not always true: why, in some cases, people *are* outraged, shocked, and angered by works of art that challenge their values and beliefs. The answers that I give to these questions pose certain important and difficult questions for the theory of criticism, and I end by attempting to resolve these difficulties.

I. Art and Anaesthesia

If I am right, some works of art not only make us suggestible, and with it susceptible, to new values, beliefs, and ideologies, but they also anaesthetize us against the pain that often attends such upheavals.[2] The philosophically interesting issue is to try to discover how this is possible: why it is that people who would normally react with hostility to any challenge to their basic beliefs and attitudes, find themselves able not merely to tolerate but to welcome this in literature, drama, or the cinema.

It is important to distinguish this phenomenon from some of the other ways in which art blunts the emotions. It is often claimed, for instance, that some violent and erotic works of art desensitize us to violence, nudity, explicit sex, and offensive language. And so they do, for we often find that our emotional responses to violent scenes in the movies or on television become tempered with repeated exposure to the representation of such acts. However, the phenomenon that I wish to explain is very different from this. For in the aforementioned cases, people *do* respond emotionally to works of art—even though these works subsequently help desensitize the emotions that they evoke. My concern, by contrast, is to explain how works of art can altogether *prevent* us from responding emotionally to ideas that would normally upset us, not how they can temper or blunt the emotional responses that we already have to works of art. So, whatever the explanation of the anaesthetics of emotion, it cannot be given by showing how art desensitizes the emotions.[3] Nor, I should add, can it be given by appealing to catharsis, for however catharsis actually works, it always works therapeutically to rid us of emotions, and it does so, in part, by exciting corresponding emotional states in us.[4] What catharsis does not do is prevent us from having these emotions in the first place.

An entirely different explanation will have to be given of the way works of art anaesthetize the emotions. A first point to notice, by way of developing such an explanation, is that any work of art that attempts to give us good reasons for abandoning certain core values and beliefs at once alerts us to the fact that our deep convictions are being threatened, and this will very likely excite an emotional response. Rational persuasion suffers from a certain candor: to persuade you rationally, I must make you aware of reasons for believing or doing differently, and in the process I must explicitly challenge what you already believe. There is no subterfuge here; if I challenge your beliefs by giving reasons against them, I have to do so explicitly—and this will often disturb you.

Artists who are honest in this way frequently excite the hostility of those who attend to their works. This was certainly true of William Blake, who was considered mad for his pains; it is true, as well, of Alexander Solzhenitsyn, André Brink, and Alice Walker (in *The Temple of My Familiar*)—all of whom are just too open in their advocacy of particular social views. But not all artists are honest in this way. Those whose works anaesthetize the emotions do not attempt to give reasons for the views that they tacitly advocate; they persuade us at a deeper and a darker level by exploiting the conventions of the medium in ways that sometimes contrive to play on our vulnerabilities. In effect, they entice us to abandon specific beliefs and values and to adopt others. Such artworks persuade, but do not do so through force of reason. If anything, they seduce. Theirs is a nonrational and nonthreatening form of persuasion: a form of persuasion that entices by touching the right emotional chords, but that never threatens or coerces. Readers of fiction or movie-goers may simply discover that their values or deep beliefs about the world have shifted or are somehow less stable, and while they may trace these changes back to specific works of art, they often do not know precisely why they have come to think and behave differently. Whereas the price people pay for rational persuasion is a full-blooded awareness of what is going on and why, with the consequent likelihood of a strong emotional reaction, the price that one pays for seductive persuasion is a kind of bemusement—an inability to understand precisely how one has come to think and act in the way that one now does.

Elsewhere I have argued that there is no more effective way of seducing people than by convincing them, sincerely or otherwise, that we share their interests and wish them well, and that it is in all other respects a matter of indifference to us whether or not they adopt our beliefs and values.[5] Claims that embody these sentiments have often been made on behalf of the arts. The great paintings and literary works of our age were said, in the wake of the aesthetic movement, to exist simply for our pleasure, edification, and delight. They were seen as engaging, entertaining—even as intellectually stimulating— but as having no lasting cognitive effects, and so as incapable of destabilizing our commitments and allegiances. The same is true of the popular arts: movies are usually seen as frivolous but generally harmless entertainments; so are magazines, comic books, television dramas, and romances. And the vital issue here is not whether these claims are true or false; it is that if we subscribe to this view of art—and many of us do—we are more (rather than less) likely to be seduced by such artworks.[6]

Those works of art that challenge our core values through a process of seduction do not upset us emotionally. Trivially, this is because seduction is a nonthreatening form of persuasion that entices by playing on our desires. Of itself, though, this does little to explain the different ways in which art seduces. While I cannot hope to explain all the mechanisms at play, there is one fairly obvious mechanism in the case of fictional literature, drama, and the cinema. For the conventions that govern what Peter Lamarque and Stein Olsen call "the practice of fiction" require us to identify imaginatively and emotionally with creatures of fiction.[7] It is by imagining the details of Dorothea Brooke's situation that we, as readers, are able to understand her situation not from our own point of view, but from hers—and, in this sense, identify imaginatively and emotionally with her. Our sympathies are engaged and enlarged; we are brought (always through the medium of our own beliefs and values) to understand and eventually "inhabit" a new world to which our established ways of thinking are not always entirely adequate, so that we become susceptible, for the moment at least, to different beliefs, moral standards, religious values, and so on.[8]

Since these new ways of thinking and feeling are arrived at through our own imaginative endeavor and through our own sympathetic engagement with characters in the fiction, we are not threatened by them. If anything, such involvement in the fiction is engaging and enjoyable, and tends as a result to prevent us from attending to the consequences for ourselves of possible shifts in attitude and opinion. And for so long as we fail to dwell on these, and are absorbed instead by the fortunes and misfortunes of Dorothea and her attempts to resolve the problems that beset her, we will not be threatened by the novel and so will have no obvious reason to protect our earlier commitments and convictions, or to respond with emotion to any challenge to them.

In this way, we find that people who might previously have praised the ideal of wifely devotion and dismissed with contempt the idea of extramarital love are gradually able to understand and sympathize with aspects of Dorothea's feelings for Will Ladislaw, while at the same time despising her self-imposed, unendurably dutiful devotion to Casaubon. Readers of The Color Purple may find that their attitudes to the traditional nuclear family have imperceptibly altered, that they are no longer hostile to sexual love between women, and that they are suspicious of male figures in the family. All of these attitudinal changes, moreover, can be achieved without our being made aware of them, so that as time passes we may discover that our commitments have changed, and, on reflection, we may trace these shifts back to our exposure to certain literary or dramatic works of art.

Although all of this is achieved without the emotional responses that one would normally expect from people whose core beliefs and values are under duress, this is not to say that the process does not involve the emotions. It does. For whenever we identify with creatures of fiction, we do so feelingly—either by sharing certain of their emotions, or by having a range of feelings about them. We share Martha Quest's contempt for her first husband, and we are mildly amused by, and disdainful of, David Copperfield's fawning love for Dora Spenlow. Our emotional absorption in these works marks our interest in, and concern for, the lives of Martha Quest and David Copperfield, and hides, for the moment at least, the interest that we have in retaining the beliefs and values that lend order to our world and help secure our place within it.

This poses an obvious question, for if all of this is true, why is it that people nonetheless read fiction? After all, if we know that it can threaten and even subvert important structural beliefs, and with it one's values and one's way of life, the rational thing to do (supposing that one wants stability and equanimity in one's life) is to avoid fictional literature, rather than to seek it out. The fact that people continue to flock to the theater and the movies, and to buy and read novels; the fact, too, that they watch television drama as frequently as they do, suggests that much of what I have so far said is simply wrong or else greatly exaggerated.

People read fictional literature, go to the theater and the movies, or memorize and recite poetry for a variety of reasons—reasons, I want to suggest, that together outweigh any fear that they might have of the subversion of their values and beliefs. For one thing, the activity of reading and of responding to fiction, like the activity of going to the movies or the theater, is intrinsically pleasurable. For, as Aristotle tells, we just do take pleasure in representations of familiar scenes, people, and situations.[9] Still more, we take pleasure in being emotionally engaged with creatures of fiction; we enjoy good tragedy, as we do the affection we feel for Elizabeth Bennett or Marianne Dashwood and the loathing we feel for Uriah Heep.[10] Equally important, people are fascinated by, and are deeply curious about, other human beings and other ways of life. Novels, drama, and poetry offer insight and understanding without the costs and upheavals that might otherwise accompany the acquisition of such knowledge.

While there are all these inducements, it is nonetheless the case that people are unlikely to engage with fiction, or to develop an extensive fictional literature, unless the practice of fiction is socially countenanced and encouraged. And this, we know from the fate of Salman Rushdie and others, is not always the case.[11] Even those societies that welcome and celebrate artistic innovation and good literature have a cautious respect—evidenced by censorship laws—for works of art that challenge our more important beliefs and values. Even so, such works are seldom treated censoriously in the West—perhaps, I have already suggested, because of a tendency bred of the Aesthetic Movement to treat art as an end in itself, as a source of gratification and delight, but never as a means of instruction or moral elevation, and certainly not as a threat to the social fabric.[12] Art, on this view, has nothing to say and so is never a genuine challenge to the deeply held views that rule our lives. The irony, we have now seen, is that it is this belief in the harmlessness of art that makes people more rather than less susceptible to its charms, more rather than less likely to submit to its challenges.

II. Art, Anger, and the Critical Paradox

Despite all of this, it is just a fact that many people—far more than I have so far allowed—react with shock, indignation, hostility, and anger to those works of fiction that threaten their core beliefs, and it is plain that in such cases art fails to anaesthetize. Many Irish Catholics were scandalised by James Joyce's *A Portrait of the Artist as a Young Man* on account, no doubt, of the threat that it posed to their beliefs about education and the Catholic Church. Others have been angered by the criticisms of Hasidic Judaism implied in Chaim Potok's *The Promise*; yet others were shocked and dismayed by the challenge that Doris Lessing's *Martha Quest* posed to traditional views of marriage. And, on one level at least, it is easy to understand why this happens: those who respond angrily to these works simply decline to respond to them *as* fiction. They see them instead as genuine threats to a favored way of life.

For, as we now know, the conventions that demarcate the practice of fiction require readers or viewers to respond to fictional works in very definite ways. Instead of attending to novels, movies, or stage plays with a mind to their effects on prevailing beliefs and values, the practice of fiction requires one to attend to certain sentences, images, or gestures by imagining the scenes they delineate, and by making believe that certain states of affairs obtain. The reader, we saw earlier, is required to become imaginatively and emotionally involved in the world of the fiction.

Sometimes people fail to do this simply because they are not properly acquainted with the practice of fiction and genuinely do not know how to respond to novels, plays, and poems. More frequently, perhaps, people fail to respond properly to novels and plays because they are impatient with the imaginative and emotional demands that fiction makes on them—perhaps because of a felt insecurity that makes them reluctant to imagine different worlds and ways of life. Quite frequently, too, the refusal to engage with fiction is motivated by one's values, by one's ideological allegiances, or by commitments to particular social movements. Whatever the cause, a failure to respond properly to fiction is a failure to understand it aright, for by failing to become emotionally and imaginatively caught up in the fiction, we are prevented from experiencing "from the inside" the particular situations that confront creatures of fiction. As a result, we fail to have that heightened sense of awareness that allows us to know what is and is not salient to the action of the story; an omission that prevents us from having appropriate expectations about characters, their behavior, and the states of affairs that govern their lives.

According to Lamarque and Olsen, one consequence of adopting this stance—what they call the "fictive stance"—toward fiction

> is that many (though probably not all) inferences are blocked from a fictive utterance back to the speaker or writer, notably inferences about the speaker's or writer's beliefs. This disengagement from normal conversational commitments highlights the idea of "cognitive distance" associated with fiction.[13]

If this is right, then those who respond with anger to what are taken to be the author's beliefs and values have responded inappropriately to the fiction. Put differently, they will have failed to respond to it as fiction.

This seems odd. For among other things, it suggests that it is inappropriate—and in some way the product of a misunderstanding—to criticize a work for its racist or sexist views, for its challenge to humane and liberal attitudes, for its advocacy of pedophilia, or for its shocking anti-Semitism. But we know that works of art can create fashions of thought that sweep across the intellectual landscape and that lure many thousands of people to new, sometimes dangerous, points of view.[14] Because of this, it seems entirely appropriate to respond critically and with emotion to some works of art on account of their promulgation or subversion of certain beliefs and values.

The problem for art criticism is clear. On the one hand, an appropriate response to fictional literature (and, as we shall see, to other art forms as well) requires us to ignore the challenges that these works present to our core beliefs and values. On the other, it is simply irresponsible to overlook the effects that certain works can have on our attitudes and beliefs, and accordingly, on the fabric of our society. It is thus entirely appropriate to respond angrily to some works of art and to do so on account of the threat that they pose to our systems of beliefs and value. From which it follows that it is critically appropriate to respond inappropriately to specific works. This I call the critical paradox.

III. Addressing the Critical Paradox

The quick way to resolve the critical paradox is to point out that it confuses a *critically* appropriate response to a work (namely, the sort of response that will enable us best to understand the content of the work) with what can loosely be called a *morally* appropriate response (namely, a response that will best enable us to grasp the effects that a work may have on its audience and its community). It is because different kinds of appropriateness are appealed to that we have a spurious, or at best a superficial, paradox.

However, the trouble with this attempt to resolve the paradox is that it is by no means clear to a growing majority of people why a critical response to a work of art cannot also take moral issues into account. Nor is it clear why it should be regarded as inappropriate, on the basis of one's critical assessment, to be angry at, or frustrated and annoyed by, a novel. While there may have been a time during the New Criticism when literary criticism was thought to stand aloof from moral issues, this was no more than a literary convention tailored to suit a particular theory of literature. In today's world of heightened moral and political sensitivities, it is thought proper to respond critically to the moral, the gendered, the political, and the religious dimensions of literary fictions. It is now a well-established part of the practice of art criticism to point to the "suppression of particular voices" in the text, to isolate the "point of view" not just of the implied but of the actual author, and in this way to point to the subtle advocacy of particular attitudes and beliefs.[15]

But if this is right, and if it is indeed the case that an appropriate critical response, say, to a novel, requires *both* that we respond to it as fiction *and* that we respond to it morally, then the paradox of criticism seems genuine enough. For although our anger and moral outrage seem to breach the requirements for an appropriate response to the work as fiction, they do not breach the requirements of art criticism — at least as currently practiced by a growing number of scholars.

The proper way to address and resolve the paradox is with the observation that a critic can respond to a novel *as* fiction without becoming locked forever in the fictive stance. We can read a story as fiction, but this need not stop us from responding to it in other ways. It is just a fact that we do not, indeed that we cannot, sustain our imaginative involvement with fiction indefinitely; rather, we move in and out of the fiction, we reflect on our responses, and, in so doing, we may wonder about the moral and political implications of our empathic experiences. Alternatively, we may pause to admire the technical brilliance of the language and the imagery, and then return once more to a full-blooded involvement with the fiction. This to-and-fro movement is part of what is involved in reading fiction, and it helps explain why it is that critics can both respond to a fictional work *as fiction*, and, on other occasions, respond to and remark on its ethical, political, or religious dimensions.

When this is realized, the critical paradox simply disappears. For we can now see that it is premised on the false assumption that an appropriate response to fiction *as fiction* excludes all other responses to the fiction. It plainly does not. One can respond appropriately to a work as fiction and still allow one's understanding of the fiction to become the object of moral or political reflection. And when critics do this, they strive to gauge the impact of the fiction on their systems of value and belief.

It is one thing to respond to *Forrest Gump* imaginatively, to become caught up in Forrest's innocent world of childish affection and misplaced trust. It is another to reflect on its implications for the viewer's beliefs about, and attitudes toward, free-enterprise economic systems and American society. A critic viewing the movie may take delight in Forrest's unwitting commercial triumphs, may cringe when he is bullied as a child and teased for his stupidity. Even so, and on reflection, the critic may be outraged by the subtle propaganda of the movie, by its seeming advocacy of capitalism and apparent glorification of the American way of life.

There is no paradox in all of this. While it is true that some fictional works of art anaesthetize us against certain sorts of emotional upheaval, it is also the case that an appropriate critical response to the work need do nothing of the sort. It may very well expose the ways in which the work lures us to certain points of view, or brings us to engage with the dominant values in our society. And this, in its turn, may quite properly be the occasion of an emotional response.

So, despite the lessons of the Aesthetic Movement and the New Criticism, it is appropriate for an art critic to attend, with feeling, to the subversion and promulgation of values and beliefs through art. Certainly, novels, paintings, poetry, and movies do not usually encourage critical reflection of this sort and, as we have seen, often work to prevent it, but, if I am right, the conventions of criticism that tend to prevent such responses do no more than regulate the practice and determine the fashions of criticism; they certainly do not define that practice and so make it conceptually inappropriate to respond to works of art in this way.[16]

IV. André Brink and Paul Gauguin

In order better to understand the robust complexity of our responses to works of art, it will be helpful to consider the example of two very different artists: one, a nineteenth-century painter whose works have become the object of un-abashed admiration in this century; another, a twentieth-century author whose novels were a source of considerable irritation to many Afrikaners during the heyday of apartheid.

When Paul Gauguin chose to leave his family, to reject Western civiliza-tion, and to paint against the backdrop of palm trees and the golden sands of Tahiti, each of his subsequent paintings conveyed a clear message about his sacrifice to genius and to the dedicated pursuit of his calling as an artist. And when, after the banning of his Afrikaans novel *Kennis van die Aand*, the South African novelist André Brink refused to continue writing in Afrikaans, each of his subsequent English novels stood as a rebuke to a government that, until then, had pretended to be the guardian of Afrikaner culture. As a result, his later novels sent a clear message about the actions of the South African gover-nent to those Afrikaners who sought to promote an Afrikaans literature and who regarded Anglo-Saxon culture as a threat to Afrikanerdom.

It is important to see, though, that these are messages in a rather special sense, for they do not properly attach to, and cannot be derived from, the content of any of Gauguin's Tahitian paintings or Brink's English novels—that is, from the various plots and themes of the novels or from the pictorial imag-ery and symbolism of the paintings. For it is plain that novels as diverse as *A Dry White Season*, *States of Emergency*, *The Wall of the Plague*, and *A Chain of Voices* all share this same message; and that paintings with entirely different motifs—from *Nafea Foa Ipoipo* (*When Will You Be Married?*), to *Mahana Maa* (*Shopping Day*), *Tapera Mahana* (*Sunset*), and *Nevermore O Taiti*—are all thought to convey a single message about Gauguin's great sacrifice to ge-nius. As a result, it is difficult to think of such messages as somehow contained within these artworks: they are not messages *in* art and are not to be found in the artworks themselves. Rather, they are messages conveyed *by means* of art, and are what I have elsewhere called messages "through" (rather than messages "in") art.[17]

What is more, the shared message of Gauguin's Tahitian paintings can properly be considered a message even if it was not intended or believed by Gauguin. For it does not take much, in the context of today's widespread disenchantment with individualism, to see Gauguin's paintings as a testament not so much to his genius as to his selfishness and his unfeeling betrayal of his wife and family.[18] This is one message that can be taken from the work; an unspoken and an unintended message to be sure, but a message nonetheless.[19]

The distinction between messages "in" and "through" art is crucial if we are to be able to distinguish, as our solution to the critical paradox suggests we must, between a response to a work of art that enables us to grasp its content and derive insights about the world from that content, and a response to the same work that enables us to gauge the work's effects on the beliefs and values of people, and hence on the social fabric. If I am right, messages "in" novels and paintings are derived by responding to a work in terms of the conventions that govern the medium. Messages "through" art, on the other hand, are discerned by suspending those conventions, and looking to the ways in which the work affects the core beliefs and values of those who attend to it.

Can this distinction be defended? One might think not—if only because the messages about the world that we take from the content of a novel are so often interlaced with higher order moral and political responses to the novel. But the fact that messages "in" art are often discerned in close temporal proximity to messages "through" art certainly does not entail that there is no difference between the two or that they are discerned in the same way.

Normally, a message "in" a work of art derives from but is not about the content of the work. It is not a message in *Nafea Foa Ipoipo*, for instance, that two Tahitian woman, one in tribal dress and one in Western dress, are sitting one in front of the other. What may be a message "in" this painting is the idea, derived from a proper apprehension of its content, that the Western way of life is slowly intruding on tribal life in Tahiti. So, whenever we speak of messages "in" art, the messages that we are concerned with are about the actual world, not about the imaginary world of the work. Furthermore, such messages are "in" a work of art only if the work, because of what is taken to be its content, can reasonably be thought to say something about, or otherwise inform us of, the actual world.

This, it must be stressed, is not to suggest that the message "in" a work is whatever one is seduced into believing.[20] Messages "in" may be discerned without our being seduced and without our core beliefs and values being affected in any way at all, for, quite plainly, a reader may already have, and so agree with, the beliefs and values suggested by the message "in" a work. The connection between the seduction of a reader by a work and the discernment of messages "in" a work is this: just as seduction, when it occurs, occurs only if the reader complies with the conventions that govern the medium, so messages "in" art are discerned only by responding to the work in terms of those conventions that are appropriate to it and that will allow the reader to grasp its content.

But, as I have already suggested, works of art may convey messages that do not properly arise because of their content. The Seurat in my office may tell people how wealthy I am; the tattoo of a dragon on my forehead may tell you how silly I am; and *Nafea Foa Ipoipo* may remind you how damaging Gauguin's pursuit of artistic fame was to his family. These are messages that cannot be taken from the content of any of these works but are the function of certain widely held beliefs and values that surround the production and display of those works. Messages "through" art have everything to do with the social location of works of art but have nothing directly to do with what we regard as the content of these works.

This is more easily understood when we attend to the backdrop of "deep" attitudes, values, and beliefs against which a work and its action unfolds, and to which almost everyone who understands the work subscribes. These, I said earlier, are sometimes the core beliefs and attitudes that, in Wittgenstein's words, "stand fast" for everyone in that society or "form of life."[21] There are occasions, however, when intellectual trends encourage us to attend to the "deep" beliefs and attitudes assumed by the work. Those who respond to the work in this way do so because they have acquired a new range of beliefs and values that are either admiring of, or (as is more usually the case) critical of, what they and the many works of art produced in their community had previously taken for granted. In the process, the work is sometimes considered to assert or to convey what, up until then, it had merely assumed. And this, of course, can happen quite independently of what the author might have wanted, intended, or believed.

One implication of this is that a message "in" a work may, in certain circumstances, be productive of messages "through" that work. This we have already seen, is true of *Forrest Gump*. It is true as well of *Nafea Foa Ipoipo*, for the message "in" that work, namely that Western manners and values are slowly displacing the indigenous way of life on Tahiti, may incline us to attend to certain background beliefs and values about assimilation, tribal life, and colonialism. Depending on which beliefs we foreground, and on our attitude toward them, we may construe the painting as conveying the message that European influence in Tahiti is a beneficial force for civilization, or alternatively, that it is intrusive, disruptive, and harmful. And although these messages are indirectly the product of a message that is "in" the work, they are not themselves messages "in" *Nafea Foa Ipoipo*: they cannot be discerned in its pictorial imagery, in its content, and so are messages "through" the painting that depend for their existence on the beliefs and values that surround its display.

Of course, there are many messages "through" art that are not in any sense a product of messages "in" art. A Degas sculpture in my servants' quarters tells you how boastful I am, not because of its content but because we attend (in a certain way) to deeply held views about the economic value of the sculpture and about the low status of servants' quarters in any home. There are, then, two kinds of messages "through" art: those that are indirectly produced by the content of the work, and those that do not depend on the work's content in any manner or form. Both have this in common: they depend on a tendency at certain times in our history to foreground, either in an approving or disapproving way, certain widely held values and beliefs.

It seems plain, then, that there is a distinction to be drawn between messages "in" and "through" art, although, in saying this, I do not wish to maintain that it is always obvious which messages are "in" and which "through" art. There are occasions when the boundaries between the two are blurred.[22] Even so, fuzzy boundaries cannot establish that there is no distinction to be drawn. The fact, as we have seen, is that it can easily be drawn in many cases, and that in these situations it is often useful to draw it.

In order to see this more clearly, think for a moment of the jokes made about and leveled at Al in the television comedy *Married with Children* — jokes about his incompetence as a husband and father, about his sexuality and unintelligence. One deep and largely unquestioned assumption that runs throughout the series is that Peg's jokes are harmless good fun. Now there are certain groups of people who would prefer to question this assumption. They see jokes of this sort as subversive of the male role within the family, as ridiculing, and so as undermining men everywhere. From time to time, members of such groups maintain that the denigration of males and of the role of men within the family is part of what *Married with Children* celebrates—part of its message and content, part of what it is about.

This, however, strikes others as at best misleading, at worst implausibly puritanical. *Married with Children*, they want to say, is a comedy; feminist triumphalism and the denigration of men is not a part of its message. The battle lines are drawn, but if my distinction is correct, this sort of disagreement can easily be resolved. For while it is implausible to suggest that the denigration of men is a message "in" *Married with Children*—that this is part of its content (its plot or theme)—it is by no means implausible to see it as a message "through" *Married with Children*, as a message that is inadvertently (or advertently) conveyed by means of the TV series on account of its uncritical endorsement of, or its implied challenge to, certain widely held background assumptions.

The distinction that I have advocated thus helps ground the feminist claim that some works of art—whether it be *Hamlet* or *Death and the Maiden*— contain messages damaging to women. But these messages, we can now see, need not be part of the action, theme, or plot of these works; nor need they be intended. They are, for all that, extremely influential and in some cases harmful. This is a distinction, then, that gives us a way of explaining the complicated emotional effects that works may have on certain audiences at certain times, where this effect, although partly cognitive, is not properly taken from what the work explicitly says. It also gives us a way of addressing a persistent dispute in the theory of criticism; a dispute that is reflected, I think, in what I earlier called the critical paradox.

V. The Death of the Artist

Messages "in" art, I have said, often work to hide those messages that are conveyed "through" art. This stands to reason, since (as we now know) the way in which one is meant to respond to a work of art in order properly to grasp the messages "in" it is quite different from the ways in which one responds to a work when one discovers messages "through" it. Messages "through" art can, of course, be insidious, but this is so only because readers and viewers are prevented by the conventions of the medium from attending to the effects of the work on their structural beliefs and values. It is only by defying these conventions that we discern messages "through" art, and respond with emotion to them.

A failure to draw a distinction between the different sorts of messages that we discern in art has contributed importantly to some of the strong claims that emerged in the wake of the "death-of-the-author" debate; a debate that arose out of Roland Barthes's well-known observation that "the birth of the reader will be at the cost of the death of the Author."[23] It was a debate that was largely intent on debunking the widespread idea of the artist as an inventive romantic genius who holds complete sway over what can legitimately be taken from the work.[24]

While there certainly is something deeply mistaken about confining the critical discussion of a work to what its author intended to convey, the death-of-the-author debate led to a number of silly excesses — excesses, I believe, that could have been avoided by marking the distinction between messages "in" and "through" art. It was soon maintained, for instance, that authorial intention, like the structural forms created by the author, should be allowed to determine neither the meaning nor the limits of a work, and certainly should not be allowed to constrain the viewer's or reader's response to it. Rather, the work and its content were to be seen as the product of the reader's or viewer's own creativity and imaginative virtuosity, or otherwise (and much more radically) as the result of the unconstrained play of signs within the text.[25]

According to Barthes, to "give a text an Author is to impose a limit on that text, to furnish it with a final signified, to close the writing."[26] And it is this limit that those who emphasize the virtuosity of the reader, and the essential creativity of critical interpretation, wish to transcend. On this view, those who look for suppressed voices in a text, who discover the valorization of the American way of life, say, in *Forrest Gump*, or the advocacy of alcohol consumption in *Coronation Street*, all offer equally "valid" or "plausible" accounts of what the work "says," for what it "says" is what the reader or viewer can imaginatively impute to it.

But this, I have already said, is implausible. We need to distinguish the province of artistic control from that of readerly contribution. In my terms, artists *are* usually responsible for messages "in" art — that is, for those messages about the world that can properly be taken from the content of the work. Still more, as we have seen, artists often exploit the conventions of the medium in order to anaesthetize their viewers or readers from those emotions that might otherwise accompany the challenges that such artworks pose to some of their deeply held beliefs or values. Consider once again the case of Paul Gauguin. In an article entitled "Paul Gauguin, or Symbolism in Painting" that appeared in *Mercure de France* in March 1891, Albert Aurier relayed Gauguin's view of what a painting should aim to be. In distinct contrast to the Impressionists, Gauguin thought that a painting should "be centred upon an idea, since the expression of the idea should be its only ideal." Such an idea would convey the subjective perception of the artist, and would do so by means of decorative symbols or forms "according to a method that [could] generally be understood." [27]

Gauguin does not just tell us what he strives to achieve in a painting but, by inventing and establishing the conventions of synthetism, tells us what his viewers ought to look for in his paintings. On his view, and on the view of anyone who is adequately informed about the genre, a proper response to his later works involves looking at the marks and colors on the canvas as symbols and decorative forms that convey a determinate idea—one derived from his own inventive perception of the world. And so, in *Nafea Foa Ipoipo*, it is appropriate to look at dress as a symbol—something that conveys the artist's subjective perception, and that tells us about the absorption of the South Sea Islands into European culture.

This is why messages "in" art are much more a product of the artist's creative endeavors than they are the result of the reader's, the viewer's, or the critic's. When we respect the author's constraints on how we are meant to view *Nafea Foa Ipoipo*, it becomes inappropriate to view it as a testament to Gauguin's betrayal of his wife, hence as containing a message about male attitudes to females. After all, none of the forms and symbols in the painting so much as hint at this; nor, of course, was this the subjective perception that Gauguin sought to convey in the painting. In order to interpret the painting in this way, the reader would have to attend critically and creatively to a wealth of detail external to the work that has nothing to do with the conventions of synthetism: to Gauguin's family history; to the deep beliefs that people had about the importance of art and the cultivation of genius in nineteenth-century Europe; to contemporary beliefs and values about art, the family, women, men, children, fidelity; and so on. Only then can one derive this message from *Nafea Foa Ipoipo*, and it will be a message "through" the painting, not a message "in" it.

So it is not true that the artist is dead, only that the artist is often ignored. There is no need for this, however, for there remains a perfectly proper sphere for the influence and determinations—for the authority—of the artist. There is also a sphere for the creative determinations of the reader. The one need not exclude the other.

If we attend only to messages "in" art, a "readerly" response to the work is effectively arrested, and the artist or author does become something like the sole authority who holds complete sway over what can properly be derived from the work. Criticism, however, addresses all sorts of issues and questions regarding a work; here readers decide what they want to know and think about in light of the work. And there is nothing improper about this.[28] It only becomes improper when we confuse messages "through" art with messages that are properly to be found "in" it.

VI. Conclusion

I began by pointing to and explaining the anaesthetic qualities of art. Some novels, poems, plays, and paintings, I said, prevent those who attend to them from experiencing the emotional responses that normally accompany strong challenges to deeply held values and beliefs. Using examples from fictional literature and painting, I argued that this is achieved only because viewers and readers are required to respond to these works in ways stipulated by the conventions of the medium. It is such a response that also allows them to understand the work properly, to grasp its content, and so to discover those messages about the world, if any, that are "in" the work: there to be discovered by the attentive but not very inventive viewer or reader.

But I also argued that a reader does not always have to respond to a novel, a painting, or a play in terms of the conventions that govern these art forms. Were this not so, much that now passes for art criticism would be disallowed, for readers frequently attend not just to the action of the narrative, but also to the challenges that it poses to certain of their core beliefs and values. And when one responds to a work in this way, one may very well feel all the emotion that is consequent on a threat to one's beliefs and values.

These observations suggest that it is somehow appropriate to respond inappropriately to works of art. The air of paradox, I said, is easily resolved, for it is plain that one can respond imaginatively to a literary fiction without becoming transfixed in this response. Rather, one moves "in" and "out" of the fiction, and, on moving beyond the conventional constraints of the medium, one assesses its challenges to one's values and one's view of the world.

It is only when we take the critical paradox seriously that we are forced to "take sides" and to assert either the total authority of the artist, or, alternatively, the "death" of the artist and the "birth of the reader." The former position inclines us to see art as an enduring anaesthetic, one that forces us to respond in terms of the conventions of the medium, that lowers our rational and emotional defenses, and that lures us, in just the way that Socrates supposed drama must do, to dangerous, unbidden, and rationally indefensible points of view.[29] The "birth of the reader," on the other hand, emphasizes the reader's creative response to the work. In so doing, it consigns the artist to an untimely death, and does so by altogether eliminating the artist's voice in much that currently passes for art criticism.

Neither extreme is necessary. It was by drawing a distinction between messages "in" and messages "through" art that I hoped to distinguish the domain of the artist from that of the reader, arguing that much art does indeed anaesthetize and that it does so on account of the artist's exploitation of the conventions that govern the medium. However, I also argued that we can move beyond the conventions of the medium, that we can assess them and their influence on us, and that when we do, we can respond with the full range of emotions that art sometimes seeks to suppress.

NOTES

I am grateful to Stephen Davies, Paisley Livingston, William Lyons, and Steven Stich for comments on earlier versions of this paper.

1. For some of the mechanisms involved in this, see my *Knowledge, Fiction and Imagination* (1987), chap. 6. Cf. Gregory Currie 1995(b).

2. On this, see my *The Boundaries of Art* (1992), chap. 9, where I illustrate the social dimensions of this phenomenon, arguing that it effectively converts art into an instrument of policy that can succeed where other instruments of persuasion fail.

3. Such an explanation would best be given in terms of the concepts of cognitive and affective dissonance. See, for example, L. Festinger 1957 and 1980, in which the author gives empirical evidence for the view that people adjust their beliefs to suit their feelings. See, as well, William Sargant's landmark, if somewhat anecdotal, book on brainwashing, *Battle for the Mind* (1956).

4. This is all rather more complicated than I here suggest. For more on catharsis, see Martha C. Nussbaum 1986, esp. 388–91.

5. *The Boundaries of Art* (1992), chap. 10. See, as well, Jean-Paul Sartre 1972, 254–57. See also, Søren Kierkegaard 1946, esp. 291–371.

6. I argue that these claims are false. See my *The Boundaries of Art* (1992), chaps. 1–4 and 8–10.

7. See Peter Lamarque and Stein Haugom Olsen 1994, 32–47, who treat fiction as a practice that is constituted by certain conventions.

8. For more on this, see Hilary Putnam 1978, 83–96.

9. Aristotle, *On the Art of Poetry* (1962), section 4, 29.

10. This phenomenon is discussed by Susan Feagin, 1983, 95–104, and by Noël Carroll 1990, chap. 4.

11. Think here of the effects of the Catholic Index, and of the Muslim *fatwa* issued in response not just to Salman Rushdie's *The Satanic Verses*, but to authors as diverse as the feminist doctor Taslima Nasrin in Bangladesh and Nobel Prizewinner Naguib Mahfouz in Egypt.

12. For more on the origins of this view, see my "Ways of Artmaking: The High and the Popular in Art" (1989). For examples of the view, see James McNeill Whistler 1888, and Oscar Wilde 1908, 241–77. Wilde tells us at one point that "Into the true and sacred house of Beauty the true artist will admit nothing that is harsh or disturbing, nothing that gives pain, nothing that is debatable, nothing about which men argue" (257). And he goes on to say that "to the poet all times and places are one . . . for him there is but one time, the artistic moment; but one law, the law of form; but one land, the land of Beauty—a land removed indeed from the real world" (258).

13. Lamarque and Olsen, *Truth, Fiction, and Literature* (1994), 43–44. See, as well, 44–52.

14. I have in mind literary works like William Blake's "Songs of Innocence and Experience," Charlotte Brontë's *Jane Eyre*, Henrik Ibsen's *A Doll's House*, the works of Charles Dickens and Emile Zola, Leo Tolstoy's *The Resurrection*, Alan Paton's *Cry, the Beloved Country*, and Doris Lessing's *Martha Quest*. The list can be projected indefinitely.

15. See, for example, Mary Devereaux 1990 and Ismay Barwell 1995.

16. Here I take issue with Lamarque and Olsen (1994), who claim that considerations of truth play no part in a critically appropriate response to fictional literature. See my critical study of their book, "The Trouble with Truth: A Critical Study of Peter Lamarque and Stein Haugom Olsen, *Truth, Fiction, and Literature*" (1995b).

17. See my "Messages 'In' and Messages 'Through' Art" (1995a). The Brink example is borrowed from this paper.

18. The *Collins Concise English Dictionary* gives as one of the entries for "message," "an implicit meaning, as in a work of art." This sense of the word is in current usage, even though it is not to be found as an entry in the *Oxford English Dictionary*, and is one sense of the word "message" that I try to elaborate in this paper.

19. It is true that Gauguin's Tahitian paintings are not widely construed in this way, and this remains, for the moment at least, a matter of his very good luck. With comments like mine, however, I suspect that Gauguin's luck may be about to run out. On this, see Bernard Williams 1981, esp. 22.

20. Here I am indebted to Stephen Stich, who alerted me to this possible misunderstanding.

21. Ludwig Wittgenstein 1974, para. 234.

22. I explain this in more detail in "Messages 'In' and Messages 'Through' Art" (1995a), 202–2.

23. Roland Barthes 1977, 148.

24. On this, see Roland Barthes 1972, xvii–xviii.

25. Roman Ingarden 1973 is an early exponent of this view. A more recent exponent is Stanley Fish 1980. It is a view, of course, that takes strength from the writings of Jacques Derrida. On this, see my *Knowledge, Fiction and Imagination* (1987), 42–55. See, as well, Joseph Margolis's earlier writings on this topic in 1980, 122–27.

26. Barthes 1977, 147.

27. On this, see Georges Boudaille 1964, 152–55.

28. I argue that it is an inevitable and necessary part of criticism. See *Knowledge, Fiction and Imagination* (1987), chap. 5.

29. Plato, *The Republic* (1923), Book X.

16

Emotions and Identification

Connections Between Readers and Fiction

KEITH OATLEY & MITRA GHOLAMAIN

Much is known about what connects people to each other. There are many kinds of connections—attachment, love, friendship, shared purpose, competition—for humans are members of the most social of vertebrate species. But what connects people to the texts of fiction?

In this chapter we suggest that the links that easily form between reader and story throw light both on the properties of narrative and on human psychology. We concentrate mainly on readers and texts, but some of our discussion also concerns the theater and the cinema.

I. Dreams and Fiction

In order to make our argument about the connection of readers to fiction, we need first to vote in a debate. The debate is about the nature of fiction: is fiction an imitation of life?

In his most influential piece of literary criticism, "The Art of Fiction" (1884), Henry James argued that a novel is "a direct impression of life" (398). With this claim, James added a gloss to that venerable work of literary criticism, the *Poetics*, in which Aristotle proposed that fictional narrative is based on "mimesis." This term has generally been translated into English as "representation" (the term used by James), or "imitation," or "copying." James was arguing against the idea that fiction is just make-believe. Instead, he asserted, a novelist seeks truth according to certain premises, every bit as much as does a historian.

James's article was followed by a rejoinder by Robert Louis Stevenson, who argued that far from being "a direct impression of life," art, whether literary or visual, is an abstraction [1884, 182]. One cannot do without the idea of a perfect circle, but one encounters it only in the domain of geometrical abstraction. By analogy, Stevenson suggests, we cannot do without the idea of character and other literary phenomena, but we encounter them in pure form only in fictional abstraction.

Abstractions are made for specific purposes. Stevenson identified three in fiction, each giving rise to a recognizable genre: stories of adventure, novels to discover the essence of a character, and novels written for readers to experience the dramatic potential of a certain passion. And, contradicting James, he contrasted life with art:

> Life is monstrous, infinite, illogical, abrupt and poignant; a work of art, in comparison, is neat, finite, self-contained, rational, flowing, and emasculate. Life imposes by brute energy, like inarticulate thunder; art catches the ear, among the far louder noises of experience, like an air artificially made by a discreet musician. (182)

Stevenson extends some of the thoughts of his earlier essay in the wonderfully artful "A Chapter on Dreams" (1888):

> The past is all of one texture—whether feigned or suffered—whether acted out in three dimensions or only witnessed in that small theatre of the brain which we keep brightly lighted all night long, after the jets are down, and darkness and sleep reign undisturbed in the remainder of the body . . . which of them is what we call true, and which a dream, there is not one hair to prove. (189)

Stevenson goes on to explain that, when he was a child, he was a dreamer. When he became a writer, his stories tended to come to him not from ordinary life, but as dreams in which characters and situations suggested themselves, and started to become actual in the theater of his brain. His dream characters were much more creative than he, or so he claimed. A corollary of this idea, which was later taken up and developed by Gardner (1984), is that what a fictional text does for a reader is to start up, and then sustain, a certain kind of dream.

Let us pursue this idea about dreaming and perception. It is a theme that fascinated not just Stevenson, but other nineteenth-century writers. Here, for instance, is Hippolyte Taine (1882):

> Ainsi notre perception extérieure est un rêve du dedans qui se trouve en harmonie avec les choses du dehors; et, au lieu de dire que l'hallucination est une perception extérieure fausse, il faut dire que la perception extérieure est une *hallucination vraie*. (13, emphasis in original)

> (So our ordinary perception is an inward dream which happens to correspond to things outside; and, instead of saying that a hallucination is a perception that is false, we must say that perception is a *hallucination that is of the truth*.)

In this striking metaphor, Taine confronts us with the constructive nature of perception, with the idea that when we perceive, it is not that the world outside is somehow able to enter the mind; the world stays obstinately where it is. The machinery for constructing vivid and convincing perceptions is present within us; it is what Stevenson calls "the small theatre of the brain." When we see the ordinary world, this machinery takes in fragmentary pieces of evidence of patterns of excitation on the retina, and these patterns guide it in constructing what we experience as reality. We know some such machinery is responsible, because dreams can produce coordinated visual scenes independently of any impingement on the senses.

The machinery that is capable of being guided by nerve signals from the retina is also capable of being guided in other ways. So, what a writer of fiction provides is verbal guidance that will start up the theaters of our brains, stimulating them to construct a certain coherent experience, start up a kind of dream, and sustain it. When we read, the effects are not entirely visual. There is perhaps the sense of a voice when reading, as Welty (1983) describes, or of voices in conversation; but in one way or another, for a novel or short story to work, the reader must construct, from bare clues of ink and page, scenes, characters, and actions, a constructed, imagined, world that becomes fascinating.

A constructed dream, we believe, provides a firmer basis than the impression of life for thinking about the art of fiction. So here are two issues. First, what else is it possible to say, from the standpoint of cognitive psychology or literature, about the process of the constructed dream which is the experience of reading? Second, what is there about this process that sustains the connections that people make with the text, and what is the value of these connections?

II. Reading as Simulation

We think this issue, like so much in understanding fiction, is best approached via Aristotle's *Poetics*, particularly by way of his term mimesis. As we said above, the word is usually translated in English as something like "imitation" or "representation," and that is how Henry James took it. Risking anachronism, however, Oatley (1992 and 1994) proposed that what Aristotle really meant by mimesis was not anything like imitation, but something closer to what we now talk of as "simulation." Aristotle's notion was that a tragic drama is a simulation of human actions. Actions are portrayed by actors in the theater and—more importantly—the whole play must run on the minds of the audience, as a computer simulation runs on a computer.

We have argued above that novels and plays work by guiding the dreammaking process, but the idea of simulation takes us further. The idea itself is at least as old as the classical Greek concept of the human microcosm as a mirror of the macrocosm. In more modern times, C. S. Peirce, the founder of pragmatism and semiotics, asserted that the mind parallels reality: ". . . there can be no reasonable doubt that man's mind, having been developed under the influence of the laws of nature, for that reason naturally thinks somewhat after nature's pattern" (1929, 269). Craik (1943) brought the idea into the age of information technology, and stated it with admirable clarity: human minds have the potentiality for making models of the world (that is, for simulation) and for operating with these models. This indeed is what our minds do generally. So, minds are constructed to parallel the workings of the world, both the physical world and the world of human actions. Our language is thick with ideas pointing to this mental function: simile, metaphor, schema, parallel, analogy, theory, hypothesis, explanation, model, and many others.

Although the idea of simulation by computer is new, the idea that the mind performs simulations is not. Having put the matter in this way, it is easy to see when rereading Aristotle's *Poetics* that this is what he was talking about. "Imitation" and "representation" are much too empirical as translations of mimesis. They imply copying and one-to-one correspondences between the movements and speech of (for example) an actor and what has happened in real life. In the *Poetics*, Aristotle makes it clear that this is not essential to mimesis. He discusses great drama as being in poetic verse, though no one ever spoke verse in real life. He writes of a day compressed into the few hours of a play's performance. And he asks: is it such things as the costumes that make a play moving (as if such correspondences might be the cause for the effectiveness of drama)? No, it is the plot that is "the heart and soul, as it were, of tragedy . . . it is the mimesis of an action and [simulates] persons primarily for the sake of their action" (28, our substitution of the new translation of *mimesis*).

Fiction does not even copy that aspect of life that many writers, including Stevenson, have asserted to be most indigenous to fiction, namely, conversation. Oatley (1994) gives a transcription of a fairly ordinary piece of conversation, and shows how such transcriptions would be hopelessly unintelligible in any narrative account. But if altered—fictionalized, as one might say—they can become comprehensible. Fiction leaves out accidental "ums," "ers," diversions, repetitions, and repairs. It provides context to understand the elliptical. It transforms ordinary life. It indicates purpose. It implies the coherence and direction that a transcription or any other recording of "real life" leaves out.

In fiction based on mimesis, it is good, of course, to have some imitative correspondence with the real world. Without it, any fiction would founder. But, more fundamentally, such correspondence is always in the service of the larger structure. In a copy, the emphasis is on exact correspondences, piece by piece, between elements of the world and elements of the copy. But in a work of art that is a simulation, two other kinds of relationships are more important: the cohering relationships among elements within the whole of the work of art, and the relationship between the work of art and its audience. We could say that whereas science prioritizes a correspondence theory of truth, narrative fiction prioritizes a coherence theory.

Aristotle makes it clear that what a tragic drama achieves is a focus on essentials of human action. For any simulation to work, nonessentials must be excluded. As Aristotle put it: "A poetic mimesis, then, ought to be . . . unified and complete, and the component events ought to be so firmly compacted that if any one of them is shifted to another place, or removed, the whole is loosened up and dislocated" (32). Was Stevenson in mind of this passage when he wrote that "a work of art, in comparison [to life], is neat, finite, self-contained, rational" (182)?

One further point: fiction is much concerned with emotions. Oatley and Johnson-Laird (1996) have argued that humans prefer being in emotional states. In fiction, people can experience such states without many of the usual consequences.

In the *Poetics*, Aristotle used the term "katharsis" in relation to the emotions of pity and fear that are aroused in the audience during tragedies. This term has also had a confusing career with the translators. It is generally translated in English either with a quasi-religious sense of "purification" or with a quasi-medical sense of "purgation." In either case, the implication is that when people go to the theater, they experience emotions that can either be improved (purified) or eliminated (purged), so that, on return to real life, these unfortunate elements will no longer have the effect of disturbing rational thought and judgment.

But there is no evidence that either of these meanings is what Aristotle intended. In fact, they would be inconsistent with the tenor of Aristotle's writings about both emotions and art. Nussbaum (1986) has shown that the central meaning of katharsis (and related words e.g., "kathairo," "katharos"), common before Aristotle, used frequently by Plato and Aristotle, and continuing after Aristotle's time, was that of clearing up or clarification, including the cognitive meaning of understanding clearly and without obstacles. The spiritual term "purification" is a derivation, indicating an absence of obscuring blemish. The medical one, "purgation," is also secondary, indicating freeing the body from internal obstructions.

Nussbaum argues that katharsis in the theater was a cognitive process: "The function of tragedy is to accomplish through pity and fear, a clarification (or illumination) concerning experiences of the pitiable and fearful kind" (1986, 391). And this, as she then adds, is an appropriate translation of Aristotle's famous passage (*Poetics* 1449b) in which katharsis is mentioned.

A cognitive hypothesis is that emotions have evolved to manage action and goals (aims, concerns, motivations), and that they are further shaped by culture to fulfil social versions of these same functions (Oatley 1992). In everyday life, however, emotions often occur without our fully understanding their significance (Oatley and Duncan 1992). Prompted by the Aristotelian considerations indicated above, one may hypothesize as follows: by engaging with the art of the theater or of the novel, we are induced to run on ourselves narrative simulations of actions, with their consequences and emotional effects.

In the theater or in a novel, we can concentrate on our emotions and reflect upon them in a safe place away from the ordinary world; this being so, we can come to a better understanding of their relation to our beliefs, desires, and actions. We are able to achieve clarification of some of the complex relationships that obtain among our emotions, our goals, and the actions for which we are responsible, even though we undertake them in a world that we only partly understand and can only partly control. Thereby, we can begin to observe the Delphic injunction, "Know thyself"; that is, we can begin to form conscious representations of ourselves, of our goals, and of their relation to our actions.

III. Five Processes in Reading or Watching Fictional Narrative

Next, we indicate some distinct psychological processes in reading fiction that connect the reader to the text, or theater and movie audiences to what is seen and heard. The first three are ordinary psychological processes, each of which plays a particular role in our responses to fiction. The last two are aspects of the fictional presentation to the reader or audience. These five processes, as discussed in the following paragraphs, are modified and extended from the set of processes proposed by Oatley (1994).

Identification

Identification is not the only psychological process occurring when we read fiction or watch a play or film, but it may be one without which a fictional narrative would not work. Identification provides a principal basis for thinking about what connects the reader to the text. If fiction is a kind of dream, as Stevenson gently suggested and as Freud later insisted, then it contains an element of wishing. In fiction, there is the wish to be elsewhere. The story and the text are designed to gratify this wish by allowing the reader to become, at least in part, a character in the story.

In "Psychopathic Characters on the Stage" (1904), Freud argued that being a member of an audience at the theater,

> does for adults what play does for children. . . . The spectator . . . is "a poor wretch to whom nothing of importance can happen," who has long been obliged to damp down, or rather displace, his ambition to stand at the hub of world affairs; he longs to feel and to act and to arrange things according to his own desires—in short, to be a hero. And the playwright and actor enable him to do this by allowing him *to identify himself* with the hero. (122, emphasis in original)

At the time he wrote this passage, Freud had dreams much in mind; his idea was that once upon a time each of us truly was at the hub of our world's affairs. Each was the focus of interest of a parent who was all the world to us, and for whom we were the world's center. Art, literature, the theater, films, and other cultural phenomena, come to fill the gap as we gradually separate from our parents (Winnicott 1971). What Freud was postulating is that the gap that is left always involves a good deal of longing to be elsewhere than here. Even in its most ordinary connotations in English, "dream" has this sense of something wished for. Hence, if Stevenson is right, part of the function of fiction is to provide something of an alternative world that we inhabit.

In some forms of literary identification, the reader becomes the character. Here for instance is Léon, in Flaubert's *Madame Bovary* (1857):

[I]s there anything better, really, than sitting by the fire with a book? . . . The hours go by. Without leaving your chair you stroll through imagined landscapes as if they were real, and your thoughts interweave with the story, lingering over details or leaping ahead with the plot. Your imagination confuses itself with the characters, and it seems as if it were your own heart beating inside their clothes. (96–97)

The idea of identification connects closely to the idea of mimesis as simulation, because following a plot requires that actions be understood as steps in plans. Oatley (1992) has argued that the basic modality of the fictional simulation is, therefore, that the actions of the protagonist are run on the planning processor of the reader or audience member. In real-world planning, we have a goal, and we arrange actions as steps in the plan to achieve it. In running a fictional simulation, we allow the text to guide our planning process, to steer us through the actions of the narrative. Emotions are then experienced in relation to the goals and plans we have adopted, much as emotions occur in relation to goals in everyday life, happiness with achievements, sadness with losses, anger at frustrations, and so forth.

Reading has some of the same bases as enjoyment of games. *Pace* Wittgenstein (1953, who said that games had no clear definition), a game can be defined as an activity that affords a person a goal, for instance to win against an opponent, together with an outline script and resources for accomplishing it. In the same way, in a plot-based story, the reader takes on the goals and plans of a character, which are then run in the planning simulator of the mind.

According to this idea, understanding narratives of human intentions involves a specific mode of thinking with its own characteristics that relate actions and outcomes of actions to goals and plans. From the age of four or five, when they become keen on playing games involving roles—doctors and patients, cops and robbers, husbands and wives—children listening to a story, or watching a movie, say spontaneously, "I will be that one." They are very clear about the role with which they want to identify. From this age onward, in their encounters with narratives, people identify with a character, or with different characters in turn, and simulate characters' actions on their own planning processes to make sense of these sequences and to experience the emotions that the actions bring about.

Sympathy

What fictional writing and, perhaps even more immediately, fictional film can do, is to inject us into a drama as unobserved observers. As Lawton (1992) has pointed out, the modern style of film gives the impression that what is presented is free of style—natural. In fact, what this means is having the camera and microphone at exactly the right place, at exactly the right moment, so that what is most essential to each action in terms relevant to the plot is captured on film from the best possible angle. Again, note the contrast to real life, where, apart from close conversation and its cognates, we are seldom quite in the right place at the right time to get an ideal view of what is going on. If, in making a shot in a movie, the director judges that camera, actors, or props, are not quite right, then another take is ordered, and another, until the image is quite right.

Camera and fictional technique allow a sympathetic, or empathetic, response to what goes on. The idea of reader as sympathetic spectator was proposed by Adam Smith (1759). More recently, the idea has been developed by Nussbaum (1995), and by Tan (1994 and 1996). As reader or member of an audience, each of us becomes the ideal fly on the wall. Tan addresses his argument directly to the elicitatation of emotions, calling film "an emotion machine." His argument is as follows: the reader-watcher sees, up close, events of high emotional significance, associated with such context(s) as the writer chooses to present to us. If, in real life, we were in a café when an angry brawl started, or in a basement and overheard a plan to rob a bank, or in a bedroom when a couple undressed each other eager to make love, we would be affected by the perceptions, which would then arouse emotions in us. In the same way, in the novel or the movie the writer has arranged for us to be in the café, in the basement, or in the bedroom, at just the right time and with the right point of view to make these scenes vivid. So we are affected by the visual and auditory patterns just as we would be if these events were taking place in real life. According to this approach, the emotions are not really about what happens to us. They are based on a sympathy for those to whom the events happen: for the man who is assaulted in the café, for the one who runs the most risk in the bank heist, for the woman on the bed who is the source of such passion. In fiction, we see but are not seen, and this allows a certain freedom of emotion. And in fiction, the writer selects and directs, so we experience more frequent, more intense, more unusual episodes of emotion-arousing potential than we ever witness in real life.

Autobiographical Memory

A third basic psychological process occurs in fictional texts and in drama. A story can act as a cue to the explicit or implicit recall of fragments of our own autobiographical memory. In a novel, a leave-taking on the platform of a railway station may be a poignant reminder of a parting we once experienced. Perhaps even more powerfully, as Scheff (1979) argues, events of which we are reminded may not be so explicitly conscious, but we are nevertheless induced to relive them:

> When we cry over the fate of Romeo and Juliet, we are reliving our own personal experiences of overwhelming loss, but under new and less severe conditions. The experience of vicarious loss, in a properly designed drama, is sufficiently distressful to awaken the old distress. It is also sufficiently vicarious, however, so that the emotion does not feel overwhelming. (13)

Thus, not only do many actors follow Stanislavski's (1936) injunctions to draw on their autobiographical experience to give their performances emotional authenticity, but the audience (or readers) draw from their memories consciously or unconsciously as they respond to the movements and turns of the story.

Reaction to the Aesthetic Object

As well as these three personally involving processes—identification, sympathy, memory—which provide raw material for our emotional responses to fiction, other processes contribute to our emotional reaction in less direct ways. An important one that has commanded much attention, might be called the direct aesthetic response to the book, play, or film (Cupchik 1994).

Though the nature of aesthetic response has been a topic of eager study in the West for two hundred years, and of more intermittent interest for two thousand, the idea remains elusive. Let us put it like this: some expressions—for instance, those that articulate a particular thought in poetry—seem flat, conventional, or trite, while others, perhaps aiming at the same thought, soar on wings, and seem not just right, but astonishingly right, as if coming not from any human mind but from a realm of the ideal. They achieve what Longinus called "the sublime," which involves profound thought, intensity of emotion, and material for reflection.

Though Longinus gives many examples of achieved and failed sublimity, we can identify its salient features most easily by comparing authentic and corrupted texts. Some of the most famous soliloquies in all literature, for instance, are from *Hamlet*. The text of the edition with the earliest date (the First Quarto) was probably pirated, perhaps by the actor who played Marcellus in one of Shakespeare's productions. The pirate had quite a good memory, and is accurate on his own lines; but he is not so good on the lines for the Prince. Here are five lines from the pirated (First Quarto) manuscript:

> To be or not to be, ay there's the point,
> To die, to sleep, is that all? Ay all:
> No, to sleep, to dream, ay marry there it goes
> For in that dream of death when we awake
> And borne before an everlasting judge . . .[1]

Compare this from the authentic, collated Second Quarto and First Folio, manuscript:

> To be or not to be, that is the question:
> Whether 'tis nobler in the mind to suffer
> The slings and arrows of outrageous fortune,
> Or to take arms against a sea of troubles,
> And by opposing end them.[2]

Alternatively, we can look at a poet gradually converging on something sublime: here for instance, as recounted by Booth (1988) is a draft of the first four lines of a poem by W. B. Yeats:

> Your hair is white
> My hair is white

Come let us talk of love
What other theme do we know . . .

The poem subsequently became "After Long Silence," and its first four lines were:

Speech after long silence, it is right,
All other lovers being estranged or dead,
Unfriendly lamplight hid under its shade
The curtains drawn upon unfriendly night . . .

There are two difficulties with instances of the sublime. One is that they make us believe in some abstract realm of Platonic ideals—too magical, and too far from our human state. The other is that, since we are not accustomed inhabitants of that realm, we seem merely able to point to such instances. We are unable to say much, psychologically speaking, to explain either how such instances come to be in this almost extra-human space, or why they affect us as they do.

Response to the Discourse Level

Without in any way exhausting the elements of fictional narrative, we mention one more kind here: the address of the writer or narrator to the reader—most famously in English, perhaps, in the first sentence of the last chapter of *Jane Eyre*: "Reader, I married him" (Brontë 1847). This modality has, we believe, been much misunderstood. If we return to Henry James, for instance, he became known for arguing that such intrusions are inevitably clumsy. Yet, as European and American novels became more inward, such intrusions did not disappear. Here, for instance, is Proust (1913–1927) explaining directly to the reader the theory of art embodied in the novel that the reader is reading, and going on to explain how the relation of writer to reader is as a kind of "translator" of the readers own thoughts:

[W]hat we call reality is a certain connexion between these immediate sensations and the memories which envelop us simultaneously with them . . . a unique connexion which the writer has to rediscover to link for ever in his phrase the two sets of phenomena.
[E]very reader is, while he is reading, the reader of his own self. (924, 949)

All fiction, indeed, as Todorov (1977) has pointed out, is made up not of one structure, but of at least two. One structure constitutes a set of events and happenings in the story world, which Todorov calls the "narrative level." The other, which Todorov calls the "discourse level," is a set of direct and indirect speech acts to the reader, which serve to present the narrative to the reader in a particular way. A speech act involves a speaker who intends to influence the listener in some way, and a listener who may be influenced; the theory of speech acts is, in other words, a modern version of the classical theory of rhetoric. What modern ideas have emphasized more clearly than ancient ones are the reception and response to the discourse level, and the ways in which, with a constructivist theory of understanding, especially with great writing, the reader does become the writer of the text that he or she reads (Barthes 1975).

IV. What Fiction Really Is

A derogatory connotation of ordinary language is that "fiction" is untrue, whereas "fact" is true. But this tells us almost nothing about fiction, or indeed about fact. Fiction is a complex of many elements in which, we would argue, there is first of all a narrative of human action. Bruner (1986) has argued that at the core of narrative are "the vicissitudes of human intentions" (16); we wish to add: "and emotions." Secondly, we propose that fiction involves a discourse level and a range of techniques that allow the simulation to run properly on the human mind. These techniques have been invented by playwrights, novelists, and moviemakers, at specific points in time, and they continue to be invented. They depend on the psychological processes of identification, sympathy, and memory, and on the representational processes that give rise to aesthetic response and response to the writer's discourse.

In fiction, there is often the depiction of dialogue. This depiction is an ancient invention already present in some of the oldest manuscripts, such as the four-thousand-year-old Sumerian stories of Gilgamesh. Also present, typically, is the prioritization not just of human agency but of the idea that humans are responsible for their actions. This was an invention of Aeschylus and Sophocles. Responsible action, as we now understand it, involves characters with certain psychological attributes thinking and being affected by what they think. The depiction of this too was an invention of Shakespeare in the soliloquies (Bloom 1994), one of which we discussed above. The modern novel uses the technique of "stream of consciousness," a phrase of Henry James's brother, William, and introduced first by Dorothy Richardson and James Joyce.

Many other inventions contribute to the methods of fiction. Such techniques have been objects of explicit attention, and they are now used not just in fiction, but in journalism. Wolfe (1975), names four: (1) scene-by-scene construction and avoidance of sequential description, so that the writing comes close to the filmmaker's idea of (apparently) having the spectator in the scene; (2) dialogue—depicting dialogue in an apparently direct way; (3) third-person point of view, the Henry Jamesian idea of giving the reader the sense of presenting scenes through the eyes of some character; and (4) "the recording of everyday gestures, habits, customs, manners . . . [that are] symbolic, generally, of people's *status life*" (46–47, emphasis in original).

All such techniques depend for their success, in degrees that vary among the different modes and genres, on the psychological processes that we have discussed above. So, for instance, as Tan (1996) argues, film relies most on sympathy and on the elicitation of witness emotions. Most filmmakers, for instance, eschew the idea of a narrator's voice-over addressing an audience; it is seen as clumsy. The fantasy of such filmmakers is to create direct experience. If the technology of virtual reality were easily available to add the senses of proprioception, touch, smell, and so on to film's basic repertoire of sight and sound, then filmmakers would grasp the possibility eagerly. Moreover, most authors of tutorials on how to write fiction (Hall 1989; Stein 1993) somewhat uncritically accept the slogan "show don't tell," and exhort the reader to strive for the production of filmic images. More thoughtfully, we believe, Wolfe (1975) suggests that written text, being an indirect medium, may rely more on prompting readers' memories than on creating direct images.

We propose a variation, following Stevenson's idea that all fiction is a kind of dream. If a filmmaker manages to convey a strong impression of reality, this means that she has succeeded in making a film that appears to be realistic to a particular audience; it does not mean that she has indeed confronted the audience with the real. All fiction—on the stage, in film, in books—we would argue, relies to some extent on the constructive abilities of the watcher or reader. With a few exceptions, such as the first eight minutes of Altman's film "The Player" (which starts with a single unbroken tracking shot lasting eight minutes), movies do not represent a view that any one person could possibly have in ordinary life. As an example: film editing produces cuts between points of view in a fraction of a second that would take any real observer seconds to accomplish. In general, even the most "realistic" effects are constructions, put together from the writer's suggestions and manufactured in the spectator's or reader's "theatre of the brain," where the simulation machinery runs to produce a seamless experience.

Genre Fiction and Art

Let us close this section by distinguishing non-art and art in fiction, and let us follow contemporary publishing practice and call the kind of fiction that is not art "genre fiction"—the thriller, the romantic love story, the weepie, and so on. Genre fiction is put together using techniques that allow the reader or spectator to disappear into the story, to experience the emotions that are intended by the writer (Collingwood 1938).

With a thriller or a roller-coaster, the writer or the designer is almost entirely in control. The sights, the sounds, the shocks—all have been designed. All you have to do as a consumer is to get in, take the ride, and feel excited. Then you get off again. If you doubt the parallel between roller-coaster and fiction, then visit the most recent Disneyland attraction, "Indiana Jones," which reenacts one of the exciting action sequences of the movie with you in a jeep plunging over uneven terrain and threatened in various ways. In such experiences, emotions are produced technically, to order. They are parallel to the way in which the food industry produces tastes to order, using effects of known chemicals in certain combinations.

In artistic fiction, the writer or director uses the basic psychological processes discussed above (identification, sympathy, memory), together with aesthetic sublimity and speech acts from writer to reader, in ways that contrast two or more of them. In this way, the reader's imagination is set in motion, and new possibilities arise of the kind that Proust talked of, or indeed that Aristotle intended when he talked of katharsis. The reader or spectator of literary art makes a creative construction to connect the experience of emotions with their meaning.

One way to prompt the reader's imagination in this way is to set the narrative and discourse structures into a relation with each other that is known as "ironic." Ironic is here understood not as a derogatory notion, but on the contrary, as Frye (1957) has argued, as one of the more profound modes of response to life.

Here, for instance, is the famous first sentence of Jane Austen's *Pride and Prejudice* (1813): "It is a truth universally acknowledged, that a single man in possession of a good fortune must be in want of a wife." This sentence, and, indeed, the whole of the first chapter, rise to exactly that pitch of perfection that we previously referred to as "sublime." Austen accomplishes her feat by a contrast between the narrative structure and the discourse structure. The narrative world is indicated in this first sentence: this is a book about fortunes and about marrying. The discourse structure, which in the subtlety of Jane Austen's art cannot be disentangled from the narrative structure, indicates that the narrator will not be taking the narrative events at face value.

In general, as Oatley (1992) has argued, great authors achieve their effects by presenting not a monologic view, but something of a challenge to easy assimilation. Artists present juxtapositions and interweavings of elements from which the reader creatively makes a gestalt construction. Each of the three psychological modes discussed above offers possibilities for elements that can contribute to such effects. So, identification allows an experience from within a character, and this may contrast with a spectator stance toward the person's actions seen from outside. Oatley (1992) has argued that this is an effect often accomplished by George Eliot in her novels. With film, as Tan (1996) has argued, ironies can be created in which the spectator and the characters have different degrees of knowledge about what is occurring. Drama and novels allow the prompting of emotional memories at what Scheff (1979) calls the "best aesthetic distance," neither too overwhelming nor too uninvolving. In this way, connections are formed between the experience of emotions and their meanings.

Genre fiction typically provides us with a simplified experience of a certain kind; reading or watching is like taking a ride on a roller-coaster. But except for a fleeting memory of excitement or terror, little remains behind. Barthes (1975) calls this kind of reading "readerly." By contrast, a novel that is a work of art enables the reader to make what Barthes calls a "writerly" reading, a construction from a number of elements, in which experience and different levels of meaning can become connected. Barthes describes five such levels. Writerly constructions make not for a simplified understanding of life, but for an amplified one that has the potential to improve our understanding of ourselves and others, and of the ways in which human action, its vicissitudes, and its emotions, are connected.

In a novel that is a work of art, the emotions that emerge are not preprogrammed. Just as beauty is in the eye of the beholder, meaning is in the mind of the reader. Concerns and images implied by the text can resonate with each reader's idiosyncratic life experience and conception of life and society. Thus, the interaction of text and reader can provide raw materials for what George Eliot called moral sentiment (1856).

V. Psychological Value of the Reading Dream: An Augmented Theory of Identification

With this idea of the reader's or spectator's constructive role in mind, we propose an augmented theory of identification that will enable us to contrast the fictional roller-coaster ride with the idea of construction.

In the form we have indicated above, the idea of identification as meaning taking on the goals of a character is a relatively simple process. In this final section, we suggest that there is some complexity to identification. We consider how identificatory processes allow readers to reenact conflictual emotional issues in relation to the story's themes. With this idea in place, we reexamine the contrast between genre fiction and art in order to try to discern the psychological value of each.

Types of Identification

Harding (1968) has pointed out that there are difficulties with the term "identification" in reading, because it is not always clear which of several different processes it signifies. The reader may perceive similarities between himself or herself and a fictional character, only to regret them (and perhaps aspire to be different); is this recognition of similarities identification? He or she may desire enviously to mirror a fictional character so different from him- or herself that all possibility of attaining the character's status is dismissed; is this admiration identification? Other readers may idealize, or may empathize with the predicament of, a character.

What this suggests is that identification is a family of psychological processes that includes empathy, imitation, admiration, and recognition of similarities. One way forward, then, is to classify some of these processes. Schoenmakers (1988) has made a useful start in this direction.

In Schoenmakers's first category, "similarity identification," the subject (reader) adopts characteristics of a protagonist because of a perceived likeness between him- or herself and the object of identification. Affinity develops based on perceived similarity of experience. Such identification involves processes such as introjection (taking in desirable attributes of a character) and projection (disowning the unwanted aspects of self by projecting them onto other characters).

The second category is "wish identification," a process in which the subject strives to become like the idealized object. The subject admires the positive attributes of a character and wishes to emulate these. The feeling of affinity in wish identification is the consequence of identification. Fictional characters may be idealized, or the reader may develop erotic fantasies about them.

Third, Schoenmakers suggests a particular type of identification in films that he calls "primary cinematic identification." In cinema, the camera typically permits the spectator a view from several angles. At times, the spectator assumes the perspective of a character. At other times, however, the spectator adopts the perspective of an omniscient observer: when the camera's gaze predominates, the spectator identifies with the filmmaker's viewpoint, rather than with the character's. In reading, a similar phenomenon occurs, with subjects identifying with the author to understand the evolving dynamics in the fiction through the author's perspective. So, the subjects have fantasies about the author's feelings and thoughts.

Last, Schoenmakers refers to what he terms "theatrical projective identification." In this process, the theatrical set allows some spectators to project their desires into a fictional character much more intensely than they ever would in real life.

The Issue of Escapism

Perhaps the most provocative issue in the literature on identification is the extent to which reading, and the emotions induced by it, are escapist, or whether they might conceivably change the reader in some way. This is a recurrent question. It arises acutely from the idea that fiction is a kind of dream, and from the fact that people in large numbers flock to films and read genre books. Is all talk of anything other than escapism merely the pious hope of a few artists and theorists? Are reading, the theater, the cinema, in the end, nothing more than taking a ride on a character's goals and plans, just as we take a ride on a roller-coaster? Or could we, in our attraction to fiction with its focus on individual action, be molding our minds in important ways (Nussbaum 1995)?

There is some empirical research on escapist reading. Nell (1988) studied a group of what he calls "ludic readers," who read several books a week for pleasure. Nell's subjects each liked reading books of a particular genre. So he had each person choose a book he or she would like to read and bring it to his laboratory, where he recorded electroencephalograph (EEG) patterns as they read it. He found that these readers entered a state of EEG arousal, which the readers described as deeply relaxed. Nell characterizes it as a kind of trance state, and he discusses this phenomenon in terms of dream and fantasy.

In relation to film, the idea that movies are akin to dreams is commonplace (Lawton 1992). Based on a method called "activity sampling," in which people were signaled by a pager (of the kind used to summon doctors) at intervals throughout the day and asked to rate their mood, Kubey and Csikszentmihalyi (1990) found that people watching television rated it neither very pleasant, nor very unpleasant. It was simply a way of passing the time. Kubey and Csikszentmihalyi conclude that television is a kind of guided daydream.

So, genre novels, of the kind that in such numbers occupy the shelves of chain bookstores—thrillers, adventures, romances—and most films and television dramas, probably function psychologically by providing a means of escapism, a daydream guided along the rails of known technique toward predictable emotional effects. Television serves this function for more of the time, and with more of the people, than anything in print.

Theoretical, as opposed to empirical, research into these issues has been undertaken primarily by psychoanalytic writers. We present some of these ideas here because psychoanalysis is concerned with dream, fantasy, and identification, and because its formulations may be suggestive for theories of response to reading and film.

Some psychoanalytic theorists have suggested that the experience of reading evokes memories of early attachment experiences, and that in some ways reading may allow a kind of therapeutic regression. For Winnicott (1971) the world of the text links each of us to those parts of ourselves from which we have separated. The text serves (as do other forms of art) to mediate the distance between self and other, for just as in Taine's metaphor of perception as hallucination, its meaning is externally prompted but internally sustained. According to Grumet (1992), the romance of reading invites us to recuperate our losses. As we pass through the fictive world and emerge from it, we experience the opportunity to reconsider the boundaries and exclusions that sustain our social identities.

Consider Radaway's (1984) study of women for whom reading romantic fiction is an escape from the demanding task of caring for the needs of their families. The fictions offer the reader a chance to identify with a heroine "who gains the attention and recognition of a male and in the tender and protective love of this idealized male the reader can also relive her childhood experience of being the exclusive object of her mother's profoundly nurturing love" (123). One plausible hypothesis offered by Radaway is that escapist reading is:

> [a] regression, temporary or habitual, to childhood forms of pleasure. After we have left the dream vision of early childhood, romance is the first form of story that we became conscious of as a paradigm of our lives. Our earliest vision of ourselves confronting danger and emerging successfully are packaged in the conventions of romance. Reverting regularly to romance from the midst of our adult problems may be something we do compulsively, a distorted ritualization of experience that we cannot do without, but it may also be a temporary, expedient retreat from the complexities of more demanding reading or from the exigencies of adult life. (124)

Identification as a Complex Process

In order to understand the concept of identification in literature, let us examine the psychoanalytic idea of identification more closely. For Freud, identification was instrumental in the formation of personality. Therefore, if identification takes place in reading fiction, reading, too, might play a formative role in shaping our personality.

According to Freud, the most important form of identification occurs with the loss of a loved one. Freud suggests that in the global, undifferentiated state of early infancy, objects are treated solely as sources of pleasure. They are thoroughly engulfed to achieve gratification. But insofar as the object is unavailable or frustrating, it has to be relinquished. Hence, identification in the early stages of development involves taking in aspects of the desired object so that the object itself can be given up. Freud suggests that when the id desires what is unattainable, the ego must try to incorporate characteristics of the object through identification: "[I]t may be that this identification is the sole condition under which the id can give up its objects" (1923, 368). Suggestively, he continues: "[T]he character of the ego is a precipitate of abandoned object choices." Translated from Freud's somewhat arcane language, this means that an individual's character or personality is built up from layers of identifications with aspects of those whom he or she has loved, and, in losing them, has made part of him- or herself. This idea is echoed by a contemporary theme in cognitive science: if some resource is reliably available in the environment, we do not learn much about it. Only if it is absent or unreliable do we need to form internal representations of it.

Meissner (1972) distinguishes introjection from identification. Introjection is taking the desired object in whole, but without any processing. It is primarily driven by instinctual dynamics and governed by primary processes of unconscious fantasies. Identification is less influenced by instinctual derivatives. It is governed by secondary processes such as conscious, meaning-based thoughts. Identification, in this framework, refers to the integrative tendencies of the ego toward self-cohesion and meaningful relatedness. Through identification, we internalize selective aspects of social and cultural life that serve our adaptive functioning. In early development, attachment experiences are dominated by introjections. With increasing differentiation of psychic structure, "internalization becomes less introjective and more identificative, less global and more selective, less a matter of indiscriminately taking in the objects and more a matter of selective production of internal structures" (Meissner 1972, 250).

During the Oedipal crisis, according to Freud, the child recognizes the impossibility of defeating the rival parent and represses the incestuous desire for the loved parent by identification with the rival. The child does not abandon the object, but surrenders incestuous ties to form a more mature affectionate bond to his or her parents, and does so by becoming more like them. So, identification requires a certain disengagement from the desired parent. Developmentally appropriate identification will not occur if the desired object continues to be filled with erotic charge.

Davis (1987) proposed that the indiscriminate way in which we form emotional ties to fictional characters indicates a process of repetition compulsion, which allows readers to reenact experiences such as that of detachment from the loved parent, in an attempt to render the separation less painful. Novels perform this function "by endlessly creating displacing erotic objects (that is characters) with whom we can form cathexis or bonds without much fear or danger" (129).

All this suggests a link to the two kinds of reading we discussed earlier.

Escapist reading of genre works is like introjection: we simply fuse regressively with characters. In Scheff's (1979) terms, we are underdistanced; in Proust's terms we have emotional experiences but without their meaning. We recapitulate early experiences that are "magic in nature, they represent only a temporary, partial or total blending of magic self and object images, founded on fantasies and even the temporary belief of being one with and of becoming the object, regardless of reality" (Meissner 1972, 250). This type of novelistic introjection, although potent at times, is entirely transient. It gratifies, but leaves intact the self and its unconscious emotional fantasies.

The second kind of reading, which Barthes calls "writerly," can potentially be transformative. Even though identifications with fiction are brief in comparison with those of real life, sometimes they can enable us to take small steps in development. But just as important identifications take place in early development, when parents do not correspond exactly to infantile wishes, so, in reading, useful identification is only possible if the text includes something that prevents complete merging. This second type of reading is based on combining, for instance, identification and a spectator stance, which enables both engagement with and detachment from literary characters. It lends itself to selective, meaning-based, internalization. It may include conscious idealization of social, moral, or intellectual causes. Although the unconscious origins of such identifications may not be conscious, their products often are. Readers are often able to articulate why they admire, empathize with, or idealize a character. Their reflections can provide material for empirical investigation of these phenomena.

Our proposal is that the great writers offer works that vary aesthetic distance and that include crucial scenes at what Scheff (1979) calls "optimal distance." One way in which this is achieved is by using several of the psychological processes outlined earlier in ways that afford contrast, paradox, irony, and reflection. The texts have an incompleteness that challenges the reader to engage in creative, and imaginative, construction.

So, we conclude that escapist reading is like merging with fictional characters. It can be thought of as reenacting primordial sequences such as the anxieties of separation, the excitements of autonomous action, or the bliss of symbiosis with loved objects. The author or movie director succeeds in introducing whole, ready-made scenes into the dream-theaters of our brain, that entrain our emotions. Imagination is unnecessary, because everything is supplied. But the corollary is that nothing much changes. The same events can be reenacted again and again. No residues from the experiences remain.

But in another kind of reading, experience and meaning are imaginatively connected by the reader. We start merely with the author's partial script (for the scripts of art are always incomplete). Scenes in the dream-theater of the brain are as yet not fully realized, but as they are constructed they may be understood. Something can change. Small increments of personal development can occur. Our conceptions of ourselves can be affected as we take something from a character, or from a clarifying katharsis of an emotion, into our schemas of self.

ᶜES

ᵃration of this paper was supported by a grant to Keith Oatley from the Social nces and Humanities Research Council of Canada.

. Shakespeare, *Hamlet* (1963).
. Shakespeare, *Hamlet* (1981).

References

Ackermann, Felicia. 1991. "Imaginary Toads and Real Gardens: On the Ethics of Basing Fiction on Actual People." In *Philosophy and the Arts*, 142–51, Midwest Studies in Philosophy; vol. 16, edited by Peter A. French, Theodore E. Uehling, Jr., and Howard K. Wettstein. Notre Dame, Ind.: University of Notre Dame Press.

Allen, R. T. 1986. "The Reality of Responses to Fiction." *British Journal of Aesthetics* 26: 64–68.

Aristotle. 1962. *On the Art of Poetry*. Translated by Ingram Bywater. Oxford: Clarendon Press.

———. 1970. *Poetics*. Translated by G. F. Else. Ann Arbor: University of Michigan Press.

Armon-Jones, Claire. 1991. *Varieties of Affect*. Hemel Hempstead, England: Harvester Wheatsheaf.

Artaud, Antonin. 1958. *The Theater and Its Double*. Translated by Mary Caroline Richards. New York: Grove Press.

Auerbach, Erich. 1959. "The Aesthetic Dignity of the *Fleurs du Mal*." In *Scenes from the Drama of European Literature: Six Essays*, 199–226. New York: Meridian.

Austen, Jane. [1813] 1906. *Pride and Prejudice*. London: Dent.

Austin, J. L. 1962. *How to Do Things with Words*. Cambridge, Mass.: Harvard University Press.

Bach, Kent. 1994. "Emotional Disorder and Attention." In *Philosophical Pathology*, 51–72, edited by George Graham and G. Lynn Stephens. Cambridge, Mass.: MIT Press.

Banes, Sally. 1983. *Democracy's Body: Judson Dance Theater 1962–1964*. Ann Arbor: UMI Research Press.

Banner, Angela. 1962. *Ant and Bee and the Rainbow*. London: Heinemann.

Barish, Jonas. 1981. *The Antitheatrical Prejudice*. Berkeley: University of California Press.

Barnden, John. 1995. "Simulative Reasoning, Common-Sense Psychology, and Artificial Intelligence." In Davies and Stone 1995b, 247–73. Oxford: Blackwell.

Barnes, Jonathan, ed. 1984. *The Complete Works of Aristotle*, vol. 2. Princeton, N.J.: Princeton University Press.

Barthes, Roland. 1972. *Critical Essays*. Evanston, Ill.: Northwestern University Press.

———. 1975. *S/Z*. Translated by R. Miller. London: Cape.

———. 1977. "The Death of the Author." In *Image-Music-Text*, 142–48. Translated by Stephen Heath. New York: Hill and Wang.

Barwell, Ismay. 1986. "How Does Art Express Emotion?" *Journal of Aesthetics and Art Criticism* 45: 175–81.

———. 1995. "Who's Telling this Story, Anyway? Or, How to Tell The Gender of a Storyteller." *Australasian Journal of Philosophy* 73: 227–38.

Baudelaire, Charles. 1924. *Les Fleurs du Mal*, edited by Jacques Crépet and Georges Blin. Paris: José Corti.

Beardsley, Monroe C. 1982. "The Aesthetic Problem of Justification." In *The Aesthetic Point of View: Selected Essays*, 65–77, edited by Michael J. Wreen and Donald M. Callen. Ithaca, N.Y.: Cornell University Press.

Beck, Aaron T. 1976. *Cognitive Therapy and the Emotional Disorders*. New York: International Universities Press.

Belfiore, Elizabeth. 1985. "Pleasure, Tragedy and Aristotelian Psychology." *Classical Quarterly* 35: 349–61.

Benjamin, Walter. 1968. "The Work of Art in the Age of Mechanical Reproduction." In *Illuminations*, 217–51, edited and introduced by Hannah Arendt, and translated by Harry Zohn. New York: Harcourt, Brace and World.

Berenson, F. M. 1993. "Interpreting the Emotional Content of Music." In *The Interpretation of Music: Philosophical Essays*, 61–72, edited by M. Krausz. Oxford: Clarendon Press.

Best, David. 1985. *Feeling and Reason in the Arts*. London: George Allen and Unwin.

Biadene, Susanna, ed. 1990. *Titian: Prince of Painters*. Munich: Prestel-Verlag.

Blair, Fredrika. 1986. *Isadora: Portrait of the Artist as a Woman*. New York: McGraw-Hill.

Bloom, Harold. 1994. *The Western Canon: The Books and School of the Ages*. New York: Harcourt Brace.

Booth, Wayne C. 1961. *The Rhetoric of Fiction*. Chicago: University of Chicago Press.

———. 1988. *The Company We Keep: An Ethics of Fiction*. Berkeley: University of California Press.

Boruah, Bijoy H. 1988. *Fiction and Emotion*. Oxford: Clarendon Press.

Boudaille, Georges. 1964. *Gauguin*. Translated by Alisa Jaffa. London: Thames and Hudson.

Brecht, Bertolt. 1957. *Brecht on Theater: The Development of an Aesthetic*. Edited and translated by John Willett. New York: Hill and Wang.

Brink, David O. 1989. *Moral Realism and the Foundations of Ethics*. Cambridge: Cambridge University Press.

Brontë, Charlotte. [1847] 1966. *Jane Eyre*. London: Penguin.

Brooks, Peter. 1976. *The Melodramatic Imagination: Balzac, Henry James, Melodrama, and the Mode of Excess*. New Haven, Conn.: Yale University Press.

Bruner, Jerome S. 1986. *Actual Minds, Possible Worlds*. Cambridge, Mass.: Harvard University Press.

Byrne, Alex. 1993. "Truth in Fiction: The Story Continued." *Australasian Journal of Philosophy* 71: 23–35.

Budd, Malcolm. 1985. *Music and the Emotions: The Philosophical Theories*. London: Routledge and Kegan Paul.

———. 1995. *Values of Art: Pictures, Poetry, and Music*. London: Penguin.

Bullough, Edward. [1912] 1957. " 'Psychical Distance' as a Factor in Art and an Aesthetic Principle." In *Aesthetics: Lectures and Essays*, 91–130. London: Bowes and Bowes.

Calcineau, Matei. 1977. *Faces of Modernity: Avant-Garde, Decadence, Kitsch*. Bloomington: Indiana University Press.

Callen, Donald. 1982. "The Sentiment in Musical Sensibility." *Journal of Aesthetics and Art Criticism* 40: 381–93.

Canaday, John. 1959. *Mainstreams of Modern Art*. New York: Holt.

Carroll, Noël. 1986. "Art and Interaction." *Journal of Aesthetics and Art Criticism* 45: 57–68.

———. 1987. "The Nature of Horror." *Journal of Aesthetics and Art Criticism* 46: 51–59.

———. 1990a. "The Image of Women in Film: A Defense of a Paradigm." *Journal of Aesthetics and Art Criticism* 48: 349–60.

———. 1990b. *The Philosophy of Horror, or, Paradoxes of the Heart*. London: Routledge.

———. 1995. "Critical Study: Kendall L. Walton, *Mimesis as Make-Believe*." *The Philosophical Quarterly* 45: 93–99.

———. 1996. "The Paradox of Suspense." In *Suspense: Conceptualizations, Theoretical Analyses and Empirical Explorations*, 71–91, edited by Peter Vorderer, Hans Wulf, and Mike Friedrichsen. Hillsdale, N.J.: Lawrence Erlbaum.

———. Forthcoming. *A Philosophy of Mass Art*. Oxford: Oxford University Press.

Chalfa Ruyter, and Nancy Lee. 1979. *Reformers and Visionaries*. New York: Dance Horizons.

Charlton, William. 1984. "Feeling for the Fictitious." *British Journal of Aesthetics* 24: 206–16.

Chesters, Graham. 1988. *Baudelaire and the Poetics of Craft*. Cambridge: Cambridge University Press.

Churchland, Paul. 1984. *Matter and Consciousness*. Cambridge, Mass.: The MIT Press.

———. 1985. "Reduction, Qualia, and the Direct Introspection of Brain States." *The Journal of Philosophy* 82: 8–28.

Citron, Paula. 1995. "Don't Be Afraid of Contemporary Dance." *Club for Dance Update*.

Clark, Herbert H. 1996. *Using Language*. Cambridge: Cambridge University Press.

Clark, Herbert H., and Gerrig, Richard J. 1990. "Quotations as Demonstrations." *Language* 66: 764–805.

Collingwood, R. G. 1938. *Principles of Art*. Oxford: Clarendon Press.

The Collins Concise English Dictionary. 1992. 3rd ed. Glasgow: Harper Collins.

Cone, Edward T. 1974. *The Composer's Voice*. Berkeley: University of California Press.

Conter, David. 1991. "Fictional Names and Narrating Characters." *Australasian Journal of Philosophy* 69: 319–28.

Craik, Kenneth J. W. 1943. *The Nature of Explanation*. Cambridge: Cambridge University Press.

Crimmins, Mark. 1995. "Quasi-singular Propositions: The Semantics of Belief Reports." *The Aristotelian Society,* supp. vol. 69: 195–209.

Cunningham, Merce, and Jacqueline Lesschaeve. 1985. *The Dancer and the Dance.* New York: Marion Boyars.

Cupchik, Gerald C. 1994. "Emotion in Aesthetics: Reactive and Reflective Models." *Poetics* 23: 177–88.

Currie, Gregory. 1990. *The Nature of Fiction.* Cambridge: Cambridge University Press.

———. 1991. "Visual Fictions." *Philosophical Quarterly* 41: 129–43.

———. 1993. "Interpretation and Objectivity." *Mind* 102: 413–28.

———. 1995a. "Imagination and Simulation: Aesthetics Meets Cognitive Science." In Davies and Stone 1995b, 151–69. Oxford: Blackwell.

———. 1995b. "The Moral Psychology of Fiction." *The Australasian Journal of Philosophy* 73: 250–59.

———. 1995c. "Simulation-Theory, Theory-Theory, and the Evidence from Autism." In *Theories of Theories of Mind,* edited by Peter Carruthers and Peter K. Smith, 242–56. Cambridge: Cambridge University Press.

———. 1995d. "Visual Imagery as the Simulation of Vision." *Mind and Language* 10: 25–44.

———. "Simulation and Cognitive Architecture." In preparation.

Damasio, Antonio R. 1994. *Descartes' Error: Emotion, Reason, and the Human Brain.* New York: G. Putnam and Sons.

Dammann, R. M. J. 1992. "Emotion and Fiction." *British Journal of Aesthetics* 32: 13–20.

Dancy, Jonathan. 1993. *Moral Reasons.* Oxford: Blackwell.

D'Andrade, Roy. 1980. "The Cultural Part of Cognition." Paper presented at the Second Annual Cognitive Science Conference. New Haven, Conn.

———. 1995. *The Development of Cognitive Anthropology.* Cambridge: Cambridge University Press.

Davidson, Donald. 1970, 1980. "How is Weakness of the Will Possible?" In *Essays on Action and Events,* 21–42. Oxford: Oxford University Press.

Davies, John Booth. 1978. *The Psychology of Music.* London: Hutchinson.

Davies, Martin, and Tony Stone, eds. 1995a. *Folk Psychology: The Theory of Mind Debate.* Oxford: Blackwell.

———. 1995b. *Mental Simulation: Evaluations and Applications.* Oxford: Blackwell.

Davies, Stephen. 1980. "The Expression of Emotion in Music." *Mind* 89: 67–86.

———. 1994. *Musical Meaning and Expression.* Ithaca, N.Y.: Cornell University Press.

Davis, Lennard J. 1987. *Resisting Novels: Ideology and Fiction.* New York: Methuen.

Deigh, John. 1994. "Cognitivism in the Theory of Emotions." *Ethics* 104: 824–54.

De Mille, Agnes. 1991. *Martha: The Life and Work of Martha Graham.* New York: Random House.

Dennett, Daniel C. 1990. "Quining Qualia." In *Mind and Cognition: A Reader,* 519–47, edited by William G. Lycan. Oxford: Blackwell.

Derrida, Jacques. 1976. *Of Grammatology.* Translated by Gayatri Chakravorty Spivak. Baltimore: Johns Hopkins University Press.

De Sausmarez, Maurice. 1970. *Bridget Riley.* London: Studio Vista.

De Sousa, Ronald. 1976. "Rational homunculi." In *The Identities of Persons,* 217–38, edited by Amélie Oksenberg Rorty. Berkeley: University of California Press.

———. 1987. *The Rationality of Emotion.* Cambridge, Mass.: MIT Press.

Devereaux, Mary. 1990. "Oppressive Texts, Resisting Readers and the Gendered Spectator: The New Aesthetics." *The Journal of Aesthetics and Art Criticism* 48: 337–48.

Dickie, George. 1974. *Art and the Aesthetic*. Ithaca, N.Y.: Cornell University Press.

Dickinson, Emily. 1970. *The Complete Poems*, edited by Thomas H. Johnson. London: Faber and Faber.

Diderot, Denis. 1957. *The Paradox of Acting*. New York: Hill and Wang.

———. *Paradoxe sur le comédien*. [1906] 1958. Paris: Libraire Théâtrale.

Dissanayake, Ellen. 1988. *What is Art For?* Seattle: University of Washington Press.

Drotner, Kirsten. 1991. "Intensities of Feeling: Modernity, Melodrama, and Adolescence." *Theory, Culture and Society* 8: 57–87.

Dutta, Satrajit, and Rabindra Nath Kanungo. 1975. *Affect and Memory: A Reformulation*. Oxford: Pergamon Press.

Dyer, Gwynne. 1987. *War*. New York: Time-Life Books.

Eaton, Marcia M. 1982. "A Strange Kind of Sadness." *Journal of Aesthetics and Art Criticism* 41: 51–63.

Ekman, Paul, Robert W. Levenson, and Wallace V. Friesen. 1983. "Autonomic Nervous System Activity Distinguishes Among Emotions." *Science* 221: 1208–10.

Eliot, George. [1856] 1963. "The Natural History of German Life." In *Essays of George Eliot*, 266–99, edited by Thomas Pinney. New York: Columbia University Press.

Feagin, Susan L. 1983. "The Pleasures of Tragedy." *American Philosophical Quarterly* 20: 95–104.

———. 1994. "Valuing the Artworld." In *Institutions of Art: Reconsiderations of George Dickie's Philosophy*, 51–72, edited by Robert J. Yanal. University Park: Pennsylvania State University Press.

———. 1996. *Reading with Feeling: The Aesthetics of Appreciation*. Ithaca, N.Y.: Cornell University Press.

Festinger, Leon. 1957. *A Theory of Cognitive Dissonance*. Stanford, Calif.: Stanford University Press.

———. 1980. *Retrospections on Social Psychology*. New York: Oxford University Press.

Fish, Stanley. 1980. *Is There a Text in this Class? The Authority of Interpretive Communities*. Cambridge, Mass.: Harvard University Press.

Fisher, Shirley, and James Reason. 1988. *Handbook of Life Stress, Cognition, and Health*. Chichester, England: Wiley and Sons Ltd.

Flaubert, Gustav. [1857] 1964. *Madame Bovary*. Translated by M. Marmur. Introduction by Mary McCarthy. New York: New American Library.

Freud, Sigmund. [1904] 1985. "Psychopathic Characters on the Stage." In *Art and Literature*, 120–27, Pelican Freud Library, vol. 14, edited by A. Dickson. London: Penguin.

———. [1915] 1984. "Mourning and Melancholia." In *On Metapsychology*, 247–67, Pelican Freud Library, vol. 11, edited by Angela Richards. Harmondsworth: Penguin.

———. [1923] 1984. "The Ego and the Id." In *On Metapsychology*, 341–407, Pelican Freud Library, vol. 11, edited by James Strachey. London: Penguin.

———, and J. Breuer. [1895] 1922. *Stüdien über Hysterie*. Leipzig: Deuticke.

Frijda, Nico H. 1986. *The Emotions*. Cambridge: Cambridge University Press.

Frye, Northrop. 1957. *Anatomy of Criticism: Four Essays*. Princeton, N.J.: Princeton University Press.

Garber, Judy E., and Martin E. P. Seligman, eds. 1980. *Human Helplessness: Theory and Applications*. New York: Academic Press.

Gardner, J. 1984. *The Art of Fiction*. New York: Knopf.

Gaut, Berys. 1992. "Book Review of Kendall L. Walton, *Mimesis as Make-Believe: On the Foundations of the Representational Arts*." *The Journal of Value Inquiry* 26: 297–300.

Gaut, Berys. 1993. "The Paradox of Horror." *British Journal of Aesthetics* 33: 333–45.

Genette, Gérard. 1988. "Implied Author, Implied Reader?" In *Narrative Discourse Revisited*, 135–54. Ithaca, N.Y.: Cornell University Press.

Gibbard, Allan. 1990. *Wise Choices, Apt Feelings: A Theory of Normative Judgment.* Cambridge, Mass.: Harvard University Press.

Gilligan, Stephen G., and Gordon H. Bower. 1984. "Cognitive Consequences of Emotional Arousal." In *Emotions, Cognition, and Behavior*, 547–88, edited by Carroll E. Izard, Jerome Kagan, and Robert B. Zajonc. Cambridge: Cambridge University Press.

Goldman, Alan. 1995. "Emotions in Music: (A Postscript)." *Journal of Aesthetics and Art Criticism* 53: 59–69.

Goldman, Alvin I. 1995. "Empathy, Mind, and Morals." In Davies and Stone 1995b, 185–208. Oxford: Blackwell.

Goleman, Daniel. 1995. *Emotional Intelligence.* New York: Bantam Books.

Gombrich, E. H. 1966. *The Story of Art.* 11th ed. London: Phaidon.

Goodman, Nelson. 1968, 1976. 2nd ed. *Languages of Art: An Approach to a Theory of Symbols.* Indianapolis: Hackett.

Gordon, Robert M. 1974. "The Aboutness of Emotions." *American Philosophical Quarterly* 11: 27–36.

———. 1980. "Fear." *The Philosophical Review* 89: 560–78.

———. 1986. "Folk Psychology as Simulation." *Mind and Language* 1: 158–71.

———. 1987. *The Structure of Emotions: Investigations in Cognitive Philosophy.* Cambridge: Cambridge University Press.

———. 1995. "Simulation without Introspection or Inference from Me to You." In Davies and Stone 1995b, 53–67. Oxford: Blackwell.

Graham, Martha. 1991. *Blood Memory.* New York: Doubleday.

Green, O. H. 1972. "Emotions and Belief." In *Studies in the Philosophy of Mind*, 24–40, American Philosophical Quarterly Monograph 6, edited by Nicholas Rescher. Oxford: Basil Blackwell.

———. 1992. *The Emotions: A Philosophical Theory.* Dordrecht: Kluwer Academic Publishers.

Greenberg, Clement. 1965. *Art and Culture: Critical Essays.* Boston: Beacon.

Greenspan, Patricia S. 1980. "A Case of Mixed Feelings: Ambivalence and the Logic of Emotion." In *Explaining Emotions*, 223–50, edited by Amélie Oksenberg Rorty. Berkeley: University of California Press.

———. 1988. *Emotions and Reasons: An Inquiry into Emotional Justification.* New York and London: Routledge.

Griffiths, P. 1997. *What Emotions Really Are: From Evolution to Social Construction.* Chicago: University of Chicago Press.

Grumet, M. R. 1992. "Romantic Research: Why We Love to Read." In *Literacy Research, Theory, and Practice: Views From Many Perspectives. Forty-first Yearbook of the National Reading Conference.* Chicago, Ill.: The National Reading Conference, Inc.

Guck, Marion. 1994. "Analytical Fictions." *Music Theory Spectrum* 16: 217–30.

Hall, Oakley. 1989. *The Art and Craft of Novel Writing.* Cincinnati: Writers Digest Books.

Hamilton, Edith, and Huntington Cairns, eds. 1961. *The Collected Dialogues of Plato.* Princeton, N.J.: Princeton University Press.

Hanna, Judith Lynne. 1983. *The Performer-Audience Connection: Emotion to Metaphor in Dance and Society.* Austin: University of Texas Press.

————. 1988. *Dance, Sex and Gender.* Chicago: University of Chicago Press.

Hanslick, Eduard. [1854] 1980. *On the Musically Beautiful.* Translated by Geoffrey Payzant. Indianapolis: Indiana University Press.

Harding, D. W. 1968. "Psychological Processes in the Reading of Fiction." In *Aesthetics in the Modern World,* edited by Harold Osborne, 300–17. London: Thames and Hudson.

Harré, Rom. 1986. "An Outline of the Social Constructionist Viewpoint." In *The Social Construction of Emotions,* edited by Rom Harré, 2–14. Oxford: Basil Blackwell.

Harries, Karsten. 1968. *The Meaning of Modern Art: A Philosophical Interpretation.* Evanston, Ill.: Northwestern University Press.

Heal, Jane. 1986. "Replication and Functionalism." In *Language, Mind, and Logic,* 135–50, edited by Jeremy Butterfield. New York: Cambridge University Press.

Higgins, Kathleen M. 1991. *The Music of Our Lives.* Philadelphia: Temple University Press.

————. 1992. "Sweet Kitsch." In *The Philosophy of the Visual Arts,* 568–81, edited by Philip Alperson. New York: Oxford University Press.

Hjort, Mette. 1993. *The Strategy of Letters.* Cambridge, Mass.: Harvard University Press.

Horosko, Marian, ed. 1991. *Martha Graham: The Evolution of Her Dance Theory and Training.* New York: a cappella books.

Hume, David. [1888] 1978. *A Treatise on Human Nature.* Edited by L. A. Selby-Bigge. Oxford: Clarendon Press.

————. [1757] 1985. "Of the Standard of Taste." In *Essays Moral, Political, and Literary,* 226–49, edited by Eugene F. Miller. Indianapolis: Liberty Fund, Inc.

Humphrey, Nicholas. 1983. *Consciousness Regained: Chapters in the Development of Mind.* Oxford: Oxford University Press.

Ingarden, Roman. 1973. *The Cognition of the Literary Work of Art.* Translated by Ruth Ann Crowley and Kenneth Olson. Evanston, Ill.: Northwestern University Press.

Isenberg, Arnold. 1949. "Critical Communication." *Philosophical Review* 58: 330–44.

Izard, Carroll E. 1977. *Human Emotions.* New York: Plenum Press.

————, Jerome Kagan, and Robert B. Zajonc, eds. 1984. *Emotions, Cognition, and Behavior.* Cambridge: Cambridge University Press.

James, Henry. [1884] 1951. "The Art of Fiction." In *The Portable Henry James,* edited by M. D. Zabel, 391–418. New York: Viking.

James, William. [1890] 1950. *The Principles of Psychology,* vol. 2. New York: Dover.

Jefferson, Mark. 1983. "What is Wrong With Sentimentality?" *Mind* 92: 519–29.

Johnson, Mark. 1987. *The Body in the Mind: The Bodily Basis of Meaning, Imagination, and Reason.* Chicago: University of Chicago Press.

Johnson-Laird, P. N. 1983. *Mental Models: Towards a Cognitive Science of Language, Inference, and Consciousness.* Cambridge: Cambridge University Press.

Kahneman, Daniel, and Amos Tversky. 1982. "The Simulation Heuristic." In *Judgment Under Uncertainty: Heuristics and Biases,* 201–7, edited by Daniel Kahneman, P. Slovic, and Amos Tversky. Cambridge: Cambridge University Press.

Kant, Immanuel. [1790] 1952. *Critique of Judgement.* Translated by J. C. Meredith. Oxford: Clarendon Press.

Kant, Immanuel. [1785] 1964. *Groundwork of the Metaphysic of Morals,* 2nd German ed. Translated by H. J. Paton. New York: Harper and Row.

Kierkegaard, Søren. 1946. "Diary of the Seducer." In *Either/Or: A Fragment of Life,* vol. 1, 249–371. Translated by David F. Swenson and Lillian Marvin Swenson. London: Oxford University Press.

Kivy, Peter. 1980. *The Corded Shell: Reflections on Musical Expression.* Princeton, N.J.: Princeton University Press.

———. 1989. *Sound Sentiment: An Essay on the Musical Emotions.* Philadelphia: Temple University Press.

———. 1990a. *Music Alone: Philosophical Reflections on the Purely Musical Experience.* Ithaca, N.Y.: Cornell University Press.

———. 1990b. "A New Music Criticism." *Monist* 73: 247–68.

Klinger, Eric. 1993. "Clinical Approaches to Mood Control." In *Handbook of Mental Control,* 344–69, edited by Daniel Wegner and James Pennebaker. Englewood Cliffs, N.J.: Prentice Hall.

Koriat, Asher et al. 1972. "The Self-Control of Emotional Reactions to a Stressful Film." *Journal of Personality* 40: 601–19.

Korsmeyer, Carolyn. 1977. "On Distinguishing 'Aesthetic' from 'Artistic'." *Journal of Aesthetic Education* 11: 45–57.

Kubey, Robert W., and Mihaly Csikszentmihalyi. 1990. *Television and the Quality of Life: How Viewing Shapes Everyday Experience.* Hillsdale, N.J.: Erlbaum.

Kundera, Milan. 1984. *The Unbearable Lightness of Being.* New York: Harper and Row.

———. 1985. "Lecture in Jerusalem." *Mishkenot Sha'ananim Newsletter* 3: 5.

Laird, James D. et al. 1982. "Remembering What You Feel: Effects of Emotion on Memory." *Journal of Personality and Social Psychology* 42: 646–57.

Lamarque, Peter. 1981. "How Can We Fear and Pity Fictions?" *British Journal of Aesthetics* 21: 291–304.

———. 1991. "Essay Review of *Mimesis as Make-Believe.*" *Journal of Aesthetics and Art Criticism* 49: 161–66.

———, and Stein Haugom Olsen. 1994. *Truth, Fiction, and Literature: A Philosophical Perspective.* Oxford: Clarendon Press.

Lang, Peter et al. 1980. "Emotional Imagery: Conceptual Structure and Pattern of Somato-visceral Response." *Psychophysiology* 17: 179–92.

Laplanche, Jean, and J. B. Pontalis. 1972. *Das Vokabular der Psychoanalyse.* Frankfurt: Suhrkamp.

Lawton, Henry. 1992. "Towards a Psychohistorical Theory of Film." *Journal of Psychohistory* 20: 85–114.

Lazarus, Richard S. 1991. *Emotion and Adaptation.* Oxford: Oxford University Press.

Lee, Vernon. 1970. "Empathy." From *The Beautiful,* reprinted in *Problems in Aesthetics,* 757–61, edited by Morris Weitz, 2nd ed. New York: Macmillan.

Leibowitz, Flo. 1996. "Apt Feelings, or Why 'Women's Films' Aren't Trivial." In *Post-Theory: Reconstructing Film Studies,* edited by David Bordwell and Noël Carroll, 219–29. Madison: University of Wisconsin Press.

Levinson, Jerrold. 1982. "Music and Negative Emotion." *Pacific Philosophical Quarterly* 63: 327–46.

———. 1990a. "Hope in 'The Hebrides.'" In *Music, Art, and Metaphysics.* Ithaca: Cornell University Press.

———. 1990b. *Music, Art, and Metaphysics: Essays in Philosophical Aesthetics.* Ithaca, N.Y.: Cornell University Press.

———. 1990c. "Music and Negative Emotion." In *Music, Art, and Metaphysics.* Ithaca, N.Y.: Cornell University Press.

———. 1990d. "The Place of Real Emotion in Response to Fictions." *Journal of Aesthetics and Art Criticism* 48: 79–80.

———. 1992. "Intention and Interpretation: A Last Look." In *Intention and Interpretation,* edited by Gary Iseminger, 221–56. Philadelphia: Temple University Press.

————. 1994. "Seeing, Imaginarily, at the Movies." *Philosophical Quarterly* 43: 71–78.

————. 1996a. "Making Believe." In *The Pleasures of Aesthetics.* Ithaca, N.Y.: Cornell University Press.

————. 1996b. "Musical Expressiveness." In *The Pleasures of Aesthetics.* Ithaca, N.Y.: Cornell University Press.

————. 1996c. *The Pleasures of Aesthetics.* Ithaca, N.Y.: Cornell University Press.

————. 1996d. "What Is Aesthetic Pleasure?" In *The Pleasures of Aesthetics.* Ithaca, N.Y.: Cornell University Press.

Lewis, David. 1980. "Psychophysical and Theoretical Identifications." In *Readings in Philosophy of Psychology,* vol. 1, 207–22, edited by Ned Block. Cambridge, Mass.: Harvard University Press.

————. 1983. "Truth in Fiction." In *Philosophical Papers,* vol. 1, 261–80. New York: Oxford University Press.

Livingston, Paisley. 1988. *Literary Knowledge: Humanistic Inquiry and the Philosophy of Science.* Ithaca, N.Y.: Cornell University Press.

————, and Alfred R. Mele. 1992. "Intention and Literature." *Stanford French Review* 16: 173–96.

Longinus. 1965. "On the Sublime." In *Aristotle, Horace, Longinus: Classical Literary Criticism,* 99–158, translated by T.S. Dorsch. Harmondsworth, England: Penguin.

Lutz, Catherine. 1995. "Need, Nurturance, and the Emotions on a Pacific Atoll." In *Emotions in Asian Thought: A Dialogue in Comparative Philosophy,* 235–52, edited by Joel Marks and Roger T. Ames. Albany: State University of New York Press.

Lyons, William E. 1980. *Emotion.* Cambridge: Cambridge University Press.

Mandler, George. 1975. *Mind and Emotion.* New York: John Wiley and Sons.

————. 1984. *Mind and Body: Psychology of Emotion and Stress.* New York: Norton.

Mannison, Don. 1985. "On Being Moved by Fiction." *Philosophy* 60: 71–87.

Margolis, Joseph. 1980. *Art and Philosophy.* Atlantic Highlands, N.J.: Humanities Press.

————. 1993. "Music and Ordered Sound." In *The Interpretation of Music: Philosophical Essays,* 141–53, edited by M. Krausz. Oxford: Clarendon Press.

Marks, Isaac M. 1969. *Fears and Phobias.* New York: Academic Press.

Martins, Daniel. 1982. "Influence of Affect on Comprehension of a Text." *Text* 2: 141–54.

Masson, J. L., and M. V. Patwardhan. 1970. *Aesthetic Rapture: The Rasâdhyâya of the Nâtyaśâstra.* Poona, India: Deccan College Postgraduate and Research Institute.

Matravers, Derek. 1995. "Beliefs and the Fictional Narrator." *Analysis* 55: 121–22.

Mattheson, Johann. 1739. *Der vollkommene Capellmeister.* Hamburg: Christian Herold.

Maus, Fred. 1988. "Music as Drama." *Music Theory Spectrum* 10: 56–73.

Meissner, W. W. 1972. "Notes on Identification." *Psychoanalytic Quarterly* 41: 224–59.

Mele, Alfred R. 1995. *Autonomous Agents: From Self-Control to Autonomy.* New York: Oxford University Press.

————, and Paisley Livingston. 1992. "Intentions and Interpretations." *Modern Language Notes* 107: 931–49.

Merleau-Ponty, Maurice. 1962. *Phenomenology of Perception.* Translated by Colin Smith. International Library of Philosophy and Scientific Method. London: Routledge and Kegan Paul.

Miall, David S., and Don Kuiken. 1994. "Beyond Text Theory: Understanding Literary Response." *Discourse Processes* 17: 337–52.

Midgley, Mary. 1979. "Brutality and Sentimentality." *Philosophy* 54: 385–90.

Moran, Richard. 1994. "The Expression of Feeling in Imagination." *Philosophical Review* 103: 75–106.

Morreall, John. 1985. "Enjoying Negative Emotions in Fiction." *Philosophy and Literature* 9: 95–103.

———. 1993. "Fear Without Belief." *The Journal of Philosophy* 90: 359–66.

Morton, Adam. 1980. *Frames of Mind: Constraints on the Common Sense Conception of the Mental.* New York: Oxford University Press.

Mothersill, Mary. 1984. *Beauty Restored.* Oxford: Oxford University Press.

———. 1993. "Character and Taste." Paper presented to the APA Pacific Division. Unpublished.

Myers, Gerald E. 1986. *William James: His Life and Thought.* New Haven, Conn.: Yale University Press.

Neill, Alex. 1991. "Fear, Fiction, and Make-Believe." *Journal of Aesthetics and Art Criticism* 49: 47–56.

———. 1993. "Fiction and the Emotions." *American Philosophical Quarterly* 30: 1–13.

———. 1995. "Fear and Belief." *Philosophy and Literature* 19: 94–101.

Nell, Victor. 1988. *Lost in a Book: The Psychology of Reading for Pleasure.* New Haven, Conn.: Yale University Press.

Nesse, Randolph M. 1990. "Evolutionary Explanations of Emotions." *Human Nature* 1: 261–89.

Neu, Jerome. 1980. "Jealous Thoughts." In *Explaining Emotions,* edited by Amélie Oksenberg Rorty, 425–63. Los Angeles: University of California Press.

Newcomb, Anthony. 1983. "Those Images That Yet Fresh Images Beget." *Journal of Musicology* 2: 227–45.

———. 1984a. "Once More 'Between Absolute and Program Music': Schumann's Second Symphony." *Nineteenth Century Music* 7: 233–50.

———. 1984b. "Sound and Feeling." *Critical Inquiry* 10: 614–43.

Nicole, Pierre. [1667] 1971. *Traité de la comédie.* In *Essais de morale,* vol. 3. Geneva: Slatkine Reprints, vol. 1, 265–78.

Novitz, David. 1980. "Fiction, Imagination and Emotion." *Journal of Aesthetics and Art Criticism* 38: 279–88.

———. 1987. *Knowledge, Fiction and Imagination.* Philadelphia: Temple University Press.

———. 1989. "Ways of Artmaking: The High and the Popular in Art." *British Journal of Aesthetics* 29: 213–229.

———. 1990. "The Integrity of Aesthetics." *Journal of Aesthetics and Art Criticism* 48: 9–20.

———. 1992. *The Boundaries of Art.* Philadelphia: Temple University Press.

———. 1995a. "Messages 'In' and Messages 'Through' Art." *Australasian Journal of Philosophy* 73: 199–203.

———. 1995b. "The Trouble with Truth: A Critical Study of Peter Lamarque and Stein Haugom Olsen, *Truth, Fiction, and Literature.*" *Philosophy and Literature* 19: 350–59.

Nussbaum, Martha C. 1986. *The Fragility of Goodness: Luck and Ethics in Greek Tragedy and Philosophy.* Cambridge: Cambridge University Press.

———. 1994. *The Therapy of Desire: Theory and Practice in Hellenistic Ethics.* Princeton: Princeton University Press.

———. 1995. *Poetic Justice: The Literary Imagination and Public Life.* Boston: Beacon.

Oakley, Justin. 1992. *Morality and the Emotions.* London: Routledge.

Oatley, Keith. 1992. *Best Laid Schemes: The Psychology of Emotions.* New York: Cambridge University Press.

———. 1994. "A Taxonomy of the Emotions of Literary Response and a Theory of Identification in Fictional Narrative." *Poetics* 23: 53–74.

———, and E. Duncan. 1992. "Incidents of Emotion in Daily Life." In *International Review of Studies in Emotion*, vol. 2, 249–93, edited by K. Strongman. Chichester, England: Wiley.

———, and P. N. Johnson-Laird. 1996. "The Communicative Theory of Emotions: Empirical Tests, Mental Models, and Implications for Social Interaction." In *Striving and Feeling: Interactions Among Goals, Affect, and Self-Regulation*, 363–93, edited by L. L. Martin and A. Tesser. Mahwah, N.J.: Erlbaum.

Packer, Mark. 1989. "Dissolving the Paradox of Tragedy." *Journal of Aesthetics and Art Criticism* 47: 212–19.

Packman, Janet L., and William F. Battig. 1978. "Effects of Different Kinds of Semantic Processing on Memory for Words." *Memory and Cognition* 6: 502–8.

Paulhan, Frederic. 1930. *The Laws of Feeling*. Translated by C. K. Ogden. New York: Harcourt, Brace and Company.

Pavel, Thomas G. 1986. *Fictional Worlds*. Cambridge, Mass.: Harvard University Press.

Peirce, C. S. 1929. "Guessing." *The Hound and Horn* 2: 268–82.

Perkins, D. N. 1981. *The Mind's Best Work*. Cambridge, Mass.: Harvard University Press.

Perner, Josef, and Deborrah Howes. 1995. " 'He Thinks He Knows': And More Developmental Evidence Against the Simulation (Role-taking) Theory." In Davies and Stone 1995a, 159–73. Oxford: Blackwell.

Plato. 1923. *The Republic*. Translated by Benjamin Jowett. New York: Random House.

———. 1987. *The Republic*. Translated by Desmond Lee. Harmondsworth, England: Penguin.

Plutchik, Robert, and Henry Kellerman, eds. 1980. *Emotion: Theory, Research, and Experience*, vol 1: *Theories of Emotion*. New York: Academic Press.

Poe, Edgar Allan. [1839] 1967. "The Fall of the House of Usher." In *The Complete Poems and Stories of Edgar Allan Poe*, vol. 1, 262–77. New York: Alfred A. Knopf.

Proust, Marcel. [1913–1927] 1954. *A la recherche du temps perdu (Remembrance of Things Past)*, vol. III, *Time Regained*. Translated by C. K. Scott-Moncrief, Terence Kilmartin, and Andreas Mayor. London: Penguin.

Prynne, William. [1633] 1972. *Histrio-Mastix, The Player's Scourge or, Actor's Tragedy*. 2 vols. Introductory note by Peter Davison. New York and London: Johnson Reprint Corporation and Johnson Reprint Company Limited.

Putnam, Hilary. 1978. "Literature, Science, and Reflection." In *Meaning and the Moral Sciences*, 83–94. London: Routledge and Kegan Paul.

Radaway, Janice A. 1984. *Reading the Romance: Women, Patriarchy, and Popular Literature*. Chapel Hill: University of North Carolina Press.

Radford, Colin. 1989. "Emotions and Music: A Reply to the Cognitivists." *Journal of Aesthetics and Art Criticism* 47: 69–76.

———. 1995. "Fiction, Pity, Fear, and Jealousy." *Journal of Aesthetics and Art Criticism* 53: 71–75.

———, and Michael Weston. 1975. "How Can We Be Moved By The Fate of Anna Karenina?" *Proceedings of the Aristotelian Society* suppl. vol. 49: 67–93.

Rey, George. 1980. "Functionalism and the Emotions." In *Explaining Emotions*, 163–96, edited by Amélie Oksenberg Rorty. Berkeley: University of California Press.

Ridley, Aaron. 1992. "Desire in the Experience of Fiction." *Philosophy and Literature* 16: 279–91.

———. 1995. *Music, Value, and the Passions*. Ithaca, N.Y.: Cornell University Press.

Robinson, Jenefer. 1983. "Emotion, Judgment, and Desire." *The Journal of Philosophy* 80: 731–41.

———. 1985. "Style and Personality in the Literary Work." *Philosophical Review* 94: 227–47.

———. 1990. "Experiencing Art." *Proceedings of the 11th International Congress of Aesthetics*, 156–60, edited by Richard Woodfield. Nottingham: Nottingham Polytechnic Press.

———. 1994. "The Expression and Arousal of Emotion in Music." *Journal of Aesthetics and Art Criticism* 52: 13–22.

———. 1995a. "L'Education sentimentale." *Australasian Journal of Philosophy* 73: 212–26.

———. 1995b. "Startle." *The Journal of Philosophy* 92: 53–74.

———, and Gregory Karl. 1995. "Shostakovitch's Tenth Symphony and the Musical Expression of Cognitively Complex Emotions." *Journal of Aesthetics and Art Criticism* 53: 401–15.

Robinson, John A. 1980. "Affect and Retrieval of Personal Memories." *Motivation and Emotion* 4: 149–74.

Rölleke, Heinz, ed. 1985. *Kinder- und Hausmärchen Gesammelt durch die Brüder Grimm*. Frankfurt: Deutscher Klassiker.

Rorty, Amélie Oksenberg. 1980. "Explaining Emotions." In *Explaining Emotions*, edited by Amélie Oksenberg Rorty, 103–26. Berkeley: University of California Press.

Roseman, Ira J. 1991. "Appraisal Determinants of Discrete Emotions." *Cognition and Emotion* 5: 161–200.

Rosen, Gideon. 1994. "What Is Constructive Empiricism?" *Philosophical Studies* 74: 143–78.

Rosenblum, Robert. 1967. *Transformations in Late Eighteenth Century Art*. Princeton: Princeton University Press.

Rosenfield, Israel. 1992. *The Strange, Familiar and Forgotten: An Anatomy of Consciousness*. New York: Alfred A. Knopf.

Ryle, Gilbert. 1949. *The Concept of Mind*. New York: Barnes and Noble.

Salkever, Stephen G. 1986. "Tragedy and the Education of the Demos: Aristotle's Response to Plato." In *Greek Tragedy and Political Theory*, 274–303, edited by J. Peter Euben. Berkeley: University of California Press.

Salovey, Peter, and John D. Mayer. 1990. "Emotional Intelligence." *Imagination, Cognition, and Personality* 9: 185–211.

Sargant, William. 1956. *Battle for the Mind: A Physiology of Conversion and Brainwashing*. Pan Books: London.

Sartre, Jean-Paul. 1948. *The Emotions: Outline of a Theory*. New York: Philosophical Library.

———. 1971. *L'Idiot de la famille*, vol. 1, 785–90. Paris: Gallimard.

———. 1972. "The Self-Alienation of the Lover's Freedom." In *Sexual Love and Western Morality: A Philosophical Anthology*, 254–57, edited by D. P. Verene. New York: Harper Torchbooks.

Saxena, Sushil Kumar. 1991. *Swinging Syllables: Aesthetics of Kathak Dance*. New Delhi: Sangeet Natak Akademi.

Schaper, Eva. 1978. "Fiction and the Suspension of Disbelief." *British Journal of Aesthetics* 18: 31–44.

Scheff, Thomas J. 1979. *Catharsis in Healing, Ritual, and Drama*. Berkeley: University of California Press.

Schoenmakers, H. 1988. "To Be, Wanting to Be, Forced to Be: Identification Processes in Theatrical Situations." In *Tijdschrift voor Theaterwetenschap 24/25, No. 1/2: New Directions in Audience Research 2*. Utrecht: Instituut voor Theaterwetenschap.

Schwartz, Robert. 1978. "Infinite Sets, Unbounded Consequences, and Models of Mind." In *Perception and Cognition: Issues in the Foundations of Psychology*, 183–200, Minnesota Studies in the Philosophy of Science, vol. 9, edited by C. Wade Savage. Minneapolis: University of Minnesota Press.

Scruton, Roger. 1971. "Attitudes, Beliefs and Reasons." In *Morality and Moral Reasoning*, 25–100, edited by John Casey. London: Methuen.

————. 1983. "Understanding Music." In *The Aesthetic Understanding: Essays in the Philosophy of Art and Culture*. London: Methuen.

Shakespeare, William. 1963. *Hamlet*. Edited by E. Hubler. New York: New American Library.

————. 1981. *Hamlet*. In *The Arden Shakespeare*. Edited by J. Jenkins. London: Methuen.

————. 1974a. *Macbeth*. In *The Riverside Shakespeare*. Boston: Houghton Mifflin.

————. 1974b. *Romeo and Juliet*. In *The Riverside Shakespeare*. Boston: Houghton Mifflin.

Sharpe, R. A. 1986. "Review of M. Budd, *Music and the Emotions*." *British Journal of Aesthetics* 26: 397–99.

Shawn, Ted. 1968. *Every Little Movement: A Book About François Delsarte*. New York: Dance Horizons.

Shelton, Suzanne. 1981. *Divine Dancer: A Biography of Ruth St. Denis*. Garden City: Doubleday.

Simon, Herbert A. 1983. *Reason in Human Affairs*. Stanford: Stanford University Press.

Skinner, B. F. 1953. *Science and Human Behavior*. New York: Macmillan.

Slater, Hartley. 1993. "The Incoherence of the Aesthetic Response." *British Journal of Aesthetics* 33: 168–72.

Smith, Adam. [1759] 1976. *The Theory of Moral Sentiments*. Oxford: Oxford University Press.

Smith, Murray. 1996. "The Logic and Legacy of Brechtianism." In *Post-Theory: Reconstructing Film Studies*, 130–48, edited by Noël Carroll and David Bordwell. Madison: University of Wisconsin Press.

Solomon, Robert C. 1976. *The Passions*. Garden City, N.Y.: Anchor Press/Doubleday.

————. 1980. "Emotions and Choice." In *Explaining Emotions*, 251–81, edited by Amélie Oksenberg Rorty. Berkeley: University of California Press.

————. 1989. "The Virtue of Love." In *Ethical Theory: Character and Virtue*, 12–31, Midwest Studies in Philosophy, vol. 13, edited by Peter A. French, Theodore E. Uehling, Jr., and Howard K. Wettstein. Notre Dame, Ind.: University of Notre Dame Press. Reprinted as "The Virtue of (Erotic) Love" in *The Philosophy of (Erotic) Love*, 492–518, edited by Kathleen Higgins and Robert Solomon. Lawrence, Kans.: University Press of Kansas, 1991.

————. 1990. "Review of Bijoy H. Borouah's *Fiction and Emotion*." *The Review of Metaphysics* 43: 620–21.

————. 1992. "The Philosophy of Horror." In *Entertaining Ideas: Popular Philosophical Essays*, 119–30. Buffalo, N.Y.: Prometheus Books.

————. 1993. *The Passions: Emotions and the Meaning of Life*. Indianapolis: Hackett.

————. 1995a. "The Cross-Cultural Comparison of Emotion." In *Emotions in Asian Thought: A Dialogue in Comparative Philosophy*, 253–308, edited by Joel Marks and Roger T. Ames. Albany: State University of New York Press.

————. 1995b. *Passion for Justice*. Lanham, MD: Rowman and Littlefield.

————, and Cheshire Calhoun, eds. 1984. *What is an Emotion?* New York: Oxford University Press.

Sorell, Walter, ed. and trans. 1975. *The Mary Wigman Book.* Middletown, Conn.: Wesleyan University Press.

Sparshott, Francis. 1981. "The Problem of the Problem of Criticism." In *What Is Criticism?*, 3–14, edited by Paul Hernadi. Bloomington: Indiana University Press.

————. 1982. *The Theory of the Arts.* Princeton, N.J.: Princeton University Press.

————. 1988. *Off the Ground.* Princeton, N.J.: Princeton University Press.

————. 1993. "How Can I Know What Dancing Is?" In *Primum Philosophari*, 148–61, edited by Jolanty Brach-Czainy. Warsaw: Oficyna Naukowa.

————. 1994. "Music and Feeling." *Journal of Aesthetics and Art Criticism* 52: 23–35.

————. 1995. *A Measured Pace: Toward a Philosophical Understanding of the Arts of Dance.* Toronto: University of Toronto Press.

Stanislavski, Constantin. 1936. *An Actor Prepares.* Translated by Elizabeth R. Hapgood. New York: Theatre Arts Books.

Stearns, Peter N., and Carol Z. Stearns. 1988. *Emotion in History.* New York: Holmes and Meier.

Stecker, Robert. 1987. "Apparent, Implied, and Postulated Authors." *Philosophy and Literature* 11: 258–71.

————. 1994a. "Art Interpretation." *Journal of Aesthetics and Art Criticism* 52: 193–206.

————. 1994b. "The Role of Intention and Convention in Interpreting Artworks." *Southern Journal of Philosophy* 31: 471–89.

————. 1996. *Artworks: Definition, Meaning, Value.* University Park, Penn.: Pennsylvania State University Press.

Stein, S. 1993. *FictionMaster.* CD-ROM. Ossining, N.Y.: WritePro.

Stevenson, Robert Louis. [1884] 1992. "A Humble Remonstrance." In *R. L. Stevenson Essays and Poems*, 179–88, edited by C. Harman. London: Dent Everyman's Library.

————. [1888] 1992, "A Chapter on Dreams." In *R. L. Stevenson Essays and Poems*, 189–99, edited by C. Harman. London: Dent Everyman's Library.

Stich, Stephen P. 1983. *From Folk Psychology to Cognitive Science: The Case Against Belief.* Cambridge, Mass.: The MIT Press.

————, and Shaun Nichols. 1995. "Folk Psychology: Simulation or Tacit Theory?" In Davies and Stone 1995a, 123–58. Oxford: Blackwell.

Stodelle, Ernestine. 1984. *Deep Song: The Dance Story of Martha Graham.* New York: Schirmer Books.

Strawson, P. F. 1963. *Individuals: An Essay in Descriptive Metaphysics.* Garden City, N.Y.: Doubleday, Anchor.

Strongman, K. T. 1973. *The Psychology of Emotion.* London: John Wiley and Sons.

Taine, Hippolyte. 1882. *De l'intelligence.* Tome 2. Paris: Hachette.

Tan, Ed S.-H. 1994. "Film-induced Affect as a Witness Emotion." *Poetics* 23: 7–32.

————. 1996. *Emotion and the Structure of Film: Film as an Emotion Machine.* Mahwah, N.J.: Erlbaum.

Tanner, Michael. 1976. "Sentimentality." *Proceedings of the Aristotelian Society* 77: 127–47.

Tatar, Maria. 1987. *The Hard Facts of the Grimms' Fairy Tales.* Princeton, N.J.: Princeton University Press.

Taylor, Charles. 1989. *Sources of the Self: The Making of the Modern Identity.* Cambridge, Mass.: Harvard University Press.

Taylor, Gabriele. 1985. *Pride, Shame, and Guilt: Emotions of Self-Assessment*. Oxford: Clarendon Press.

Thalberg, Irving. 1964. "Emotion and Thought." *American Philosophical Quarterly* 1: 45–55.

———. 1980. "Avoiding the Emotion-Thought Conundrum." *Philosophy* 55: 396–402.

Thom, Paul. 1993. *For an Audience*. Philadelphia: Temple University Press.

Tice, Dianne, and Roy Baumeister. 1993. "Controlling Anger: Self-Induced Emotion Change." In *Handbook of Mental Control*, 393–409, edited by Daniel Wegner and James Pennebaker. Englewood Cliffs, N.J.: Prentice-Hall.

Todorov, Tzvetan. 1977. *The Poetics of Prose*. Translated by Richard Howard. Ithaca, N.Y.: Cornell University Press.

Tolstoy, Leo. [1898] 1960. *What is Art?* Translated by Aylmer Maude. Indianapolis: Hackett Publishing Company.

Tomkins, Silvan S. 1979. "Script Theory: Differential Magnification of Affects." *Nebraska Symposium on Motivation* 26: 201–36.

Tompkins, Jane. 1985. *Sensational Designs: The Cultural Work of American Fiction 1790–1860*. New York: Oxford University Press.

Tsur, Reuven. 1992. *Toward a Theory of Cognitive Poetics*. Amsterdam and New York: North-Holland.

Tye, Michael. 1986. "The Subjective Qualities of Experience." *Mind* 95: 1–17.

Van Peer, Willie. 1986. *Stylistics and Psychology: Investigations of Foregrounding*. London: Croom Helm.

———. 1992. "Literary Theory and Reader Response." In *Reader Response to Literature: The Empirical Dimension*, 137–52, edited by Elaine F. Nardocchio. Berlin and New York: Mouton de Gruyter.

———. 1994. "Emotional Functions of Reading Literature." In *Literature and the New Interdisciplinarity: Poetics, Linguistics, History*, 209–20, edited by Roger D. Sell and Peter Verdonk. Amsterdam: Rodopi.

———. 1995a. "The Historical Non-Triviality of Art. A Rejoinder to Jerome Stolnitz." *British Journal of Aesthetics* 35: 168–72.

———. 1995b. "Literature, Imagination and Human Rights." *Philosophy and Literature* 19: 276–91.

———. 1996. "The Ethics of Literature: Two Research Models." *The Journal of Literary Semantics* 25: 154–72.

Vermazen, Bruce. 1986. "Expression as Expression." *Pacific Philosophical Quarterly* 67: 196–224.

Walton, Kendall. 1976. "Points of View in Narrative and Depictive Representation." *Noûs* 10: 49–61.

———. 1978. "Fearing Fictions." *The Journal of Philosophy* 75: 5–27.

———. 1979, 1987. "Style and the Products and Processes of Art." In *The Concept of Style*, 72–103, edited by Berel Lang. Ithaca, N.Y.: Cornell University Press.

———. 1988. "What is Abstract About the Art of Music?" *Journal of Aesthetics and Art Criticism* 46: 351–64.

———. 1990. *Mimesis as Make-Believe: On the Foundations of the Representational Arts*. Cambridge, Mass.: Harvard University Press.

———. 1994. "Listening with Imagination: Is Music Representational?" *Journal of Aesthetics and Art Criticism* 52: 47–61.

Weaver, John. [1717] 1985. *Loves of Mars and Venus*. In *The Life and Works of John Weaver*, 735–62, edited by Richard Ralph. London: Dance Books.

Welty, Eudora. 1983. *One Writer's Beginnings*. New York: Warner Books.

Whistler, James McNeill. 1888. "Ten O'Clock Lecture." London: Chatto and Windus.

Wierzbicka, Anna. 1992. *Semantics, Culture, and Cognition: Universal Human Concepts*. New York: Oxford University Press.

Wilde, Oscar. 1908. "The English Renaissance of Art." In *Miscellanies*, 241–77. London: Methuen and Co.

Williams, Bernard. 1981. "Moral Luck." In *Moral Luck: Philosophical Papers 1973–1980*, 20–39. Cambridge: Cambridge University Press.

Wilson, George M. 1991. "Comments on *Mimesis as Make-Believe*." *Philosophy and Phenomenological Research* 51: 395–400.

Winnicott, D. W. 1971. *Playing and Reality*. Harmondsworth, England: Penguin.

Wittgenstein, Ludwig. [1969] 1974. *On Certainty*, edited by G. E. M. Anscombe and G. H. von Wright and translated by Denis Paul and G. E. M. Anscombe. Oxford: Blackwell.

———. 1953. *Philosophical Investigations*. Translated by G. E. M. Anscombe. Oxford: Blackwell.

Wolfe, Tom. 1975. "The New Journalism." In *The New Journalism*, 13–68, edited by Tom Wolfe and E. W. Johnson. London: Picador.

Wollheim, Richard. 1980. "On Persons and Their Lives." In *Explaining Emotions*, 299–321, edited by Amélie Oksenberg Rorty. Berkeley: University of California Press.

Woodfield, Andrew. 1982. "Desire, Intentional Content and Teleological Explanation." *Proceedings of the Aristotelian Society* 82: 69–87.

Woolf, Virginia. [1931] 1990. *The Waves*. London: Hogarth.

Yanal, Robert J. 1994. "The Paradox of Emotion and Fiction." *Pacific Philosophical Quarterly* 75: 54–75.

Contributors

NOËL CARROLL is the Monroe C. Beardsley Professor of the Philosopy of Art at the University of Wisconsin at Madison. He is the author of *The Philosophy of Horror, or, Paradoxes of the Heart* (Routledge, 1990), *Philosophical Problems of Classical Film Theory* (Princeton University Press, 1988), and *Mystifying Movies: Fads and Fallacies in Contemporary Film Theory* (Columbia University Press, 1988). He is also the coeditor, with David Bordwell, of *Post-Theory: Reconstructing Film Studies* (University of Wisconsin Press, 1996).

GREGORY CURRIE is Professor of Philosophy and Head of the School of Arts, Flinders University, Adelaide. His publications include *An Ontology of Art* (St. Martin's Press, 1989) and *The Nature of Fiction* (Cambridge University Press, 1990). His most recent book is *Image and Mind: Philosophy, Film and Cognitive Science* (Cambridge University Press, 1995). He is currently working on the psychology of the imagination.

STEPHEN DAVIES teaches philosophy at the University of Auckland. He is the author of *Definitions of Art* (Cambridge University Press, 1991) and *Musical Meaning and Expression* (Cornell University Press, 1994), as well as many papers in the philosophy of art.

RONALD DE SOUSA is Professor of Philosophy at the University of Toronto. He is the author of *The Rationality of Emotion* (MIT Press, 1987). His research interests range from cognitive science, through the philosophy of sexuality and the philosophy of biology, to Chinese language and philosophy.

SUSAN L. FEAGIN is Professor of Philosophy at the University of Missouri — Kansas City. She is the author of *Reading with Feeling: The Aesthetics of Appreciation* (Cornell University Press, 1996), as well as numerous articles in aesthetics and the philosophy of art. Her current interests include the concept of appreciation, drawing, and pictorial representation, and the role played by emotional and other affective responses in our appreciation of art.

MITRA GHOLAMAIN is a doctoral student in the Department of Human Development and Applied Psychology at the Ontario Institute for Studies in Education, University of Toronto. She is conducting research on the ways in which readers' attachment states affect their responses to narrative.

ROM HARRÉ is Emeritus Fellow of Linacre College, Oxford University, Professor of Psychology at Georgetown University, Washington, D.C., and Adjunct Professor in the program for Philosophy, Computers, and Cognitive Science at Binghamton University. His published work includes studies in the philosophy of both natural and human sciences, such as *Varieties of Realism* (Blackwell, 1986) and the trilogy *Social Being* (Blackwell, 1979), *Personal Being* (Harvard University Press, 1984), and *Physical Being* (Blackwell, 1991). He is the author of *The Explanation of Social Behaviour* (Blackwell, 1973), and the editor of *The Social Construction of Emotions* (Blackwell, 1986). His current research interests concern the ways in which language enters into all aspects of human life. His most recent books in this area are, with Grant Gillett, *The Discursive Mind* (Sage, 1994), and with W. G. Parrott, *The Emotions* (Sage, 1996).

METTE HJORT is Associate Professor of English at McGill University. She is the author of *The Strategy of Letters* (Harvard University Press, 1993), and the editor of *Rules and Conventions: Literature, Philosophy, Social Theory* (The Johns Hopkins University Press, 1992).

SUE LAVER is a doctoral candidate in the Department of English at McGill University, where she is currently completing her dissertation, entitled "Poets, Philosophers, and Priests: Modernism, Formalism, and the Social Authority of Art."

JERROLD LEVINSON is Professor of Philosophy at the University of Maryland, College Park. He is the author of *Music, Art, and Metaphysics* (Cornell University Press, 1990), *The Pleasures of Aesthetics* (Cornell University Press, 1996), and the forthcoming *Music in the Moment* (Cornell University Press, 1977). He is also the coeditor, with Arto Haapala and Veikko Rantala, of *The End of Art and Beyond: Essays After Danto* (Humanities Press, 1997), and editor of the forthcoming *Aesthetics and Ethics: Essays at the Intersection* (Cambridge University Press, 1998).

PAISLEY LIVINGSTON teaches philosophy at Roskilde University in Denmark. He is the author of *Ingmar Bergman and the Rituals of Art* (Cornell University Press, 1982), *Literary Knowledge: Humanistic Inquiry and the Philosophy of Science* (Cornell University Press, 1988), *Literature and Rationality: Ideas of Agency in Theory and Fiction* (Cambridge University Press, 1991), and *Models of Desire: René Girard and the Psychology of Mimesis* (The Johns Hopkins University Press, 1992). He is also the editor of *Disorder and Order* (Anma Libri, 1984).

WILLIAM LYONS is Professor of Moral Philosophy in the School of Mental and Moral Science at Trinity College, Dublin, and a Member of the Royal Irish Academy. His publications include *Gilbert Ryle: An Introduction to His Philosophy* (Harvester and Humanities Presses, 1980), *Emotion* (Cambridge University Press, 1980), *The Disappearance of Introspection* (MIT Press, 1986), and *Approaches to Intentionality* (Clarendon Press, 1995). He is also the editor of *Modern Philosophy of Mind* (Everyman, 1995).

DEREK MATRAVERS lectures in philosophy at the Open University, Milton Keynes. He is the author of several articles in aesthetics and the philosophy of art. His primary research interests are in ethics and aesthetics. He is currently working on his forthcoming book, *Art and Emotion* (Oxford University Press).

ALFRED R. MELE is Vail Professor of Philosophy at Davidson College. He is the author of *Irrationality* (Oxford University Press, 1987), *Springs of Action* (Oxford University Press, 1992), and *Autonomous Agents* (Oxford University Press, 1995). He is also the editor of *The Philosophy of Action* (Oxford University Press, 1997), and coeditor, with John Heil, of *Mental Causation* (Clarendon, 1993).

DAVID NOVITZ is Reader in Philosophy at the University of Canterbury, New Zealand. He is the author of *Pictures and their Use in Communication* (Nijhoff, 1977), *Knowledge, Fiction and Imagination* (Temple University Press, 1987), and *The Boundaries of Art* (Temple University Press, 1992), as well as many journal articles in aesthetics and the philosophy of literature.

KEITH OATLEY is Professor of Applied Psychology at the Ontario Institute for Studies in Education, and at the Department of Psychology, University of Toronto. His primary area of research is emotions and people's responses to literary narrative. His numerous publications include *Perceptions and Representations: The Theoretical Bases of Brain Research and Psychology* (Free Press, 1979), *Brain Mechanisms and Mind* (Thames and Hudson, 1972), and *Best Laid Schemes: The Psychology of Emotions* (Cambridge University Press, 1992). He also has written a novel, *The Case of Emily V*, which won the Commonwealth Writer's Prize for best first novel in 1994.

ROBERT C. SOLOMON is Quincy Lee Professor of Philosophy at the University of Texas at Austin. His numerous publications include *From Rationalism to Existentialism* (Harper and Row, 1972), *The Passions* (Doubleday, 1976, and Hackett, 1993), *In the Spirit of Hegel* (Oxford University Press, 1983), *About Love* (Simon and Schuster, 1988), *From Hegel to Existentialism* (Oxford University Press, 1988), and *A Passion for Justice* (Rowman and Littlefield, 1994). He is also the author, with Kathleen Higgins, of *A Short History of Philosophy* (Oxford University Press, 1996) and *From Africa to Zen: An Invitation to World Philosophy* (Rowman and Littlefield, 1994), and the editor, with Cheshire Calhoun, of *What is an Emotion?* (Oxford University Press, 1984).

FRANCIS SPARSHOTT is Professor Emeritus of Philosophy at the University of Toronto. He has published nine books of poetry and eight of philosophy, including two on the philosophy of dance, *Off the Ground* (Princeton University Press, 1988) and *A Measured Pace* (Toronto University Press, 1995). His other publications include *The Concept of Criticism: An Essay* (Clarendon Press, 1967) and *The Theory of the Arts* (Princeton University Press, 1982).

WILLIE VAN PEER teaches theory of literature at Utrecht University in The Netherlands. His many publications include *Stylistics and Psychology: Investigations of Foregrounding* (Croom Helm, 1986). He is also the editor of several volumes, including *The Taming of the Text: Explorations in Language, Literature and Culture* (Routledge, 1988). His latest book is *Foundations of Literary Theory.* He is currently working on problems of evaluation in literary studies.

KENDALL WALTON is James B. and Grace J. Nelson Professor of Philosophy at the University of Michigan. He is the author of *Mimesis as Make-Believe: On the Foundations of the Representational Arts* (Harvard University Press, 1990), as well as numerous articles in aesthetics and the philosophy of art.

Printed in the United States
32331LVS00003B/66

9 780195 111057

3225